THE ICSA CHARITIES HANDBOOK

THE ICSA
CHARITIES HANDBOOK

EDITOR

Kirsty Semple

Published by ICSA Publishing Ltd
16 Park Crescent
London W1B 1AH

© ICSA Information & Training Ltd, 2010

All rights reserved. No part of this publication may be reproduced, stored in a retrieval system, or transmitted, in any form, or by any means, electronic, mechanical, photocopying, recording or otherwise, without prior permission, in writing from the publisher.

The right of Kirsty Semple to be identified as author of the general editor's part of the work has been asserted by her in accordance with sections 77 and 78 of the Copyright, Designs and Patents Act 1988.

The rights of the following contributors to be identified as authors of their work have been asserted by them in accordance with sections 77 and 78 of the Copyright, Designs and Patents Act 1988: Jane Ascroft, Val King, Chris Priestley and Richard Reger.

Designed and typeset by Paul Barrett Book Production, Cambridge
Printed in Great Britain by Hobbs the Printers Ltd, Totton, Hampshire

British Library Cataloguing in Publication Data
A catalogue record for this book is available from the British Library

ISBN 978-186072-404-6

Contents

Preface		vi
Contributors		viii
Abbreviations		x

Section A The charity's structure and legal framework

1	Charity law and regulation *Adrian Pashley*	3
2	Legal forms and structures *Adrian Pashley*	27
3	Setting up a charity *Adrian Pashley*	85

Section B The charity's compliance

1	Records and registers *Kirsty Semple*	101
2	Compliance and filing requirements *Kirsty Semple*	119
3	Contracts, signing and sealing *Kirsty Semple*	141

Section C The charity's governance

1	Principles of governance *Richard Reger*	157
2	Roles and relationships *Richard Reger*	175
3	Charity meetings *Kirsty Semple*	219

Section D The charity's business

1	Employment *Val King*	249
2	Fundraising and trading *Chris Priestley*	285
3	Data protection and e-commerce *Mandy Webster*	311

Section E The charity's assets

1	Use of charitable assets *Jane Ascroft*	331
2	Risk management and internal controls *Jane Ascroft*	355
3	Accounting and audit *Jane Ascroft*	381

Appendix A	Directory	415
Appendix B	Outline document retention checklist	420
Index		425

Preface

The task of administering a charity, and having regard to all the relevant laws and regulations, is a difficult one. Charities are governed not just by charity law but by the laws that relate to their legal form; the laws that govern how businesses and employers operate; and the laws that relate to their specific area of work. The range of charities, in terms of size, legal structure and governance, is also very wide. It can therefore seem like an almost impossible task to provide a handbook that will be useful to them all. However, it is vital that there is such a handbook that can act as a source of information for all charities. This is what we have tried to pull together here.

This book aims to give an overview of the rules and procedures governing how a charity works. It covers the requirements under charity law, including the changes brought about following the Charities Act 2006. The type of legal form that a charity takes will also affect how it operates. With most new charities now being registered as companies, this book covers the requirements under company law, and reflects the new Companies Act 2006. However, there are a wide range of other legal forms that charities take and we will also deal with those requirements. There is then a host of other legislation, regulations and best practice that can impact on charities – from employment law to data protection – which is also covered.

In recent years one of the significant changes in the way charities are regulated has been the development of charity legislation in Scotland and Northern Ireland, and the establishment of regulatory bodies for both of those countries. These different requirements are touched on to some extent, as charities registered in England and Wales sometimes work in these other countries. However, references to charities in this book are to charities recognised as such under the law of England and Wales, unless otherwise specified. Where it is relevant, reference is made to the comparable law or regulatory requirements in Scotland (as Northern Ireland's new regime in not yet fully in force).

Whilst there are still some areas due to be implemented (for example Charitable Incorporated Organisations) the Charities Act 2006 has now been broadly implemented and references to the Charities Act are to that Act, unless otherwise specified.

The Companies Act 2006 has been completely implemented and references to the Companies Act are to that Act, unless otherwise specified.

The chapters in Section A cover charity law and regulation. They examine key issues such as the definition of a charity and the public benefit test, along with the role of the Charity Commission. The core changes that there have been as a result of the Charities Act 2006 are covered in detail. We then move on in Section B to discuss the different legal forms and structures that charities can take. These include trusts, companies, Industrial and Provident Societies and other forms. We also consider Charitable Incorporated Organisations and how these will operate when they are introduced. Whilst most new charities are set up as companies, and we cover the requirements in detail, the ways of working and requirements of other legal forms are also considered. The relevant chapter will also guide you through the ways of setting up a charity.

The next set of chapters concern compliance and the requirements faced in regard to record keeping and accountability to regulators. There is also a short chapter on contracts and how they are signed and sealed. Whilst this book cannot provide a detailed review of contract law, it does provide an overview of use to a charity administrator.

A core area of importance to charities is governance, and the chapters in Section C deal with this. First, we outline some of the core principles of governance and discuss how these have recently been developed. We then focus on roles and relationships within a charity and charity meetings.

Section D focuses on a charity's business. This covers issues such as the employment of staff; fundraising and trading; and key matters such as data protection.

The book then concludes in the core area of finance and the use of the charity's assets.

Kirsty Semple
January 2010

Contributors

Jane Ascroft is a Chartered Accountant with over 10 years' experience of working with charities. She runs her own accountancy practice in County Durham which specialises in the charity sector and is also a trustee for a local medium-sized charity. She wrote the accountancy and tax chapters for *The ICSA Charity Trustee's Guide*, 2nd edition.

Val King is the editor of ICSA's *Employment Law and Practice*. She was a solicitor in private practice for many years before specialising as a consultant in employment law. She is heavily involved in tribunal work and regularly advises charities on a wide range of issues with particular emphasis on restructures and TUPE.

Adrian Pashley is a senior solicitor in the Charities Team at Blake Lapthorn, providing practical legal and business solutions to charities and social enterprises. Adrian's particular areas of expertise are governance; legal structures and charity registrations; reorganisations, incorporations and mergers; and all aspects of fundraising and trading. He is a visiting university lecturer and is regularly asked to speak and write articles on issues affecting charities.

Chris Priestley is a partner at Withers LLP, where he specialises in advising on company and commercial matters for domestic and international charities. Particular specialities are fundraising law and advice to charities on all kinds of collaborative working arrangements. His practice encompasses a wide variety of constitutional and restructuring work for charities (including mergers) and the preparation and negotiation of commercial arrangements (including contracts with public bodies).

Richard Reger studied classics at Cambridge, where he volunteered for a children's charity, and he worked as an accountant in an ice cream factory before changing career direction and qualifying as a Chartered Secretary. He has been company secretary at a number of major housing associations, head of governance at the National Housing Federation and company secretary at Guide Dogs for the Blind.

Kirsty Semple ACIS LLM is a Chartered Secretary in public practice and has worked in this capacity since 2001. She works as a consultant and trainer for the voluntary sector, specialising in the fields of corporate governance compliance and company secretarial work. As well as consultancy, Kirsty also acts as company secretary for a number of organisations, including charities; a housing association and a professional body. Before going into public practice Kirsty was company secretary for Scope.

Mandy Webster is a Chartered Secretary and a non-practising barrister and has built up a wealth of business experience during her career as a company secretary and in-house lawyer. She set up Data Protection Consulting offering audit, advice and training on data protection and e-commerce in 1999 and is a well-known writer, commentator and speaker on data protection issues.

Abbreviations

ACAS – Advisory, Conciliation and Arbitration Service
BACS – Bankers Automated Clearing System
BSI – British Standards Institute
CSCI – Commission for Social Care Inspection
CEMVO – Council of Ethnic Minority Voluntary Organisations
CRB – Criminal Records Bureau
DCSF – Department for Children, Schools and Families
ET – Employment Tribunal
EAT – Employment Appeal Tribunal
EMF – Ethnic Minority Fund
ECJ – European Court of Justice
FSA – Financial Services Authority
FRSB – Fundraising Standards Board
HSC – Health and Safety Commission
HSE – Health and Safety Executive
HMRC – Her Majesty's Revenue & Customs
ICSA – Institute of Chartered Secretaries and Administrators
IIA – Institute of Internal Auditors
NCVO – National Council for Voluntary Organisations
NHF – National Housing Federation
NMW – National Minimum Wage
OSCR – Office of the Scottish Charity Regulator
SSP – Statutory Sick Pay
TUPE – Transfer of Undertakings and Protection of Employment
RNIB – The Royal National Institute of Blind People
RNLI – The Royal National Lifeboat Institution
WTR – Working Time Regulations

SECTION A

The charity's structure and legal framework

A1
Charity law and regulation

1 The meaning of charity and legal frameworks

1.1 What is a charity?

1.1.1 An essential concept to grasp is that a charity is not a type of legal structure, it is a status conferred on an organisation because of the activities it carries out. Charitable status is completely separate from the organisation's legal structure (see chapter A2).

1.1.2 In England and Wales an organisation is a charity and has charitable status if:

- it is established wholly and exclusively for charitable purposes (also known as 'objects'); and
- it provides a public benefit.

1.1.3 Registration with the Charity Commission and entry in the Central Register of Charities (which provides the organisation with a charity registration number) confirms charitable status. However, an organisation does not have to be recognised by the Charity Commission, HM Revenue & Customs or any other body to be a charity; this is a matter of fact and law. If the organisation fulfils the criteria it is a charity. There are a large number of charities which fall below the charity registration threshold (see chapter A3, paragraph 6.2 below) which are not obliged to register with the Charity Commission. There are also a number of charities which are exempt or excepted from registration (see chapter A3, section 6.16 below). However, the trustees of a charity which fulfils the registration criteria have a legal duty to apply to the Charity Commission for registration.

 1.1.4 Key features of a charity in England and Wales:

- It has to be established for exclusively charitable purposes (see paragraph 1.2 below).

- It has a body of trustees who are responsible for its administration and management. Its trustees will normally be unpaid volunteers, although it is possible to have paid trustees if the constitution or Charity Commission allows. If it is an unincorporated charity (see chapter A2), the Charity Commission will expect the majority of its trustees to be resident in the UK to ensure that it has jurisdiction over them.
- Any profits or surplus it makes cannot be paid out to its members or (except in limited circumstances) its trustees; they must be re-invested in the charity and used to fulfil its charitable aims.
- It is established to benefit the public (see paragraphs 1.3 to 1.12 below) and must not therefore give disproportionate levels of private benefit to any particular group or person. Any private (personal or commercial) benefit must be incidental. Significant non-charitable activities should be carried out through a non charitable subsidiary.
- Its assets must always be used to further its charitable purposes: 'once a charity, always a charity.'
- With some exceptions, it is regulated by the Charity Commission and (provided its gross annual income exceeds £5,000) it is registered with the Charity Commission.

The main advantages of charity status can be summarised as follows:
- Public recognition and support – funders and the general public are greatly reassured by an organisation being a charity. Charity status provides kudos and signifies integrity. Many grant funders will or can only provide funding to charitable organisations.
- Tax advantages – the UK has one of the most generous tax regimes in the world for charities. There are tax advantages both for UK charities and for UK taxpayers (individuals and businesses) who give to them. A detailed description of these tax advantages is beyond the scope of this Handbook.
- Charities do not pay tax on profits derived exclusively from activities which are in pursuit of its charitable purpose (known as 'primary purpose trading').
- Eighty per cent mandatory relief from business rates is available for property occupied by a charity and 'wholly or mainly used for charitable purposes' (and the local authority has discretion to relieve the remaining 20 per cent).
- Charities are exempt from stamp duty land tax on all acquisitions of land and buildings, whether by gift or purchase, that are used for qualifying charitable purposes.
- Gifts of any amount of cash to UK charities by individuals or organisations that pay UK income or profits taxes are eligible for relief under the Gift Aid scheme. Gift Aid relief is available whether a gift is made regularly or

as a one off payment, if the individual donor is a UK resident for tax purposes or the donor organisation pays UK corporation tax. For donations by individuals, the Gift Aid scheme enables the charity to recover income tax on the amount of the gift received, for which the donor must account to HM Revenue & Customs. In addition, individuals who pay income tax at the higher rate (currently 40 per cent) are entitled to claim the difference between the higher rate (40 per cent) and the basic rate of tax (20 per cent) on the total (gross) value of the donation. For donations made by individuals between 6 April 2008 and 5 April 2011 the charity is also entitled to a separate government supplement of 3p on every pound given under the Gift Aid Scheme.

1.2 Charitable purposes

1.2.1 The Charities Act 2006 has introduced for the first time a statutory definition of charitable purposes to the law of England and Wales.

1.2.2 A charitable purpose is:

- one which falls within any of the descriptions of purposes set out in the 2006 Act; and
- is for the public benefit.

1.2.3 The following descriptions of charitable purposes are set out in the 2006 Act:

(a) the prevention or relief of poverty;
(b) the advancement of education;
(c) the advancement of religion;
(d) the advancement of health (which includes the prevention or relief of sickness, disease or human suffering) or the saving of lives;
(e) the advancement of citizenship or community development (which includes rural or urban regeneration and the promotion of civic responsibility, volunteering, the voluntary sector or the effectiveness or efficiency of charities);
(f) the advancement of the arts, culture, heritage or science;
(g) the advancement of amateur sports;
(h) the advancement of human rights, conflict resolution or reconciliation or the promotion of religious or racial harmony or equality and diversity;
(i) the advancement of environmental protection or improvement;

(j) the relief of those in need by reason of youth, age, ill-health, disability, financial hardship or other disadvantage (which includes relief by the provision of accommodation or care);
(k) the advancement of animal welfare;
(l) the promotion of the efficiency of the armed forces of the crown, or of the efficiency of the police, fire and rescue services or ambulance services;
(m) any other purposes which:
   i. are not included in the list above, but are recognised under the existing law or the Recreational Charities Act 1958 as charitable purposes; or
   ii. may reasonably be regarded as analogous to, or within the spirit of, the charitable purposes listed above or those recognised under the existing law as charitable purposes.

1.3 Before the 2006 Act: the public benefit presumption

1.3.1 Before the Charities Act 2006 provided us with a definition of charity the definition was set out in case law. To be a charity an organisation had to have exclusively charitable purposes and be established for the public benefit (this has not changed).

1.3.2 Accepted charitable purposes were originally derived from the Statute of Elizabeth, dating from 1601, which over the years was refined by the courts to four heads of charitable purposes:

1. the relief of poverty;
2. the advancement of education;
3. the advancement of religion; and
4. any other purposes beneficial to the community.

1.3.3 The advantage of this approach was that the scope of what were considered to be charitable purposes could be expanded and altered by the courts (and the Charity Commission) to take account of changes in social and economic circumstances. For example, during the First World War, cigarettes were provided to sick or wounded service men by a number of major charities as part of their charitable activities. Cigarettes were seen as a 'useful sedative'. The provision of cigarettes to hospital patients would obviously no longer be regarded as a charitable activity for the public benefit.

1.3.4 Charities which fell within the first three heads of charitable purposes (the relief of poverty, the advancement of education and the advancement of religion) were presumed to provide a public benefit. In practice this meant that the public benefit credentials of an organisation were only really tested where it fell within the fourth, catch-all head of charitable purposes.

1.4 The public benefit requirement

1.4.1 Following the 2006 Act all organisations, without exception, wishing to be recognised or wishing to continue to be recognised as charities must demonstrate that their aims are for the public benefit and that they meet the 'public benefit requirement'.

1.4.2 Following consultation, the Charity Commission has published the following guidance (together with statements of the legal analysis underpinning its guidance):

- **Charities and Public Benefit:** general guidance on public benefit;
- guidance on the advancement of education for the public benefit;
- guidance on public benefit and fee-charging;
- guidance on the prevention or relief of poverty for the public benefit; and
- guidance on the advancement of religion for the public benefit.

1.5 General guidance

1.5.1 In its top-level general guidance the Charity Commission breaks the public benefit requirement down into two main principles, with a number of important factors within each principle:

 1.5.2 Charity Commission principles
Principle 1: There must be an identifiable benefit

1a *It must be clear what the benefits to the public are*
- Such benefits should be capable of being recognised, identified, defined or described although they do not have to be quantifiable or measurable.
- Where benefits are debatable or depend on the circumstances, evidence will need to be shown.

1b *The benefits must be related to the aims of the charity*
- The only benefits that will be taken into account are those which arise as a result of the organisation pursuing its charitable aims.
- Where an organisation has more than one aim, each aim must be for the public benefit.
- Other 'incidental' activities will not be count towards the public benefit assessment.
- An organisation which provides significant benefits which are not related to its charitable aims may be required to widen or restate its aims or cease such activities.

1c *Any benefit(s) must be balanced against any detriment or harm*
- If detrimental or harmful consequences outweigh the benefits, the organisation would not be charitable.
- Examples of detriment or harm include: the harm caused to the environment by providing motorised transport to the disabled; and the inherent risks involved in most sports.
- The Charity Commission will take into account steps taken by an organisation to minimise and reduce detrimental or harmful consequences of its activities but, however much reduced, these may still not outweigh the benefits if the organisation is to be deemed charitable.

Principle 2: Benefit must be to the public or a section of the public

2a *The beneficiaries must be appropriate to the aims of the charity.*

2b *Where benefits are provided to a section of the public, the opportunity to benefit must not be unreasonably restricted:*
- by geographical or other restrictions; or
- by ability to pay any fees charged.

2c *People 'in poverty' must not be excluded from the opportunity to benefit.*

2d *Any private benefit must be incidental.*

1.5.3 A detailed exploration of the Charity Commission's guidance is beyond the scope of this Handbook. However, we set out below some of the main issues dealt with in detail in the Charity Commission's general guidance.

1.6 Reasonable restrictions (Principle 2b)

1.6.1 The starting point is that charities should provide as much benefit as possible, given the nature of their aims and the resources available to them. In general, the greater the individual need of a charity's beneficiaries or the more limited the resources available to it, the greater the justification for benefiting a smaller number of beneficiaries.

1.6.2 Where a section of the public benefits from a charity, any restriction on who can benefit must be legitimate, proportionate, rational and justifiable given the nature of the charity's aims.

1.6.3 The Charity Commission's guidance includes the following broad principles:

- Restrictions based upon geographical areas (such as a village, town, city, council or country) or charitable need (for example, poverty, ill-health or disability) are likely to be reasonable.
- Restrictions based upon personal characteristics, for example gender, race, ethnic origin, religion or sexual orientation, will only be reasonable where there is a rational link between any such restriction and the charitable aims to be carried out.
- Any restrictions on public access to facilities should be reasonable, appropriate in the circumstances and lawful.
- Where you must be a member of a charity in order to benefit, any restrictions on who may join must be reasonable and justifiable in the circumstances. In particular, charities must not be seen as exclusive clubs that only a few can join. The more open, outward looking and inclusive the aims, the greater the public benefit.
- Where a charity's trustees have discretion as to who may benefit, the public benefit requirement is satisfied if the exercise of the discretion is within the charity's objects and those who can benefit are a 'section of the public'. However, the charity must not exclude people 'in poverty' from the opportunity to access its benefits (see further below).

1.7 Fee-charging charities

1.7.1 It has long been established that a charity is able to charge for its services and continue to be regarded as a charity. The key case is Re Resch's Will Trusts (*Le Cras v The Perpetual Trustee Company Limited and Others*) [1969] 1 AC 514, which concerned a gift which had been made to an independent hospital which charged fees at a 'substantial' level, although these were approximately at cost price.

1.7.2 The general guidance (which should be read in conjunction with the specific detailed guidance) sets out the following principles (derived from Re Resch and other relevant cases):

- Charities can charge more than cost price for services or facilities, provided such charges are reasonable and necessary in order to carry out the charity's aims, for example maintaining or developing the service provided.
- If access to the benefits provided by a charity is not dependent on payment of a financial contribution, then this will not affect public benefit. For example, in the case of religious charities whose core beliefs involve financial contributions from followers, such payments will not affect public benefit unless, in practice, the financial contribution is used as a way of restricting who can join or benefit from the charity.

- In assessing public benefit, the Charity Commission will take into account the totality of the benefits provided by the fee-charging charity.
- The fact that services or facilities are provided mainly to those who can afford them does not necessarily mean that the organisation is not operating for the public benefit.
- However, an organisation which excludes people from the opportunity to benefit because of their inability to pay any fees charged would not be operating for the public benefit.
- The public benefit requirement will not be met by providing some token (meaning minimal or nominal) benefit to those who are unable to pay the fees; they must be able to benefit in some material way related to the charity's aims.
- People who are unable to pay the fees do not have to actually take up the benefit; they must not be excluded from the opportunity to benefit.

1.7.3 The guidance states that the Charity Commission will consider the following four issues:

1. whether the levels at which fees are set have the effect of preventing people who are unable to pay the fees from benefiting from the services or facilities. The Commission will look not just at the level of fees but at the overall financial commitment;
2. if this is the case, whether it is possible to show that people who are unable to pay the fees are not excluded from the opportunity to benefit. The guidance encourages charities to be positive, innovative and imaginative in considering how to maximise benefits to the public;
3. whether and how people who are unable to pay the fees may otherwise benefit from those services or facilities; and
4. the nature and extent of the other benefits provided.

1.8 People 'in poverty' must not be excluded (Principle 2c)

1.8.1 Irrespective of the restrictions placed on who can benefit, in order to meet the public benefit requirement a charity must not exclude people 'in poverty' from the opportunity to benefit in some material way from each of the charity's aims. However, this does not mean that people in poverty actually have to benefit, nor does it introduce an element of relieving poverty into all charitable purposes.

1.8.2 Not entirely helpfully, the guidance states that there is no absolute definition of what 'in poverty' means, although it does give three examples, including the charity law meaning of 'people who are financially disadvantaged'. What is clear is that the meaning of 'in poverty' needs to be considered in the context of a charity's aims, whom those aims are intended to benefit and where it carries out its aims (one size will not fit all).

1.9 Assessing public benefit

1.9.1 New organisations seeking charity registration will be required to explain how their aims are for the public benefit and how they propose to carry them out as part of the registration process. The Charity Commission may ask for supporting evidence.

1.9.2 In assessing public benefit the Charity Commission has stated that it will follow the principles of better regulation: proportionate; accountable; consistent; transparent; and targeted.

1.9.3 The Charity Commission will carry out rolling reviews to ensure that the public benefit requirement is being met and will use the following tools for assessing public benefit:

- Public benefit reporting by trustees in their annual reports.
- Public benefit research studies – these will start with: charities for the relief of poverty; educational charities; religious charities; and fee-charging charities.
- Working with professional and umbrella bodies to establish good practice and encourage innovation.
- Carrying out detailed assessment of individual charities – desk-top assessments; assessments by telephone; and/or visits to charities.

1.9.4 Failure by the trustees to report properly in annual reports is likely to trigger an individual assessment and other regulatory action.

1.10 Not meeting the requirement

1.10.1 Trustees of a charity cannot opt out of the charitable sector if they consider that their responsibilities to meet the public benefit requirement are too onerous. If charities are found not to be meeting the requirement, the Commission will take appropriate action including:

- Seeking agreement with the trustees to alter their charity's objects or the way in which they carry out their aims.
- Taking regulatory action to ensure that the trusts are carried out, for example removing trustees, appointing new trustees or giving directions to trustees.
- Applying the assets for other similar charitable aims for the public benefit.
- If the aims were never for the public benefit and the organisation was mistakenly registered as a charity the Commission can ask the trustees to restructure the organisation; amend the aims; or remove it from the register. This option is rarely used.

1.11 The Charity Commission and public benefit

1.11.1 The Charity Commission has a new objective to promote awareness and understanding of the operation of the public benefit test and has new duties:

- to issue guidance in pursuance of its public benefit objective;
- from time to time to revise its public benefit guidance; and
- to carry out such public and other consultations as it considers appropriate before issuing or revising its guidance.

1.11.2 Charity trustees have the following new duties:

- to ensure that their charity's aims are carried out for the public benefit;
- to have regard to the Charity Commission's public benefit guidance; and
- with effect from 1 April 2008, to report on how their charity carries out its purposes for the public benefit and to confirm that they have paid due regard to the Charity Commission's guidance in deciding what activities the charity should undertake.

1.12 The reporting obligation

1.12.1 The extent of the reporting obligation depends on the size of the charity:

Large charities: gross income in the financial year + £500,000; or income + £100,000 and aggregate value of assets + £2.8 million	Full explanation in the trustees' Annual Report of the significant activities undertaken in order to carry out the charity's aims for the public benefit.
Small charities: gross income in financial year ≤ £500,000; or income ≤ £100,00 and aggregate value of assets ≤ £2.8 million	Brief summary in the trustees' Annual Report of the main activities undertaken in order to carry out the charity's aims for the public benefit.

2 Charity Commission role and responsibilities

2.1 The Charity Commission is the body which regulates charities in England and Wales. It was originally set up in 1853, as an unincorporated body of individual Charity Commissioners. Its responsibilities have widened over the years.

2.2 The Charities Act 2006 has put the Charity Commission onto a formal statutory footing for the first time.

2.3 One of the key aims of the Charities Act 2006 was to make the role and status of the Charity Commission clearer and more appropriate to modern conditions and to set out its objectives and duties comprehensively in statute for the first time.

A1 CHARITY LAW AND REGULATION

 2.4 Key features of the reformed Charity Commission:

It is a corporate body:

- Prior to the Charities Act 2006 the responsibility for regulating the charity sector was in the hands of 'The Charity Commissioners', a collection of up to 5 individuals. The new Act has transferred their assets, activities and functions to a new corporate body known as 'the Charity Commission for England and Wales' or, in Welsh, 'Comisiwn Elusennau Cymru a Lloegr'.
- The new corporate Charity Commission consists of a chairman and between 4 and 8 other members, who are appointed by the Minister for the Cabinet Office. The Charities Act 2006 stipulates criteria that some of the members must meet, the length of terms they may serve (maximum 3 years for each term, subject to a maximum of 10 years in total) and the knowledge and experience they should have. Members can be paid.

It is accountable to Parliament, but largely independent of government control:

- The Charity Commission's status in relation to government was not altered by the Charities Act 2006. It is a 'non-ministerial government department', accountable to Parliament but not subject to the control of any Minister or other government department.
- The Charity Commission has to prepare an annual report which must be made available to the public and also laid before Parliament. It is also required to hold an annual public meeting, within 3 months of publishing its annual report. Its financial year runs from 1 April to 31 March.

It has five objectives, these are:

1. **Public confidence:** to increase public trust and confidence in charities.
2. **Public benefit:** to promote awareness and understanding of the operation of the public benefit requirement.
3. **Compliance:** to promote compliance by charity trustees with their legal obligations in exercising control and management of the administration of their charity.
4. **Charitable resources:** to promote the effective use of charitable resources.
5. **Accountability:** to enhance the accountability of charities to donors, beneficiaries and the general public.

It has six general functions, which are:

1. to determine whether institutions are charities or not;
2. to encourage and facilitate the better administration of charities;

3. to identify and investigate apparent misconduct or mismanagement in the administration of charities and to take remedial or protective action in connection with misconduct or mismanagement in charities;
4. to determine whether public collections certificates should be issued, and remain in force, in respect of public charitable collections;
5. to obtain, evaluate and disseminate information in connection with the performance of any of the Charity Commission's functions or meeting any of its objectives (this objective includes maintaining an accurate and up-to-date register of charities); and
6. to give information or advice, or make proposals, to any Minister of the Crown on matters relating to any of the Charity Commission's functions or meeting any of its objectives.

It has six general duties, which are:

1. so far as is reasonably practicable, to act in a way which is compatible with its objectives and which it considers most appropriate for the purpose of meeting those objectives;
2. so far as is reasonably practicable, to act in a way which is compatible with the encouragement of charitable giving and voluntary participation in charity work;
3. to have regard to the need to use its resources in the most efficient, effective and economic way when performing its functions;
4. to have regard to the principles of best regulatory practice. In particular its regulatory activities should be proportionate, accountable, consistent, transparent and targeted only at cases in which action is needed;
5. to have regard to the desirability of facilitating innovation by or on behalf of charities; and
6. in managing its affairs, to have regard to such generally accepted principles of good governance as it is reasonable to regard as applicable to it.

2.5 In addition, the Charity Commission has a wide 'sweep-up' power to do anything which is calculated to facilitate, or is conducive or incidental to, the performance of any of its functions or general duties.

2.6 However, it is important to appreciate that the Charity Commission is not authorised to:

- exercise its functions as if it were a trustee of a charity; or
- directly involve itself in the administration of a charity.

2.7 The role of the Charity Commission is therefore to supervise and regulate the charity sector but also to provide guidance to and act as champion for the sector.

3 Charity Commission regulation, investigations and powers

3.1 In this section we explore the Charity Commission's dual role as regulator of charities and as a source of guidance and support to charities in more detail.

3.2 The Charity Commission as policeman

3.2.1 The Charity Commission has a number of statutory powers to investigate and supervise charities. These statutory powers have been strengthened and widened by the 2006 Act.

3.2.2 In this section we will look at the Charity Commission's powers:

- to instigate formal inquiries – commenced under section 8 Charities Act 1993;
- to act for the protection of charities – once a section 8 inquiry has been instigated; and more generally;
- to supervise charities.

3.3 Charity Commission investigations and section 8 inquiries

3.3.1 The Charity Commission's guidance on complaints is set out in its document CC47, 'Complaints about Charities', available directly from the Charity Commission or on its website.

3.3.2 On receipt of a complaint from a member of the public about the activities or affairs of a charity the Charity Commission will consider the matter reported to it, take a view as to whether it is best placed to deal with it and decide on the most appropriate form of action to take in the circumstances. The starting point will often be that the Charity Commission writes to the charity's trustees setting out details of the complaint and will determine whether the concern or allegation holds water and merits further investigation depending on the response received. In the vast majority of cases the matter will be dealt with by the Charity Commission providing advice to the charity and/or highlighting information in its guidance.

3.3.3 The Charity Commission is only likely to intervene in relation to a complaint in circumstances where it considers:

- that there is a serious risk of significant harm to or abuse of the charity, its assets, beneficiaries or reputation; and
- that its intervention is a necessary and proportionate response to protect the charity, its assets, beneficiaries or reputation.

3.3.4 In its guidance the Charity Commission states that it regards the following matters to be serious or significant and unacceptable for any charity, its trustees, employees or agents to be engaged in:

- causing significant financial loss to the charity;
- causing serious harm to beneficiaries and, in particular, vulnerable beneficiaries;
- activities which threaten national security, particularly terrorism;
- criminality within or involving a charity;
- setting up sham charities for an illegal or improper purpose;
- deliberately using charities for significant private advantage;
- activities which seriously call a charity's independence into question;
- serious compliance breaches within a charity that has damaged or has the potential to damage its reputation and/or the reputation of charities generally; and/or
- serious non-compliance in a charity which, left unchecked, could damage public trust and confidence in the Charity Commission as an effective regulator.

3.3.5 If any of these circumstances prevail the Charity Commission will almost certainly commence a formal inquiry under section 8 of the Charities Act 1993. A section 8 inquiry may involve a particular charity or a class of charities, although the Charity Commission does not have jurisdiction to investigate complaints about charities based in and operating in Scotland or Northern Ireland. The Charity Commission may carry out the inquiry itself or appoint any other person to conduct the inquiry on its behalf. In 2007/8 the Charity Commission opened 170 new cases and 19 formal statutory inquiries. In the same period it closed 171 non-inquiry cases and 29 inquiries.

3.3.6 When conducting a section 8 inquiry the Charity Commission (or its appointee) has the following powers:

- To direct any person to give written accounts and statements on the matter under investigation; to return answers in writing to questions posed; and to verify any accounts, statement or answers by making a statutory declaration.
- To enter premises and to seize documents, computer disks and other electronic storage devices, to take copies and to require any person on the premises to explain any such document or information or to state where they may be found. In order to exercise this power the Charity Commission must first obtain a magistrate's warrant.

    Before issuing a warrant the magistrate must be satisfied that there are reasonable grounds for believing: that a section 8 inquiry is underway; that documents or information relevant to the inquiry are on the premises specified; and that, if the Charity Commission were to make an order requiring the document or information to be provided to it, either the order would not be complied with, or the document or information would be removed, tampered with, concealed or destroyed.

Entry and search must take place at a reasonable hour and within one month of the warrant being issued. It is a criminal offence to obstruct the Charity Commission exercising its rights under such a warrant.

3.3.7 Once a section 8 inquiry has been instigated the Charity Commission has the following protective powers under section 18 of the Charities Act 1993:

- to suspend trustees, officers, employees or agents of the charity from their duties;
- to appoint additional trustees;
- to vest any of the charity's property in the Official Custodian for Charities;
- to freeze the charity's assets and bank accounts;
- to restrict any of the charity's transactions;
- to appoint an interim manager, who acts as receiver and manager of the property and the affairs of the charity (the Charity Commission maintains a panel of experts approved to carry out this role);
- to remove and replace trustees; and
- to issue an order directing a trustee, officer or employee of the charity, or the charity itself to take any action which the Charity Commission considers to be expedient in the interests of the charity. This is a wide new power given by the Charities Act 2006. The Charity Commission cannot order any action which would be unlawful or inimical to the charity's trusts or purposes.

3.3.8 Before it exercises any of its powers under section 18 of the Charities Act 1993 the Charity Commission must be satisfied either:

- that there is or has been misconduct or mismanagement in the administration of the charity; or
- that it is necessary or desirable to act in order to protect the property of the charity or to ensure that any property the charity has or is due to receive is properly applied for its charitable purposes.

3.3.9 The Charities Act 2006 has introduced a new power to enable the Charity Commission to suspend a trustee, officer, agent or employee of the charity from membership of the charity, to terminate his or her membership and to prohibit him or her from resuming their membership without the Charity Commission's approval. This power can only be exercised where the Charity Commission has suspended or removed that person from being a trustee, officer, agent or employee of the charity.

3.3.10 At the end of an inquiry the Charity Commission may publish the results of its investigation in a report or make a statement. In practice, reports are published on the Charity Commission's website. The organisation involved will usually be given an opportunity to review and make representations on the draft report before it is published.

3.3.11 The Charities Act 2006 has introduced a new supervisory power which can be exercised by the Charity Commission irrespective of whether a section 8 inquiry has been instigated. This is the power to direct that a charity's property be used or transferred in a particular way if those in control of it refuse to use or apply the charity's property for the purposes of the charity. This power could be used to ensure that trustees are meeting the public benefit requirement (see paragraphs 1.3 to 1.12 above).

3.3.12 It is also always worth bearing in mind that it is a criminal offence (punishable by a fine and/or imprisonment for up to two years) to knowingly or recklessly provide the Charity Commission with information which is false or misleading in a material particular or to wilfully alter, suppress, conceal or destroy any document required to be produced to the Charity Commission.

3.4 Power to disclose information about charities

3.4.1 The Charity Commission also has powers:

- to share information about charities with other public bodies (such as a local authority, the police, HM Revenue & Customs or any other government department), and such public bodies have the power to disclose information to the Charity Commission in order to assist it in the discharge of its functions; and
- to disclose information to and receive information from the principal regulators of exempt charities (see chapter A3, paragraph 6.16 below).

3.5 The Charity Commission representing the interests of charities

3.5.1 In its role as friend to and champion of charities, the Charity Commission:

- has various powers to assist charities;
- is required to maintain an up-to-date and accurate register of charities;
- publishes guidance (including its very useful operational guidance);
- carries out and publishes the results of consultations and research; and
- maintains a register of mergers.

3.6 Enabling powers

3.6.1 The Charity Commission has the following powers to assist charities:

- **Power to establish schemes:** this power in section 16 of the Charities Act 1993 gives the Charity Commission concurrent jurisdiction with the High

Court to establish schemes to alter the trusts of charities, including altering their objects cy-près. Unless the Charity Commission is satisfied that it is unnecessary to do so, before sealing a scheme the Charity Commission must give public notice of its proposal to make it, inviting representations to be made to it within the period specified in the notice.

Before sealing a scheme to remove a trustee, officer, agent or employee of a charity without his or her consent the Charity Commission must give the individual concerned not less than one month's notice of its proposals (unless that person cannot be found or has no known address in the UK).

In all other circumstances it is for the Charity Commission to decide how public notices should be timed and the manner in which they should be made. Before the introduction of the Charities Act 2006 (which relaxed the requirements for giving public notice) it was common practice, depending on the size and nature of the particular charity or charities, for the Charity Commission to require notices of schemes to be published in national or local newspapers or on public notice boards.

- **Power to authorise dealings with charity property, etc.:** this is a wide power in section 26 of the Charities Act 1993 exercised by issuing an order to sanction any action proposed or contemplated by the charity which the Charity Commission considers is expedient in the interests of the charity. This enables the Charity Commission to authorise a particular transaction or compromise, or a particular application of property, or to give a more general authority.
- **Power to authorise ex gratia payments, etc.:** this power in section 27 of the Charities Act 1993 is used to authorise trustees to waive the charity's right to receive property or to enable the trustees to apply the charity's property in circumstances where they have no power to do so, but they consider they have a moral obligation to do so.

  An example of the former is where a charity is left a substantial legacy in a will in circumstances where family members are left destitute. An example of the latter is where trustees wish to reward a member of staff for their hard work for their charity above and beyond any entitlement in the member of staff's contract of employment.

  Unless there is a specific power in their charity's governing document authorising such action (which is unlikely), the trustees will have acted in breach of trust and are personally liable to make good any loss to their charity if they take such action without obtaining authorisation from the Charity Commission.
- **Power to give advice and guidance:** this power in section 29 of the Charities Act 1993 enables the Charity Commission to assist any trustee of a charity who applies to it in writing for its opinion or advice on the performance of his or her duties as a trustee or otherwise about how his or her charity should be properly administered. A trustee who, acting in good faith, follows the Charity Commission's opinion or advice is protected from any breach of trust claim.

The scope of this power has been extended to enable the Charity Commission generally to issue advice or guidance about the administration of charities. This may be in respect of individual charities, classes of charities or charities generally.
- **Power to determine membership of charities:** this is a useful new power in section 29A of the Charities Act 1993 enabling the Charity Commission to make a determination about who the members of a charity are. The power is exercised either on receipt of an application by a charity or in connection with a section 8 inquiry. This power will be helpful where a charity has failed to maintain an accurate and/or up-to-date record of its members and is unable to take forward important business (such as amending its governing documents or winding up) without the approval of its membership. Many charity law practitioners all too often come across such situations in practice. Even with this new power, rectifying such situations is not the best use of a charity's resources and management time and can easily be avoided by maintaining proper records.
- **Powers to preserve charity documents:** including accepting documents for safe keeping.
- Power to order an assessment of a solicitor's bill of costs.
- Power to give directions about dormant bank accounts of charities.
- Power (concurrent with the High Court) to make schemes to establish common investment funds or common deposit funds.

3.7 Charity Commission visits

3.7.1 Between 2002 and 2007 the Charity Commission carried out a programme of review visits, attending charities to review their governance performance. The aim of the programme was to promote effective governance in charities and to gather information to assist with policy development. In November 2007, as part of the Charity Commission's restructuring, a decision was made to terminate this project.

4 Challenging Charity Commission decisions

4.1 Prior to the implementation of the Charities 2006 Act, the only avenues available to charities to challenge formal decisions of the Charity Commission were either to bring a complaint under the Charity Commission's internal procedures and/or to mount an appeal to the High Court.

4.2 The Charity Commission's decisions can have serious consequences for organisations, for example a decision not to register an organisation as a charity or to remove an organisation from the Central Register of Charities can have a devastating impact. Bringing an appeal against Charity Commission decisions to the High Court was prohibitively expensive and was not an option commonly pursued by charities.

4.3 In order to address this lack of an effective recourse to the courts, the Charities Act 2006 provides a new route for challenging a decision of the Charity Commission: the Charity Tribunal.

4.4 The route to challenge Charity Commission decisions is now as follows:

- Firstly, seek a review of the decision under the Charity Commission's internal 'Decision Review' process. This will result in a 'final decision' being issued.
- If this does not result in the outcome required, bring the matter before the Charity Tribunal (if the matter is within its jurisdiction).
- If grounds for appeal exist, appealing the Charity Tribunal's decision to the High Court.

4.5 Decision Review process

4.5.1 The Charity Commission's Decision Review process is a one-stage process, which it states will usually be concluded within a maximum three-month period. The decision received following this process is the Charity Commission's final decision, which will be published on its website and subject to appeal or review by the Charity Tribunal.

4.5.2 The Charity Commission will accept requests for a review within three months of the original decision having been made, although the Charity Commission may extend the deadline in exceptional circumstances and where it considers it would be fair to do so. The three months is calculated from the date on which written notification of the original decision was received. The Charity Commission deems written notification to have been received either on the second day after the letter enclosing the decision was sent by first-class post or on the same day if the decision was sent by e-mail before 5 p.m. on that day.

4.5.3 A request for a review can be made by any person or organisation able to show:

- that the relevant decision does, or could, directly affect them (for example the trustees or beneficiaries of the charity); or
- that they are an authorised agent of someone who is, or could be, directly affected by the relevant decision.

4.5.4 Decisions capable of review under this procedure will be those decisions made by the Charity Commission within its statutory powers and will include:

(a) All the decisions listed in the table in Schedule 1C of the Charities Act 1993, which are matters capable of appeal or review in the Charity Tribunal.
(b) Exceptional decisions which are not capable of appeal or review in the Charity Tribunal, for example orders made by the Charity Commission under sections 26, 36 and 38 of the Charities Act 1993 and where it exercises its power of interpretation set out in Charity Commission schemes. The Charity Commission may offer a Decision Review if its original decision:
   i. has consequences that affect either a person or the interests of a charity to a significant degree; or
   ii. relates to an issue which the court would consider, for example a decision capable of being judicially reviewed; or which involves significant matters or public interest issues.
(c) Decisions made by the Charity Commission under the Freedom of Information Act to withhold information from disclosure.

4.5.5 The Charity Commission will only consider carrying out a Decision Review if it is provided with:

- information or evidence in addition to that which was previously supplied to it by the applicant; or
- reasoned arguments from the applicant as to why the original decision was wrong; and
- an indication from the applicant of how changing the Charity Commission's original decision will better promote charitable purposes in the interests of the organisation in question.

4.5.6 If the Charity Commission's final decision made at the end of the Decision Review process is unsatisfactory it may be possible to seek an appeal or review of it by the Charity Tribunal.

4.5.7 Where a charity wishes to make a complaint about the outcome of a judgment made by a case-worker or a decision that is not made under any of the Charity Commission's statutory powers, the Charity Commission's guidance says that it may be able to offer a formal Outcome Review. This is undertaken by an Outcome Review Panel comprising members selected for their experience and expertise in the relevant area and remedies can include financial recompense if severe hardship or injustice is found to have occurred.

4.6 The Charity Tribunal

4.6.1 The Charity Tribunal was introduced by the Charities Act 2006 and became operational on 27 February 2008. The Charity Tribunal is part of the Tribunals Service, an executive agency of the Ministry of Justice. It is independent of the Charity Commission.

4.6.2 The members of the Charity Tribunal consist of a legally qualified President who is the judicial head of the Tribunal, 5 other legally qualified and 7 non-legally qualified members. Tribunal Members are appointed by the Lord Chancellor on recommendation from the Judicial Appointments Commission. Members must retire on reaching the age of 70 years. Subject to this, there is no limit on the length of term members can serve.

4.6.3 The Charity Tribunal:

- hears appeals against the decisions of the Charity Commission;
- hears applications for review of decisions of the Charity Commission; and
- considers references from the Attorney General or the Charity Commission on points of law.

4.6.4 The Charity Tribunal only has jurisdiction in respect of Charity Commission decisions made on or after 18 March 2008. The Charity Commission's Decision Review process must be exhausted before a matter can be brought before the Charity Tribunal.

4.6.5 Schedule 1C of the Charities Act 1993 (as inserted by Schedule 6 of the Charities Act 2006) includes a detailed table setting out which decisions, directions or orders of the Charity Commission are subject to appeal or review by the Charity Tribunal.

4.6.6 Not all decisions of the Charity Commission are subject to appeal or review by the Charity Tribunal. The following are some examples of decisions, directions or orders which can be brought before the Tribunal:

- a decision to register, or not to register, an organisation as a charity;
- a decision to remove, or not to remove, a charity from the register;
- a direction that a charity must change its name;
- a decision to instigate an inquiry under section 8 of the Charities Act 1993 (see paragraph 3.5 above); and
- an order to appoint an interim manager or to remove a trustee, following a section 8 inquiry.

4.6.7 The Charity Tribunal has no power to review a decision not to give formal advice or guidance under section 29 of the Charities Act 1993. It is open to debate whether the Charity Tribunal has power to review a complete failure by the Charity Commission to consider an issue, unless this falls within the category of a 'deemed decision' not to act.

4.6.8 The Charity Tribunal's remit does not cover delays by the Charity Commission or poor service. A charity affected in this way will be able to bring a complaint under the Charity Commission's internal procedures and if the matter is not resolved to the charity's satisfaction either to:

- the Independent Complaints Reviewer (see www.icrev.dcmon.co.uk); and/or
- the Parliamentary Ombudsman (see www.ombudsman.org.uk) – a complaint must be made via a Member of Parliament.

Each of these forums deals with maladministration, such as excessive delay or failure to follow proper procedures, and does not provide an avenue for reviewing or appealing legal decisions.

4.6.9 The Charity Tribunal has power:

- to quash the Charity Commission's original decision;
- to remit the matter back to the Charity Commission (with or without a direction to determine the matter in a particular way); or
- to substitute its own rulings.

4.6.10 The following parties can, in most cases, bring proceedings before the Charity Tribunal:

- the charity trustees;
- the charity itself; and
- any other person who is or may be affected by the decision.

4.6.11 In addition, the Attorney General, acting as the protector of charities on behalf of the Crown, may bring a case.

4.6.12 Both the Charity Commission and the Attorney General may refer questions of law to the Charity Tribunal.

4.6.13 The current rules regulating the practice and procedure of proceedings before the Charity Tribunal are set out in The Charity Tribunal Rules 2008 (Statutory Instrument no. 221 of 2008) which came into force on 27 February 2008.

4.6.14 Any party who brings proceedings in the Charity Tribunal must, in the first instance, bear their own costs. However, the Charity Tribunal can order one party to pay the other party's costs if the Charity Tribunal considers any party has acted 'vexatiously, frivolously or unreasonably' at any time during the proceedings.

4.6.15 In addition the Charity Tribunal can order the Charity Commission to pay all or part of the other party's costs if it considers that the decision, direction or order which is subject to the proceedings was unreasonable in the first place.

However, despite calls for one to be created, no suitors' fund has been set up to assist charities with the cost of bringing matters before the Charity Tribunal, and the Charity Tribunal has no power to award compensation to charities for losses caused by a decision of the Charity Commission which is subsequently overturned.

4.6.16 Any party can appeal Charity Tribunal decisions to the High Court, with the consent of the Charity Tribunal or of the High Court itself.

5 Charity regulation in Scotland and Northern Ireland

5.1 Scotland

5.1.1 Charities in Scotland are regulated by the Office of the Scottish Charity Regulator (OSCR), which was created by the Charities and Trustee Investment (Scotland) Act 2005. That Act sets out the powers and responsibility of OSCR, as well as defining what a 'charity' is for the purposes of Scottish law. Charities registered in Scotland are required to submit annual returns and accounts to OSCR.

5.1.2 The Scottish definition of a 'charity' is similar to the English definition, but has some notable differences. Charities required to register in both jurisdictions will have to comply with both definitions and both regulatory regimes.

5.1.3 Charities which are registered in England and Wales but which carry out activities in Scotland are required to also register with OSCR. An exception is made, however, if these activities are seen as insignificant or occasional. Charities which are administered or managed from Scotland, occupy land or premises in Scotland or carry out activities from an office, shop or other business premises are required to register with OSCR. OSCR has published detailed guidance on its website (www.oscr.org.uk).

5.1.4 As a condition of registration in Scotland, OSCR has required charities registered in England and Wales with significant activities in Scotland to make amendments to their governing documents which have the effect of making all of the charity's property subject to the narrower Scottish charity law test. This has left charities with a difficult decision to make, either:

- to make the amendments on the basis that being subject to the narrower test will have no effect on their day-to-day operations; or
- to go to the expense (in time and cost) of setting up a separate registered charity either in Scotland or in England and Wales, registering it in Scotland and transferring the charity's current operation in Scotland to it.

5.2 Northern Ireland

5.2.1 The Charities Act (Northern Ireland) 2008 received Royal Assent on 9 September 2008. It modernises and reforms charity law in Northern Ireland, establishing a Northern Ireland Charity Commission. This is the first time Northern Ireland has had a regulator specifically for the charity sector and creates the first register of charities in Northern Ireland. The Act is not yet fully in force, but the first Commencement Order was made in March 2009 establishing the Charity Commission for Northern Ireland (CCNI). Further Commencement Orders are scheduled and it is anticipated that the first charity registrations in Northern Ireland will be from April 2010.

5.2.2 English charities operating in Northern Ireland will have to prepare a financial statement and a statement of activities every financial year, in a form prescribed by the Department for Social Development. However, the legislation does not state what organisation, if any, this information should be submitted to, and we are waiting for further guidance.

5.2.3 It is also not yet clear whether such charities will have to register in Northern Ireland. The 2008 Act simply states that the Charity Commission for Northern Ireland shall keep a register of these organisations.

5.2.4 The 2008 Act introduced a new definition of 'charity' and 'charitable purpose' for Northern Ireland, which is largely in line with the English definition, but also has some key differences.

A2
Legal forms and structures

1 Introduction

1.1 In this section we will look at some of the legal forms and structures commonly adopted by charities and compare the key features of those forms which are most commonly encountered in practice.

1.2 To recap, charity is a status conferred on an organisation because of the activities that it carries out, it is not a type of legal form or structure.

1.3 Charities come in many sizes and legal forms. It is vital to understand the legal structure of a charity in order to be able to provide competent advice to it or to its trustees or management. It is good practice to start by carrying out an online search of the Central Register of Charities maintained by the Charity Commission (www.charity-commission.gsi.gov.uk). This will provide a description of the governing documents of the charity and copies of recently filed accounts; these usually provide sufficient information to identify the type of legal form which the charity takes. However, be aware that the information shown on the Central Register of Charities may be out-of-date and/or incomplete.

1.4 One of the most interesting aspects of advising charities is the number of different legal forms that are encountered in the sector, a number of which are either unique to the 'not-for-profit' sector or are rarely encountered in the mainstream commercial world.

1.5 There are a number of legal forms available to organisations wishing to be established in England and Wales. The most common legal forms for organisations that pursue charitable purposes are:

- Charitable Trusts;
- Unincorporated Associations;
- Companies Limited by Guarantee (CLG);
- Industrial and Provident Societies (IPS); and
- Royal Charter Bodies and charitable statutory corporations.

Table 1
Summary of key features of legal forms for charities

Unincorporated legal forms

	Constitution	Unlimited liability for directors/ committee	Membership separate from trustees/ directors?	Limited liability for members?	Regulator	Registration fee
Trust	Trust deed/ declaration of trust/Charity Commission scheme	Yes	No	N/A – there are no 'members'	Charity Commission	None
Unincorporated association	Constitution/ rules/ Charity Commission scheme	Yes	Yes	May be limited for some members, dependent on constitution or rules	Charity Commission	None

A2 LEGAL FORMS AND STRUCTURES

Incorporated legal forms

	Constitution	Unlimited liability for directors/committee	Separate membership?	Limited liability for members?	Regulator	Registration fee
Company Limited by Guarantee (CLG)	Memorandum and Articles of Association	No	Yes (but directors and members can be the same)	Yes	Charity Commission and Companies House	£20–£50 (Companies House)
Charitable Incorporated Organisation (CIO)	Constitution	No	Yes (but trustees and members can be the same)	Yes	Charity Commission	Not yet known
Industrial and Provident Society (IPS)	Rules	No	Yes	Yes	FSA and Charity Commission or Tenant Services Authority if Registered Provider	£100–£950 (FSA)

1.6 The Charities Act 2006 has introduced a new legal form designed specifically for charities, the Charitable Incorporated Organisation (CIO), which is due to be available in the near future.

1.7 Many charities own subsidiary trading companies. These will usually take the form of either:

- a company limited by shares; or
- a CLG; or
- (less commonly) a Community Interest Company (CIC) that is either a CLG or a company limited by shares.

1.8 Trusts and Unincorporated Associations are unincorporated (non-corporate) organisations; IPSs, CIOs and CLGs are corporate organisations. Table 1 summarises the key features and compares these key legal forms.

1.9 One of the key roles in advising charities is to guide founders and trustees in choosing the most appropriate legal form for their charitable endeavours.

1.10 Factors affecting formation

The key factors to consider whenever choosing or advising on the appropriate legal form for a charity are:

(a) **Risk and complexity:** what activities is the charity planning to undertake? If these activities involve any of the following, a limited liability corporate body (e.g. a company limited by guarantee, an Industrial and Provident Society (IPS) or a Charitable Incorporated Organisation (CIO)) is likely to be most appropriate:
   i. use of or ownership of any land (whether leasehold or freehold);
   ii. provision of goods and/or services to, or any other dealings with, members of the public;
   iii. entering into any significant contractual liabilities, for example: any secured or unsecured loans, employment contracts or funding arrangements.

(b) **Cost and administration:** it is generally perceived to be more expensive to set up and administer a corporate body than a charitable trust. However, all charities must comply with the rules on producing accounts and returns and filing them with the Charity Commission. The cost of setting up a corporate body is also likely to be justified by the advantages and by the comparable cost of converting an unincorporated organisation into a corporate body at a later stage.

(c) **Stakeholder involvement:** charitable trusts do not allow for involvement by stakeholders (often known as members) in the governance of the charity, whereas this is a key feature of a corporate organisation.

A2 LEGAL FORMS AND STRUCTURES

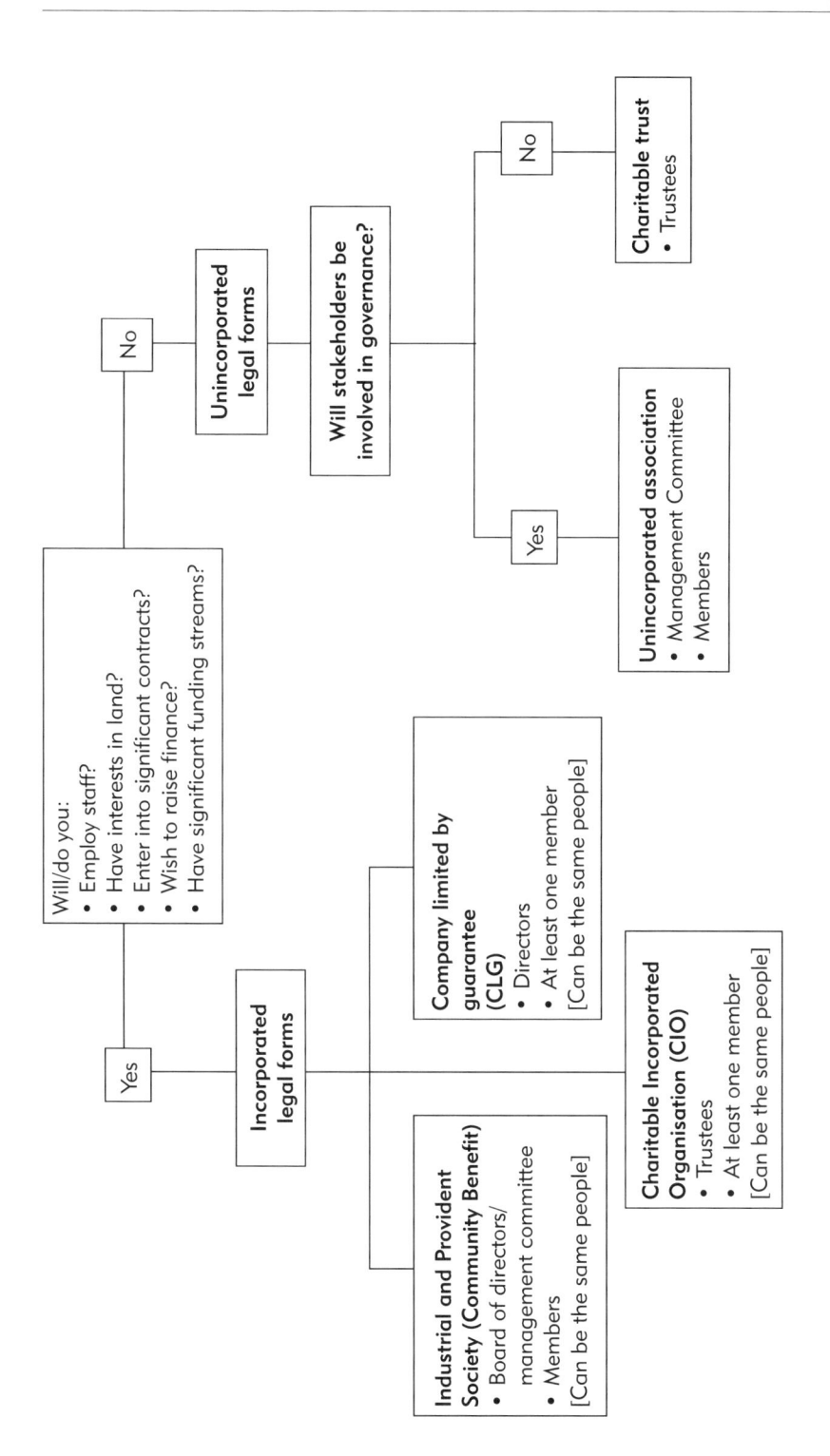

Figure 2.1: What form of charity?

1.11 Figure 2.1 is a flowchart which summarises the thought process.

2 Risk and unlimited liability

2.1 It is important to understand the practical advantages of legal forms which have a separate legal (or 'corporate') identity and how legal forms which limit liability protect against personal risk for both trustees and members.

2.2 An unincorporated charity (for example a charitable trust or unincorporated association) has no separate legal identity or personality. The assets of the charity are vested in the trustees or (in the case of an unincorporated association) the members of the charity.

2.3 Moreover, the trustees of an unincorporated charity are jointly and severally liable for the debts and liabilities of their charity. It is the trustees who are sued (or sue) in their own names as those with ultimate responsibility for the management and administration of the charity; the buck stops with them. The liability of the trustees (and the members) is unlimited. The trustees have a right to be indemnified out of the assets of the charity for all liabilities properly incurred in managing and administering the charity.

2.4 The following 'doomsday scenario' illustrates the potential practical effect of these principles:

2.5 A museum is operated as a charitable trust. As it has no separate legal personality, it is the individual trustees who own the building in which the museum is housed; their names are on the deeds, albeit in their capacity as trustees of the museum. All debts and other liabilities of the museum are the responsibility of the trustees.

2.6 During a violent storm a tree in the grounds of the museum is blown down. It topples onto a part of the museum with a glass roof; several members of the public are seriously injured. The trustees are on the receiving end of several multi-million pound claims for compensation relating to personal injuries. We will assume for the purposes of illustration that the claims are successful.

2.7 If the museum's insurances are insufficient to cover all or any part of the compensation and costs awarded to the claimants, the trustees are entitled to meet the liabilities from the assets of the charity. However, ultimately, if these liabilities exceed the value of the charity's assets, individual trustees are jointly and severally liable to meet any shortfall personally. Similar principles apply to unincorporated associations, although the members of such charities may also be personally liable (see paragraph 4.2 below).

A2 LEGAL FORMS AND STRUCTURES

2.8 Structuring the museum as a limited liability corporate form (such as a company limited by guarantee (CLG) or Charitable Incorporated Organisation (CIO)) would affect the scenario as follows:

- The museum has its own separate legal personality; the museum owns its building and is responsible for its debts and liabilities.
- If the insurances and other assets are insufficient to meet claims against it, the museum is insolvent and the trustees (subject to the points discussed in paragraphs 2.9 and 2.11 below) will not be personally liable. The members' liability will be limited to the guarantee (often £1 or £10 each) they have given in the governing document.

2.9 It is important to understand that, irrespective of the legal form their charity takes, charity trustees are vulnerable to claims by their fellow trustees, or by the Charity Commission or the Attorney General acting on behalf of the charity if they have acted in breach of duty (also known as breach of trust) and loss has been caused to the charity as a result. In practice it is highly unlikely that charity trustees will be held personally liable for breaches of trust which are made in good faith. Both the Charity Commission and the courts have power to relieve a charity trustee from personal liability for a breach of trust or duty where they consider that the trustee has acted honestly and reasonably and ought fairly to be excused. Charity trustees who have caused loss to their charity either deliberately or by acting recklessly will receive no leniency.

2.10 In addition, charity trustees who are company directors can be personally liable in the following limited circumstances:

- allowing the company to continue to trade when it is unable to meet its current liabilities out of available assets (known as unlawful trading);
- various rules under company law which have criminal sanctions; and
- corporate manslaughter.

2.11 In addition, all charity trustees, irrespective of the legal form their charity takes, can be personally prosecuted for breaches of criminal rules, including numerous health and safety rules, and for breaching competition laws.

2.12 It is possible to take out trustee indemnity insurance which, depending on the extent of the policy, will fully cover breaches of trust made in good faith and unlawful trading. Trustee indemnity insurance does not provide protection to trustees for personal liabilities to third parties where their charity is unincorporated.

3 Charitable trusts

3.1 A charitable trust is created whenever a donor gives money or other property to trusted individuals (the trustees) to be used for purposes expressed by the donor that are exclusively charitable. In its simplest form, a charitable trust can be created by word of mouth.

3.2 The terms of charitable trusts are usually set out in and governed by a trust deed or declaration of trust or Charity Commission scheme. Trusts are ideal for simple or narrow purpose charities, small-scale charities and fund-giving charities where the activities of the charity mean that the trustees are not exposed to potential personal liability.

3.3 Key features of charitable trusts

The main advantages of charitable trusts are:

- They are often quick and easy (and therefore relatively inexpensive) to set up.
- They are often relatively inexpensive to run.
- Some commentators consider that they are flexible and 'forgiving' to run (although other charity law practitioners would disagree).
- They are less rigorously regulated than corporate bodies.

The main disadvantages of charitable trusts are:

- **Unincorporated:** a charitable trust is not a legal entity in its own right; it has no 'separate legal personality'. It is the trustees who enter into contracts, employ staff, lease property, are sued and sue and enter into obligations and liabilities in their own names on behalf of the trust. This can create legal and administrative difficulties when trustees resign and new trustees are appointed.
- **Unlimited liability:** trustees of a charitable trust are jointly and severally personally liable for the debts and other liabilities of the trust. This means that if the charitable trust suffers a loss that is not covered by insurance or the realisable assets of the trust, the trustees' personal assets are at risk (see section 2).

4 Unincorporated associations

4.1 An unincorporated association is formed whenever several people join together to carry out a mutual purpose, otherwise than for profit. There are no rules in legislation governing unincorporated associations and, like charitable trusts, they can be created by word of mouth.

4.2 Key features of unincorporated associations

- They are membership organisations where the relationship between members is governed by contract, usually in the form of a constitution or set of rules.
- A board (often called a management committee) is usually elected by the members to run the unincorporated association on behalf of its members.

The main advantages of unincorporated associations are:

- They can operate relatively informally, as they are governed only by their constitution or rules.
- They enable and promote stakeholder involvement via their membership.

The main disadvantages of unincorporated associations are the same as those of a charitable trust:

- **Unincorporated:** unlike a company, an unincorporated association has no separate legal identity apart from the members of which it is composed. It exists for and by its members. The individual members of the management committee enter into obligations and liabilities in their own name on behalf of the members.
- **Unlimited liability:** depending on what the rules say, either the members of the management committee or individual members of the unincorporated association are jointly and severally liable for the debts or liabilities of the unincorporated association, and their personal assets are at risk. In practice it would be those who have delegated responsibility for the general management of the affairs of the unincorporated association (i.e. the trustees or members of the management committee) whom a well-advised litigant would be most likely to commence proceedings against.

5 Companies limited by guarantee (CLG)

5.1 For a company to be registered as a charity it must be formed as a CLG.

5.2 They are incorporated – they are legal entities in their own right and have 'separate legal personality'. They own property, hold land, employ staff, enter into contracts and can sue and be sued in their own corporate name.

5.3 They have a two-tier structure:

(a) **Members:** to whom the directors are accountable. The members give a guarantee to cover the company's liabilities. However, the guarantee is nominal, normally being limited to £1 or £10.

The members of a CLG have broadly the same powers as shareholders in a company limited by shares. However, the purpose of members within a charitable company is very different from that of shareholders, who are principally interested in protecting the value of their investment. Ideally, the members of a charitable company are stakeholders who are actively interested and involved in the work of the charity.

Providing a membership separate from management is intended to provide a layer of accountability.

Members of a CLG have various powers or rights (see below for more detail). In practice, the most important of these are:
i. to vote to remove directors;
ii. to receive a copy of the annual accounts, the directors' report and the constitution of the company;
iii. to attend general meetings of the company at which the directors may be held to account and to requisition such meetings if the directors fail to call them;
iv. to approve changes to the constitution of the company; and
v. in many cases, where the constitution specifically provides for it, to elect directors.

(b) **Directors:** who are responsible for the day-to-day management of the company. Where a CLG has charitable status, its directors are also charity trustees.

However, it is possible to structure a CLG with the directors and members as one and the same people, sometimes called an 'oligarchy' or 'all members are directors' model. This is common practice where separate stakeholder involvement in the charity is not required.

5.4 Personal liability is limited. The debts and obligations of the CLG are the responsibility of the corporate organisation and not of individual directors or (subject to their 'guarantee', see paragraph 5.3(a)) of members.

Incorporation does not provide a blanket protection against liability. Individual officers and employees of the company can be sued personally by others for their acts or omissions. In the vast majority of circumstances the company's insurances will cover the negligent acts and omissions of its employees and officers.

There are also limited circumstances when the managers of a business may be personally liable; for example, company directors who allow the company to trade whilst insolvent, corporate manslaughter, certain competition law offences and wilful or reckless breaches of trust by charity trustees (see paragraphs 2.9 to 2.12).

5.5 The *ultra vires* rule applies – a person who, acting in good faith, enters into a transaction with a non-charitable company is entitled to assume that the directors have power to bind the company and that the company has legal capacity to carry out the activity irrespective of what it says in the company's constitution. This does not apply to charitable companies, to which the *ultra vires* rule does apply. The directors/trustees of any charity must ensure that all of the charity's activities are authorised by its objects and the powers it has to achieve those objects. The members of a charitable company can, however, ratify acts of the directors which are beyond the company's capacity, but only with the Charity Commission's prior written consent.

5.6 They are constituted and governed by Memorandum and Articles of Association:

- The Memorandum of Association establishes the formal charitable and corporate limited liability status of the CLG. It used to set out its objects and the powers it has to achieve those objects. Since the Companies Act 2006 was fully implemented the Memorandum of Association has become a short statement establishing the company signed by the first member(s), and the Articles of Association contains details of how the company will be organised.
- The Articles of Association contain all of the key rules regulating a company. They regulate the internal management of the CLG and set out procedural rules for meetings of the directors and the members. The members have power to amend any provision in the Articles of Association by special resolution. Companies are able to conditionally entrench provisions within their Articles. These are provisions that can be altered or removed only when certain conditions have been met (e.g. with written consent of the Charity Commission). It is not possible to absolutely entrench provisions in a company's Articles (i.e. include provisions that can never be changed) unless such provisions already existed in the company's Memorandum and/or Articles and are unchangeable.

5.7 They are registered with Companies House and regulated by company law.

5.8 In order to be a charitable company, a CLG must:

- have objects that are charitable;
- have a provision in its constitution (which cannot be altered or removed) that prevents any profits from being distributed to its members by way of dividend and requires profits to be retained for application towards its charitable purposes (known as a 'non-distribution' clause or an asset lock); and
- have a provision in its constitution that in the event of its dissolution any surplus will not be divided among the members but will go to an organisation or organisations with the same or similar charitable objects.

5.9 The main advantages of incorporating as a CLG are:

- **separate legal personality** (see paragraph 5.2 above);
- **limitation of liability** (see paragraph 5.4 above);
- **clear ownership/governance structure:** the CLG is a tried and tested legal structure that has been in existence for many years. There is a clear legislative framework governing CLGs and powers, and processes for decision-making are well understood;
- **increased public accountability/transparency:** CLGs have to have a registered office, file their constitutions, annual returns, members' resolutions and prescribed details of their directors and (if they choose to have one) company secretary with Companies House and are accessible to the public; and
- **recognition by financial institutions, investors and donors:** financial institutions, investors and major donors will understand the nature and mechanics of a company better than any other legal form currently available.

5.10 Membership: in more detail

5.10.1 Members have the following rights:

(a) To receive notice of, attend, speak and vote at all general meetings of the company and to appoint proxies to attend, speak and vote at meetings of the company.
(b) Only if required by the company's Articles, to hold an Annual General Meeting (AGM) in every calendar year.
(c) If the company's Articles require an AGM, the Articles will often give members the following rights in relation to each AGM:
    i. to receive the accounts of the company for the previous financial year;
    ii. to receive the directors' reports on the activities of the company since the previous AGM;
    iii. to accept the retirement of directors; and
    iv. to appoint auditors.
(d) To inspect the minutes and resolutions of general meetings free of charge and to receive a copy, for which they pay a fee.
(e) To inspect the register of members free of charge and to receive a copy, for which they pay a fee.
(f) To reject the reports of the directors; this operates as a vote of censure on the directors, but has no other effect.

5.11 The Companies Act 1985 (repealed in its entirety by 1 October 2009) provided members with the following powers, exercisable by members passing a special resolution:

- to alter the objects of the company;
- to amend certain clauses in the Memorandum of Association;
- to change the name of the company; and
- to amend any provision in the Articles of Association.

5.12 Of these, only the power to amend any provision in the Articles of Association is retained by the Companies Act 2006. From 1 October 2009 all of the rules on how the company is managed and organised, including its objects and powers, will either be contained in or be deemed to be contained in the Articles.

5.13 Members also have certain statutory powers which cannot be taken away from them. These include:

- power to remove a director by passing an ordinary resolution at a meeting at which special notice has been given;
- power to petition for a compulsory liquidation;
- power to require circulation of written resolutions and statements;
- power to require the directors to call a general meeting;
- the right to inspect directors' service contracts and to approve contracts for more than two years by resolution. This is unlikely to be relevant where directors are unpaid;
- the right to approve substantial non-cash asset transactions with a director or a person connected with a director; and
- the right to approve loans to directors.

5.14 Members may also in normal circumstances use ordinary resolutions to appoint directors and sometimes to ratify certain actions that the directors have taken (subject to obtaining the prior written approval of the Charity Commission).

5.15 Resolutions (whether special or ordinary) that the members can pass at a general meeting may also be passed as written resolutions. The process for these was simplified by the Companies Act 2006, the requirements now being:

- **ordinary resolution:** simple majority: over 50 per cent of members eligible to vote); or
- **special resolution:** not less than 75 per cent of members eligible to vote.

Companies should ensure that their Articles of Association are in line with these rules.

5.16 Written resolutions lapse if the required majority is not achieved within 28 days of its circulation date (see section 11 for more detail).

5.17 It is essential that charities structured as companies limited by guarantee ensure that their company books are kept up to date, recording details of current members. Failure to do so can create real problems in passing members' resolutions and administrating the company's membership.

6 Industrial and Provident Societies (IPS)

6.1 IPSs are societies, not companies. They take two forms:

- **community benefit societies:** set up to benefit the community as a whole; and
- **co-operative societies:** set up to benefit their members.

6.2 Because co-operatives are established for the benefit of their members rather than for the public benefit, they are not usually charitable, except where a necessary condition of membership is to be within a class of charitable beneficiaries. Most charitable IPSs are community benefit societies. Following amendments to the list of exempt charities set out in Schedule 2 to the Charities Act 1993 (as amended by the Charities Act 2006) charitable IPSs are exempt from registration with the Charity Commission if they are registered in the register of social landlords under Part 1 of the Housing Act 1996 (in other words where they are Registered Providers (RPs)). The Tenant Services Authority (which replaced the Housing Corporation on 1 December 2008) registers and regulates RSLs. During the current transitional period, IPSs which are not RPs need to register with the Charity Commission only if they have an income of over £100,000.

6.3 Key features of community benefit societies

They are corporate bodies (see paragraph 6.1 below) and the personal liability of their members and directors is limited (see paragraph 6.1 below).

As with CLGs (see paragraph 5.3 above), they have a two-tiered structure:

- **a board of directors or management committee:** who owe fiduciary duties and duties of skill and care similar to those owed by directors of companies; and
- **members:** who can be individuals, corporate organisations such as companies and other societies and nominated representatives of unincorporated associations.

Members normally have the following powers:

- to elect and dismiss the board of directors or management committee;
- to appoint and dismiss the auditors;
- to change the rules by special resolution; and
- to approve a transfer of engagements, amalgamation or conversion.

They are registered with the FSA, rather than Companies House.

6.4 Their constitutions are known as 'rules', which are either bespoke or model rules registered by one of the recognised sponsoring bodies, for example the National Housing Federation. A society's rules and any amendments to rules are subject to approval by and registration with the FSA.

6.5 The rules of a charitable community benefit society will include the following provisions:

- what powers members have generally;
- that no benefits are to be returned to members by way of dividend;
- that each member has one vote; and
- that on a winding up members have no right to a share of the assets of the society, and any surplus must be applied for the same or similar charitable purposes to those pursued by the society.

6.6 The main advantages of IPSs are similar to those of CLGs, namely:

- **Incorporated:** they are separate legal entities in their own right which own assets, employ staff, sue or are sued, enter into contracts and other liabilities in the their corporate name; and
- **Limited liability:** the debts and obligations of the IPS are the responsibility of the corporate organisation and not individual directors. The personal liability of the members of a community benefit society is limited to the value of their shareholding, which will be a nominal value (e.g. £1).

6.7 Although IPSs are corporate bodies which provide limited liability for their directors and members they are not commonly found outside the social housing sector. They are comparatively expensive to set up and are generally considered not to be well understood by financial institutions, investors, donors and professionals, particularly outside the circle of experienced advisers to the third sector.

6.8 HM Treasury has carried out a consultation on reforming the law governing Industrial and Provident Societies and Credit Unions. Responses to the consultation have now been published. On 14 April 2009 HM Treasury published for consultation a draft Regulatory Reform Order to amend the legislation for IPSs and Credit Unions. The main changes proposed which are relevant to charitable IPSs are as follows.

6.9 Currently those under the age of 16 cannot become members of an IPS and those under the age of 18 cannot become an officer (a member of the committee, trustee, manager or treasurer). It is proposed to remove the restriction on the age of members and to make the minimum age for an officer 16. This will bring IPSs into line with limited companies.

6.10 Currently, IPSs are obliged to provide any individual with a copy of their rules on payment of a sum not exceeding 10p. This creates an administrative burden for the society, which has to charge for each copy of the rules they supply. The proposed change will enable IPSs to provide copies of their rules free of charge to members and to charge non-members up to £1.

6.11 It is also proposed to relax the requirements for dissolving a dormant IPS. Currently 75 per cent of all members are required to vote in favour of a resolution to dissolve an IPS. This rule makes it very difficult to dissolve a dormant society where contact with registered members has been lost. The proposed changes will permit societies to dissolve if they pass a 'special resolution' agreed by two-thirds of those present at a general meeting. Only dormant IPSs will be able to use this procedure.

6.12 IPSs will be able to choose their own accounting year end provided they notify the FSA and they will no longer be required to have their interim accounts audited if they chose to publish interim accounts.

7 Charitable Incorporated Organisations (CIO)

7.1 The CIO is a new corporate structure specifically designed for charities which is expected to be introduced into the law of England and Wales in late spring 2010. The aim is that the CIO will be a simpler and cheaper alternative to other corporate structures.

7.2 The CIO was developed by the Charity Law Association working with the University of Liverpool. The intention is to provide a corporate structure specifically for charities, with the benefits of limited liability, but without the burden of dual registration with both the Charity Commission and Companies House. A CIO will have to be registered with and report to only the Charity Commission.

7.3 The rules on CIOs are found in the following:

- Part 8A of the Charities Act 1993 as updated by the Charities Act 2006;
- Draft Charitable Incorporated Organisations (General) Regulations;
- Draft Charitable Incorporated Organisations (Insolvency and Dissolution) Regulations; and
- Draft Charity Tribunal (Amendment) Order.

7.4 Key features of CIO

(a) It is a corporate entity with separate legal personality.
(b) It provides limited liability protection for its trustees and members.
(c) It has a constitution, which is similar to the Memorandum and Articles of Association of a company.

A2 LEGAL FORMS AND STRUCTURES

(d) It has a principal office in England or Wales.
(e) It has at least one member.
(f) Like a CLG, it has a two-tier structure:
   i. trustees; and
   ii. members.

7.5 CIOs are obliged to adopt a constitution in or as near as possible to a form prescribed by the Act. There are two forms:

(1) an Association CIO: which has a body of members distinct from the trustees who may be required to pay subscriptions; and
(2) a Foundation CIO: in which the members and trustees are one and the same persons (as is possible in a company limited by guarantee – see paragraph 5.3 above).

7.6 The draft Regulations contain a model form constitution for each type of CIO. Where it is proposed to establish a CIO with a bespoke constitution which deviates from the model forms, its constitution must contain the following as a bare minimum:

- a statement of the CIO's purpose (which must be charitable);
- a clause preventing the distribution of profits;
- a clause restricting the extent to which trustees can derive benefit from their position;
- provisions covering the appointment and retirement of members and of trustees; and
- provisions on what will happen to any surplus funds if the CIO is wound up solvent.

7.7 The Charity Commission has warned that CIOs wishing to depart from the model form constitutions can expect their applications for registration to be delayed. As the anticipated timescale for the Charity Commission to process an application is 40 days, this may be important for founders considering what form of constitution is appropriate when setting up a CIO.

7.8 Subsequent amendments to a CIO's constitution which would alter:

- the CIO's purposes;
- any application of CIO property on winding up; or
- any provision authorising benefits to members, trustee or any person connected to them

will require the Charity Commission's prior written consent.

7.9 The process to be followed to establish a new CIO is as follows:

- Application to be made to the Charity Commission to be assessed by the 'Registrations Unit';
- Submission of the proposed constitution and other documentation for approval; and
- Provided the application and documents are approved, the Charity Commission will add the CIO to the Register of Charities, and the CIO will become a charity and a body corporate without any requirement for it to also be registered at Companies House.

7.10 The Charities Act 1993 (as amended) contains mechanisms for converting charitable companies and IPSs to CIOs. The existing body is simply re-registered as a CIO; there is no new corporate body to be set up and the organisation's legal personality and relationships remain unchanged and it is likely that it will retain the same registered charity number.

7.11 There is no specific mechanism in the Charities Act 1993 (as amended) for the conversion of trusts or unincorporated associations to CIOs. However, the Charity Commission has published guidance stating that trustees of unincorporated charities must establish a CIO, transfer the assets of the unincorporated charity to the CIO and wind up the unincorporated charity. The CIO will be a new legal entity, with a new registered charity number and all existing contracts will need to be transferred to the CIO.

7.12 CICs (see section 10 below) will also be able to convert to become a CIO, although no mechanism is provided in the Charities Act 1993 (as amended), and the Charity Commission has not yet published any guidance on this.

7.13 There are also mechanisms in the Charities Act 1993 (as amended) to facilitate mergers of CIOs.

7.14 Whilst CIOs have been introduced to provide an alternative, simpler legal form for charities wishing to receive the benefits of incorporation, it remains to be seen whether in practice the CIO will provide significant advantages in comparison with operating as a CLG. Although CIOs will have only one regulator (the Charity Commission) it is highly likely that the technical rules governing CIOs will be the same as or very similar to those governing CLGs. Unlike CLGs, which have been available under English law for many years, CIOs are untried and untested, and it may take some time following their introduction for commercial lenders, funders, donors and professional advisers to become comfortable with dealing with them.

8 Other legal forms

8.1 Charities can (but in practice relatively rarely do) take the following forms:

- company limited by shares;
- Royal Charter body; or
- statutory corporation/Act of Parliament body.

8.2 The company limited by shares (CLS) is the norm in the field of commercial activity. A CLS has shareholders who each purchase at least one share in the company. The CLS is generally not a suitable legal form for charities. They are designed for returning profit to their shareholders and are not well suited to 'not for profits'. It is extremely unusual to structure a charity as a CLS, and registration is permitted only in exceptional circumstances (for example The Charity Bank Ltd, registered by the Charity Commission in 2002 on the basis that the share structure was necessary for the bank to achieve its objects and that there would be no distributions made to non-charitable shareholders without the Commission's consent). Trading companies set up by charities are, however, usually private companies limited by shares; the charity, or someone appointed by the charity, will normally own all the shares (see section 13 below).

8.3 A Royal Charter is the exercise of the Royal Prerogative of the Sovereign. This is an ancient format bestowed (rarely) by the Privy Council which gives corporate status. In modern times, incorporation by Royal Charter has generally been confined to professional, charitable, scientific, educational or learned non-profit-making institutions or societies. The constitution of a Royal Charter body is bespoke and, along with any variation of it, subject to approval by the Privy Council Office. The process of obtaining a Royal Charter and making constitutional changes is very slow and costly. Examples of charities established by Royal Charter include The Royal National Institute of Blind People (RNIB), registered charity number 226227, and The Royal National Lifeboat Institution (RNLI), registered charity number 209603.

8.4 A number of charitable organisations are established as corporations by statute. They are governed by the statute creating them and by any supplemental rules set out in secondary legislation. For example, Further Education Corporations, which operate many Further Education Colleges, are statutory corporations established under the Further and Higher Education Act 1992 and are governed by rules in that Act and by Instruments and Articles of Government prescribed by Statutory Instrument. Further Education Corporations are exempt charities (see chapter A3, paragraph 6.16 below). A very few charities are established as corporate bodies by their own individual Act of Parliament. The terms of the statute govern the charity. An example of a charity established by Act of Parliament is the Board of Trustees of the Armouries, usually known as the Royal Armouries (a charity exempt from registration with the Charity Commission), which is governed by provisions in the National Heritage Act 1983.

9 Incorporation of charity trustees

9.1 Part VII of the Charities Act 1993 enables the trustees of a charity to apply to the Charity Commission for a certificate of incorporation of the trustees as a body corporate.

9.2 Once the certificate is granted the trustees become a body corporate. This is different from the charity itself becoming incorporated (for example as a company limited by guarantee, see section 5, above), and has the following advantages.

9.3 The charity's property is vested in the name of the corporate body, avoiding the need to transfer title to land and investments into the names of new trustees whenever appointed. Once issued by the Charity Commission, the certificate of incorporation automatically vests all of the charity's property in the corporate body.

9.4 In addition, the trustees are able to enter into contracts, sue and be sued in the name of the corporate body, rather than in their own name.

9.5 However, it is important to appreciate that this procedure does not provide charity trustees with the protection of limited liability. The trustees remain as personally liable for the acts and omissions of the charity as they were before a certificate of incorporation was issued. This procedure is therefore of limited appeal to charity trustees.

9.6 To apply for a certificate of incorporation of the trustees, a case for incorporation must be put to the Charity Commission, together with a form (currently CSD-1093A) signed by all of the trustees. The trustees need to decide on the following:

- (subject to the Charity Commission's approval) the name of the corporate body; and
- whether they wish to have a common seal. This is not compulsory, but if they wish to have one, they need to give details to the Charity Commission and confirm that they have agreed proper measures for its safekeeping and made regulations for its use.

9.7 Once a certificate of incorporation has been issued, the trustees can sign documents either:

- by using the common seal – if they have decide to have one; or
- by signing by a majority expressed as executives by the corporate body; or
- by giving any two or more trustees authority in writing or by resolution to execute the documents in the name of, and on behalf of, the corporate body.

10 Community Interest Companies (CIC)

10.1 The Community Interest Company (CIC) was recently developed to address the lack of an appropriate legal vehicle for *non-charitable* social enterprises. CICs provide a legal form for businesses that trade with social purposes, and, like charities, they allow for an organisation's assets to be locked, preventing their distribution to members or shareholders. Unlike charities, however, they are suited to social entrepreneurs who wish both to control the organisation and to receive a salary from it. They also offer (albeit limited) opportunities for social investors to inject long-term share capital.

10.2 Whilst a CIC cannot be a charity, it is possible for an English or Welsh charity to convert to a CIC, subject to the approval of the Charity Commission and a restriction to use the pre-conversion assets for the original charitable purposes. Scottish charities are not currently able to convert to a CIC.

10.3 Whilst CICs are free from the red tape which comes with charitable status, they do not benefit from any of the tax incentives available to charities. CICs can benefit from Community Interest Tax Relief but otherwise do not have any special tax status.

10.4 A CIC is a type of company. There are three main types of CIC:

(1) Those that are limited by guarantee which cannot declare dividends; all profits go back into the company.
(2) Those that are limited by shares but have a limited shareholding and no ability to declare a dividend.
(3) Those that are limited by shares which do have a (limited) ability to declare a dividend.

10.5 A CIC may be a public limited company.

10.6 Key features of CICs

They must pass a 'community interest test' – the test is whether a reasonable person would consider that the company's activities are for the benefit of the community. The test is objective, transparent and 'light touch'.

The definition of 'community' includes sections of the community. Political parties, the promotion of or opposition to changes in applicable law or policy and activities which benefit only the employees of a single employer or members of a particular body are excluded.

They are regulated by the CIC Regulator – the Regulator is responsible for ensuring that CICs operate for the benefit of the community, both at registration and ongoing. The CIC Regulator has power to appoint, suspend or remove directors of CICs. The CIC regulator can investigate complaints from stakeholders and has power to act if it finds that a CIC is not working in the interest of the community or the asset lock is not being observed.

They have an asset lock – this ensures that any profits made by the CIC are reinvested for the benefit of the community and are not distributed to its members or shareholders. The asset lock does not, however, prevent CICs from using their assets efficiently in pursuit of community benefit: for example, a CIC can use its assets as collateral for finance, can receive grant funding and take out secured and unsecured loans.

If assets of a CIC are to be transferred to another, they must be transferred for full value unless the transfer is to another asset-locked body, either as specified in the CIC's constitution or as approved by the CIC Regulator, or otherwise for the benefit of the community. A CIC may buy back its shares from investors at par.

CICs limited by shares are subject to a dividend cap – CICs can distribute profits by declaring dividends on shares, subject to a cap set by the CIC Regulator. The cap is expressed to be a percentage of the paid-up value of the share. Because the level of the cap can be changed by the CIC Regulator, the cap applicable is that set by the CIC Regulator at the time the share was issued or the date the company became a CIC (whichever is the later).

At the time of publishing this, a dual cap applies:

- no dividend as a percentage of the paid-up value of the share can be higher than 5 per cent above the Bank of England base rate; and
- the aggregate dividend paid must not be greater than 35 per cent of the CIC's distributable profit.

An interest payment cap – this relates to any debts or debentures on which interest is to be paid by the CIC at a performance-related rate (i.e. limited to the CIC's profits, turnover or balance sheet). The cap is calculated on the average amount of the debt over the 12 months running to the day before the interest due date. The cap is set by reference to an index, for example the Bank of England base rate.

10.7 As with any limited company, a CIC is governed by Memorandum and Articles of Association. However, these have to include various provisions depending on the type of CIC, and it is prudent to base these on the model forms published on the CIC Regulator's website. The process for registering a CIC is similar to registering a standard limited company.

11 Constitutions

11.1 Types of constitution

11.1.1 As we have seen, different legal forms have different types of governing document or governing instrument, the most common being:

- **Charitable trusts:** which have deeds or declarations of trust, or may be governed by Charity Commission schemes or a bequest in a will.
- **Unincorporated associations:** which have rules or constitutions, these being a contract between members.
- **Industrial and provident societies:** which have rules which must include certain provisions prescribed by the Industrial and Provident Societies Act 1965 and often take the form of model rules prescribed by a promoting body, for example the National Housing Federation.
- **Companies limited by guarantee:** which have Memorandum and Articles of Association which must include certain provisions prescribed by the Companies Acts.
- **Charitable Incorporated Organisations:** which will have a constitution which must include certain provisions prescribed by the Charities Act 1993 (as amended by the Charities Act 2006).
- **Royal Charter body:** which have a Royal Charter or Letters Patent handed down by the Sovereign or Privy Council.

11.1.2 Whilst it is possible in law to create both a charitable trust and an unincorporated association without setting out in writing any of the rules by which it operates, it is good practice to do so in order to provide clarity and to help avoid disputes over the purposes, powers and internal management of the organisation. Corporate bodies such as companies incorporated under the Companies Acts, Industrial and Provident Societies and Royal Charter bodies cannot be created without a written constitution in a particular form.

11.1.3 A number of organisations offer model governing documents of charities; for example, the Charity Commission's model documents for a charitable trust, an unincorporated association and a charitable company limited by guarantee are available (together with guidance notes) on its website. It is common practice for solicitors who are members of the Charity Law Association (CLA) to promote the use of model documents prepared by that Association.

11.2 Nature and purpose of constitution

11.2.1 The constitution or governing instrument of a charity is its most important document. It sets out its charitable purposes, the powers it has (or its trustees have) to achieve these purposes and the internal rules governing the board of trustees and, where relevant, the relationship between the board and the charity's membership.

11.2.2 For an unincorporated association, a company and an Industrial and Provident Society the constitution is a legally enforceable contract which sets out:

- the rights and obligations of members in relation to the charity;
- the rights and obligations of members in relation to each other; and
- the powers and obligations of the board of trustees in relation to the members and to the charity itself.

11.2.3 For an unincorporated trust, the declaration, deed of trust, Charity Commission scheme or bequest in a will sets out the rules which the charity trustees must follow in managing their charity. The Charity Commission and, ultimately, the courts have power to interpret and enforce these rules.

11.2.4 It is worth bearing in mind, however, that the written constitution of a charity may not always contain all of the rules applicable to it. The express terms of the constitution are often supplemented or even overridden by:

- rules contained in legislation – for example the Companies Acts for limited companies; and the Trustee Act 2000, which applies to trustees of charitable trusts and unincorporated associations;
- case law or common law.

Before creating or amending the constitution of a charity you should be aware of these rules.

11.2.5 One of the key duties of charity trustees is to ensure that their charity is governed in accordance with its constitution. Trustees who abuse their charity's funds (for example, by allowing the charity to engage in activities not in pursuance of its charitable objects or in which the charity has no power to engage) or who are guilty of mismanagement may be in breach of trust and could be held personally liable for making good any loss caused to the charity as a result.

11.3 Contents of constitutions

11.3.1 As a general rule it is prudent to ensure that a charity's constitution sets out the rules governing it in full, using plain English so that the trustees can both follow them without seeking legal advice at every turn and be reasonably confident that the rules are complete and can be relied on without reference to legislation or other law except where absolutely necessary (for example, the rules in the Charities Act 1993 on disposing or mortgaging land, see below for further detail).

11.3.2 Whilst the declaration of trust or trust deed of a charitable trust, the constitution of an unincorporated association, the rules of an Industrial and Provident Society and the Memorandum and Articles of Association of a company limited by guarantee will include significant differences in both content and drafting style, they should cover the matters set out in the following checklist.

11.4 Name

11.4.1 Care should be taken to ensure that the name proposed (either for a new charity or for a name change of an existing charity):

- is not the same or confusingly similar to a charity already registered with the Charity Commission;
- where it is a company, is not the same or confusingly similar to a company already registered with Companies House;
- where it is an Industrial and Provident Society, is not the same or confusingly similar to an Industrial and Provident Society already registered with the Financial Services Authority; and
- does not include a word or words which cannot be used without the prior approval of the Secretary of State or a specified body. The Company and Business Names Regulations 1981 (SI 1981/1685) as amended contains lists of these words.

11.5 Charitable companies

11.5.1 Under section 60 of the Companies Act 2006 a charitable company may be exempt from the usual requirement to include the word 'limited' as part of its name provided the requirements of the section are satisfied.

11.5.2 The exemption is obtained by completing a statutory declaration and filing it with Companies House, currently using Form NEO 1.

11.6 Location

11.6.1 Companies limited by guarantee and industrial and provident societies must state the country of domicile of their registered office: either 'England and Wales' or 'England' or 'Wales'.

11.7 Objects

11.7.1 This is the most important clause in a charity's constitution. As we have seen, the objects must be exclusively charitable and care must be taken when drafting.

11.7.2 It is, generally, good practice to frame the objects as broadly as possible to help ensure that both the current and future activities of the charity are within the objects. This will help reduce the risk of the charity inadvertently carrying out activities which are not within the objects and the trustees being in breach of trust as a result.

11.8 Powers

11.8.1 This clause will set out the means by which the charity fulfils its charitable objects. These should be carefully considered to ensure that the charity has power to carry out all its current and future activities.

11.8.2 If the trustees allow the charity to carry out any activity which is outside the powers expressly set out in the constitution, given by statute or implied by case law then they have acted *ultra vires* (outside their powers) and may be personally liable for any loss caused to the charity.

11.8.3 It is vital to appreciate that the powers a charity has must be exercised only in furtherance of its charitable purposes. For example:

- A power to make grants or loans must only be exercised by making grants or loans either to individuals or to other organisations within the purposes of the charity.
- A power to purchase property must either be exercised to directly further the purposes of the charity (for example, a charity for the advancement of education which purchases a building for use as a place of worship) or on an investment basis with the intention of improving the financial position of the charity so that it can better further its purposes (for example, the same charity purchases retail units in order to provide a rental income to help fund its work).

11.8.4 A modern, forward-thinking charity should have a full suite of powers.

11.8.5 The following are all examples of powers which are included in the Charity Law Association's model trust deed for a charitable trust and its model Memorandum and Articles of Association of a charitable company:

(a) general powers – for example: to promote or carry out research; to publish or distribute information; to co-operate with other bodies; to support, administer or set up other charities; to make grants or loans of money and to give guarantees; to set aside funds for special purposes or as reserves against future expenditure; and to pay for the costs of forming the charity.

(b) powers in relation to property, for example:
   i. power to acquire or to hire property of any kind;
   ii. subject to the restrictions imposed by the Charities Acts, power to borrow and charge property – to raise funds by loans or other forms of borrowing and to mortgage or charge the charity's property for this purpose. Banks will require reassurance that a charity's constitution includes an express power as a prerequisite for any borrowing (secured or unsecured);
   the trustees' power to mortgage their charity's land is subject to the restrictions set out in sections 38 and 39 of the Charities Act 1993 (as amended by the Charities Act 2006). If the trustees are unable to take advantage of the procedure in section 38 a Charity Commission Order will be required to authorise the borrowing;
   iii. subject to the restrictions imposed by the Charities Acts, power to let or dispose of property – before entering into any legally binding agreement to sell, lease, make a gift of or otherwise dispose of their charity's land (or any interest in the land, which includes granting easements, wayleaves and options) the trustees must either follow the procedures in section 36 of the Charities Act 1993 (as amended by the Charities Act 2006) or obtain an Order from the Charity Commission specifically authorising the disposal;
   In particular a Charity Commission Order will always be required before any of the charity's land can lawfully be disposed of to any person who, or organisation which, has a connection with either the trustees or with the charity itself;

(c) powers in relation to fundraising and trading – including:
   i. power to establish or to acquire subsidiary companies;
   ii. power to raise funds but not by means of taxable trading;

(d) standard commercial powers – for example:
   i. to employ (paid or unpaid) staff, agents or advisers – this should cover employees, volunteers, consultants and other independent contractors and enable the charity to provide pensions and other employee benefits;
   ii. to insure the charity's property and to take out such other insurance policies as may be required to protect the charity (for example, public liability insurance, employers' liability cover, product liability insurance and motor risks cover);
   iii. to enter into contracts to provide services to or on behalf of other bodies;

(e) to purchase indemnity insurance for the charity's trustees (see further details below);

(f) powers in relation to investments – it is important that express powers to deposit and invest funds and to delegate the management of the charity's investments to a financial expert are provided for corporate charities. For unincorporated charities, if an express power is not included, the position will be governed by the statutory power of investment in the Trustee Act 2000; however, this does not give power to invest in land outside the UK and it is always prudent to set out the trustees' powers in full.

The power should set out the terms on which the management of investments can be delegated to a financial expert, including: a requirement to set out the trustees' investment policy in writing; for transactions to be reported promptly to the trustees; for the investment policy and the delegation arrangements to be reviewed at least annually; and the ability for the trustees to cancel the delegation arrangements at any time;

(g) a final 'blanket' power – to do all such other lawful things which further the objects of the charity.

11.9 Benefits to trustees

11.9.1 The general rule is that charity trustees can receive a benefit from the charity they administer only in the following circumstances:

- express constitutional power: if and to the extent that the charity's constitution expressly permits it;
- with the authority of the regulator: if the Charity Commission (or ultimately the courts) permit it; or
- statutory permission: if and to the extent that it is permitted by a statutory provision.

11.9.2 A benefit will include a straightforward payment of money and any other benefit which has a monetary value. The rules extend not just to trustees but to any individual or business connected with a trustee. The 'connected person' rules extend to:

- relatives: a spouse, partner, brother, sister, child, parent, grandchild or grandparent of a trustee; and
- businesses: any partnership in which a trustee is a member or employee; or any company of which a trustee is a director or an employee or of which a trustee has the benefit of more than 1 per cent of the share capital.

11.9.3 If a trustee (or any connected person) receives a benefit from their charity which is not authorised or permitted by one of the routes described above, they will have received that benefit in breach of trust and may be required to repay it to the charity. In addition, any fellow trustee who was aware of and/or acquiesced in the trustee receiving the benefit may also be personally liable for making good any loss to the charity as a result.

11.9.4 It is therefore essential that the charity's constitution sets out in full any circumstances in which its trustees may receive a benefit. It is standard practice to provide for the following benefits to trustee as a minimum:

- Reimbursement of any expenses properly incurred in performing their duties as trustees (e.g. necessary travel and accommodation costs in order to attend trustee meetings).
- A reasonable interest rate on any money lent by a trustee to their charity.
- A reasonable rent or hiring fee on any property let or hired by a trustee to their charity.
- An indemnity for any liabilities a trustee might incur in running their charity. This would therefore cover any costs personally incurred by trustees in successfully defending a criminal prosecution brought against them, perhaps for a breach of health and safety rules. Obviously, such an indemnity cannot cover a trustee's personal liability for wilful or reckless breaches of trust.
- Payment of premiums for trustees' indemnity insurance – such insurance covers trustees against potential personal liability resulting from innocent breaches of trust or duty and is therefore a benefit to trustees rather than to the charity itself (although the availability of such insurance is often helpful in recruiting trustees).
- Payment to any company in which a trustee has no more than a very small (usually 1 per cent) shareholding – this enables the charity to enter into contracts with companies, such as utility companies, in which a trustee may own a small number of shares.
- Any other exceptional payments or benefits as approved in writing by the Charity Commission in advance of them being made.

11.9.5 In addition, it has until recently been common practice to provide an express power for the charity to enter into a contract with a trustee (or a connected person) for the provision of goods and services in return for payment or any other benefit in the following limited circumstances:

- where the goods and/or services are actually required for the charity;
- where the level of payment or benefit is no more than reasonable in relation to the value of the goods and services to be provided;
- where the decision to enter into the contract has been made following the charity's procedures for managing conflicts of interest (see further below) and a written agreement is entered into; and
- where no more than a specified number or proportion of the trustees, up to one half of their total number, have an interest in such a contract in any one financial year.

11.9.6 The Charity Commission has recently been rejecting applications for registration where constitutions provide scope for trustees to receive benefits for providing goods to their charity as well as for services. The Commission's rationale is that the scope of such power goes beyond that expressly provided by a new provision in the Charities Act 2006. Unless and until there is a change in the Commission's policy the safest course is to provide a power which goes no further than section 73A of the Charities Act 1993 (as amended).

11.9.7 In the absence of an express power section 73A of the Charities Act 1993 (inserted by the Charities Act 2006) provides a statutory power to enable a charity to remunerate a trustee or a person connected to a trustee (see above for more details on 'connected persons') for services provided to the charity subject to similar safeguards to those described above. This power cannot be used where the governing documents of a charity contain any express provision that prohibits the trustee or connected person from receiving such remuneration. This is the norm in the Memorandum and Articles of Association of existing charitable companies, which usually include wording along the following lines: 'a trustee must not receive any payment of money or other material benefit (whether directly or indirectly) from the charity' followed by a list of exceptions to the general rule setting out limited circumstances where a trustee or connected person may receive a benefit.

11.10 Paid trustees

11.10.1 It is important to appreciate that none of the powers discussed above enable a trustee to be paid either for being a trustee or as an employee of the charity. It remains relatively rare, particularly for small to medium-sized charities, for paid employees to sit on the board of trustees. For a charity to have an employee who is also a trustee its constitution must contain an express power to this effect (which will require Charity Commission approval) or the prior approval of the Charity Commission must be obtained. This restriction also applies to payments by a charity's trading subsidiary to a director who is also a trustee of the charity.

11.10.2 If a trustee wishes to resign in order to take up paid employment with their charity care needs to be taken. The trustee must avoid receiving any unauthorised benefit from the charity and there should be no suggestion that they have been preferred or benefited in any way during the recruitment process. In practice this means:

- that the trustee should have resigned before they had any knowledge of the position becoming available;
- that, if they were aware of the potential position whilst still a trustee, they must resign immediately and have no part in: any decision by the charity to create the position; any discussion of the job description or skills specification; any aspect of the recruitment process; and any decision on pay and conditions; and

- that an Order should be obtained from the Charity Commission authorising the ex-trustee to take up such a position in any circumstances where they could be seen to have benefited from having been a trustee.

11.11 Conflicts of interest

11.11.1 Charity trustees have a general duty to avoid conflicts of interest. A conflict of interest is any situation in which a trustee's personal interests, or interests which they owe to another body, and those of the charity arise simultaneously or appear to conflict.

11.11.2 In addition to the common law duties which trustees are subject to by virtue of their position as charity trustees, trustees of charitable companies are also subject to the duties set out in the Companies Act 2006. To comply with the Companies Act 2006 company directors will need to check and, if necessary, modify their Articles if they intend to authorise certain directors' conflicts of interests. For charity trustees of charitable companies, those conflicts that may be authorised should be restricted to conflicts of loyalty. Unless the governing document, Charity Commission, courts or the law provides for a trustee to benefit from their position, the general rule is that trustees have a duty to avoid conflicts, act in the best interests of the charity and not benefit from their position.

11.11.3 As such, ICSA recommends that charitable companies should consider including the authorisation clause and take the opportunity to do so as part of their annual review and consequential updating of their Articles, as a matter of best practice. Given the numerous changes in legislation impacting on charitable companies, it would be prudent for the charity's secretary to highlight and update the Articles to ensure that they are making the most of the opportunities currently available to them within the legal framework.

11.12 Non-distribution clause (or asset lock)

11.12.1 The constitution must contain a clause stating that the property of the charity does not belong to the individual trustees (of a charitable trust) or to the members (of a company limited by guarantee or an unincorporated association) but must be held on trust for the objects of the charity.

11.12.2 This clause needs to be coupled with a clause setting out the limited extent to which the trustees (see above for further detail) and, for a company limited by guarantee or an unincorporated association, the members are able to benefit from the charity.

11.13 For charitable companies, a limited liability clause and a guarantee clause

11.13.1 Both of these clauses are required by company law:

- the former establishes the limited liability status of the charitable company; and
- the latter sets out the extent to which each of the members provides a personal guarantee to contribute to the assets of the charitable company if it is dissolved whilst he or she is a member. The amount of the guarantee is usually £1 or £10.

11.14 A dissolution clause

11.14.1 The dissolution clause sets out the rules that must be followed when a charity has reached the end of its useful life, is solvent and is to be dissolved.

11.14.2 It is essential that any assets remaining, after all outstanding debts and liabilities have been satisfied, are used for furthering the charity's objects or for charitable purposes which are within or similar to the charity's objects.

11.15 Rules for members

11.15.1 Where a charity has a separate membership, the constitution should set out the rules which govern the membership.

11.15.2 A well-drafted constitution will include detailed rules on at least the following:

- who is eligible to be a member – for example, is membership open to individuals and/or to member organisations? In an oligarchy, only the trustees will be members;
- the rights and obligations of members;
- mechanisms for applying for membership and for the resignation and removal of members; and
- procedures for calling members' meetings and rules governing such meetings – for example rules on: how notice is given; quorums; voting rights (including proxies); chairing meetings; and voting majorities.

11.15.3 The members of companies limited by guarantee benefit from rights and rules about their meetings which are set out in legislation, some of which cannot be amended by provisions in the charity's constitution. It is vital to have a detailed understanding of these statutory rules before drafting constitutions for charitable companies or substantially amending the rules set out in model documents. If in doubt, seek specialist advice.

11.15.4 It is possible to draft the rules for members of a company limited by guarantee by reference to the default rules for companies limited by guarantee published by Companies House (known as model articles for companies limited by guarantee). However, it is good practice to set the rules out in detail in the Articles of Association to prevent the need to cross-refer.

11.15.5 The relationship of the members of an unincorporated association between themselves and their association are governed entirely by the rules set out in the constitution. If the rules are silent on an issue affecting the membership there are no statutory rules and very few common law rules to fill the void. It is therefore essential that a full suite of rules governing membership is set out.

11.16 Rules for trustees

11.16.1 The constitution should set out in detail the rules which the trustees must follow in governing their charity.

11.16.2 A well-drafted constitution will include the following:

(a) minimum and maximum numbers of trustees;
(b) mechanisms for appointing trustees and any qualifications necessary to be a trustee;
(c) provisions on resigning and removal of trustees;
(d) terms of office of trustees – it is common to provide for retirement by rotation or a maximum number of terms of office that a trustee can serve before taking at least a 12-month break. Such rules are designed to encourage 'fresh blood' onto the board;
(e) rules for trustees' meetings:
   i. how many meetings are to be held each year?
   ii. length of notice for calling meetings;
   iii. quorum for trustees' meetings;
   iv. voting on resolutions – majority rule is the norm. It is common for a casting vote to be given to the chair in the event of deadlock;
(f) if appropriate to the particular circumstances, power to pass resolutions in writing and power to hold meetings by video or telephone conferences or by any other means when all trustees can communicate together simultaneously (note that it is not possible for trustees to meet by consecutive email communication or separate telephone calls);
(g) power to delegate to committees:
   i. if an express power is not provided in the constitution of an unincorporated charity the position is governed by the Trustee Act 2000. Section 11 of the Trustee Act 2000 sets out the limited circumstances in which trustees can delegate to committees;
   ii. the trustees of corporate charities (such as companies limited by

guarantee) are not governed by the Trustee Act 2000 and it is essential if the trustees are to delegate to committees to include a specific provision in the constitution.

It is prudent for at least one trustee to be a member of each committee and committees must report back to the board of trustees;
(h) power to delegate to staff:
  i. where it is impractical for trustees to personally undertake all of their duties, they may delegate certain tasks to employees of the charity. Any such delegation must be authorised by the charity's governing document or by the Trustee Act 2000.
  ii. it is good practice to ensure that delegated tasks and limits of delegated authority are also reflected in the relevant employees' job descriptions;
(i) rules governing conflicts of interest (see above).

11.17 Amending constitutions

11.17.1 The power and procedure for amending a charity's constitution depends both on the legal form it takes and the nature of the provision in the constitution to be amended.

11.17.2 As a general rule, provided it has an express power either in its constitution or in legislation to make amendments, a charity is able to amend the administrative provisions in its constitution without obtaining Charity Commission consent.

11.17.3 The process for amending a charity's objects is dependent on its legal structure.

- The objects of an unincorporated charity can be amended without the Charity Commission's consent where there is express power to do so in the constitution.
- Charitable companies must always obtain the prior written approval, under section 64 of the Charities Act 1993, of the Charity Commission to any proposed amendment to their objects.

11.17.4 However, the amendment clause in the constitution may specify that consent is required from another body, for example another regulator or sponsoring body. These rules must be followed to ensure that amendments are lawfully made.

11.17.5 Different rules may apply where a charity wishes:

- if it is a charitable company or a larger unincorporated charity without express power to do so, to amend its objects; and/or

A2 LEGAL FORMS AND STRUCTURES

- to amend its constitution to provide benefits to its trustee (in excess of the power provided by section 73A of the Charities Act 1993); and/or
- to amend its dissolution clause; and/or
- commonly (if it is an unincorporated charity) to spend its permanent endowment.

11.17.6 As a general rule, any such amendment will either require prior written approval from the Charity Commission before it takes effect or the Charity Commission must concur with the trustees' decision.

11.17.7 The following table sets out details of the powers of amendment available to charities depending on the legal form they take:

Legal form	Power of amendment
Charitable trust	**Express power** The trust deed, declaration of trust or Charity Commission scheme may give the trustees an express power of amendment. This power may be wide enough to enable amendments to be made to the charitable objects without reference to the Charity Commission. The constitution may require the prior consent of the Charity Commission or another third party (such as a local authority, a founder or sponsoring body) before any or a particular amendment can be made. It is common for the governing documents of charitable trusts to specifically state that the objects clause cannot be amended without the Charity Commission's prior written approval. **Statutory power (administrative provisions)** The new section 74D of the Charities Act 1993 gives the trustees of an unincorporated charity (i.e. a charitable trust or unincorporated association) power to modify any provision in their charity's governing documents which is either an administrative power or an administrative procedure. It is important to appreciate that this power cannot be used: - to modify the objects clause (see below) or to give the trustees power to modify the objects; or - to provide any benefit to the trustees of the charity or connected persons; or - to spend capital held as permanent endowment; or

Charitable trust

- to change provisions giving third parties rights to nominate trustees.

Procedure
To take advantage of this power, the trustees should:

- pass the resolution following the decision-making rules in their charity's constitution and record the decision in writing;
- send a copy of the resolution to the Charity Commission (the Charity Commission's approval is not required and it is not necessary to give public notice of amendments).

Statutory power to change purposes (smaller charities)
The new section 74C of the Charities Act 1993 provides power for the trustees of an unincorporated charity with gross income in its last financial year of £10,000 or less to change their charity's purposes.

The trustees can pass a resolution to change all or any part of the purposes of their charity, provided that:

- the amended objects are charitable;
- they are satisfied that it is in the best interests of their charity to make the changes; and
- the new purposes, so far as is reasonably practicable, are similar in character to those they replace.

The trustees must pass the resolution by not less than a two-thirds majority and send a copy of it to the Charity Commission together with a statement of their reasons for passing it.

The Charity Commission can ask for additional information or explanation from the trustees or require them to give public notice of the resolution.

If the Charity Commission does not object or seek further information or require public notice the resolution will automatically take effect 60 days after they have received a copy of it.

Charity Commission
The Charity Commission's assistance will be required:

- to change the purposes of larger charities where the trustees of a charitable trust with an annual income of over £10,000 have no express power in their charity's governing document to amend the purposes of their charity. The trustees will need to apply for a Charity Commission scheme to make the amendments;

A2 LEGAL FORMS AND STRUCTURES 63

Charitable trust	■ where the constitution expressly states that the Charity Commission's consent to any or a particular amendment is required; ■ where the statutory powers of amendment cannot be used.
Unincorporated association	**Express power** The rules may include an express power to amend. The approval of the membership will commonly be required, depending on what the rules say. **Statutory power (administrative provisions)** The new power in section 74D of the Charities Act 1993 to amend administrative provisions in the constitutions of unincorporated charities is available to trustees of an unincorporated association (see the comments above in relation to charitable trusts). The resolution must be approved by the members of the association in general meeting, either by: ■ a majority of two-thirds of those voting on the matter; or ■ by a decision taken without a formal vote but without any expression of dissent when the matter is put to the meeting. **Statutory power to change purposes (smaller charities)** The new power in section 74C of the Charities Act 1993 to change purposes is available to trustees of unincorporated associations with an annual income of £10,000 or less. **Charity Commission power** See comments above in relation to charitable trusts.
Company limited by guarantee	**Statutory powers** Subject to section 63 of the Charities Act 1993, the members of the company have power to make amendments to a company's Memorandum and Articles of Association by passing a special resolution either at a members' meeting or by signing a written resolution. Prior to 1 October 2009, the Companies Act 1985 set out the provisions within a company's Memorandum of Association which could be lawfully altered by the members. These included: the name; the objects clause; and any other provision which could have been included in the Articles of Association. In practice this meant that the majority of the provisions in the Memorandum of Association could be

Company limited by guarantee

amended, but some care was needed to identify those provisions which could not be amended.

The Companies Act 2006 has simplified the situation. With effect from 1 October 2009, the Memorandum of Association contains a statement by the subscribers of their wish to be formed into a company, and all other provisions will be contained in the Articles of Association. It is no longer possible to amend or update the Memorandum of Association; it is simply a historical record of the subscribers' details. All provisions contained in the Memorandum of Association of existing companies (other than the subscriber details) are deemed to be part of the Articles and capable of amendment by the members by special resolution. It is possible to entrench provisions in the Articles by making any alteration or removal of the provision conditional on certain conditions being met (for example, obtaining the prior consent of the Charity Commission).

Section 64 of the Charities Act 1993 provides that a charity which is a company must obtain the consent of the Charity Commission before it can make a 'regulated alteration' to the Memorandum or Articles of Association. Regulated alterations are:

- any alteration of the objects clause;
- any alteration of any provision directing the application of property of the charity on its dissolution; and
- any alteration which authorises a director or member (or persons connected to them) to obtain a benefit. Only amendments which will provide a benefit to a director, member or connected person beyond the extent to which they can obtain benefits under section 73A of the Charities Act 1993 (see above) require Charity Commission consent.

Care must be taken to seek such prior consent in good time (well in advance of putting the issue to the vote) using Application Form CSD 1388A. The Charity Commission will endorse its consent on the draft altered Memorandum and/or Articles of Association and the special or written resolution of the members to make the alteration.

In addition, Charity Commission consent will be required in the following circumstances:

- **Pre-1982 companies:** the Memorandum and Articles of Association of some companies incorporated before 1982 include a requirement to obtain the Charity Commission's consent to all changes. This requirement must continue to be followed until removed by the members.
- **Express prohibition on paying trustees:** any alteration which removes an express prohibition on paying trustees of the charity will require prior authorisation by Charity Commission Order under section 26 of the Charities Act 1993 where either all of the directors of the charitable company are also its members or where the company does not have a sufficient number of members who are not directors to form a quorum to vote on the resolution.

Company law procedures

A special resolution can either be passed at a members' meeting or by the members passing a written resolution. The following procedure must be followed for a members' meeting:

- either 14 clear days' notice of the meeting at which it is proposed to pass the resolution must be given to *all* members or, if longer, the length of notice required by the company's Articles of Association (commonly 21 clear days);
- the notice must: state that it is a special resolution; contain the precise wording of the resolution; and include a statement informing members of their right to appoint a proxy to attend, speak and vote in their place at the meeting. Members should be provided with sufficient information about the proposed amendments to be able to make an informed decision whether or not to agree to them. It is therefore good practice to provide members with an explanatory note on the amendments proposed if they are not self explanatory and they have not previously been consulted about the proposed amendments;
- a majority of at least 75 per cent of the members who either attend in person or by proxy and are entitled to vote at the meeting must vote in favour of the resolution;
- a copy of the special resolution (certified by a director or the company secretary), together with a copy of the Memorandum and/or Articles of Association must be filed at Companies House within 15 days of the resolution being passed. Technically, it is a criminal offence punishable by a fine not to file within the timescales;

- a copy of the Memorandum and/or Articles of Association and the special resolution should also be filed with the Charity Commission. The originals should be kept with the company books.

To pass a special resolution in writing, the following procedure must be followed:

- The written resolution setting out the amendments to be made to the Memorandum and/or Articles of Association must be sent to all members at the same time or by submitting the same copy to each member in turn if this can be done without 'undue delay'. The resolution must state on the face of it that it is proposed as a special resolution.
- The circulated resolution must in all cases be accompanied by a statement as to how members should signify their agreement and the date by which the resolution must be passed or will otherwise lapse (it is a criminal offence not to comply with this requirement, although the validity of the resolution itself is not affected).
- The circulated resolution is passed if and when at least 75 per cent of the members sign it within a period of 28 days from either the date it was sent out or the first date on which it was sent out for circulation. After this period, a resolution with insufficient support will lapse.
- All the signatures do not need to be on the same document, so long as each is written on a document which accurately states the terms of the resolution.
- The company's auditors are entitled to receive a copy of the written resolution.
- A copy of the signed written resolution (certified by either a director or the company secretary), together with a copy of the Memorandum and/or Articles of Association should be filed with Companies House within 15 days of it being passed and should also be sent to the Charity Commission. Originals should be kept with the company books.

Industrial and Provident Society (IPS)

Express power
The rules of the IPS will include a provision on amending them. All amendments will need to be made by the members at a general meeting. It is usual to require at least a two-thirds majority vote by the members to adopt the amendments.

Industrial and Provident Society (IPS)	**Statutory rules** Section 10 of the Industrial and Provident Societies Act 1965 provides rules applicable to how IPSs amend their rules: - No amendment of rules is valid until the Financial Services Authority (FSA) has registered the amendment. - All amendments to the IPS's rules must be notified to the FSA by providing two printed copies of the amended rules signed by three members and the secretary of the society. - The Secretary of the IPS must sign and complete an application (available from the FSA's website: www.fsa.gov.uk/Pages/Doing/small_firms/MSR/Societies/index.shtml) outlining details of the rule changes and send this to the FSA together with a statutory declaration by an officer of the IPS and a copy of the amended rules. IPSs which are Registered Providers (RPs) require the prior consent of the Tenant Services Authority to any amendment to their rules. The FSA will not register rule amendments of an RP without the Tenant Services Authority's sealed consent.
Charitable Incorporated Organisation (CIO)	**Statutory power** Members of a CIO will be able to alter the CIO's constitution by passing a resolution of 75 per cent of votes cast at a general meeting or by passing a written resolution provided the amendment does not result in the CIO ceasing to be a charity. Any amendments to provisions in the CIO's constitution which relate to any of the following will, in addition, require the prior written consent of the Charity Commission: - the CIO's purposes; - any application of the CIO's property on winding-up; or - any authorisation of benefits to trustees, members or those connected to them.
Royal Charter body	A Royal Charter body's charter and/or by-laws can be altered only with the agreement of the Privy Council. The Privy Council's website (www.privy-council.org.uk) contains detailed guidance on the procedure. A detailed checklist can be found at: www.privy-council.org.uk/files/pdf/AMENDMENDING_A_ROYAL_CHARTER_CHECKLIST.pdf. If the Royal Charter body is a registered charity, the Charity Commission (or OSCR for Scottish charities) will need to be consulted about proposed amendments which have a bearing on charity law; for example, any change to the objects or to the trustees' powers.

Royal Charter body	Where significant changes which have charity law implications are proposed to a Royal Charter the Charity Commission may make a scheme which is then given effect by the Privy Council. The following should be sent to the Privy Council in order to apply for its agreement to the proposed amendments: ■ the text of the proposed amendments; ■ a note setting out as concisely as possible the purpose and effect of the proposed amendments. This should briefly explain the reasons why the change is considered desirable, the changes that are proposed and an explanation of how the amendments achieve this; ■ full details of any consultation with the Charity Commission (including details of the outcome and contact details of the person dealt with); ■ full details of any consultation with government departments or any other institution which may be required; ■ an electronic version of the amendments formatted in accordance with the Privy Council's particular requirements (see the website: www.privy-council.org.uk/output/Page46.asp); ■ details of the timetable for passing formal resolutions to make the amendments; ■ copies of the formal resolutions required to make the amendments, which should include a 'latitude' clause enabling textual amendments to be agreed without the need to repeat all the formalities provided for in the Charter. For example *'subject to such changes as the Privy Council may require and which are agreed by the* [Royal Charter Body]*'*; ■ a signed and sealed certificate confirming that the resolutions were duly passed in accordance with the by-laws.

11.18 Notification

11.18.1 Details of any changes to the constitution of a registered charity (apart from those made by Charity Commission scheme) must be sent to the Charity Commission, who will update the Register of Charities.

11.18.2 All amendments to the constitutions of Scottish charities must be notified to OSCR within three months. Where charities are dual registered OSCR's requirements in relation to amendments to constitutions will have to be complied with as well as any English charity law requirements.

11.19 Registered Providers

11.19.1 All charities which are Registered Providers (RPs) generally require the prior consent of the Tenant Services Authority to any change to their governing documents. Guidance on what changes require notification can be found on their website at www.tenantservicesauthority.org/upload/pdf/Regulatory_framework_ for_social_housing_-_annexes.pdf. Failure to obtain such consent renders many amendments invalid, as detailed in pages 6–8 of the guidance. Typically RPs are Industrial and Provident Societies or companies limited by guarantee.

12 Branches, networks and group structures

12.1 Many charities have a straightforward legal structure: either all activities will be carried out through the charity itself or the activities will be split between primary-purpose trading activities and certain fundraising events carried out through the charity and commercial trading activities carried out through one or more wholly-owned trading subsidiaries (see section 13 below).

12.2 However, some charities have complex structures comprising several different legal entities carrying out a variety of different charitable and non-charitable activities. The need to adopt or preserve a complex structure is likely to be driven by direct tax and Value Added Tax considerations and a desire to ring-fence risk. Mergers of charities frequently result in 'groups' of charities with any number of separate charities under common control (see section 14 below).

12.3 Projects and branches

12.3.1 Problems can occur where a 'parent' charity is unclear of the status of projects or branches associated with it. It is important to establish whether such projects or branches are in fact separate, independent organisations (with their own duties, responsibilities and liabilities) or are activities of the parent charity. This is not always easy to establish.

12.3.2 Difficulties can arise where a project or branch is operating autonomously and has no accountability to the parent. A project or branch may have use of premises, employ staff, have its own bank account and provide services. Where the project or branch is not a separate organisation its activities are those of the parent, which, ultimately, is responsible and can be held to account. Particular problems can arise where the project or branch is pursuing activities which are not within the charitable purposes or the powers of the parent and are therefore being carried on in breach of trust.

12.3.3 Where a project or a branch is not a separate organisation, or its status is in any doubt, it is advisable that the parent charity requires the project or branch to sign up to written terms of reference. Depending on the particular circumstances, the terms might cover:

- its status as a non-autonomous project or branch of the parent;
- the authorised scope of its activities and area of operation;
- compliance with the parent's charitable purposes and strategy;
- requirements for reporting and accounting to the parent;
- implementation of policies and procedures of the parent;
- the composition of any local committee, how members are appointed and removed and how they are to manage their meetings;
- managing the relationship between any local committee of the branch or project and the parent (the parent should have the right to attend meetings and to receive minutes);
- any restrictions or controls on funds and fundraising;
- controls on bank accounts;
- restrictions on entering into contracts in the parent charity's name; and
- dissolution of the project or branch.

12.3.4 Where a project or branch is a separate charity, responsibility for managing and administering the charity rests with its trustees. Depending on the particular circumstances, it may choose to affiliate with the parent charity or to form a group with the parent for accounting, taxation or VAT purposes or to become a subsidiary of the parent (where the parent charity has ultimate control).

12.4 Networks of independent charities

12.4.1 There are many ways in which separate independent charities work together. These range from formal affiliation and federal structures through licensing and franchising arrangements to looser partnering arrangements. A detailed discussion of such structures and arrangements are beyond the scope of this Handbook.

12.4.2 However, we will look in a little more detail at:

- affiliated structures; and
- federal structures.

12.4.3 In each of these, a parent charity provides strategic guidance and central services to its affiliates or members. The parent is also usually able to exercise a degree of control over how the affiliates or members operate.

12.4.4 An affiliated structure is created when a number of independent charities agree to be bound by the rules of a main charity. Each independent charity may be required to adopt a common form of governing document and/or operate within a framework prescribed by the main charity.

12.4.5 A typical affiliation arrangement between a main charity and its affiliates might include the following terms:

- where the affiliates use any name and/or logo belonging to the main charity, a licence to use that name and/or logo. To include a right to withdraw the licence and require the affiliate to change its name and to cease using the name and/or logo if the agreement is breached;
- a description of the relationship between the main charity and its affiliates;
- requirements to obtain the main charity's consent to change its charitable objects and to make other changes to its governing document;
- rights of the main charity to appoint trustees or to attend trustees' meetings;
- details any policies or procedures to be followed by affiliates;
- obligations on the affiliate to report or account to the main charity;
- any restrictions on activities or controls on fundraising;
- any obligations to pay an affiliation fee (which may have VAT implications);
- any obligation to transfer funds to the main charity on dissolution of the affiliate or otherwise;
- any obligations on the main charity to provide support (financial or otherwise), guidance or assistance to its affiliates; and
- rights of the main charity and of affiliates to terminate the relationship and the consequences of doing so.

12.4.6 A federal or umbrella structure is created where separate independent charities become members of a central charity to pursue a common purpose. This enables each charity to benefit from centralised administration, training and information sharing and to co-ordinate activities, particularly campaigns. Each separate charity will have rights as members of the federation and may pay a fee for funding the central charity (which may have VAT implications).

13 Trading subsidiaries

13.1 A basic rule of charity law is that charities can only carry on trading activities which are either directly in pursuance of their objects or which are ancillary to their objects (together known as primary-purpose trading). The amount of other non-primary-purpose trading they can carry on is strictly limited.

13.2 A charity's profits from primary-purpose trading activities are exempt from tax as are profits made from lotteries and from certain other types of fund-raising event. In each case, exemption is subject to conditions relating to the application of the profits received by the charity. In addition, income received by a charity from the sale of goods that have been donated to it is not generally regarded as trading profits and is not taxable.

13.3 Whilst charities may trade more or less freely in pursuance of their charitable purposes, charities should not engage in non-primary-purpose trades which would result in a significant risk to the assets of the charity. Such trade should be undertaken by a trading subsidiary established as a separate company.

13.4 Before establishing a trading subsidiary it is highly recommended that advice is sought on the direct tax and VAT implications for the charity.

13.5 The most common legal form for a trading subsidiary is a company limited by shares; the charity will usually by the sole member owning the entire issued share capital and have the sole right to appoint and remove the directors. However, with charities increasingly becoming involved in 'social enterprise' activities, establishing trading subsidiaries as companies limited by guarantees or Community Interest Companies is become increasingly popular.

13.6 The trading subsidiary must be wholly separate from the charity and the entire relationship must be kept at arm's length. This means:

(a) there should be no subsidy in the form of money, staff time, cost of shared facilities, interest free loans, guaranteeing of loans, etc.;
(b) there should be no mixing of funds – the charity and its trading subsidiary should have separate bank accounts;
(c) the charity should make a management charge for the use of shared resources;
(d) the trading subsidiary must have separate company books and business stationery and must itself comply with all Companies Acts requirements;
(e) the trading subsidiary must keep separate minutes of its members' and directors' meetings, even if the meetings take place at the same time as the charity trustees' or members' meetings;
(f) whilst it is common for trustees of a charity to also be directors of its trading subsidiary, it is important to consider that sometimes the interests of the two entities may be in conflict. The Charity Commission therefore recommends that, in the interests of good governance, there should be:
    i. at least one person who is a trustee, but not a director or employee of the trading subsidiary; and
    ii. at least one person who is a director of the trading subsidiary, but not a trustee or employee of the charity;
(g) finally, a trustee of the charity cannot be paid for their services as a director (or employee) of its trading subsidiary unless specifically provided for by the charity's governing document, or specifically authorised by the Charity Commission.

13.7 The trading subsidiary will commonly require initial start-up or working capital. The usual practice is for the charity to provide this by way of loan. Such a loan must be treated by the trustees of the charity as a form of investment, irrespective of the close connection between the two entities. This means that the charity should:

- consider and decide whether the investment is one which the charity should make having regard to risk and the need to diversify its investment portfolio;
- enter into a loan agreement under which the trading subsidiary is charged a commercial rate of interest and commits to repayment terms (usually on demand); and
- take security in the form of a fixed and floating charge over all the assets of the trading subsidiary.

13.8 In order to avoid adverse tax consequences for the charity it is important that the loan between the charity and the trading subsidiary will be a qualifying loan for the purposes of section 505 and 506 of the Income and Corporation Taxes Act 1988. Where there is any doubt about this advice from a tax adviser should be sought, and in the case of loans of large sums the charity should consider obtaining prior clearance from HM Revenue & Customs.

13.9 The trading subsidiary will usually pass its taxable profits to the charity using Gift Aid. This amount is paid gross and the company claims tax relief when calculating its profits for Corporation Tax. The charity cannot reclaim tax on donations made by the trading subsidiary. The donation needs to be paid over to the charity within nine months of the trading company's year end, in order to obtain tax relief for the financial year in question. The working capital requirements of the trading company may prevent the full year's profits being donated to the charity.

13.10 Ideally the relationship between the charity and its trading subsidiary should be recorded in a trading agreement; this will include arrangements for cross-charging between the two entities.

13.11 Other subsidiaries

13.11.1 A charity may wish to set up other subsidiaries and these may be charitable or non-charitable. Charities often choose to hive off some of their operations to a subsidiary in the interests of good governance. It can be a useful way of ring-fencing non-core activities or activities involving some form of risk, be that risk financial, reputational or otherwise.

14 Mergers and restructuring

14.1 A merger occurs when two or more charities come together to form one organisation (either one single charity or a group of charities under common control). The primary drivers for mergers between charities normally include: carrying out the merging charities' charitable purposes more effectively; better meeting the charitable needs of the merging charities' users and beneficiaries; and making best use of charitable funds by pooling resources and taking advantage of economies of scale.

14.2 Mergers and collaborative working between charities are encouraged by the Charity Commission. The Charity Commission's guidance can be found in its publication CC34, 'Collaborative Working and Mergers: An Introduction'.

14.3 Mergers typically involve a number of areas of law, some of which can be technical. Trustees of charities proposing to merge would be well advised to seek expert legal advice from the outset.

14.4 There are three main types of merger:

(a) Transfer to existing charity (type one) – where one or more charities transfer assets (subject to the liabilities) to another already existing charity.
(b) Transfer to new charity (type two) – where a new charity (usually a corporate body) is set up to receive the assets (subject to the liabilities) of one or more charities.
(c) By change of control (type three) – where one charity takes legal control of another (creating a parent/subsidiary relationship) either:
   i. by being appointed at trustee level; or
   ii. through the membership of the charity.

14.5 Examples of each of these three types are illustrated in Figures 2.2 to 2.4.

14.6 A type-one merger often saves time and expense as there is no need to set up a new charity to receive the transferred assets. However, it is possible only where the objects of the receiving charity are wide enough to incorporate the objects of the charity being transferred. In addition, this type of merger can be

Welfare fund → Transfer assets (subject to liabilities) and dissolve → Benevolent charity

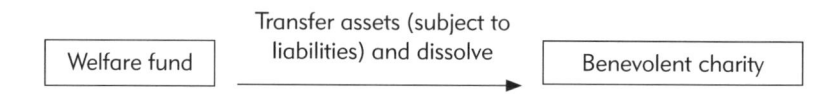

Figure 2.2: Type-one merger: transfer to an existing charity

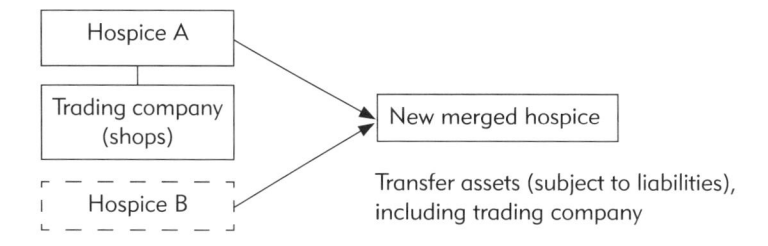

Figure 2.3: Type-two merger: transfer to a new charity

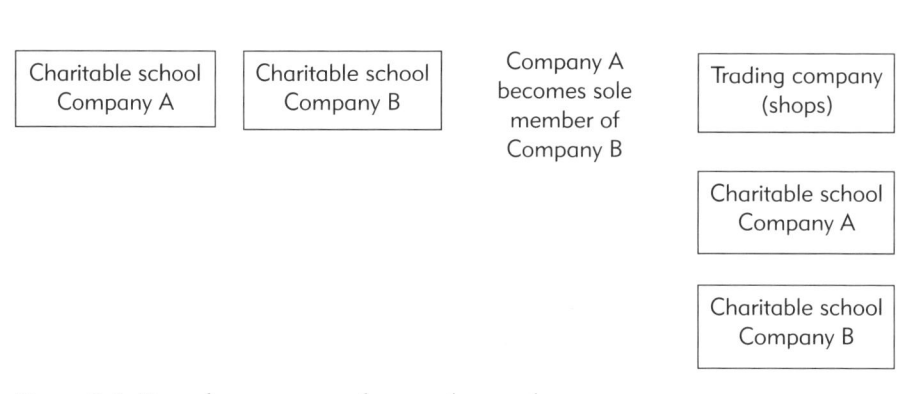

Figure 2.4: Type-three merger: change of control

perceived as a takeover of one charity (or more) by another, which is often an important consideration for the trustees and members, who may be concerned about reputational implications.

14.7 Where the merging charities are unincorporated it is likely to be advisable to pursue a type-two merger and set up a new corporate charity. This will provide the benefits of incorporation discussed in chapter A3, section 7 below. (It is worth noting that restructuring an unincorporated charity as a corporate charity – 'incorporation' – is in fact a type-two merger. See chapter A3, section 7 below.)

14.8 Merging by change of control (type three) creates a group structure where the 'merged' charities each continue to exist in the same legal form but are controlled by one of their number acting as a 'parent' charity. This type of merger may be appropriate where it is not practical to achieve a transfer of assets and liabilities in the timescales available or there are sound commercial reasons for assets and liabilities to remain within each merged organisation; for example there are concerns about liabilities which the parent wishes to remain ring-fenced. The legal mechanisms for merging by change of control tend to be more straightforward than those for effecting an asset transfer. However, each charity remains a separate legal entity accountable to the Charity Commission and any other relevant regulator (for example Companies House) and must be administered as such. This obviously has cost implications and inter-relationships within the group can be complex to manage.

14.9 The merger process

14.9.1 Like any marriage, mergers of charities should not be entered into lightly, and the merger process needs to be carefully managed. It is always advisable for the board of trustees of each party to the merger to appoint a working party (which would typically include at least one trustee and one senior member of staff) with delegated authority to take the merger negotiations forward and to make recommendations to the board. The ultimate decision as to whether to merge must be reserved to the board (or members, depending on the decision-making powers set out in the charity's governing document) and may be subject to Charity Commission approval.

14.9.2 It is prudent to provide written terms of reference for the merger working party. From a legal point of view the merger process can be broken down into four main components:

1. agree the structure;
2. due diligence;
3. negotiating the merger documents; and
4. practical steps to achieve merger (both before and after the merger has legal effect).

14.9.3 The structure of the merger needs to be settled early on. In order to do this, the following issues need to be addressed:

- **Legal structures:** if all parties to the merger are unincorporated it may well be advisable to set up a new corporate charity (e.g. a company limited by guarantee or a charitable incorporated organisation, when this is available) to transfer the assets of the merging charities to.
- **Charitable objects:** the charitable objects of all of the merging charities must be sufficiently compatible to enable the merger to take place. If there is any doubt on this issue, specialist legal advice should be sought, and it may be necessary to obtain guidance from the Charity Commission. If the objects of the receiving charity are wider (but include) those of the transferring charity any assets transferred must be ring-fenced within the receiving charity following merger for the original narrower purposes. It may be necessary or desirable to amend the charitable objects of one or more parties before the merger takes place. Charity Commission consent to any amendments will be required.
- **Power to transfer assets:** each charity which is to transfer its assets to achieve merger must have power to do so. The governing document may either

provide an express power to transfer assets or a power to dissolve or wind up. Depending on the wording of the governing document it may be necessary to obtain the approval of the members and/or the Charity Commission to exercise these powers.

Where express powers are absent, the trustees of an unincorporated charity may seek to rely on the powers set out in the Trustee Act 2000 and/or, in relation to land, the Trusts of Land and Appointment of Trustees Act 1996 to transfer assets. In cases of doubt it may be necessary or desirable to amend the governing document to provide them (this may require the involvement of the Charity Commission and/or any membership) or to seek a vesting order from the Charity Commission.

In the absence of express powers, the trustees of an incorporated charity can ask the members to pass a resolution to amend the constitution to include the necessary power.

14.10 Other restrictions on assets

14.10.1 If any of the merging charities have property (usually land or funds) which are permanent endowment, specie land (this is land which is given in trust for a specific charitable purpose, for example to operate a school or a nursing home) or subject to other restrictions imposed by trust law this is likely to have an effect on the legal structure. We recommend that specialist legal advice is sought (see further in paragraph 14.13.2).

14.11 Due diligence

14.11.1 From a legal point of view due diligence is the process of investigating the nature and extent of the assets and liabilities of the charities to be merged. The transferring charity will investigate the receiving charity and vice versa. The legal due diligence exercise will often run alongside (and may well be secondary to) a financial due diligence exercise, usually carried out by a firm of accountants on behalf of each charity. The overall due diligence process should also cover strategic and operational issues.

14.11.2 The trustees of all parties to the merger need to be satisfied that it is in the best interests of their charity to merge. The outcome of the legal due diligence exercise should be a report which assists the trustees in reaching their decision whether to go ahead with the merger. The purpose of the legal due diligence exercise is twofold:

- to highlight any significant risks and/or liabilities which might prevent the merger going ahead either at all or on the basis agreed; and
- to understand the nature of the assets and liabilities of the merging charities and identify the legal mechanisms which need to take place to achieve the merger (whether by transfer of assets or by change of control).

It is important at the outset that the parties (with guidance from their advisers) agree the scope of the due diligence exercise to ensure that the work carried out is in proportion to the potential risks being assessed and to avoid unnecessary costs being incurred. In particular, the parties will need to consider the nature of their activities (what material risks/liabilities are involved?) and the extent to which they are currently aware of each other's operations and enjoy a positive working relationship. It may be appropriate to agree to limit the scope of the due diligence exercise to a level which is proportion to the scale of the merger and the risks involved.

14.12 Merger documents

14.12.1 The documents required to document the merger will depend on the type of merger and the nature of any assets to be transferred.

14.12.2 In a typical type-one and type-two (asset-transfer merger) the following documents would be entered into:

- A transfer agreement identifying the assets to be transferred and setting out the contractual terms on which the transfer will take place.
- Resolutions (usually set out in board minutes) of the trustees of each party to the merger agreeing to either transfer or receive the transfer of assets, as appropriate, and to approve and enter into the agreed form merger documents.
- Any property documents such as freehold transfers or consents and assignments of leases.
- Any additional documents required to transfer ownership of assets of the transferring charity such as consents to assign or formal novations of significant contracts, releases of mortgages, charges and other loans.

14.13 Practical steps

14.13.1 Depending on the type of merger, the nature of the assets and liabilities of the merging charities and any issues of confidentiality it may be necessary or prudent to consult with the following prior to entering into a legally binding agreement to merge:

- **employees:** all transferring employees must be consulted in accordance with the TUPE regulations;
- **banks:** to agree how any loan or overdraft facilities and security is to be dealt with on merger;
- **pensions providers:** where a pension debt will be triggered on merger, to agree how that debt can be dealt with under the pension scheme rules. Specialist legal advice should be sought;

- **regulators:** to ensure that any necessary regulatory consents or registrations are obtained. This may include obtaining regulatory consents from for example: the Department for Children, Schools and Families (DCSF) where the merging charities are independent schools; and from the Care Quality Commission (CQC) where the merging charities are providers of care services;
- **members:** where their approval is required to any necessary amendments to governing documents or to a transfer of assets or where their status or rights are to be affected by the merger;
- **beneficiaries and stakeholders:** particularly where the merger will affect the provision of any services charged for by a party to the merger.
- **major funders and contractors:** where their prior consent is required to transfer funding arrangements and/or contracts or to a change in control of the relevant charity; and
- **insurers:** to ensure that the liabilities of the merged charities are fully covered following merger.

14.13.2 The following may need to be dealt with depending on the type of merger and the assets and liabilities involved:

- **Employees:** the Transfer of Undertakings (Protection of Employment) Regulations 2006 (TUPE) apply, and all employees whose employment is to transfer on merger must be consulted in accordance with the TUPE rules. Under TUPE all employees will automatically transfer on their existing terms and conditions of employment.

  If redundancies, dismissals or changes in terms and conditions of employment are contemplated as part of the merger early legal advice should be sought to ensure that such proposals do not amount to constructive unfair dismissal.
- **Contracts and grants:** the general legal principle is that, subject to the specific terms that have been agreed between the parties, only the benefit of a contract can be transferred (or 'assigned') to a third party (i.e. the receiving company) without the consent of the other party or parties to the contract. To transfer the obligations (known as 'the burden') under a contract to a third party requires the consent of all the other parties to the contract. It is therefore necessary to review all the terms and conditions of all significant contracts and grants of the transferring charity or charities to identify any clauses which either permit assignment (with or without the other party's consent) or prohibit assignment.

  The types of contract that will typically need to be reviewed include: all leases (see below), banking arrangements (see below), funding arrangements, hire purchase and equipment leasing agreements, significant contracts for the supply of goods and or services (example e.g. cleaning, catering, IT maintenance) and construction contracts (including any collateral warranties).

Some contracts and grants (for example the Big Lottery Fund) also include conditions which require the grant or contract maker's prior consent to any change of control, amalgamation or other form of reorganisation. The contracts and funding arrangements of each transferring charity and (where relevant) the receiving charity should be reviewed. Subject to any issues of confidentiality, to avoid being in breach of these conditions, the specific terms should be followed and prior consent obtained where necessary and practicable.

- **Property:** title to all of the transferring charity's leasehold and freehold properties should be investigated. Landlord's consent will almost certainly be required to assign any leases to the receiving charity (this process has cost implications). Where any of the transferring charity's properties are unregistered, transferring them to the receiving charity is likely to trigger first registration of title, and any transfer of registered land will need to be registered at the Land Registry. It is also vital to investigate and identify any land which is permanent endowment (see below). The trustees of the transferring charity must ensure that they comply with the requirements of section 36 of the Charities Act 1993 in respect of all disposals of property to the receiving charity and the appropriate statements required under section 37 of the Charities Act 1993 must be included in the merger or transfer agreement (see below). It is strongly recommended that legal advice is sought on dealing with legal formalities in relation to property.
- **Permanent endowment:** if any of the charity's property (usually land or funds) is permanent endowment it cannot be held absolutely by a corporate body (such as a company limited by guarantee, a Royal Charter body, an Industrial and Provident Society or, when available, a Charitable Incorporated Organisation) as part of its corporate property. It may be appropriate to appoint the corporate body as sole corporate trustee and a Charity Commission scheme may be required, or it may be possible to remove restrictions on capital removed using the new powers in the Charities Act 2006. Permanent endowment is a technical area and it is strongly recommended that specialist legal advice is sought.
- **Pensions:** transferring all the transferring charity's employees to the receiving charity may trigger an exit by the charity from pension arrangements it participates in on behalf of its employees. Depending on the type of scheme, if the underlying pension scheme is under-funded this can have the nasty consequence of triggering a debt payable by the charity on exiting; the level of debt can either prevent a merger or incorporation going ahead or seriously delay it. This is a technical area and it is strongly recommended that specialist legal advice is sought.
- **Banking arrangements:** each charity's bank will need to be consulted about the proposed merger. Where a new charity has been established it will be necessary for the trustees to open new accounts. Where a bank has taken a mortgage or charge to secure a loan over the assets of a transferring charity the bank's consent will be required to transfer any property which is subject to

such mortgage or charge. This will have timing and cost implications. The trustees must comply with sections 38 and 39 of the Charities Act 1993 where any new charge is to be put in place as a result of the merger. Any new charge or mortgage taken over the assets of a charitable company must be registered at Companies House within a short period of time; failure to comply with the timescale could jeopardise the security. Any charges granted by a merging charity over the assets of its trading subsidiary may also need to be transferred. It is strongly recommended that legal advice is sought whenever transferring property which is subject to a mortgage or charge.

14.14 Mergers register

14.14.1 On 28 November 2007 the Charities Act 2006 introduced the mergers register maintained by the Charity Commission. This contains details of any 'relevant charity mergers' notified to the Charity Commission. It can be accessed via the Charity Commission's website.

14.14.2 The intention of the mergers register is to deal with a difficult legal issue encountered on merging or restructuring charities. Before the mergers register, where a charity ceased to exist following merger or restructuring any potential legacy made in a will to benefit that charity could fail for lack of a beneficiary. Where merging charities were likely to receive legacies the unpalatable potential risk of losing significant funds lead to the common practice of keeping merged charities in existence as 'shell' charities to receive legacies.

14.14.3 Now, if a charity merger is included in the register of mergers, a legacy to the transferring charity may be saved (or the costs of defending a legacy which is challenged saved) and the transferring charity can be wound up. Once included on the register, all future income to the transferring charity passes automatically to the receiving charity.

14.14.4 However, a technical problem has been highlighted with this new tool. Registration on the mergers register will not save legacies which are worded so that the gift is not left to the named charity where it has ceased to exist. It is thought that it is not common practice to word legacies in this way. Following merger or restructuring trustees need to decide whether to dissolve a transferring charity. They should weigh up the risk of losing legacies that have been made using such wording against the administration cost of maintaining a charity within the merged structure. This may not be an easy decision to make.

14.14.5 What constitutes a 'relevant charity merger' is defined in the Charities Act 2006. The following are all examples of relevant charity mergers which can be registered on the mergers register:

- where all of the assets of one or more charities have been transferred to an existing charity and the transferring charities have subsequently ceased to exist (type-one merger, see 14.4 above); and
- where all of the assets of one or more charities have been transferred to a newly established charity and the transferring charities have subsequently ceased to exist (type-two merger, see 14.4 above).

14.14.6 A merger where the transferring charity does not cease to exist is not a relevant charity merger capable of registration. It is only obligatory to register a relevant charity merger where a vesting declaration has been made in respect of the merger or restructuring; otherwise it is voluntary. The trustees of the receiving charity can apply to register a relevant charity merger by completing Form CSD-1162 and submitting it to the Charity Commission.

14.15 Vesting declarations

14.15.1 The Charities Act 2006 has introduced a new tool to assist charity mergers; the vesting declaration. Where the trustees of a transferring charity pass a vesting declaration the assets named in it are automatically transferred from one charity to another.

14.15.2 However, a vesting declaration can be used only in mergers and restructuring projects which fall within the definition of a 'relevant charity merger', and they are available to transfer only a limited range of assets specified in the Charities Act 1993 (as amended by the Charities Act 2006); for example, unmortgaged freehold land (where any consent required under covenants on assignment have been obtained prior to transfer); unmortgaged leases (where any consent to assign has been obtained from the landlord prior to transfer); cash; equipment and stock; and vehicles. Vesting declarations cannot be used to transfer liabilities, stocks and shares, mortgaged land, permanent endowment or to assign contracts and funding arrangements.

14.15.3 In practice it is likely that the vesting declaration will be of only limited use in the most straightforward of mergers or restructuring projects.

14.16 Small unincorporated charities provisions

14.16.1 Any unincorporated charity with gross annual income of less than £10,000 can use new powers in sections 74 and 74A of the Charities Act 1993 (as amended) to transfer all of its expendable capital to another charity provided:
- that the transferring charity has no designated land (being land held on trust for the particular purpose or purposes of the charity); and
- that the trustees of the transferring charity consider the transfer to be expedient in the interests of furthering the purposes for which the property is held, and

all or any of the charitable purposes of the receiving charity (or charities) are substantially similar to all or any of the purposes of the transferring charity.

14.16.2 This power can be used only to transfer all of the charity's property, not part of it. The property can be transferred to more than one charity. Because not all of purposes of the transferring and receiving charity need be similar, the receiving charity may have wider purposes.

14.16.3 The trustees exercise the power by passing a resolution at a properly constituted trustees' meeting by a two-thirds majority. The trustees must send a copy of the resolution to the Charity Commission, which has a period of 60 days in which to concur with the trustees' decision, to ask for further information about the trustees' reasons for passing the resolution or to require public notice. If the Charity Commission seeks further information or requires public notice the timetable is suspended; the resolution is treated as if it was never made if the timetable is suspended for a period or periods of more than 120 days.

14.16.4 If the Charity Commission raises no objections, the resolution takes effect at the end of the 60-day period, and the trustees of the transferring charity must then transfer the property in accordance with the resolution.

14.16.5 Section 74B of the Charities Act 1993 (as amended) provides a similar power for small unincorporated charities to transfer permanent endowment. The procedure for passing a resolution and seeking concurrence from the Charity Commission is the same. Where permanent endowment property is to be transferred, the receiving charity (or charities) must have purposes which are substantially similar to all of the purposes of the transferring charity.

14.16.6 The main purpose of these powers is to help charities rationalise small funds and to ease administration. It is important to appreciate:

- that property transferred using sections 74 and 74A will continue to be subject to any restricted purposes applicable to it prior to the transfer when held by the receiving charity. Trustees may be able to use the power in section 74C of the Charities Act 1993 (as amended) to alter the purposes; and
- that property transferred using section 74B will continue to be permanent endowment and subject to the same restrictions on capital expenditure when held by the receiving charity. Trustees may be able to use the power in section 75 of the Charities Act 1993 (as amended) to enable permanent endowment to be spent out.

14.17 Industrial and Provident Societies

14.17.1 The Industrial and Provident Societies Act 1965 provides powers to enable Industrial and Provident Societies (IPSs) to amalgamate with another IPS or a company, to transfer its business to another IPS or company or convert into a company.

14.17.2 The members must pass a special resolution either:

- by two-thirds of votes cast in person or by proxy at a general meeting to amalgamate with or transfer its business to another IPS; or
- by three-quarters of votes cast in person or by proxy at a general meeting to amalgamate with, transfer its business to or to convert into a company.

14.17.3 This special resolution must be confirmed by a second resolution passed by a majority of the votes cast or by proxy at a general meeting held between two weeks and one month after the first.

A3
Setting up a charity

1 Setting up a charity

1.1 Setting up a new organisation as a charity usually involves two stages:

- Establishing a legal form; and
- Applying to the Charity Commission to register it as a charity.

1.2 We have looked at key features of the types of legal form commonly used to structure charities. In this next section we will look in more detail at setting up the three most common forms used in practice:

- charitable trusts;
- unincorporated associations; and
- companies limited by guarantee.

1.3 This Handbook does not deal with Industrial and Provident Societies in any more detail for the following reasons:

- Where an Industrial and Provident Society is created, model rules or a model constitution will often be prescribed by a promoting body. The promoting body will provide advice and guidance on using their model documents.
- Unless model rules are to be used, because of the specialist nature of Industrial and Provident Societies we recommend that legal advice is sought before seeking to set one up.

1.4 This Handbook will be updated to include the detailed rules and procedures of setting up a Charitable Incorporated Organisation (CIO) as they become available.

2 Establishing a charitable trust

2.1 It is possible to create a charitable trust without putting anything in writing; anyone who receives property on the condition that it is used for a purpose which is charitable in law holds that property on trust and is accountable for it.

For example, a participant in a fundraising event such as the London Marathon holds the sponsorship money they collect on trust for the charity or cause they are running in aid of.

2.2 However, it is best practice to set out the rules for governing a charitable trust in writing in a deed or declaration of trust. Where rules are not set out in writing the trust will be governed by rules set out in case law and in statute.

2.3 When the first trustees have agreed the wording of the trust deed or declaration of trust, it should be signed by each of them in the presence of a witness, who should sign, date and print their name, address and occupation. The document should be dated on the date that it is signed.

2.4 There are no requirements to have the deed or declaration of trust stamped and there is no separate register for trusts; the trust will be constituted on the date that the deed or declaration of trust is formally adopted by the trustees signing it.

2.5 The Charity Commission provides a Model Trust Deed (GD2) which includes a range of alternative clauses designed to cover most simple situations.

3   Establishing an unincorporated association

3.1 An unincorporated association is formed whenever several people agree to join together to carry out a mutual purpose, other than for profit. The unincorporated association will be a charity if those purposes fall within one of the purposes recognised as charitable in law and are pursued for the benefit of the public.

3.2 Unincorporated associations come in many different shapes and sizes, and there is no legal requirement to adopt a written set of rules for an unincorporated association to have been formed. Unincorporated associations are based on contract, which can be oral. However, some form of rules must be in place.

3.3 Obviously, it is advisable to set out the rules governing the unincorporated association in writing in a form of constitution. The general law relating to unincorporated associations can be complex and is not settled; it is better to rely on a clear set of written rules in a constitution. This will also help in the event of a disagreement and can help protect trustees and officers from personal liability.

3.4 The rules in the constitution bind the members of the unincorporated association, and the members control the unincorporated association. It is therefore very important that a full and up-to-date list of members is kept at all times and that the rules include clear provisions on the admission and retirement of members. No specific case law or statutes regulate the form or contents of the rules, but it is advisable that they are carefully drafted and tailored to the particular requirements of the association.

3.5 A model form of constitution for an unincorporated charitable association is available from the Charity Commission (reference GD3). A number of other organisations have forms of charitable constitutions which have been approved by the Charity Commission.

3.6 It is usual practice for the form of rules or constitution to be adopted by a formal resolution of the members at their first meeting.

4 Establishing a company limited by guarantee

4.1 Formation

4.1.1 A company limited by guarantee can be formed either by sending the following to Companies House or by using a company formation agent to set up the company electronically (e.g. to use a same-day, paper-free service):

- Memorandum and Articles of Association signed by the first subscribers (i.e. members) and their signatures witnessed.
- Form NE01: a statutory declaration allowing the charity to omit the word 'limited' from its name (see further below).
- Form IN01: application to register a company, which includes attached forms to provide details of the directors, the company secretary (if the company is to have one) and the subscribers.
- Fee: £20 for standard service (7–10 days), £50 for 24-hour service, or where a company formation agent is used to set up the company electronically £15 for the standard service or £30 for the 24-hour service.

4.1.2 Where an agent is used to form a company electronically the Memorandum and Articles of Association, and forms do not need to be signed and sent to Companies House. Instead, each of the first directors, the company secretary (if there is to be one) and the members must provide three different pieces of unique personal information about themselves. All details are completed online and the Memorandum and Articles of Association filed electronically.

4.1.3 The company is formed on the date specified in the Certificate of Incorporation. As with any private company, the directors of a company limited by guarantee are required to maintain and keep up-to-date company (or 'statutory') books containing a register of members, register of directors, etc.

4.1.4 A company must be formed with at least one director who is a natural person (i.e. an individual). It is no longer possible to have a sole corporate director. It is good practice for a charitable company to have at least three directors on the board from the outset. It is not necessary for any of the directors of a charitable company to be resident in the UK; because the company is registered in England and/or Wales, the Charity Commission and the courts have jurisdiction over it and can take such action as may be necessary against the company without the directors having to be UK residents. This is not the same as for a charitable trust or unincorporated association, where (because the charity has no legal identity separate from its trustees) at least a majority of the trustees are usually expected to be resident in the UK so that the Charity Commission and the courts have jurisdiction over them.

4.1.5 It is no longer necessary to appoint a company secretary, but it is advisable for charitable companies to appoint one. If a company secretary is appointed their details must be filed with Companies House.

5 Names

5.1 Before setting up a charity with a particular name, the following should (as a minimum) be checked to make sure that the name proposed is available and that no other organisation is either registered with or using a name which is confusingly similar:

- the Register of Companies maintained by Companies House;
- the Register of Charities maintained by the Charity Commission; and
- the internet.

Where the trustees of a charity are adamant that a particular name is used because of the importance of it to their charity's work they would be well advised to seek specialist branding advice to ensure that they can use the name without infringing prior intellectual property rights.

5.2 In addition, the Company and Business Names Regulations 1981 (SI 1981/1685), as amended, should be checked to make sure that either the name proposed for the charity, or any trading name the trustees may wish to use in connection with the activities of their charity, does not contain any of the words prescribed by these Regulations which can only be used with the approval of the Secretary of State or specified body. Companies House and the Charity Commission will not register a charity which contains one of the prescribed words without evidence that approval has been obtained.

◆ 5.3 Charity Commission powers

The Charity Commission has power to require a charity to change its name where that name:

- is either the same as, or, in the Charity Commission's opinion, too like a name of any other charity (whether registered or not); or
- is, in the Charity Commission's opinion, likely to mislead the public as to the true nature of the purposes of the charity or of the activities to be carried out in furtherance of those purposes; or
- includes a word or expression prescribed by the regulations discussed above and will, in the Charity Commission's opinion, mislead the public as to the status of the charity; or
- is, in the Charity Commission's opinion, likely to give the impression that the charity is connected in some way with the Government, any local authority or any other body or individual, when it is not so connected; or
- is, in the Charity Commission's opinion, offensive.

6 Registration with the Charity Commission

6.1 With the exception of a Charitable Incorporated Organisation (CIO), it is not necessary to register an organisation with the Charity Commission for it to be charitable in law. (A CIO will not exist in law until it is registered with the Charity Commission.) A significant number of charities either do not meet the threshold for compulsory registration or are exempt or excepted from registration with the Charity Commission. Over time, new rules are being introduced:

- to significantly reduce the number of exempt charities;
- to remove excepted charity status; and
- to enable small charities to register voluntarily.

The intention is to boost public trust and confidence in the sector by ensuring that information about charities and their trustees is available to the public and that they are properly regulated. Being registered as a charity with the Charity Commission, and being able to provide a registered charity number, is also extremely helpful when a charity is seeking to raise funds either from the general public or from potential grant makers.

6.2 The current criteria for registration with the Charity Commission are:

(a) The organisation is a charity in law. To recap this means:
  i. it must be established exclusively for purposes which are recognised as charitable in the law of England and Wales; and

ii. its activities are pursued for the benefit of the public (see chapter A1, paragraphs 1.3 to 1.12 above).
(b) It has, or reasonably considers it will have, an annual income of at least £5,000.

> **6.3 Charity Commission checklist**
>
> To apply to register an organisation as a charity the following need to be sent to the Charity Commission – it is now possible to register online:
>
> (a) a completed application form (currently Form CC5a, which is accompanied by Guidance Notes CC5b);
> (b) a declaration form signed by each trustee of the organisation (currently Form CC5c);
> (c) a copy of the governing document of the organisation. To recap on the most common legal forms:
>   i. for a company limited by guarantee – the Memorandum and Articles of Association;
>   ii. for a charitable trust – the declaration of trust;
>   iii. for an unincorporated association – the constitution or rules;
>   iv. when available, for a Charitable Incorporated Organisation (CIO) – the constitution.

6.4 The trustees are required to state in the application whether their charity works with children and/or vulnerable adults. In each of these circumstances the trustees will either be required by law to have or should as a matter of best practice have Criminal Records Bureau (CRB) background checks carried out on them. The Charity Commission's guidance on completing the application form includes a helpful section on the law relating to background checking, which can be complex. The trustees are required to confirm in the declaration form that CRB checks have been carried out and that they are suitable to act and to confirm in the application form that their charity has a policy for working with children and/or vulnerable adults (as appropriate).

6.5 The Charity Commission's guidance asks applicants for registration not to enclose any papers or information other than that set out in paragraph 6.3 above. If the Charity Commission requires further information they will request it, having carried out a preliminary assessment of the application. It is therefore advisable to ensure that the application form is as complete, comprehensive and persuasive as possible. Whilst, ultimately, it is the courts who determine what is or is not charitable in law, it will often be prohibitively expensive, time-consuming and difficult to challenge a decision by the Charity Commission that an organisation is not charitable because it does not meet the criteria. The Charity Tribunal is intended to make the process of challenging Charity Commission decisions less expensive and more accessible; however, it remains to be seen whether this will be the case in practice.

6.6 Examples of additional information that the Charity Commission may request in support of an application include:

- evidence that the organisation has an income of over £5,000: for example accounts or a copy bank statement; and/or
- copies of information about the charitable or fundraising activities of the organisation: for example, a business plan, fundraising materials or minutes of meetings.

6.7 The application form and trustee declaration form, together with helpful guidance on registering as a charity, can be obtained from the Charity Commission's website or by telephoning their information line.

6.8 At the time of writing, no fee is payable to the Charity Commission to apply to register a charity.

6.9 Applications can be sent to the Charity Commission either by post to its Liverpool address, by email or by following the online application process. The Charity Commission has said it aims to respond to an application within 15 working days of receipt; this will often consist of an acknowledgement of receipt.

6.10 How long it will take from receipt for the Charity Commission to approve an application and register a charity will depend to a large degree on whether the organisation in question clearly meets the criteria for registration and on the quality of the information provided in the application. It is safest to work on the basis that it will take several weeks rather than days. The Charity Commission will treat applications as urgent if the circumstances merit it (for example if the organisation in question is negotiating to purchase property and is seeking to take advantage of the stamp duty exemption available to charities or is about to launch a major fundraising appeal).

6.11 If all the criteria for registration are satisfied, the Charity Commission will confirm this by letter to the correspondent named in the application form and provide a registered charity number. Details of the charity usually appear on the Register of Charities (accessible via the Charity Commission website) within a few days. It is prudent to check the details showing on the Register carefully to ensure that accurate entries have been made.

6.12 Under normal circumstances, the trustees' names (but not their addresses or other personal details) will appear on the public register of charities. A dispensation can, however, be granted by the Charity Commission if it is considered that the publication of trustees' names may put them at risk. In such cases, an alternative contact will be published on the Register, for example a firm of solicitors.

6.13 Similarly, where appropriate, Companies House may agree to keep personal details of trustees off their public registers (see Legal Form and Structures, chapter A2, above). Under s.723B of the Companies Act 1985 it was possible to make an application to the Secretary of State for a Confidentiality Order if the availability of the usual residential addresses on the Companies House public register was likely to create a serious risk of violence or intimidation. However, as from 1 October 2009, Confidentiality Orders ceased to be effective. Trustee directors still have to provide their residential address but also have the option of providing an alternative service address. The service address will be on the public record, but the residential address will be protected and held on a private register available only to selected organisations (specified public authorities and credit reference agencies). Trustee directors deemed vulnerable by virtue of risk of violence or connection to the police or security services will be able to apply to the Registrar for their addresses not to be provided to credit reference agencies.

6.14 Rules on charity information on materials

6.14.1 All registered charities with an income in their last financial year of over £10,000 must clearly state the fact that the charity is a registered charity in:

- all fundraising material and any other documents either issued by or on behalf of the charity which solicit money or other property for the charity's benefit;
- all bills of exchange, promissory notes, endorsements, cheques and orders for money or goods purporting to be signed on behalf of the charity; and
- all bills rendered by it and in all its invoices, receipts and letters of credit.

There is no legal requirement to state the registered charity number although many charities choose to do so.

6.14.2 In addition, where the charity is a company, the following rules apply:

(a) The full name of the company as registered at Companies House must be disclosed on:
    i. all business letters, notices and other official publications of the company;
    ii. all bills of exchange, cheques, orders and invoices;
    iii. all applications for licences to carry on a trade or activity;
    iv. all other forms of its business correspondence and documentation; and
    v. on its website.

These requirements extend to a charitable company's emails which are business correspondence.

(b) All its business letters (including emails), order forms and its websites must also state the company's place of registration, the number with which it is registered and the address of its registered office. Where the company's name does not include the word 'limited' they must also indicate that the charity is a limited company.

This information is normally shown in the form of a footnote as follows: [*Full name of charitable company*], a limited company, registered in England and Wales under number [*company number*], registered office: [*address*]. Registered charity number [charity number];

(c) The registered name of the company must be displayed at its registered office, at any place where it keeps its company records for inspection and at any other business location(s) in a conspicuous position so that it may be easily seen by visitors.

6.15 Keeping the Charity Commission informed

6.15.1 The trustees of a registered charity have a duty to notify the Charity Commission if their charity ceases to exist or if any changes are made to its governing document or to any of the details shown on the Register of Charities and to provide copies of any amendments to governing documents (except where these have been made by Charity Commission scheme).

6.16 Excepted and exempt charities

6.16.1 A number of charities have historically not been required to register with the Charity Commission because they were either exempt or excepted from registration. These charities enjoyed the tax and status benefits of being charities and are required to comply with the general law relating to charities. However, they were not subject to regulation by the Charity Commission in the same way as registered charities. The rationale behind this was that they were all regulated by some other body, whether an umbrella body or another arm of government.

6.16.2 However, it was felt that these anomalies have confused the public and that exempt and excepted charities and their regulating bodies may not have been fully aware of and followed the requirements of charity law, particularly in relation to governance and benefits to trustees.

6.16.3 The Charities Act 2006 has therefore changed the law to remove exempt and excepted status from many charities or groups of charities, and excepted status will in time be abolished entirely. Transitional arrangements are currently in place to help charities and the Charity Commission manage the change in status and the process of registration.

6.16.4 Exempt charities are those charities listed in Schedule 2 to the Charities Act 1993 (as amended by the Charities Act 2006). They currently include the universities of Oxford, Cambridge, London, Durham and Newcastle and their colleges; higher and further education corporations; various prestigious national galleries, museums and institutions (including the National Gallery, the Tate, the Victoria and Albert Museum, the Science Museum and Imperial War Museum, the British Library and the Royal Botanic Gardens, Kew) and Industrial and Provident Societies which are Registered Providers (i.e. housing associations).

6.16.5 The Charities Act 2006 has significantly reduced the number of charities exempted from registration. The following are no longer exempt:

- students' unions;
- Eton and Winchester Colleges;
- voluntary aided schools and foundation schools (both types of school within the state sector); and
- Industrial and Provident Societies which are charities but are not registered social landlords.

In addition, the Secretary of State has power to make orders to either remove charities from or add charities to the list of exempt charities in Schedule 2. This power is to be used in the near future to remove exempt charity status from the halls and colleges of the Universities of Oxford, Cambridge and Durham.

6.16.6 In order to help previously exempt charities deal with their change in status and to help the Charity Commission cope with the increase in registrations, only those previously exempt charities with income exceeding £100,000 per annum will initially be required to register. The same threshold applies for excepted charities. A timetable is in place for registering both previously exempt and excepted charities which are now subject to registration.

6.16.7 Excepted charities are those charities which historically have been excepted from registration either by regulation or by Charity Commission order. These include some religious charities, scout and guide groups and some armed forces charities.

6.16.8 For the time being, the Charity Commission orders excepting these charities from registration remain in force, however, those with gross income exceeding £100,000 per annum are now required to register, and a process is underway to register these.

6.16.9 The Government's intention is that all exempt and excepted charities with annual income of £100,000 or less and all small charities with annual income of less than £5,000 will be able to register voluntarily. This will help ensure that information about them is readily available to the public.

6.16.10 In time, provisions in the Charities Act 2006 will come into force to enable all charities falling below the income thresholds to register voluntarily with the Charity Commission; this will enable both excepted charities with incomes under £100,000 per annum and any charity with an income under £5,000 per annum to register.

7 Incorporation

7.1 The process of converting an unincorporated charity into a corporate charity is known as 'incorporation'. At present, unincorporated charities most commonly incorporate as companies limited by guarantee. When the Charitable Incorporated Organisation (CIO) is available it will be possible to convert to this form (see chapter A2, section 7 above).

7.2 The process of incorporating an unincorporated charity as a company limited by guarantee normally involves setting up a charitable company and transferring all of the assets (subject to the liabilities) of the unincorporated charity to it. The legal process is the same as that for a type-two merger and this section should be read together with chapter A2, section 14. It is advisable to seek legal advice on the incorporation process.

7.3 Before they make a decision to go ahead with incorporation the trustees need to decide whether it is in the best interests of their charity to do so, taking into consideration the following:

7.3.1 The advantages of incorporation include that a company is a separate legal person and can therefore hold property and enter into contracts in its own name, without having to act through the medium of trustees. This avoids the need to transfer ownership of property and other assets when trustees change and makes the company, rather than the trustees, the employer of the charity's employees and the contracting party in contracts of all kinds between the charity and third parties. However, the trustees need to understand that incorporation does not exclude them from all personal liability. They remain trustees of a charity, and as such they remain responsible for any breaches of trust resulting in losses to the charity itself. The company structure creates a shield against claims by third parties against the trustees, but does not shield the trustees from claims by the charity itself or from statutory liabilities of directors and officers.

7.3.2 The disadvantages of incorporation are the added administrative burden and associated costs of reporting to Companies House as well as to the Charity Commission. However, these should not be substantial and the same form of accounts can be submitted to both regulators. A company has to comply with the requirements of the Companies Act with regard also to the passing of resolutions, the keeping of minutes, disqualification of directors, liquidation, etc., but these requirements, where not specified by charity law, contribute to good practice.

7.4 When the decision to proceed has been made the following steps need to take place:

7.4.1 Preparing the constitution, assets and liabilities of the unincorporated charity (a process known as 'due diligence') in order to identify the legal formalities to be followed in order to transfer the assets to the new charitable company. For example, the following need to be investigated:

- **Power to transfer:** the constitution of the unincorporated charity needs to be checked to ensure that the trustees have power to transfer the charity's assets to the charitable company. If no express power is provided, the constitution may need to be amended (which may require a resolution to be passed by any membership) before any transfer can take effect.
- **Employees:** the Transfer of Undertakings (Protection of Employment) Regulations 2006 (TUPE) apply and all employees must be consulted about the transfer of their employment to the charitable company. Under TUPE all employees will automatically transfer to the charitable company on their existing terms and conditions of employment.
- **Contracts and grants:** it is necessary to review all the terms and conditions of all significant contracts and grants of the unincorporated charity to identify any clauses which either permit assignment (with or without the other party's consent) or prohibit assignment.

    Some contracts and grants include conditions (known as change of control provisions) which require the grant or contract-makers' prior consent to any form of reorganisation. To avoid being in breach of these conditions the specific terms should be followed and consent obtained.
- **Property:** title to all of the charity's leasehold and freehold properties should be investigated. Landlord's consent will almost certainly be required to assign any leases to the new charitable company (this process has cost implications). Where any of the charity's properties are unregistered, transferring them to the new charitable company is likely to trigger first registration of title and any transfer of registered land will need to be registered at the Land Registry. It is also vital to investigate and identify any land which is permanent endowment (see below). It is recommended that legal advice is sought on dealing with these formalities.
- **Permanent endowment:** if any of the charity's property (usually land or funds) is permanent endowment it cannot be held absolutely by the new charitable company as part of its corporate property. It may be appropriate to appoint the company as trustee and a Charity Commission scheme may be required, or it may be possible to remove restrictions on capital removed using the new powers in the Charities Act 2006. Permanent endowment is a technical area and it is strongly recommended that specialist legal advice is sought.
- **Pensions:** transferring all the charity's employees to the new charitable company may trigger an exit by the charity from pension arrangements it

participates in on behalf of its employees. Depending on the type of scheme, if the underlying pension scheme is under-funded this can the nasty consequence of triggering a debt payable by the charity on exiting; the level of debt can either prevent an incorporation going ahead or seriously delay it. This is a technical area and it is strongly recommended that specialist legal advice is sought.
- **Banking arrangements:** the charity's bank will need to be consulted about the proposed incorporation: it may be necessary for the new charitable company to open new accounts and the bank's consent will be required to transfer any secured or unsecured loans and other banking facilities to the new charitable company. This will have timing and cost implications. It is strongly recommended that legal advice is sought.

7.4.2 Setting up a company: this involves drafting Memorandum and Articles of Association for the charitable company and incorporating it at Companies House in the usual way (see section 4 above). Typically the Memorandum and Articles of Association will incorporate the objects and other details from the existing charity's constitution/trust deed, but the trustees and/or members may wish to take this opportunity to review and update these details. If the charitable company is to have objects which differ from those of the unincorporated charity or if the constitution of the charitable company will enable trustees to obtain benefits which they were not previously entitled to, the trustees should seek specialist legal advice and/or guidance from the Charity Commission.

7.4.3 Registering the company as a charity: an application is made to the Charity Commission to register the company as a charity in the usual way (see section 6 above). The application form for registering as a charity enables the applicant to indicate that the registration is sought in relation to incorporation. The charitable company will be given a new charity registration number to be used when the incorporation is complete.

7.4.4 Carrying out any consultations or notifications and/or obtaining any consents that may be necessary before the transfer of assets takes place (as identified by the due diligence process).

7.4.5 Transferring the assets of the unincorporated charity to the new charitable company. It is usual for the following documents to be entered into to record the transfer:

(a) a formal transfer agreement between the unincorporated charity and the new charitable company;
(b) minutes of the trustees of the unincorporated charity;
(c) minutes of the trustees/directors of the new charitable company;

(d) where necessary, any members' resolutions;
(e) where necessary:
  i. freehold property transfer documents;
  ii. lease assignment documents;
  iii. novations of major contracts;
  iv. banking documents.

7.4.6 Registering the transfer on the Mergers Register – where all of the assets of the unincorporated charity have been transferred to the new charitable company (see chapter A2, paragraph 14.4).

7.4.7 If appropriate, asking the Charity Commission to remove the unincorporated charity from the register.

SECTION B

The charity's compliance

B1

Records and registers

1 Records and registers

1.1 A charity needs to keep adequate records just to ensure that it is well administered. For example, even if there were not legal requirements to be fulfilled, it is of core importance to know who the trustees are and were; who the members are and were; and what decisions have been taken by the trustees over the period of the charity's existence. Charitable companies are the most heavily governed in terms of the legal requirements for records and registers, but all charities need to keep them to ensure that they can work effectively.

1.2 There are two general points to note with regard to the registers that will be kept by the charity. The first key element to note with regard to registers is that they are historical documents, that is they should record the past position and not just the present position. A register that just records who the current trustees are is not sufficient as a register of trustees. It must also include who the past trustees were and the date that they ceased to be trustees. Therefore when a trustee's term ceases, the termination date should be entered on the register of trustees, but his or her entry should remain upon it. You should be able to look at the register of trustees and ascertain who the trustees were during any period.

1.3 The second key point to note is that care needs to be taken in regard to the security of the registers. They need to be kept in such a way that data cannot be deleted or changed without record. For charitable companies these are legal requirements, but it is important for all charities that there is security over their registers. This is a matter to consider in deciding in what format to retain registers. It means that for many charities a hard copy register will be preferable to a computerised register. This is because in most computerised software the data can be amended or deleted without this being shown. However, in a bound book, it can be seen if a page is removed or if details have been deleted or amended.

2 Registers in charities that are not companies

2.1 The requirements for registers for a charity that is not also a company will be set out in the constitution and will depend on the type of charity. For a charity that is established under a trust deed, it is quite common for no registers to be required by the trust deed. If there are no requirements, it may still be advisable to keep a register of trustees just to assist the record-keeping of the charity. For membership charities, the most common requirement is for a register of members to be maintained. The constitution may also require a register of trustees to be kept and sometimes a register of secretaries, mirroring company law. Later on in this chapter we will discuss the right of access to registers. However, it should be noted now that for charities that are not companies, there is no legal right of access to the registers by the members or by the general public unless this is specified in the constitution.

3 Registers in charitable companies

3.1 The Companies Act 2006 is much more prescriptive about the registers that must be kept; what information they must contain; how they are kept and the rights of public access to the registers. The Companies Act 2006 requires every company to keep the following:

- a register of members (s. 113);
- a register of directors (s. 162);
- a register of directors' residential addresses (s. 163);
- a register of secretaries (s. 275); and
- a register of charges (s. 876).

3.2 In a charitable company the directors are the trustees, and so a register of directors or of directors' residential addresses is a register of trustees or of trustees' residential addresses.

4 Location and format of registers

4.1 If the charity is a company, there are legal requirements as to where the registers are kept. For other charities, this may be a requirement of the constitution. The Companies Act 2006 prescribes where the registers of companies are to be kept. It states that:

- The register of directors and secretaries and the register of charges (together with copies of any instrument creating any charge) must be kept at the registered office.
- The register of members must be kept either at the registered office or at some other place within the country of registration (England and Wales or Scotland) where the register is made up.

If the registers are not to be kept at the registered office at all times the registers may be kept at 'a single alternative inspection location' (or SAIL). A company must notify Companies House if it sets up a SAIL address or if the SAIL address is moved, and a company may have only one SAIL address for a company at a time. Once the SAIL address is set up, the company can move some or all the registers to the SAIL address by notifying Companies House.

4.2 The statutory registers and books can be kept in either electronic or hard copy form. However, there are requirements that must be met for companies regarding the security of the registers, and this may make hard copy form a better option for most charitable companies. Section 1138 of the Companies Act requires that where company records are kept otherwise than in bound books, adequate precautions must be taken to guard against falsification, and to facilitate the discovery of falsification. If a hard copy is kept bound books (and loose-leaf registers) are available from most legal stationers. A bound book is the most secure format, and so where the register is not kept in a bound book, adequate precautions must be taken. As a basic measure the registers should be kept in a secure cabinet to which access is restricted.

4.3 It is also possible for statutory registers and books to be kept on computer or in other non-legible form provided, again, that adequate precautions are taken for guarding against falsification and facilitating their discovery and, in addition, that they are capable of being reproduced in legible hard copy form (section 1135 (2)).

4.4 If the charitable company has a large membership, it may be preferable for it to keep the register of members on a computer. However, any database or other software used for this purpose must also provide adequate security for such data. If such a database is also to act as the statutory register of members it is important to ensure:

- that the information kept includes all the data necessary for a statutory register of members;
- that the register is kept in a secure form, and there is adequate protection against the deletion or amendment of data without a record being kept.
- that if it is a membership database that is kept for wider purposes, there must be consideration of the wider data held. If the database is also likely to hold data that is not part of the statutory register this needs to be considered. There is no right of public inspection over such data and so it is important to ensure that the statutory data can be extracted and made available for inspection in such a way that other data held is not revealed.

If non-statutory information is kept in the register itself, it must be held back from any copy available for public inspection. Note that the Data Protection Act 1998 does not apply to statutory registers, which are considered public documents, but that non-statutory information falls outside this exemption of the Data Protection Act 1998 if it is made available to a third party in response to a request for inspection or a copy of the register. Although the charitable company will have exemption from liability for loss caused to a member by reason of disclosure of the information required to be held on the statutory register, it will have no similar exemption for the non-statutory information. Accordingly, charities should ensure that they are able to remove any non-statutory elements of the information contained in their register of members.

4.5 Charities with a smaller membership may find it easier to maintain the register by manual methods using standardised bound books or loose-leaf printed sheets obtainable from law stationers. It is unlikely that a standard computer program will contain the security elements required, and so whilst it may seem simpler to keep an electronic copy, this could cause difficulties in meeting the legal obligations regarding security and if the register needs to be relied upon as evidence. If an electronic copy is maintained it is advisable to print out and retain a hard copy record on each occasion that the register is added to.

5 Contents of registers: charitable companies

5.1 The Companies Act is also prescriptive about the content of registers and there are legal requirements as to what information they must contain.

5.2 Register of members

5.2.1 Section 113 of the Companies Act 2006 states that the following information must be held on the register:

- the names and addresses of the members;
- the date on which each person was registered as a member; and
- the date at which any person ceased to be a member.

5.2.2 If the company has a share capital (e.g. this may apply to a trading subsidiary), there must be entered in the register a statement of the shares held by each member, distinguishing each share by its number (so long as the share has a number), and where the company has more than one class of issued shares, by its class, and the amount paid or agreed to be considered as paid on the shares of each member.

5.2.3 If the company does not have a share capital but has more than one class of members (as is the case in some companies limited by guarantee), there must be entered in the register, with the names and addresses of the members, a statement of the class to which each member belongs.

5.2.4 Whilst statutory registers are historic documents, entries relating to a former member may be removed from the register 10 years after the date on which he ceased to be a member (sections 121 and 128). However, a copy of any details that were included in the register immediately before 6 April 2008 and that are removed from the register after that date must be retained by the company until 6 April 2018, or if earlier 20 years after the member ceased to be a member.

5.2.5 If the register is not self-indexing and contains more than 50 names it must be accompanied by an index of the members.

5.2.6 If there is only one member (as is commonly the case for subsidiary companies) the register of members must contain a statement to this effect.

5.3 Register of directors

5.3.1 Section 163 of the Companies Act 2006 requires that a company's register of directors (i.e. the trustees in a charitable company) must contain the following information (SI 2007/3495, Sch. 4, para. 2, as amended by SI 2008/674, Sch. 3, para. 6):

- name and any former name of the director;
- a service address (and this may be stated to be 'the company's registered office');
- the country or state (or part of the United Kingdom) in which he is usually resident;
- nationality;
- business occupation (if any); and
- date of birth.

5.3.2 It is not necessary for the register to contain particulars of a former name in the case of a peer or an individual normally known by a British title; nor in the case of any person, where the former name was changed or disused before the person attained the age of 16 years, or has been changed or disused for 20 years or more.

5.3.3 If a director is a body corporate, or a firm, there are particular requirements as to the details that must appear on the register.

5.3.4 Under the Companies Act 1985 the requirement was for a director's residential address to be kept on the register, and this requirement still applies. These new provisions allow a service address to be used instead. As there is a right of public access to the register of directors a service address can provide privacy for the directors. For the first time directors can choose not to make their residential addresses public, without the need for a confidentiality order.

5.3.5 However, this section of the Companies Act is accompanied by the provisions of section 165, which requires a company to keep a register of directors' residential addresses. The register must state the usual residential address of each of the company's directors. The requirement to keep such a register applies even when the register of directors has only the director's residential addresses as their service addresses. Section 165 states that if a director's usual residential address is the same as his service address (as stated in the company's register of directors), the register of directors' residential addresses need contain only an entry to that effect. But the register will still need to be kept. This therefore creates a new requirement to maintain an additional register for all charitable companies, often with duplicate information.

5.3.6 Although it is not specified as a requirement, the register of directors should also include for each director the date on which he or she became a director and the date on which they ceased to be a director.

5.3.7 It should be noted that there is also a legal requirement (sections 228–229 of the Companies Act 2006) for all companies to allow members to inspect and obtain copies of directors' service contracts. However, this requirement is probably of very limited application to charitable companies, in which the vast majority of trustees, and therefore directors, will be voluntary.

5.4 Register of secretaries

5.4.1 If the charitable company has a secretary, it should maintain a register of secretaries that should include the name and address of the secretary. Unlike the register of directors the addresses of secretaries have never needed to be residential addresses, and there is also no need for a separate register of residential addresses for secretaries. As with the register of directors, it should also include the date the person was appointed as the secretary and the date on which they ceased to be the secretary.

5.5 Register of charges

5.5.1 Every company, including every charitable company, is required to keep a register of charges (whether or not it has any entries made in it). For many charitable companies this may mean keeping an empty register. The register shall include all charges specifically affecting property of the company, and all floating charges on the whole or part of the company's property or undertaking. The entry shall in each case give a short description of the property charged, the amount of the charge and, except in the cases of securities to bearer, the names of the persons entitled to it.

5.5.2 If there are any charges on the register, it is also a legal requirement for the company to keep at its registered office a copy of every instrument creating a charge requiring registration.

6 Inspection of the registers

6.1 One of the reasons for the importance of keeping registers accurate and up to date is that they are public documents. The registers of charitable companies are open to inspection by any member of the public, as the Companies Act gives a right of inspection for all of them (with the exception of the register of directors' residential addresses).

6.2 The register of the directors and of the secretaries is available for inspection by any member of the company without a charge, and by any other person on payment of a prescribed fee.

6.3 The register of charges is available for inspection by any creditor or member of the company without a charge, and by any other person on payment of a prescribed fee.

6.4 The register of members (and any index that is also maintained, see above) is also open to inspection by any member free of charge or by any other person on payment of such fee as may be prescribed. Any person may also require a copy of a company's register of members, or of any part of it, on payment of such fee as may be prescribed.

6.5 Whilst this may seem to be a very wide right, it should be noted that one of new features of the Companies Act 2006 is that it has tightened up the ability for access to the register of members and the provision of copies of it. Many company members are not happy about the right to public access, and companies have felt uncomfortable about giving such access in certain situations. Under these new provisions, access can be restricted to requests that are for 'a proper purpose'. A person wishing to inspect or obtain copies of the register of members must make a request to the company, containing the following information:

(a) in the case of an individual, his name and address;
(b) in the case of an organisation, the name and address of an individual responsible for making the request on behalf of the organisation;
(c) the purpose for which the information is to be used; and
(d) whether the information will be disclosed to any other person, and if so:
   i. where that person is an individual, his name and address;
   ii. where that person is an organisation, the name and address of an individual responsible for receiving the information on its behalf; and
   iii. the purpose for which the information is to be used by that person.

6.6 Within five working days after receiving the request the company must either comply with it or apply to the court. If the court considers that the request has not been made 'for a proper purpose' it will direct the company not to comply with it and may award costs against the person making the request. Furthermore, if the court considers that further requests for a similar purpose are likely to be made (whether or not made by the same person) the court may give an overall direction that the company is not to comply with any such requests. However, if the court does not direct the company not to comply with the request, or the application to the court is discontinued, the company must then immediately comply with the request.

6.7 The 2006 Act gives no guidance on the meaning of the term 'proper purpose' – that is for the courts to determine. However the ICSA has issued a Guidance Note, 'Access to the Register of Members: The Proper Purpose Test'. This gives an analysis of matters that may in practice be reasonably considered to be proper or improper purposes, and is likely to be of assistance in such scenarios.

7 Other registers and records

7.1 There are two other types of register that it is common for a charity to retain, although there is no statutory requirement to do so:
- a register of sealing (see chapter B3); and
- a register of trustees' interests.

7.2 Whilst there is no statutory requirement to keep such registers it should be noted that if they are kept, there may be occasions when they should be regarded as subsets of the minutes. If either register is used as a means of recording matters that would usually be minuted and referred to in this way, the register should be retained for the same period as the minutes.

7.3 A charity will also be required to keep other statutory records,. A charity that has employees will be required to keep records regarding PAYE, National Insurance; pensions and employment records. Charities also have to keep records regarding health and safety, insurance and VAT (if VAT registered – see below). There may also be legal requirements to keep records depending on the nature of the charity's work. There will be a range of inspection rights for such records, but they will generally be open to inspection by regulatory authorities and fiscal authorities.

8 Minutes

8.1 In a separate chapter we deal with meetings, but here we will discuss the minutes of meetings as they are an important record for the charity.

8.2 Minutes are sometimes thought about essentially as a short-term record – a means of quickly recording the decisions taken and the actions that are necessary. All minutes can operate in this way, and for some forms of meeting, such as informal management meetings, a short action sheet is all that is required. However, for the formal meetings of the charity – that is its board, its committees and its general meetings – the minutes will also need to provide a longer-term record of the decisions taken and in some instances the reasons for that decision. For this reason, the minutes of such meetings may need to be fuller. A short action note can be useful for the weeks following a meeting, but it is a different matter whether it will stand the test of time. A formal minute needs to be readable and clear as a stand-alone document, and it needs to be able to make sense to someone who may not have been associated with the charity at the time of the meeting and who reads it for the first time a number of years after the meeting took place.

8.3 For all charities, the keeping of minutes of the board, the general meetings and committees will often be a requirement of its constitution. It is also the clear recommendation of the Charity Commission that such records are kept for the lifetime of the charity. If you think about the work of a charity, and the role and responsibilities of its trustees, you can begin to see why it is important to keep such records. Say, for example, that the trustees took a decision that entailed some risk for the charity. They took the decision under professional advice, and after full consideration of the risks and the benefits. If the charity then suffers a loss as a result of that decision, there may be a possibility of action against the trustees for a breach of trust. If no minute has been retained of their decision-making then there will be no evidence that they gave the matter full and proper consideration. However, a minute that records the advice received, the consideration of the risks and the benefits and the reasoning behind the decisions could provide protection for the trustees by showing that they had behaved properly.

8.4 If the charity is a company – there is also a legal requirement that:

- minutes must be kept of all general meetings for 10 years (s. 355);
- minutes must be kept of all board meetings, and of board committee meetings for 10 years (s. 248); and
- records of all written resolutions of the board must also be kept for 10 years (s. 248), as must all records of written resolutions of the members, also for 10 years (s. 355).

8.5 Although the legal requirement is for minutes of companies to be kept for 10 years, it is recommended practice to retain them for the life of the charity. In addition, it may be necessary to retain agenda papers if these are necessary to understand the minutes. For example if a minute says that a policy was agreed as set out in a paper, that paper also needs to be retained. Therefore whilst it may seem cumbersome at the time to include reference to such matters in full in the minutes, or by attaching appendices, it is likely to be easier to do this than having to store all of the papers for the meeting for the life of the minutes.

8.6 If a register is used to record details of documents approved for sealing by the board, instead of recording full details in the minutes, that register should be treated as a subset of the relevant minutes. The same would also be true of any register used to record directors' declarations of interest in transactions, if those declarations were not recorded in full in the relevant minutes.

8.7 Although the Companies Act 2006 makes no provisions for the location of board minutes or their inspection by anyone other than the auditors, under common law a director has a right to inspect board minutes. A member would also have a right to inspect the minutes of the general meetings. Members, or the general public, have no right to inspect board or committee minutes unless this is given to them by the constitution.

✓ 8.8 Minutes checklist

The Charity Commission recommends that every set of minutes contains:

- the name of the charity;
- the type of meeting;
- the date and time the meeting was held;
- apologies for absence;
- the names of those present, including in what capacity they attended (e.g. trustee, adviser, etc.) and for what items on the agenda;
- the name of the chair;
- the approval of, and any changes made to, minutes of a previous meeting must be recorded, together with matters arising from the previous minutes which are not dealt with as a separate item of business

---

8.9 The minutes should also record the wording of any resolution passed. Some charities also record a proposer and seconder (if the resolution has been handled in this way) and the details of who voted. However, it is sufficient for only the result of the vote to be shown. There may be occasions when a trustee requests that their dissent or disagreement to a resolution be recorded in the minutes. If so, it should be recorded, although it should be noted that the trustee still shares responsibility for that decision.

8.10 It is advisable for the minutes to include a summary of the discussion on each item of business and the information upon which the decision was based.

8.11 A minute book needs to be used to keep a copy of all the original minutes as signed by the chair of the meeting (or the next meeting). Minute books can be in the form of either a bound volume or loose leaf. If a loose-leafed volume is kept each page should be signed or initialled by the chair. The minutes and any appendices, or explanatory notes, should be numbered to ensure that any lost or missing pages can be identified. The minute book must be kept in a safe and secure place.

8.12 A charitable company is permitted to retain its statutory books on computer. Therefore copies of minutes can be stored on a computer, but see the comments below regarding the issue of the minutes as evidence.

8.13 There is no legal requirement for the minutes to be approved by the subsequent meeting before they are signed, but this is normal practice. Minutes are usually approved at the following meeting of the board or committee and then signed by the chair of that meeting. It does not matter if the chair did not chair the meeting that was minuted, or even if the members of the meeting approving the minutes are different from the members who attended the meeting that was minutes (for example, if the board or committee membership has changed in the interim).

8.14 For general meetings, the minutes can again be signed by the chair of the meeting or the subsequent meeting. In this case, it is usually advisable for the chair of the meeting to sign them rather than them awaiting the next general meeting for approval and signature.

9 Minutes as evidence

9.1 Minutes can be authenticated by the chairman of the meeting or by the chairman of the next meeting by their signature and are evidence of the proceedings at the meeting. For charitable companies minutes signed by the chair of the meeting at which the business was transacted or by the chair of the next succeeding meeting (or by the secretary in the case of resolutions of members) are evidence of the proceedings. When minutes have been signed in this way, the meeting is deemed to have been duly convened and held and the proceedings duly transacted unless the contrary is proved (sections 249 and 356 of the Companies Act 2006).

9.2 The same issues arise with regard to the keeping of minutes as for registers, and the question as to whether this should be in electronic or hard copy form. A charity may choose to keep its minute books in computerised form; however, this is likely to reduce their value as evidence. If minutes are tendered in legal proceedings as evidence of the proceedings of a meeting, their evidential value could be undermined if there is any doubt as to whether they were signed by the chairman. If such questions are raised and it is not possible to produce an original signed copy, the company may be required to provide additional evidence as to the assertions of fact made in the minutes. As an alternative, minutes may be kept in computerised form without necessarily prejudicing their evidential value if they are signed by the chairman using an electronic signature (as defined in the Electronic Communications Act 2000). However, the type of electronic signature applied may have a bearing on the weight given by the courts to the minutes. For the majority of charities it is unlikely that they will have the mechanisms in place to apply electronic signatures. A third option is to scan manually signed minutes for retention in computerised form and to destroy the originals. However, it appears that such records will still not have the weight of original signed minutes in court. The Civil Evidence Act 1968, the Police and Criminal Evidence Act 1984 and rules of court impose special procedural rules on, for example, the contemporaneous validation of copies which may subsequently be tendered in evidence, and additional rules apply where the copies are kept in electronic form (for details see the BSI British Standard 6498 of 1991, *Guide to Preparation of Microfilm and Other Microforms That May Be Required as Evidence*). It therefore appears advisable for hard copy originals of minutes to be retained. However, they could be stored away and electronic copies used for operational purposes.

9.3 Although signed minutes are prima-facie evidence of the proceedings, they may be set aside by the court if inaccuracies can subsequently be established. No alterations should be made to minutes except to correct obvious errors and this should be done before signature, the alterations being initialled by the chair. Once signed, minutes may not be altered, and any subsequent revisions found necessary should be dealt with by an amending minute at a subsequent meeting.

10 Electronic and microfilm records

10.1 If the charity chooses to keep its statutory registers and records in computerised form there are commercially available software packages that enable this to be done. However, these packages are usually only appropriate for charitable companies rather than charities that take on other legal forms, and even in that scenario may not always be designed for companies limited by guarantee. If a suitable package is found, it is likely to be of use only to a charity with a large membership and in this scenario it is also more likely that the charity will have a membership database set up for different purposes. The importance may therefore be in ensuring that this database can also act as a register of members.

10.2 Increasingly, legislation and regulatory practice not only allows records to be created and stored on a computer, but also allows electronic copies of records to be kept instead of the originals for regulatory purposes. For example, both the Charity Commission and Companies House now provide for information to be filed electronically with them. There are still several important areas where original paper copies must be kept or where they may be preferable for evidential reasons. However, these are fast becoming the exception rather than the rule.

10.3 It is important to note that although documents stored electronically can be tendered as evidence in legal proceedings, they may not always carry the same weight as the paper original. For example, a scanned copy of a document signed under hand will not carry the same weight as the original when seeking to determine whether that signature was genuine.

10.4 If a charity is considering storing documents electronically it should note that the British Standards Institute (BSI) has published a code of practice on electronic records *Code of Practice for Legal Admissibility of Information Stored Electronically* (2004 edition). The BSI's Information Security Standard may also be relevant for these purposes. This standard is published in two parts:

- ISO/IEC 17799 *Code of Practice for Information Security Management*;
- BS 7799-2:2002 *Specification for Information Security Management*.

11 Accounting records

11.1 Charities have a legal obligation to maintain accounting records. The Charity Commission defines accounting records as 'The trustees' records of the financial transactions undertaken by the charity from which the annual statements of account are required to be prepared for each financial year.' It goes on to state that 'The term covers any books (including computer records) in which transactions and events from day to day are entered, together with all the relevant invoices, receipts, other vouchers and other associated documentation' (CC15a, 'Charity Reporting and Accounting: The Essentials').

11.2 The source of the legal duty to keep accounting records depends on whether the charity is a company. All charities that are not companies are governed by Part VI of the Charities Act 1993. Charities registered under the Companies Acts are governed by section 386 of the Companies Act 2006.

11.3 Part VI of the Charities Act 1993 states that:
11.3.1 '(1) The charity trustees of a charity shall ensure that accounting records are kept in respect of the charity which are sufficient to show and explain all the charity's transactions, and which are such as to:

(a) disclose at any time, with reasonable accuracy, the financial position of the charity at that time; and
(b) enable the trustees to ensure that, where any statements of accounts are prepared by them under section 42(1) below, those statements of accounts comply with the requirements of regulations under that provision.'

11.3.2 '(2) The accounting records shall in particular contain:

(a) entries showing from day to day all sums of money received and expended by the charity, and the matters in respect of which the receipt and expenditure takes place; and
(b) a record of the assets and liabilities of the charity.'

11.4 In accordance with this Act the trustees have a duty to maintain the accounting records for at least six years from the end of the financial year of the charity in which they are made. If the charity ceases to exist the obligation to preserve the accounting records for six years shall continue to be discharged by the last charity trustees of the charity, unless the Commissioners consent in writing to the records being destroyed or otherwise disposed of.

11.5 Charitable companies are bound by section 386 of the Companies Act 2006, which states that every company must keep adequate accounting records and that:

11.5.1 'Adequate accounting records means records that are sufficient:

(a) to show and explain the company's transactions;
(b) to disclose with reasonable accuracy, at any time, the financial position of the company at that time; and
(c) to enable the directors to ensure that any accounts required to be prepared comply with the requirements of this Act (and, where applicable, of Article 4 of the IAS Regulation);'

11.5.2 '(3) Accounting records must, in particular, contain:

(a) entries from day to day of all sums of money received and expended by the company and the matters in respect of which the receipt and expenditure takes place; and
(b) a record of the assets and liabilities of the company.'

11.6 A charitable company also has an obligation in regard to any subsidiaries, such as trading subsidiaries. The Act states that 'A parent company that has a subsidiary undertaking in relation to which the above requirements do not apply must take reasonable steps to secure that the undertaking keeps such accounting records as to enable the directors of the parent company to ensure that any accounts required to be prepared under this Part comply with the requirements of this Act (and, where applicable, of Article 4 of the IAS Regulation).'

11.7 Section 387 makes it an offence committed by every officer of the charitable company not to comply with these requirements. Section 388 states that:

'(1) A company's accounting records:

(a) must be kept at its registered office or such other place as the directors think fit; and
(b) must at all times be open to inspection by the company's officers.'

11.8 There are additional requirements if the accounting records are kept at a place outside the United Kingdom. The section goes on to state that accounting records must be preserved by a private company (which is what all charitable companies would be) for three years from the date on which they are made.

✓ 11.9 VAT records checklist

If the charity is registered for VAT it must also keep VAT records, and whilst there is no set way of keeping these, HM Revenue & Customs advises that these should include:

- Records of all the standard-rated, reduced-rated, zero-rated and exempt goods and services that are bought and sold.
- Copies of all sales invoices issued. (With the exception that retailers do not have to keep copies of any less detailed VAT invoices for items under £250 including VAT, unless the customer has asked for a VAT invoice.)
- All purchase invoices for items bought.
- All credit notes and debit notes received.
- Copies of all credit notes and debit notes issued.
- Any self-billing agreements made as a supplier.
- Copies of self-billing agreements made as a customer and name, address and VAT registration number of the supplier.
- Records of any goods given away or taken from stock for private use including rate and amount of VAT.
- Records of any goods or services bought for which the VAT cannot be reclaimed, such as business entertainment.
- Any documents dealing with special VAT treatment, such as relief or zero-rating by certificate.
- Records of any goods exported.
- Records of any taxable self-supplies made.
- Any adjustments such as corrections to the accounts or amended VAT invoices.
- A VAT account, that is a separate record that must be kept of the VAT charged on your sales and the VAT paid on your purchases.

---

12 Document retention

12.1 Throughout this chapter, and others, we refer to the legal need to retain certain documents – registers, minutes and accounting records as just a start.

The issue of document retention – what needs to be kept and how, and for how long – is a broader issue that should be considered. By not having clarity about the requirements charities can sometimes go to one of two extremes, or apply both to different documents. Either there can be a temptation to hold on to everything, forever, or the charity can aim to destroy documents and data very quickly, regardless of any need to retain them for legal or business reasons.

12.2 It is recommended that all charities should adopt a document retention policy. This should set out the core principles of document retention, and set out the minimum and maximum retention periods for key documents. The reasons for developing such a policy are:

- There is a wide range of legal requirements to retain data, with differing legal requirements as to the length of retention. A policy can summarise all these and ensure that there is clarity for staff in what must be retained and how.
- There are also commercial and business reasons for retaining data. For example, there may be a need to take action under a contract that has already been performed. If the charity contracted to have a building built and defects appear in the building during the liability period after it, the charity will want to refer back to the original contract. Another example is if a grant or legacy is given to the charity which creates a restricted fund. If that fund cannot be used for the purpose the money was given for, reference may need to be made to the original grant or legacy in order to remedy the situation.
- It is important to consider not just how long documents are retained for, but in what form. If the document may need to be relied upon as a piece of evidence, the format will be important. For example, if minutes are to be relied upon as prima-facie evidence, they should be signed by the chair of the meeting or the next meeting. An electronic version of the minutes will not usually be signed. Even if the electronic version is a scanned copy of the signed minutes, it may not have the same weight as evidence. The charity will need to take judgments and to understand the legal requirements for the form of documents to be retained and set these out in the policy.
- There are not just minimum reasons why document should be retained. If this was the case, and the charity had sufficient space, it may just decide to keep everything. However, under the Data Protection Act documents that contain personal data should not be retained for any longer than is necessary for the purpose for which they are created. There will also be practical reasons of space for not retaining everything. A document retention policy can set maximum periods for retention, highlighting what data must be kept for the lifetime of the charity. In addition, if the charity is challenged under the Data Protection Act for retaining data, reference to a policy that indicates the reason for the retention and the period of retention could help to show that this matter had been appropriately considered.

12.3 A document retention policy will:

- ensure that the legal requirements as to the method and retention period of certain documents are met;
- ensure that documents that may need to be used as evidence in legal proceedings are kept in a manner that ensure that they will be admissible;
- give clarity as to the retention of other documents, ensuring that staff know what is to be retained, and how, and what can be destroyed; and
- explain how documents should be disposed of.

12.4 The document retention policy should:

- set out the core principles of document retention;
- identify what documents should be retained;
- identify in what format these documents should be retained;
- identify minimum and maximum retention periods for these documents;
- be clear as to the reason for the above, such as whether is it a legal or business requirement;
- specify how documents should be regularly reviewed;
- specify how documents that do not need to be retained should be disposed of; and
- give clear responsibility for document retention.

12.5 Unfortunately, document retention polices can have a tendency to become over-complex, with a very long list of documents. Ideally, they should be kept as simple as possible. There should be clarity regarding core documents and documents where there are legal requirements. However, with other documents it may be simpler to prepare principles for retention that are to be applied rather than listing every possible document. This keeps the policy shorter and simpler. It is also the case that even a very long schedule of documents is still likely to have some gaps that arise from time to time – and so it is a good idea to have principles that can be applied.

B2
Compliance and filing requirements

1 Introduction

1.1 This chapter looks at the compliance and filing requirements for charities reporting to different regulatory bodies depending on what legal form they take. It also considers the legal requirements regarding stationery and the use of the charity's name. As these matters are often the responsibility of the secretary, it concludes by looking at the role of the secretary.

1.2 All charities that are registered with the Charity Commission have a range of reporting requirements, that is information that they must regularly provide to the Commission. Charities that are also companies also have to meet the reporting requirements of Companies House, and those that are Industrial and Provident Societies must also file certain records with the FSA. Other forms of charities, for example chartered bodies or unincorporated associations, have to meet only the requirements of the Charity Commission (if registered), although there may be other regulators depending on the work of the charity.

2 Charity Commission requirements

2.1 Annual returns to Charity Commission

2.1.1 All charities with an income above £10,000 that are registered with the Charity Commission need to complete and submit an annual return to the Charity Commission. However, the level of detail required in the response will depend greatly on the size of the charity. The annual return is made up of a number of parts, and the parts that need to be completed will depend upon the charity's income in the financial period that is being reported on.

2.1.2 Whilst charities with an income of £10,000 or less in the reporting period are not required to complete an annual return they are asked by the Charity Commission to complete an annual update of the information that forms part of the charity's entry on the Register.

Filing requirements: summary
L = legal requirement to file as and when applicable
A = advisable to file when known and often also required in annual return

	Charity Commission	Companies House	FSA
	All registered charities	All companies	All Industrial and Provident Societies
Name of charity	L	L	L
Registered address	A	L	L
Financial year end	A	L	–
Trustees	A	L	A
Secretary	A	L	A
Annual return	L	L	L
Annual accounts	L	L	L
Change in constitution	L	L	L
Mortgage	–	L	–
Alternative address (for registers)	–	L	–
Allotment of shares	–	L	–
Change in trustee/ secretary details	A	L	–
Bank details	A	–	–
Contact details	A	–	–
Website and email address	A	–	–

2.1.3 Charities with an income between £10,001 and £25,000 in the reporting period are required to complete an annual return. The form they have to complete is the basic Part A of the Annual Return (Charity Information). This is similar in content to the annual update required of the smallest charities. Charities of this size also need to make a declaration in regard to the trustees' legal obligation to report serious incidents (RSI) to the Charity Commission. Effectively, the signatory needs to certify that any such incident occurring in the period has been

B2 COMPLIANCE AND FILING REQUIREMENTS

reported to the Charity Commission. Charities of this size do not need to submit the annual report and accounts (for years ending after 1 April 2009).

2.1.4 Charities with an income between £25,001 and £500,000 in the reporting period must also complete this Annual Return (Part A) and submit the declaration in regard to serious incidents (RSI). They must also submit their annual report and accounts.

2.1.5 Charities with an income between £500,001 and £1,000,000 in the reporting period will be legally required to complete Part A, the statement on the reporting of serious incidents (RSI) and Part B (Financial Information). They must also submit the annual report and accounts. Part B comprises a series of questions about the charity's finances. The information required for completing this section should be available from the annual report and accounts, provided that they have been completed in accordance with the Statement of Recommended Practice. Having said this, it would be useful for the trustees to be aware of the questions to be answered before finalising the annual report and accounts, so that there is clarity in regard to what information is required. Whilst the annual report and accounts also need to be submitted, and are then available to the general public from the Charity Commission's website, some of the answers to Part B are more readily available on the accessible Register of Charities, and so it is important that these are handled correctly.

2.1.6 Charities with an income exceeding £1,000,000 in the financial period must complete Part A, the statement on the reporting of serious incidents, Part B and Part C, the Summary Information Return (SIR). They must also submit their annual report and accounts.

2.1.7 It should be noted that although only charities with an income greater than £25,000 must send in their trustees' annual report and accounts to the Commission, all charities regardless of their level of income must prepare accounts and make these available to the Commission on request.

2.1.8 Annual returns and the trustees' annual reports and accounts must be completed and submitted within 10 months of the end of the charity's financial year. The Charity Commission encourages charities to file their documents as early as possible after the end of the financial year. The Charity Commission publishes the compliance history of all charities on the Register of Charities. This shows when documents were filed for the past five years, so enables people to see how compliant the charity is in this regard. It should also be noted that annual returns filed in hard-copy form are not always acknowledged as received immediately, and so sufficient time should be allowed before the deadline.

2.1.9 Much of the information given in annual updates and annual returns is made available on the Register of Charities, which is open to public inspection at the Charity Commission's office and on its website. This does not include the information on the charity's bank details, trustees' addresses and telephone numbers or dates of birth, but the names of the trustees and summary data on the income and expenditure and financial history of the charity is available. Charities should regularly review their register entry to ensure that it is correct, and should bear in mind the data that is published when completing their annual report and accounts and the annual return. The following table sets out reporting requirements.

Charity Commission: annual returns

Income	Annual update	Part A: annual return	Statement re Serious Incidents	Part B: annual return	Summary Information Return	Annual report and accounts
<£10,000	✓					
£10,001–£25,000		✓	✓			
£25,001–£500,000		✓	✓			✓
£500,001–£1,000,000		✓	✓	✓		✓
>£1,000,000		✓	✓	✓	✓	✓

2.2 Summary Information Return

2.2.1 Large charities with an annual income of over £1,000,000 now need to complete a Summary Information Return (SIR). This requires much more detail than the other parts of the annual return. Again, it should be noted that the Summary Information Return is made available to members of the public via the Register of Charities.

2.2.2 The SIR was introduced by the Charity Commission in 2005, in response to an earlier government report *(Private Action, Public Benefit: A Review of Charities and the Wider Not-for-Profit Sector*, Cabinet Office, Strategy Unit, September 2002), which identified a lack of accessible and relevant information about charities.

2.2.3 The SIR requires charities to provide key qualitative and quantitative information about the charity's work, with information on its key aims, activities and achievements; how it sets objectives; and how it measures its outcomes and its impact. The Charity Commission advises that when completing the SIR, charities should aim to create a document that helps the public understand what the charity does and how it has performed.

2.2.4 In completing the SIR a charity should have the relevant information available in its annual report and accounts and may need to refer to other documents (e.g. business plan). The SIR asks a number of questions (those asked in 2009 are listed below) and also give the charity the opportunity to refer readers to where fuller information can be provided. In undertaking its planning for the year, and drafting its annual report, it is useful for the charity to be aware of the questions that it will need to answer so that the information is readily available. For example, is there a clear analysis of how the previous year's objectives were met; have the current year's objectives been set along with a medium to long-term strategy?

2.2.5 Care should be taken in completing the SIR as it is an important report. A great deal of care is often taken in how the charity presents itself in its annual report and accounts, but the presentation of the SIR is neglected. The SIRs of all charities that complete them are publicly available. In completing the SIR it may be advisable to review the SIR of similar charities for comparable information and guidance on how to approach the completion.

✓ 2.2.6 Summary Information Return checklist

1. What are your charity's aims?
2a. Who benefits from the charity's work?
2b. How do you respond to their needs and how do they influence the charity's development?
3a. What are the key elements of your charity's medium to long-term strategy?
3b. How does your charity measure the success of the strategy?
4. What were your charity's main annual objectives and were they achieved?
5a. What were your charity's three main fundraising activities in the year, and how much did each one generate and cost?
5b. What were your charity's most significant activities in the year, and how much did it spend on them?
6. How would you describe your charity's financial health at the end of this period?
7a. How will the overall performance last year affect your charity's medium to long-term strategy?
7b. What are your charity's main annual objectives for next year?
8. How does your charity ensure that its governance arrangements are appropriate and effective?

2.3 Electronic filing with the Charity Commission

2.3.1 The default position now for the filing of annual returns is that this is done electronically and the Charity Commission no longer provides paper forms unless they are requested. It estimates that 70 per cent of charities now file their annual returns electronically.

2.3.2 The Charity Commission provides a range of services online, allowing you to file the annual update and/or return, file accounts and update the charities details. Whereas there is no legal requirement to inform the Charity Commission of changes in the charity's trustees, other than in the annual update or return, the fact that this can now be done online means that it is good practice to update the details whenever they are amended. The details that are held by the Charity Commission that can be updated online are:

- activities of the charity;
- where the charity operates;
- contact details;
- trustees – name; address and date of birth;
- classification – what the charity does; how and to whom;
- financial year;
- main bank or building society details; and
- internet details – e.g. email and website addresses.

2.3.3 To access the online services you will require the charity registration number and a password. Passwords were generally issued to charities when the Charity Commissions moved across to the use of the online service. However, if you do not know the password or need to change it, a new password can be sent to the charity's contact address on request. If you need a new password to file the annual return online, ensure that you leave sufficient time to request it.

2.3.4 The annual report and accounts can be submitted in hard copy or electrically. If submitted electrically the annual report and accounts must be in a PDF format, but if submitted in this format the signatures do not need to appear on the document (provided that they have been signed and that you retain a signed copy).

3 Industrial and Provident Societies

3.1 Charities that are registered as Industrial and Provident Societies are often exempt from registration with the Charity Commission (see chapter A3) and therefore do not need to submit annual returns to it. However, Industrial and Provident Societies are regulated by the Financial Services Authority (FSA) and there is a requirement to submit annual returns to it. The annual return must be submitted within seven months of the year end, and failure to submit your return by the due date is an offence which may result in prosecution. It is the duty of the society's secretary to submit the annual return.

3.2 The annual return for an Industrial and Provident Society is made up of two parts. Part 1 is the form R/IP/AR30, a copy of which is available from the FSA. Part 2 is normally the annual accounts. However, societies not producing accounts to the minimum standard required by the FSA must also complete a supplementary return as part 2 of the annual return.

3.3 The FSA still sends out paper forms for completion of the annual return and there is no provision for filing electrically. However, the form can be downloaded and completed on computer before being printed, signed and sent. This is an improvement on the handwritten form that was required until recently.

3.4 Other than the completion of the annual return there is no requirement for an Industrial and Provident Society to inform the FSA of any changes in its trustees during the year. However, changes to the rules, including a change of name and change of registered office, must be filed with the FSA.

4 Notification to Companies House

4.1 There are documents that a charity that is a company will need to lodge with Companies House. These are:

- Annual report and accounts (see chapter E3); and
- Annual return (see below).

4.2 Change of accounting reference date

4.2.1 The accounting reference date is the date by reference to which the company's financial year is determined. So, for example, if a company prepares its accounts from 1 April to 31 March its accounting reference date is 1 April. A company's first accounting reference date relates to the date that it was incorporated. It will be the anniversary of the end of the month in which it was incorporated. However, companies can change their accounting reference date and most will want to do so in order to have a more regular date than that which stems from their incorporation date. The change of accounting reference date must be notified to Companies House (Form AA01).

4.3 Change of registered office

4.3.1 All companies must notify Companies house of any change in their registered office. You can change your registered office address by sending a completed Form AD01 to Companies House. The change becomes legally effective only when Companies House have registered the form. A person may validly serve any document on the company at the previously registered address for 14 days after the registration of the form.

4.4 SAIL

4.4.1 All registers may be held at the registered office address or at a single alternative inspection location (SAIL). Companies House must be notified if a company has set up a SAIL address (Form AD02) or if the SAIL address is moved (Form AD03), and a company may have only one SAIL address at a time. Once the SAIL address is set up, a company can move some or all registers to the SAIL address by notifying Companies House.

4.5 Change of directors and secretary and their details

4.5.1 Any change of a company's directors or secretaries must be notified to Companies House within 14 days of the change. Form AP01 is for the appointment of a director (AP02 for a corporate director) and AP03 is for the appointment of a secretary (AP04 for a corporate secretary). Form TM01 is for the termination of a director's appointment and TM02 for the termination of a secretary's appointment (resignation, removal, death, etc.). Form CH01 is for a change in details of a director, for example a change of name or new residential address (CH02 for a corporate director, CH03 for a secretary and CH04 for a corporate secretary).

4.6 Allotments of shares

4.6.1 If your company has shares (e.g. if it is a trading subsidiary) Companies House must be notified of an allotment of shares within one month of the allotment of shares (Form SH01).

4.7 Change of Articles

4.7.1 You must send copies of the special resolution passed to change the Articles, or adopt new ones, along with a copy of the revisions to Companies House within 15 days of them being passed by the company. If you do not comply with this requirement you will commit an offence and could be liable to a civil penalty of £200. This is in addition to any liability to criminal proceedings.

4.8 Mortgages and charges

4.8.1 You must send details of every mortgage or charge created by the company and requiring registration to Companies House within 21 days of its creation (Form MG01).

4.8.2 If a form or document submitted to the Registrar of Companies has been incorrectly completed or contains an error, the Registrar will normally return the document to the presenter for correction. If, however, a document requiring correction has been scanned (or accepted electronically) before the error is discovered, a director of the company will need to make a statutory declaration explaining the circumstances under which the error was made. This should be submitted

B2 COMPLIANCE AND FILING REQUIREMENTS

to the Registrar for his consideration along with the revised document. Even if the Registrar agrees to file a revised copy of the document it should be noted that the original document remains on the public record but a note will be placed on the file explaining that the original document has been corrected.

4.8.3 Companies House will reject any documents that contain shading or other formatting because the Companies Registrar cannot make an acceptable copy of them. The Companies House booklet *Directors and Secretaries Guide* sets out the specifications and requirements for filling in forms and completing other documents which have to be sent to the Registrar. The key point to remember is that, although colour-printed glossy accounts are attractive for members and for general publicity, the Registrar requires black print on white A4 paper with a matt finish – a typed printer's proof is ideal provided it has the necessary signatures.

4.9 Electronic filing with Companies House

4.9.1 All of the forms to be used to submit information to Companies House are available online on its website (www.companies-house.gov.uk). The forms may be completed on-screen or downloaded in Adobe's PDF file format before being signed, dated and returned by post.

4.9.2 In addition, there is now also the provision of electronic communications for the delivery of any document required to be delivered to Companies House. Companies House provides an electronic filing service (WebFiling) which may be used to file the following:

- AR01 – Annual return
- Annual accounts – audit exempt abbreviated accounts
- AA01 – Change of accounting reference date
- AA02 – Dormant company accounts
- AD01 – Change of situation or address of registered office
- AP01 – Appointment of director
- AP02 – Appointment of corporate director
- AP03 – Appointment of secretary
- AP04 – Appointment of corporate secretary
- TM01 – Terminating appointment as director
- TM02 – Terminating appointment as secretary
- CH01 – Change of particulars for director
- CH02 – Change of particulars for corporate director
- CH03 – Change of particulars for secretary
- CH04 – Change of particulars for corporate secretary
- AD02 – Notification of single alternative inspection location (SAIL)
- AD03 – Change of location of the company records to the Single Alternative Inspection Location (SAIL)

- AD04 – Change of location of the company records to the registered office
- SH01 – Return of allotment of shares

4.9.3 Most accounts still need to be filed in hard copy, although the online system can be used for the filing of audit exempt accounts and dormant company accounts.

4.9.4 To use WebFiling you must first register for a security code (which is emailed to you), and next register for an authentication code for the company (which is posted to the company's registered office address). If you are filing for more than one company you will be issued with one security code (which is personal to you) and then a different authentication code for each company.

4.9.5 When filing electronically the forms for the appointment of a director or secretary, the individual to whom the notification relates is required to indicate his or her consent to act as a director or secretary by providing three pieces of information which other people would not normally be expected to know (e.g. mother's maiden name). This information will not be displayed on the public file or checked by Companies House (in the same way that it does not check signatures). However, it will be stored electronically so that it can be retrieved should any question arise as to the authenticity of the notification. Whilst Companies House has been advised that this will satisfy the requirement that such notifications must contain a consent to act 'signed' by the person appointed, if the electronic filing method is adopted it could also be advisable to obtain a separate signed consent to act which also authorises the company to use the information supplied by the individual and required for electronic filing purposes.

4.9.6 There is a £15 fee for the filing of the annual return, which can be paid by credit card. It is also possible to use a credit account with Companies House, which will be invoiced monthly. However, to open an account the presenter must need to file 30 or more annual returns per year and so this is very unlikely to be available to a charity.

4.9.7 Companies House usually files documents that are submitted in this way very quickly. However, electronically filed documents are covered by the same five-day processing targets as paper documents received by Companies House. This should be taken into account when filing documents (e.g. annual returns) close to a deadline. All electronically filed documents are acknowledged by an acceptance or rejection message being emailed to the sender.

4.10 Protected Online Filing (PROOF) scheme

4.10.1 This scheme is a newly introduced scheme that helps to protect companies against false filings. The Protected Online Filing (PROOF) Scheme aims to provide added security for companies filing documents. Whilst paper forms (such as those changing directors or the registered office) need to be signed by a director or secretary, Companies House does not check the authenticity of those signatures. This can place a company at risk of fraud. Companies can now elect to join the online filing scheme, which improves security by using passwords, confidential authentication codes and recognised email addresses. If a company also decides to sign up to the PROOF scheme, Companies House will only accept specific statutory forms relating to changes of address or director details electronically using its WebFiling or electronic filing services. Companies House will not accept forms that can be submitted electronically on paper once a company has joined the PROOF scheme, unless the company and its directors specifically authorise it to do so by submitting a consent form.

4.11 Annual returns: companies

4.11.1 In addition to the requirement to submit an annual return to the Charity Commission, all charitable companies need to submit an annual return to Companies House. Unlike the Charity Commission procedure, the date of the annual return is not governed by the accounting reference date but by the date of the formation of the company. The return date (the latest date to which a return may be made up to) is the anniversary of the company's incorporation or, if the company's last return was made up to a different date, the anniversary of that date. Whilst the return date can be changed by the date of the filing of the last year's return, it should be noted that if a return is not delivered within the time limit, that return will not establish a new anniversary date and the date established by the last validly delivered return (or in the absence of such date, the anniversary of incorporation) will continue to apply.

4.11.2 A return must be filed with the Registrar within 28 days of the date to which it is made up. A fee of £30 is payable at the time of filing if the return is delivered in paper form. If it is delivered electronically, a reduced fee of £15 applies.

4.11.3 Whilst a paper return can be delivered, it is nowadays simpler and cheaper to file a return electronically. However, to do so the filer and the company must be registered (see paragraph 4.9.4), and so time needs to be allowed for this to happen before the annual return is due.

4.11.4 If it is submitted in paper form the annual return must be signed by a director (trustee) or the secretary. Electronic forms must still be submitted by a trustee or the secretary and they will include a statement to this effect. The electronic annual return is simper to complete as it is based on already filed information which can then be checked and then signed off. Companies House used to provide hard copy forms in this way but no longer does, so a paper copy will need to be completely filled on.

4.11.5 The annual return requires up-to-date information about the company, including:

- the name of the company;
- its registered number;
- the type of company it is, for example, private or public;
- the registered office address of the company;
- the address where the company keeps certain company registers if not at the registered office;
- the principal business activities of the company (which must be stated in accordance with a prescribed classification system based on the Standard Industrial Classification). If the classification cannot be determined, a brief verbal description of the company's principal business activity or activities may instead be given;
- the name and address of the company secretary, where applicable;
- the name, usual residential address, service address, date of birth, nationality and business occupation of all the company's directors; and
- the date to which the annual return is made up (the made-up date).

4.11.6 If the company has share capital, the annual return must also contain information about the issued share capital and details of the shareholders. The filing of changes to the list only is permitted provided that a full list of members is given every three years. This will not be applicable to charitable companies, which are companies limited by guarantee (with some rare exceptions) but may be applicable for subsidiary trading companies.

5 Legal requirements for stationery

5.1 Charities communicate in a range of ways – by letter, leaflets, email and via the website to name just some. It is common sense that in doing so they need to say who they are, so that people know who they are communicating with. However, there are also legal requirements here – it is not just a common-sense matter. It is also something that commonly gets neglected. Whilst this may seem unlikely, think about whether your charity gives its full name and the fact that it is a charity on all communications.

5.2 Charitable law obligations: England and Wales

5.2.1 Where a charity is registered with the Charity Commission there is a legal obligation to say so. Section 5 of the Charities Act 1993 as amended by the Charities Act 1993 (Substitution of Sums) Order 1995 states that charities with an income in excess of £10,000 which are registered with the Charity Commission must state that they are a 'registered charity' on:

- notices, advertisements or other documents issued by or on behalf of the charity which solicit money or property for the charity's benefit;
- bills of exchange, promissory notes, endorsements, cheques and orders for money or goods purporting to be signed on the charity's behalf;
- bills, invoices, receipts and letters of credit.

The statement must be in legible characters in English (unless the charity is Welsh). There are different ways of making the statement but common ways include 'a registered charity' or 'registered charity number XXXXXXX'.

5.3 Charities registered in Scotland

5.3.1 There are also disclosure obligations under Scottish charity law and these must be observed by charities listed on the Register of Charities in Scotland. This will therefore apply to any charity that is registered in both England and Wales and Scotland. The documents that the disclosure must be made on are letters, emails, advertisements, notices and official publications, items soliciting money or property, invoices, receipts accounts, campaign and educational documentation and documents relating to land transactions and contracts. The disclosure must include:

- the registration number;
- the name by which the charity is recorded on the Scottish Charity Register; and
- an indication of the charity's charitable status if the words 'charity' or 'charitable' do not appear in its name.

5.3.2 The requirements under Scottish Charity law are therefore potentially broader than those under English and Welsh law. A charity registered across both legislations will need to meet both – so it will need to say that it is registered in England and Wales (but not necessarily to give its registration number) and that it is registered in Scotland (and to give its registration number). Scottish charity law also explicitly covers emails (but see below).

5.4 Use of other names

5.4.1 The use of other names is governed by the Business Names Act 1985. The term 'business names' may suggest that the Business Names Act is not relevant to non-commercial bodies such as charities. However, this is not the case. The term 'business name' applies if a body is operating under any name other than its true corporate name (i.e. the name on its certificate of incorporation or governing document). In such a case the true name must be stated on all business letters, orders for goods or services, invoices, receipts and written demands for payments of debts. Any person who fails to comply with this requirement is liable to a criminal fine. The Business Names Act will therefore be relevant if a charity uses another name, or shortens its name or uses its initials only. In all of these cases there is a legal requirement to also state the full name of the charity.

5.4.2 It should also be noted that there is provision under the register of charities to record any other name that the charity is known by. Whilst this will not carry any legal weight, it could still be very useful in keeping the public informed.

5.4.3 Another matter for a charity to consider, if it regularly uses a business name, is whether it may be easier to change the name of the charity to this name. Doing so can help to prevent any breaches of the Act and the requirements under charity and company law to disclose the full name. Whilst there may be reasons why the charity wants to retain a name it does not use, in some instances consideration of changing the name could be more worthwhile.

5.5 Company law requirements

5.1.1 In addition to the charity law obligations there are requirements under company law that will apply to both charitable companies and trading subsidiaries of all types of charities.

5.5.2 Companies must:

(a) clearly show in legible characters the name on the company's certificate of incorporation on all:
  i.   business letters;
  ii. emails and a company's website;
  iii. notices and official publications;
  iv. bills of exchange, promissory notes, endorsements, cheques, orders for money or goods; and
  v.   bills of parcels, invoices, receipts, letters of credit.
  A criminal fine is liable for the company, its officers and any person who issued an incorrect document where these conditions are breached;
(b) show the address of the registered office, the place of registration (England and Wales), and the registered company number on all business letters, order forms, emails, and a company's website. Even if the registered office address is the only address used on the letterhead, it should be stated that it is the registered office; and
(c) show their 'limited' status on all business letters and order forms, in English, and in legible characters. This is usually done by having 'limited' or 'ltd' in the name. However, must charitable companies have been granted permission to omit 'limited'. In these cases, additional words must be used and the usual form is to say 'A charitable company limited by guarantee'.

5.5.3 Whilst it is not necessary to show details of share capital on letters or order forms (relevant to trading subsidiaries), where reference to share capital is made on the letters and orders, it must be to paid-up share capital only.

5.5.4 Whilst directors' details do not need to be shown on company stationery, where directors' details are included, they must be included for every director, and this information must be up to date. Having a list of trustees on the letterhead would therefore mean that it will need to be scrapped and replaced every time there is a change in the names of the trustees.

5.5.5 Failure to observe these requirements make the company and its officers (i.e. director/trustee and secretary) and those involved in issuing an incorrect letter or order liable to a criminal fine.

5.6 VAT registration

5.6.1 It is important to remember that the VAT registration number also needs to appear on invoices and receipts.

5.7 What is stationery?

5.7.1 It is also important to think about how you use other forms of stationery, such as compliments slips. If these are used to form a contract or to place an order they are likely to be subject to the above rules and need to show the full name, company registration details, etc.

5.7.2 For many charities, consideration may also need to be given to how volunteers act on their behalf. The usual practice regarding paper letters sent by volunteers is that they will use letterhead supplied by the charity. This would presumably have the correct details on it. However, in these times it is becoming more usual for volunteers to communicate by email. If this is the case, and the volunteer is acting on behalf the charity, are the legal requirements being met when an email is sent from a volunteer's home computer? If that email is forming a contract, for example, it needs all of the charity's details on it. If volunteers are authorised to act in this way it could be advisable to provide them with 'signature' inserts for their emails to be sent on behalf of the charity with all of the relevant details and instructions on use.

5.7.3 Care also needs to be taken with branches and ensuring that they are aware of the requirements and have access to the required information, again usually in a template. Conversely, independent groups or branches that are separate legal entities should not be allowed to use the charity's name and registration number in a manner which might mislead the public into believing they were dealing with the charity itself rather than a separate organisation.

5.7.4 Finally, make sure that when names or other details are changed that the old stationery is removed and new stationery is used from the date of any change.

5.8 Display of registered name

5.8.1 The registered name of a company must be displayed (in legible characters) at its registered office, at any place where company records are made available for inspection and at any other location at which the company carries on business (unless the location is primarily used for living accommodation). These requirements do not apply if the company has been dormant at all times since incorporation. Where display of the name is required, the name must be positioned so that it may be clearly seen by any visitor. Where the location is shared by six or more companies a scrolling display may be used.

6 The role of the secretary

6.1 Charities take on a range of forms – trusts, companies and chartered bodes amongst others. Not all have to have secretaries, but many do, and the role is undertaken by a range of people – from trustees, to staff members who combine it with another function and named secretaries who perform only this role. A key question is what is or should be the role of the secretary? Is there a core role, or does it depend on who is allocated the task and the type of organisation that the charity is?

6.2 There are a number of differences in the role depending on the type of charity and how it has allocated the role. No two job descriptions for a charity secretary are ever the same. However, there are some core roles and all secretaries usually share the same primary responsibilities. The charity secretary is primarily responsible for:

- the smooth and efficient running of meetings of the trustee board, any committees and general meetings;
- ensuring that all decisions made by the trustees are in accordance with the governing document and reflect the objects of the charity;
- providing assistance and support to the chair of the board of trustees; and
- compliance with various legislative and regulatory requirements affecting the charity and its activities.

6.3 Whilst a number of charities will choose to appoint a secretary even if there is no legal or constitutional requirement to do so, it is usually a requirement of the constitution. In addition, until the Companies Act 2006 came into force all companies were required to have a company secretary. Under the Companies Act 2006 private companies including charitable companies, are no longer required to have a company secretary. However, any company that refers to the appointment of a secretary in its Memorandum and Articles of Association will need to amend the Memorandum and Articles of Association if it wants to dispense with the role of company secretary. It is also arguable that given the governance standards and

B2 COMPLIANCE AND FILING REQUIREMENTS

accountability levels expected of charities along with their heavier reporting obligations it would be unwise for the board of a charitable company to dispense with a secretary. Having a secretary can make it easier in terms of the administration of some matters, as the secretary is a recognised signatory alongside directors. It should also be remembered that all of the functions and duties that will usually sit with a secretary will still need to be the responsibility of someone if a secretary is not appointed. Since the Companies Act 2006 came into force there does not appear to have been a rush amongst charities to remove the need for a secretary. Perhaps the fact that the role is still common in those types of corporate form where it has never been a legal requirement is an indication of the overall importance of the role for a charity.

6.4 The secretary must usually be appointed by the board, and this is certainly the case in a charitable company. The appointment should be minuted. There may also be particular requirements under the constitution for the appointment that need to be met. For example, the constitution may state that the secretary must, or must not, be a member. In addition, some charities have an honorary secretary under the terms of their constitution and may require that the honorary secretary also serves as a trustee.

6.5 If the charity is a company and it chooses to have a company secretary:

- it must notify Companies House of the appointment within 14 days (using Form AP03 or AP04 or by filing online);
- it must notify Companies House of any changes in details; and
- details must be recorded in the Register of Secretaries.

6.6 There is no requirement to give the Charity Commission details of the secretary. However, the secretary is very often the most appropriate person to act as correspondent for the charity, and therefore their details should normally be given to the Charity Commission in this capacity immediately.

6.7 The secretary is usually the principal administrative officer and generally reports direct to the board. In the largest charities the post of secretary will often be an employed post within the charity's staff structure, whereas in medium-sized or smaller charities it is more likely that an unpaid volunteer will act as secretary or the role is combined with another. It is possible to engage suitable professional persons or organisations independent of the charity to act as the secretary on an outsourced basis. The secretary may also be a trustee, and this is usually the case if the role is that of an honorary secretary. If a trustee performs this role, care needs to be taken to ensure that:

- if they are responsible for the minuting of board meetings (as secretaries usually are) consideration is given as to how this impacts on their participation as

a member of the meeting. They are a trustee first and foremost, and sometimes taking comprehensive minutes can affect the ability to also participate fully. If possible, the honorary secretary could retain responsibility for the minutes whilst someone else could attend the meeting to actually take the notes;
- there is consideration of the best use of a trustee's time. Many of the tasks of a secretary are essentially administrative. Is this the best use of the trustee's time? It may be that there is no one else who can perform this role, in which case there also needs to be clarity about what the trustee has responsibility for as secretary; and
- the trustee has understanding, and if necessary, training. Does the trustee understand the role and the duties? Do they require additional support and/or training in this regard?

6.8 Responsibilities of the secretary

6.8.1 The secretary's duties and responsibilities should be determined by the board and they should always be recorded in writing, in a role description or at the very least in the minutes. The nature of the exact duties and responsibilities will vary considerably from charity to charity because of diversity in the organisation's objects, activities, size and legal nature. However, the secretary will almost certainly have 'core duties' which are:

- attending trustee and general meetings;
- issuing notices, agenda and papers for meetings;
- taking minutes (or being responsible for the taking of minutes);
- having custody of registers; minute books; records;
- acting as correspondent for trustees;
- being responsible for statutory compliance (e.g. notifications to the Charity Commission and (if required) Companies House; annual returns, etc.);
- having custody of any seal and overseeing its use; and
- being the custodian of the governing document. This means not just holding a copy of the up-to-date documents (and past versions) but also understanding and interpreting it and advising the trustees on its contents.

6.8.2 Whilst these are the core duties, it is also appropriate for the secretary to be the person responsible for:

- advising on governance matters;
- the provision of legal advice. If they have the appropriate expertise themselves, they could provide it directly but this will usually mean liaising with the solicitors and obtaining such advice; and
- trustee support, training and development.

6.8.3 The secretary is an 'officer' of the charity. Unless the secretary is also a trustee, the liabilities will not be as extensive as those of trustees, but do exist. If the

B2 COMPLIANCE AND FILING REQUIREMENTS 137

charity is a company, section 1121 of the Companies Act 2006 applies, and the secretary may be criminally liable for defaults committed by the company, such as:

- failure to file change in the details of the company's directors and secretary; and
- failure to file the company's annual return.

6.9 Joint and deputy secretaries

6.9.1 A company may wish to appoint more than one secretary, for example if the incumbent secretary is going on maternity leave but wishes to remain as the office holder during the period of absence; or where a company wishes to appoint a person to the office of secretary but to have someone else carry out most of the detailed duties. The appointment of a joint secretary can sometimes be considered when there is an honorary secretary, but they are unable or unwilling to perform all of the administrative duties and a member of staff or outsourced secretary is employed to do this.

6.9.2 Care needs to be taken when making multiple appointments in order to avoid unforeseen consequences.

6.9.3 If joint secretaries are appointed, they will both be placed on the Register of Secretaries, and notified to Companies House. As the most common intention is for the secretaries to be able to act independently this needs to be made clear in the appointment (unless specified in the Articles). Otherwise, joint secretaries will be assumed to have to act jointly, i.e. a document that needs to be signed by the secretary would need to be signed by both.

6.9.4 A charity may also seek to appoint a deputy secretary. Again, for a charitable company, care needs to be taken to ensure that it is clear what powers such a person has, and when they can act. Section 274 of the Companies Act 2006 gives authority for the appointment of deputy or assistant secretaries to act should the office of secretary be vacant or if for any other reason there is no secretary capable of acting; in the absence of any deputy or assistant secretary, the functions of the secretary may be performed by any officer of the company authorised generally or specially in that regard by the directors. Apart from this statutory authority, the Articles of Association of companies frequently contain specific provisions governing the appointment of deputy or assistant secretaries. However, it should be noted that the interpretation of when a secretary is incapable of acting may be narrow, so it would be beneficial if, in making such an appointment, the board also specified when the deputy was allowed to act, for example to sign documents as the secretary. There are differing opinions on whether the appointment of deputy secretaries should also be entered on the Register of Secretaries and notified to Companies House. However, it is arguable that if they are to act as secretary, for example in signing, then they should be. Sample wording for an appointment would be:

> 'That AB be appointed as deputy/assistant secretary of the company with authority to undertake the duties of, and to exercise the powers conferred on, the secretary of the company when the secretary is incapable of acting in that capacity because of his/her absence from the company's offices.'

6.9.5 For charities that are not companies the facility to appoint a joint or deputy secretary will depend to some extent on the provisions in the constitution. If the role of the secretary is not formally outlined in the constitution, this should not be an issue. If it is, the wording will need to be considered to see if more than one person can take on the role, or if the secretary can delegate his or her responsibilities.

6.10 Charitable companies: why have a secretary?

6.10.1 Given that the Companies Act 2006 removed the need for a private company to have a secretary, it is worthwhile considering whether it is worthwhile continuing to do so. It is advisable for three reasons:

1. The charitable company will need to comply with its Memorandum and Articles of Association. If drafted before 2006 these may include a requirement to have a secretary.
2. Having a secretary can make some administrative things easier. For example, notifications of changes in director, annual returns and other statutory notification to Companies House must be made by either a director (i.e. a trustee) or a secretary. If there is no secretary, a trustee will need to take on this role. A secretary can also act as a signatory, for example on certified copies of minutes, in a way that, again, only the trustees will be able to do otherwise.
3. The decision to remove of the role of secretary was taken as it was felt that private companies did not have the same requirement as public companies regarding governance and accountability. However, although they are private companies, it is arguable that charitable companies are actually closer to public companies in this regard than to other private companies.

6.11 Cessation of office?

6.11.1 If a secretary resigns, this should be reported to the trustees immediately. Whenever possible boards should not allow a 'gap' before a new appointment is made, even if this means appointing an interim secretary until a permanent replacement can be made. (So resignations should, whenever possible, coincide with a board meeting. which will then also appoint the next secretary.)

6.11.2 As with appointments, removal can be effected only by the board and should be minuted (along with resignations).

6.11.3 For companies, resignations/removal must be notified to Companies House, and details of the resignation/removal should be entered in the register of secretaries.

B3
Contracts, signing and sealing

1 What is a contract?

1.1 The importance of contracts cannot be overestimated. They have been used since mediaeval times, are the means by which we can form an understanding between two or more parties and are used today as a legally enforceable agreement. Although there is sometimes a perception that a contract is invalid unless it is written and signed, it is possible for contracts to be oral. A contract does not have to be in writing unless there are specific legal requirements for a written form, such as a contract used for the transfer of land. They can therefore be less formal, and most people will enter into small informal contracts as they go about their regular, day-to-day business. Whilst some people may believe a contract does not exist unless there is a signed commitment to an undertaking, or may even go as far to use terms such as agreements 'not being worth the paper they are written on', it is important to understand that contracts can be made in a variety of forms.

1.2 Contracts can be made orally, for example by making a telephone order for office stationery; in writing, for example a mortgage contract; or by implication, for example in buying a rail fare from a ticket machine. The basic principles of what makes a contract, and what these examples have in common, is that they create a legally enforceable contractual obligation.

1.3 Just as an individual can enter into contracts every day, so can a charity. For example, if you just consider the arrangements needed to hold a trustee meeting, a number of contracts could be involved. In such a scenario, contracts could be set up when buying travel tickets, hiring venues for meetings, buying refreshments, printing meeting papers and posting meeting papers.

1.4 Whilst it would be unrealistic and unnecessary to have written agreements for all these contracts, written undertakings are needed for bigger transactions and ongoing matters, and verbal contracts in many of these types of situations should be avoided. If the meeting room is regularly hired with the same venue a written contract would be expected. In addition, the charity may want to ensure that it is imposing its own standard terms and conditions, or at the very least that it understands and accepts other terms and conditions that are being proposed. A written contract will enable this to happen.

2 The basics of contract law

2.1 Not every agreement is a contract, so, if we enter into contracts so often, what makes an agreement a contractual one and therefore legally enforceable? The basis of contract law is that a contract is created when there is:

- offer;
- acceptance;
- consideration; and
- intention to create legal relations.

2.2 Offer

2.2.1 An offer is made when the person making the offer (the offeror) shows an intention to enter into a binding agreement, on certain terms, whenever that offer is accepted by the person to whom it is made (the offeree). Whilst this can appear simple, it is often actually more complex to determine when an offer has been made, and it is important to distinguish an offer from an 'invitation to treat'. An 'invitation to treat' is where there is a communication that the offeror may wish to make the offer, but not a clear intention to actually do so. Sometimes it can be difficult to tell the difference between an offer and an invitation to treat. For example, many people would assume that the display of goods in a self-service store was an offer because it would seem obvious that the display of goods, with the price, was an offer that the purchaser was being asked to accept. However, in law it is actually an invitation to treat (see *Pharmaceutical Society of Great Britain v Boots Cash Chemists* [1953]). It is actually the buyer that makes the offer to purchase, not the person displaying the goods.

2.3 Acceptance

2.3.1 The offer then needs to be accepted, which can be done in writing, orally or sometimes by conduct. The acceptance generally needs to be unconditional – all of the terms included in the offer must be agreed by both parties. If the acceptance is expressed in a way that suggests different terms from those of the offer (e.g. a different price) it is usually regarded as a counter-offer. Just as the offeree must receive the offer, so the offeror must receive the acceptance, and any changes to the original means the terms of that offer have not been accepted. This points to the issue that the offeree must show or, in law, communicate that he or she has accepted the offer. This can be done verbally or non-verbally, but must be understood as a communication that completes the transaction.

2.1.3 Consideration

2.4.1 Offer and acceptance are not enough to create a contract in most scenarios. Generally speaking, for the contract to be enforceable there must be some exchange of value or benefit (for the exception see below) which is called 'consideration'. Consideration is effectively the price paid for the promise. However, whilst there must be some consideration, or 'price', this does not need to be adequate. The law is not concerned in this regard with whether the bargain is a good one. A good example of this is the term 'peppercorn rent', in which the reference to a peppercorn is to a very small payment, a nominal consideration, used to ensure that there is consideration and therefore a legal contract. A peppercorn rent may seem like a very small consideration, but it is still regarded as one and therefore is a component in creating a contract.

2.4.2 Later on we will discuss the use of the seal and deeds and the reasons for entering into contracts as a deed. One core reason is that a contract entered into as a deed is a core exception to the requirement for consideration. A key reason why a charity may want to enter into a contract as a deed is to create a legally enforceable agreement where there is no consideration, for example for a grant. If an individual or a company approaches the charity offering a grant, either in the future or perhaps payable over time, having the grantor enter into a deed can protect the charity to ensure that the grantor does not back out of this offer. Without it being a deed, there is no consideration on the behalf of the charity, and therefore it would not be a legally enforceable contract.

2.5 Intention to create legal relations

2.5.1 In contract law there must also be an intention to create legal relations for a contract to exist. In many contracts, the intention to create legal relations is expressly stated by the parties. However, in commercial contracts the intention to create legal relations will often be implied. This is in contrast to domestic agreements, for example between parent and child, or husband and wife. In such domestic agreements, the intention to create legal relations will not be implied, and should therefore always be expressed if a contract is to be created.

2.6 Unenforceable contracts

2.6.1 A contract could be unenforceable because of a lack of consideration, or if it is *ultra vires* (see below). There are also some contracts which the law will never enforce. These include:

- illegal contracts. If the purpose of the contract is illegal or if performing it requires an illegal act, the courts will not enforce it;
- contracts contrary to public policy;
- unreasonable penalties. If a contract requires one of the parties to pay a penalty if he does not perform his obligations, should non-performance happen

and the amount is regarded as unreasonable by the courts, the courts will not enforce the contract; and
- **restraint of trade:** the courts will not enforce a contract that prevents a person from earning a living. This covers situations when an employment contract may prevent a person from working for a specified time after employment, for example to prevent them working for a competitor. Such clauses can be upheld in limited circumstances, but the general rule is that the kind of contract that prevents a person from earning a living will be unenforceable.

3   Why is it important to have clarity regarding contracts?

3.1 Ensuring that the contract is entered into in written terms can help to ensure that there is clarity. A charity can enter into contracts for a variety of matters, from simple purchases to the employment of staff, the purchase of buildings and to managing ongoing business. It is vital that the charity has clarity regarding what contracts are in place, and their terms, and this is for a variety of reasons.

3.2   Ultra vires

3.2.1 A charity must not enter into a contract which is *'ultra vires'* – that is, beyond its objects or powers. It is very important that the charity's objects and powers are understood and applied in this way. When a contract is entered into that is *ultra vires* there are a number of consequences. The first is that the trustees may face personal liability for breach of trust in having acted in this way, and the charity would have an obligation to recover any losses from the trustees. The second consequence is that the contract may not be valid. The Companies Act generally protects third parties in regard to *ultra vires* contracts and allows the contract to be upheld, but this protection does not apply in the same way to charitable companies as it does to commercial companies. Charitable companies are instead covered by section 65 of the Charities Act 1993. This states that where a charitable company acts *ultra vires*, either by operating outside its objects or its powers, the contract is not enforceable by a third party unless he gave full consideration and did not know that: (i) the act was *ultra vires* or (ii) the company was a charity. It is important to note that the limited protection of the contract by section 65 of the Charities Act 1993 applies for charitable companies only. In addition, whereas a commercial company can have *ultra vires* acts ratified by the members passing a special resolution, for a charitable company, such a ratification would also require the approval of the Charity Commission.

3.3   Authority to enter into the contract

3.3.1 The person agreeing the contract on behalf of the charity, that is signing it, must be properly authorised to do so. A person cannot enter into a contract on behalf of a charity unless authorised to do so, and this authority must be delegated from the board. It can be a specific delegated authority, a general authority or, in some cases, an implied authority. An example of a specific delegated authority would be to enter into that contract, a general authority may include a delegated authority to enter into contracts up to a certain value provided that they are included within the business plan and an example of an implied authority can be a job description. Those entering into contracts must be clear that they have delegated authority to do so. Without such a delegation the individual could be placing themselves as risk by acting without authority. For this reason, it would be better to ensure that the delegation is express rather than just implied. So, a contract of employment for a chief executive may give the person authority to manage the day-to-day business of the charity, and this would carry implied delegation; it would be preferable if there was also a clear, express delegation minuted by the trustees, and perhaps set out as a scheme of delegation. For example, this could state that the chief executive had delegated authority to enter into contracts up to a certain value and/or in furtherance of the business plan agreed by the trustees.

3.3.2 It is important to make a distinction between acts that are beyond the capacity of the charity (and therefore *ultra vires*) and acts that are beyond the authority of the individual concerned, but not beyond the capacity of the charity. For example, if a charity's objects stated that it could provide a service only in Kent, a contract to provide that service in Sussex would be beyond its capacity and *ultra vires*. However, a new contract to provide the service in Kent could be entered into by a member of staff or a trustee, without any delegated authority from the board to do so. This would be beyond the authority of the individual concerned, but not beyond the capacity of the charity. In such a case, the actions could be ratified by the charity. However, there is still a risk to the individual concerned that this will not happen and that he or she is acting beyond their powers. If the person is a trustee he or she may be therefore be potentially at risk of being in a breach of trust.

3.4 Name in which the contract is entered into

3.4.1 A simple matter that is often the cause of error is the name in which the contract is entered into. It is important to get this right as it can affect the validity of the contract and determine who is the contracting party. For example, a contract entered into in the name of an organisation that does not exist can effectively be being entered into by the person signing the contract. Two issues which often occur are:

- the wrong name of the charity being given, either by its full and correct name not being used, or by a trading name being used without further reference to the full name. This sometimes arises in regard to branches, when the branch may have an informal regional name, for example also giving the name of its locality, but it is still a part of the charity. When a contract is entered into it

must be entered into in the full and correct name of the charity and not the branch's local name. Otherwise, there is a lack of clarity as to who the contracting party actually is. This can lead to a circumstance when the actual signatory becomes liable;
- a confusion as to whether it is the charity or a subsidiary which is entering into a contract. When a charity has a trading subsidiary, some contracts will need to be entered into by that subsidiary and not the charity itself. This is important where these are non-charitable contracts that are likely to be *ultra vires* the charity itself. The staff and trustees need to remember and understand when the subsidiary should be acting as the contracting party, and ensure that the contract is entered into in its name. Sometimes the existence of the subsidiary as a separate legal entity can be forgotten and the main charity's name used as a default.

3.5 Terms and conditions of the contract

3.5.1 Care needs to be taken to ensure that these are recognised, understood and agreed with. It may be beneficial for the charity to draw up its own standard terms and conditions (see below). This can give clarity to authorised signatories about what is acceptable and provide a basis for written contracts.

4 Signing of contracts

4.1 Standard contracts will usually be signed by authorised signatories of the charity on the charity's behalf. It should be noted that where the charity is unincorporated, contracts cannot be entered into by the charity itself, in its own name, as it is not a legal entity. It is therefore either the members, or more usually the trustees, who are entering into the contract. (Whether it is the members or the trustees depends upon the legal type of unincorporated charity that it is.) Where the trustees are entering into the contract, this means that contracts should either be signed by the trustees or there should be a clear delegation to the signatory from the trustees enabling him or her to sign, and it should be clearly stated in the contract that he or she is signing on behalf of the trustees.

5 Deeds

5.1 On occasions charities will need to enter into contracts as deeds, and it is important to understand what a deed is and the difference between a contract as a deed and other forms of contract. A deed is a signed, and sometimes a sealed, legal instrument in writing used to grant a right. Deeds have historically been entered into under seal. However, many organisations today choose not to have a seal, and a deed can be created without the use of a seal. There are two key reasons why a charity would want to enter into a contract as a deed:

- First, a deed differs from a simple contract in that it is enforceable without consideration. This could therefore be of significance if a charity wanted to ensure that a grant offered to it was legally binding. By asking the grantor to enter into the grant as a deed, he or she would therefore be committed to it.
- Second, a deed has a liability period which is twice as long as that of a standard contract. (The liability period is the period under which you can take legal action on the contract.) Under contract law a standard contract has a liability period that runs for 6 years, whereas a contract entered into as a deed has a liability period of 12 years. For this reason, it can be to the benefit of the organisation that is having work done for it (e.g. building work) to have the contract entered into as a deed. For the same reason, where the charity itself is to undertake the work, and is asked to enter into the deed, it may want to consider whether it would be to its advantage to do so, as the liability period would be lengthened.

5.2 Many charities own a seal, but it is increasingly common now for charities not to, and deeds can now be entered into by an organisation in other ways than just the affixing of a seal. The constitution often sets out the procedures for how the seal is used and who is authorised to sign under a seal. This will usually be a trustee and the secretary, or two trustees. However, it is also common for the governing document to also allow the board to appoint other signatories for the seal. This is one of the advantages of using a seal as a means of entering into deeds, as it means that persons who are not trustees can be authorised to do so. If a charity has to enter into a large number of deeds (as, for example, is often the case with housing associations) it can be beneficial to enable staff to sign on its behalf. Requiring every deed to be signed by one or two trustees can be difficult. With trustees being voluntary and therefore not available at the charity's main office on a regular basis the board may take the view that it would rather delegate the signing of deeds to staff. The rules of executing a deed without the use of a seal are set out below, but it can be seen that this is restricted to trustees and the secretary. The use of a seal can therefore be beneficial for those charities that would prefer delegation to staff.

5.3 Unincorporated charities execute a deed by acting in accordance with the procedure laid down by their constitutions. This will usually require the signature of all trustees. However, under section 82 of the Charities Act 1993, charity trustees of an unincorporated charity can confer authority on two or more of their number to execute documents in the names and on behalf of the trustees, for the purpose of giving effect to transactions to which the trustees are a party. This delegation can either be specific or general and should be recorded in the minutes of the board meeting. Without such a delegation, a deed will usually have to be signed by all the trustees. Also, when the trustees of the charity change, the deed will need to be updated with the new trustees as signatories. The delegation under section 82 of the Charities Act 1993 is therefore of great value to unincorporated charities.

5.4 A charitable company can enter into a deed by the affixing of its seal by the authorised officers, or by the document being declared as a deed and being signed by two trustees or one trustee and the secretary, or one trustee signing in the presence of a witness who attests the signature (Companies Act 2006). A deed, whether or not sealed, should be stated to be a deed to take effect in this way.

5.5 Other incorporated charities execute deeds in a similar way. Although they are not governed by the Companies Act in the same way as charitable companies and so do not have the same flexibility, their constitution will usually provide for the use of a seal or state how deeds are entered into.

5.6 It is good practice to maintain a record of deeds and/or the use of the seal. The constitution may require the use of a seal to be reported back to each board meeting. If this is the case the use of the seal should either be entered into the minutes, or if a register is used and circulated at the meeting, the register should be maintained as a subset of the minutes. The secretary may also consider it advisable to hold copies of all the deeds that are entered into or, at the very least, to have a record of where the originals are held.

5.7 Where a register is maintained it can be a good idea to number the use of the seal. Whenever the seal is affixed the number should be written next to it. The same number should then be entered on the register. The numbering is done simply on a continuous basis. This can make it easier to search for a record of a sealed document in the seal register. The register should normally give the date on which the seal is affixed, a short explanation of what it is for, and sometimes the value, and the names of the persons who signed the deed. If the original is not held by the secretary, it should also state where the original is held.

6   Electronic signatures

6.1 Whilst substantive contracts should be in writing, in these times much of the communication about a contract can sometimes be done electronically by email. Often the contract will be exchanged and agreed informally in this way, and then printed copies exchanged for signature. However, there is now also provision for contracts to have electronic signatures. The Electronic Communications Act 2000 makes provision to facilitate the use of electronic communications and electronic data storage. An electronic signature has a very general definition. It is defined in section 7(2) of the Electronic Communications Act 2000 as anything in electronic form as:

(a) is incorporated into or otherwise logically associated with any electronic communication or electronic data; and
(b) purports to be so incorporated or associated for the purpose of being used in establishing the authenticity of the communication or data, the integrity of the communication or data, or both.

6.2 This definition means that many different methods can be used to create an electronic signature. What is of fundamental importance is the security of the method used. In order to ensure that an electronic signature is regarded as having the same legal standing and applicability as a manual signature, it is necessary to use up-to-date cryptographic methods. For these reasons, electronic signatures are usually within the remit only of commercial organisations. Most charities will not have the facilities for creating electronic signatures in this way. There is also an issue as to the extent to which an electronic signature can be relied upon. Section 7(1) of the Electronic Communications Act 2000 states that in any legal proceedings:

> '(a) an electronic signature incorporated into or logically associated with a particular electronic communication or particular electronic data, and
> (b) the certification by any person of such a signature shall each be admissible in evidence in relation to any question as to the authenticity of the communication or data or as to the integrity of the communication or data.'

If the party that the charity is contracting with wishes to use an electronic signature, the charity will also need to consider if it places reliance on electronic signatures provided in this way. The organisations would need to able to provide a measure of assurance to the charity that an electronic signature belongs to the person that it purports to represent. It will also need to provide assurance that the signature was applied by or on behalf of its owner.

6.3 The Electronic Communications Act 2000 provides that a person may certify an electronic signature by making a statement (whether before or after the making of the communication) confirming that the signature, a means of producing, communicating or verifying the signature, or a procedure applied to the signature, is (either alone or in combination with other factors) a valid means of establishing the authenticity of the communication or data, the integrity of the communication or data, or both (section 7(3)). A person could certify an electronic signature applied using an insecure method under this procedure. Difficulties may arise, however, where there is some dispute as to the validity of the electronic signature or as to whether the electronic signature was applied by or on behalf of the person it purports to represent.

7 Standard terms and conditions

7.1 In many cases a charity will enter into a contract on standard terms and conditions. Often, these are as provided by the other contracting party. However, there are a number of advantages in the charity developing its own standard terms and conditions:

- they can ensure that the small print is dealt with quickly, and key points not neglected;
- they can place the charity in a stronger bargaining position;
- it can give clarity to staff in terms of what terms and conditions are acceptable to the charity;
- where there are a number of similar contracts it can ensure consistency; and
- standard terms and conditions can reduce legal costs. Standard contracts, or terms and conditions, can be drafted with legal advice and then used in a variety of settings.

7.2 Key features commonly covered by standard terms and conditions

- the jurisdiction that will apply, i.e. which country's law will be used?
- arbitration and how to deal with matters when there is a disagreement. This is a very good alternative to proceeding directly to court action. It can also reduce costs;
- 'force majeure' – how to deal with issues that arise that are outside the control of either party;
- notices and communications – where they should be sent, in what form and how long after being sent they are regarded as having been received;
- payment terms, e.g. when will payment be expected or made throughout the contract term;
- liability and indemnity – what liability is accepted, and what indemnity will be provided? This can be an important means of limiting the risks to the charity;
- transfer and assignment, i.e. can either party pass on their rights and obligations under the contract to another party, and, if consent is needed can it be upheld without good reason?
- intellectual property – who owns the rights? This is a key point in contracts with people undertaking work for the charity. Often, charities do not realize that work written for them is usually the intellectual property of the contractor unless the contract says otherwise;
- variation to the contract – how can it be varied, i.e. this should usually be in writing with the agreement of both parties;

- clarity that this is the entire agreement, i.e. 'what is not in this contract is not applicable';
- termination clauses – how can the contract be ceased by either party?
- confidentiality – often it is advisable to include a duty of confidentially regarding information that may be provided or shared under the contract.

7.3 Standard terms and conditions can be applicable even for a range of different contracts. However, if the charity is entering into a number of similar contracts it may also want to consider having an overall standard format for these contracts. This can reduce costs and ensure that there is a consistent approach. For example, if a charity contracts with a number of consultants it can be useful to use a common contract for all of them.

7.4 Implied terms

7.4.1 Even when a contract is clearly specified in writing there can also be implied terms that will be held to apply to it. These can be implied by fact, by law and by custom.

7.4.2 Terms implied by fact
For a term to be implied by fact it must be obvious to both parties and it must also be clear that both parties (and not just one) would have agreed to its inclusion in the original contract if they had thought of it. Terms implied by fact are terms that are often needed just to make a contract workable.

7.4.3 Terms implied by law
These are terms that are implied regardless of the intent of the parties as a result of the application of common law or statute. Usually they are imposed to further public policy. Such terms can be implied to ensure that the parties treat each other fairly or to protect an economically weaker party. A key point to note in this regard is that the terms implied by law include terms that give an obligation of good faith and fair dealing between the parties of a contract. Another key implied term is that a person with ostensible authority to enter into the contract on behalf of the organisation is taken to actually have that authority. Therefore, the charity will usually be bound to a contract that has been entered into in such a way, even if authority had not been given.

7.4.4 Terms implied by custom
This relates to particular customs that relate to a particular trade and are known to, and recognised by, the parties. Whilst this may not seen applicable to charities it should be noted that terms can also be implied by custom in circumstances where the parties have contracted with each other previously on a number of occasions and particular terms have usually applied in these past contracts.

8 Privity of contract

8.1 In any contract there will be two, or more, parties who agree to it and sign up to it. There will be the offeror and the offeree, or offerees. A key confusion arises as to the rights of anyone else under that contract. It is important to note that under English law no one other than one of the parties to the contract can acquire rights under it, or be subject to liabilities under it. The parties can agree that another party should be conferred a benefit, but that third party will never be able to enforce the contract or those benefits.

8.2 It is therefore very important that you identify from the beginning who needs to be a party to the contract. For example, if the contract is being entered into primarily by the trading subsidiary, but it is intended that the contract will also allow the use of the main charity's brand, the main charity will also need to be a party to the contract.

9 Assignment

9.1 The general principle is that a contract is not assignable (i.e. transferable) to a third party unless there is provision for this in the contract. An assignment is a transfer of the rights and obligations under the contract without the agreement of the other party. Often, when contracts are entered into, it is not envisaged that there will be any need for assignment, but this then arises at a later date. For example, if the charity were to merge with another one, or if it were an unincorporated charity that determined to become incorporated, the contract would need to be assigned to the new body. It is sometimes therefore advisable to ensure that contracts have the facility for assignment. At the very least it can be advisable to include a provision in the contract that consent to the assignment of the contract cannot be unreasonably withheld.

10 Non-performance under a contract

10.1 If there is a breach of a contract by the failure to perform an obligation there are a number of remedies that can be applicable. However, it should be noted that a breach of a contract does not always mean that the contract is terminated. In a worst-case scenario the matter may need to be placed in the hands of the courts, although this should be avoided if possible. The options for remedies that are then available are:
- damages to pay compensation to the injured party for any losses incurred as a result of the breach. This could be as a direct, or indirect, result of the breach of contract. In some scenarios even if there are no actual losses nominal

damages may sometimes be payable. Whilst damages can be payable for losses that arise indirectly, such indirect losses will need to be foreseeable for damages to be payable. Another important point to note is that the injured party is under an obligation to mitigate the losses and not just to let them mount up.
- **specific performance:** if there are no adequate damages, and the breaching party still has it in his capacity to perform, then the court can order him to do so. However, specific performance is not granted as a right, as damages can be. It would always need to be ordered by the court.
- **injunction:** this is the mirror image of specific performance, when instead of being ordered to do something the breaching party is ordered not to do something.
- **recission:** if the breach of the contract is sufficiently serous the injured party may have the right to escape from his own obligations under the contract. However, it is important to note that the right to terminate for breach does not arise in the case of every breach. In general it only arises if the breach is fundamental to the contract, that is that it lies at the heart of the agreement. Also note that the right to rescind can be waived and can be regarded as having been waived. For example, if the injured party insists on continued performance after he learned about the breach he will be regarded as having waived the right to rescind.

10.2 As you will see from the above examples there are occasions when it is necessary to rely on the courts to deal with the non-performance under a contract. Ideally, this should be avoided, and this is a key reason why it is advisable to have a standard clause regarding arbitration in every contract.

✓ 10.3 Contracts checklist

1. Is the contract within the objects of the charity? The objects will be in the constitution of the charity. A contract that is outside the objects of the charity is *ultra vires*. For example, if the objects of the charity restrict its work to a particular locality and the contract is to undertake work in a different locality, it will be *ultra vires*.
2. Does the charity have the power to enter into the contract? In the constitution the statement of the objects is usually followed by statement of the powers that it has. These must also be complied with. A contract needs to fall within the powers. Again, check the constitution of the charity and see if there is a specific power. If there is not a specific power, you can also check if there a general power, that is 'To do anything else within the law which promotes or helps to promote the Objects'. If there is no specific or general power, in some instances there may be a statutory power, but advice should be sought.

3. Are there any special statutory requirements that need to be observed? For example, contracts for the sale of land, or entering into mortgages, are bound by the requirements of the Charities Act 1993.
4. Is there delegated authority to enter into the contract from the trustees? This can be either specific or general (see above). Delegation should be recorded in writing. In addition, is there any reason why the contract should be authorised by the board? This may be because it is of very high value, or for a high-risk project, or because it is not part of the agreed business plan or normal course of business. Note as well that the Charity Commission advises that all contracts for the sale of land should be considered by the full board.
5. Are the signatories properly authorised to sign on behalf of the charity? Even if the board has authorised the contract being entered into, is it being signed by the person who was given that delegated authority?
6. Is the contract a deed, and should it be (see above)?
7. Is the contract in the correct name? Is the full and proper name of the charity being used? Should the contract actually be entered into by a subsidiary?
8. Are the terms and conditions acceptable to the charity? If the other party has referred to their standard terms and conditions are these acceptable to the charity? If the charity has its own standard terms and conditions are these incorporated into or met by the contract?

SECTION C

The charity's governance

C1
Principles of governance

1 Background to the governance of charities

1.1 It is generally acknowledged that the governance of an organisation is one of the most important factors in its long-term success. Governance is high on the agenda in both the commercial and not-for-profit sectors, and certainly public expectations of a charity's governance are high. But what do we mean by 'governance'? One short definition, quoted in *Good Governance: A Code for the Community and Voluntary Sector*, defines governance as being 'The systems and processes concerned with the overall direction, effectiveness, supervision and accountability of an organisation' (the definition comes from *The Governance of Voluntary Organisations*, Chris Cornforth, ed., Routledge, 2003).

1.2 There are number of governance roles encapsulated here.

- 'direction' – providing leadership, setting strategy and being clear about what the organisation is aiming to achieve and how it is going to do it;
- 'effectiveness' – making good use of financial and other resources to achieve the desired outcomes;
- 'supervision' – establishing and overseeing controls and risk management and monitoring performance to make sure that the organisation is on track to achieve its goals, making adjustments where necessary and learning from mistakes;
- 'accountability' – reporting to those who have an interest in what the organisation is doing and how it is doing it.

1.3 Good governance and effectiveness go hand in hand, and it is the board of trustees that is responsible for both. As the Charity Commission itself says in its publication, *Charities Back on Track*, 'Good governance arrangements really are the key to running an effective charity. Being clear about roles and responsibilities and implementing strong financial controls and record-keeping is the best way to avoid everything from disputes to financial chaos.'

1.4 The governance of charities is influenced by a range of external and internal factors. External influences include, for example:

- codes of governance for the public and private sectors as well as those explicitly for the charities;
- events in the corporate sector that have led to major failures, such as Enron, and the financial crisis of 2008/9;
- relevant legislation, such as the Companies and Charities Acts;
- regulation, such as that exercised by the Charity Commission;
- codes of practice for particular activities, such as fundraising;
- requirements of funders – particularly state funding or major trusts;
- public expectations;
- that elusive thing – 'best practice'.
- Internal influences may be more subtle, for example:
- the personalities of individual trustees and their relationships with senior staff (see below in the section on behavioural governance);
- the experience of recent successes or failures;
- dependence on volunteers or members;
- whether service users are engaged with the organisation or not;
- the size and spread of the organisation; and
- the range and types of services provided.

1.5 Sitting in both camps are the stakeholders – those people and organisations that have an interest in what the charity does. Many governance theories (see below) stem from the commercial sector and emphasise the importance of the relationship with the organisation's 'owners' rather than its stakeholders. In a charity, this boarder group of stakeholders, and in particular the beneficiaries, are of key importance, as is the concept of accountability.

2 The history of governance

2.1 There has been a great deal of change in the governance of charities since the 1990s. Much of this has arisen directly in regard to the sector, but it has also been greatly influenced by changes in the governance of the corporate and public sectors. There are three particularly influential reports: the Cadbury Report, *On Trust* and the Nolan Report.

2.2 The Cadbury Report

2.2.1 The Committee on the Financial Aspects of Corporate Governance, chaired by Sir Adrian Cadbury, was set up following the death of Robert Maxwell in 1990 and the revelation that resources had been diverted from Mirror Group's pension fund to pay for a series of risky acquisitions. The business community recognised that unless it put its own house in order, companies would be subjected to greater regulatory and legislative control. While the committee was sitting, there

C1 PRINCIPLES OF GOVERNANCE 159

were two other major corporate collapses – the Bank of Credit and Commerce International (BCCI) and Polly Peck.

2.2.2 The Cadbury Report, published in 1992, made a number of important recommendations about the responsibilities of company directors based on the principles of 'openness, integrity and accountability'. It also addressed the relationship between the chairman and chief executive, the role of non-executive directors and reporting on internal controls and on the company's financial position. The report encouraged listed companies to comply with the accompanying code of best practice or, if not, explain why they had not done so – known as 'comply or explain'.

2.2.3 Although the report was aimed at listed companies, many of its recommendations are relevant to any organisation, including charities. Of particular relevance were the recommendations for fixed terms of office for non-executive directors and recommendations for establishing audit and remuneration committees.

2.2.4 To quote from the Cadbury Report: 'The effectiveness with which boards discharge their responsibilities determines Britain's competitive position. They must be free to drive their companies forward, but exercise that freedom within a framework of effective accountability. This is the essence of any system of good corporate governance.'

2.2.5 Over the years, the recommendations in the Cadbury Report have been added to. For example, in 1995 the Greenbury Report made recommendations on directors' remuneration. In addition, in 1996 the Hampel Committee was established to review the recommendations of the Cadbury and Greenbury Committees. Its report emphasised the principles of good governance. By concentrating on the principles rather than specific rules, it tried to reduce the regulatory burden on companies and be flexible enough to apply to all companies, whatever their size. The Cadbury and Greenbury Reports had focused on preventing senior managers from abusing their power. The Hampel Report, in contrast, looked at governance from the perspective of enhancing long-term shareholder value and so gave greater emphasis to shareholder involvement and the board's accountability, emphasising its responsibility for all aspects of risk management and the system of internal controls.

2.2.6 The Combined Code was published in 1998, consolidating the underlying principles and recommendations of the Cadbury, Greenbury and Hampel Reports. In 1999 the Turnbull guidance provided directors with guidance on internal controls, following on from the work of the Hampel Committee.

2.2.7 Following scandals in the United States involving WorldCom and Enron, the Combined Code was updated in 2003 to incorporate recommendations from the Higgs Report on the role of non-executive directors and the Smith Report on the role of the audit committee. At the same time, the Financial Reporting Council (FRC) took on responsibility for publishing and updating the Code. Further minor changes to the Code followed in 2006.

2.2.8 In 2004 the Myners Report, *Review of the Impediments to Voting UK Shares*, was published, promoting the use of electronic voting. Although this has not yet been taken up to any great degree by the charity sector, it seems likely that charities, particularly those with large memberships, will take advantage of changes in legislation and improved software and start using electronic voting.

2.3 On Trust

2.3.1 Often, when charity governance is considered, it is assumed that everything about it stems from the commercial sector and that all the charity sector has done is to accept the principles of the Combined Code and adapt them. However, the Cadbury Report was not the only report published in 1992. In that year a governance report of direct relevance to charities was published. The NCVO published a key report, *On Trust*, concerned with increasing the effectiveness of charity trustees and management committees. This report and its conclusions were key influences on corporate governance in the charity sector.

2.3.2 The report was from a working party that had been established to consider trustee training, but its outcomes were wider than this. It had a list of strong recommendations, many of which encapsulated for the first time themes that would become common in charity governance, and many of which were implemented in some form. The recommendations included:

- the need for clarity in the main roles and responsibilities of trustees, including the role of the chair, treasurer and secretary;
- the need for advice, support and training for trustees covering a range of topics, and recommendations on how that training be approached;
- that general information packs should be provided for trustees;
- that a senior staff member or the chair should take responsibility for training;
- that there was a need for clear guidelines on the charity's expectation of trustees and job descriptions for trustees;
- that charities should have a policy on the composition, recruitment and appointment of their trustees;
- that attention be give to induction for trustees;
- that training needs be regularly assessed, with a rolling programme of advice and support;
- that there should be clarity about who the trustees of a charity were, and their role;

C1 PRINCIPLES OF GOVERNANCE 161

- that the Charity Commission should publish a leaflet on the roles and responsible of trustees;
- that NCVO should give much higher priority to working with trustees, particularly chairs, and ensure that its services were accessible to them;
- that funders should establish a mechanism for monitoring the governance of organisations that they fund;
- that trustees should sigh a statement accepting their responsibilities.

2.3.3 A review of these recommendations 17 years later shows how influential they were. Whilst the focus began with training, the principles had far wider application, and many of the ideas that they encapsulated are now common practice for charities. The principles of clarity regarding roles and responsibilities, and the idea that charities should have job descriptions for trustees, are widely espoused. The concept of regular assessment has grown into the idea of regular performance review and skills audits. The importance of having a policy in the composition of the board and who is recruited has also been developed, with charities now having to report on such matters in their annual reports.

2.4 The Nolan Report

2.4.1 The Committee on Standards in Public Life, under the chairmanship of Lord Nolan, was established in October 1994 by the then Prime Minister, John Major, in the wake of the 'Cash for Questions' affair. It was given wide terms of reference to examine concerns about the standards of conduct of all those who hold public office.

2.4.2 The Nolan Report expanded the list of principles included in the Cadbury Report to seven. These are: Selflessness, Integrity, Objectivity, Accountability, Openness, Honesty and Leadership (the Seven Principles).

2.4.3 Although drafted for public sector bodies, the Seven Principles address a fundamental problem faced by all organisations and have been used within the voluntary sector. How do you know that those who are in charge of the organisation are doing a good job and acting in the best interests of the organisation? Just as individual shareholders do not run a public company, donors and service users do not run charities. The answer is that those who have been made responsible for the running of an organisation have to report on what they have done and their stewardship of the organisation's resources. This is being accountable. The next question is 'Who are trustees accountable to?' The answer most trustees will now give is, 'To our stakeholders'.

2.5 Good Governance Standard for Public Services

2.5.1 The Good Governance Standard for Public Services was jointly published in January 2005 by the Office for Public Management and the Chartered Institute of Public Finance and Accountancy. It was the result of work done by the specially constituted Independent Commission for Good Governance in Public Services. The Good Governance Standard was intended to build on the Nolan Report and set a common benchmark for what good governance means for public service organisations. Its six standards mark an interesting development from the Seven Principles of Nolan, as they are more outward-looking and participative. Instead of just being accountable and open, organisations are encouraged to take 'an active and planned approach to dialogue with and accountability to the public' and focus on 'the organisation's purpose and on outcomes for citizens and service users'.

2.5.2 The Good Governance Standard for Public Services

1. **Good governance means focusing on the organisation's purpose and on outcomes for citizens and service users**
    - Being clear about the organisation's purpose and its intended outcomes for citizens and service users
    - Making sure that users receive a high-quality service
    - Making sure that taxpayers receive value for money
2. **Good governance means performing effectively in clearly defined functions and roles**
    - Being clear about the functions of the governing body
    - Being clear about the responsibilities of non-executives and the executive, and making sure that those responsibilities are carried out
    - Being clear about relationships between governors and the public
3. **Good governance means promoting values for the whole organisation and demonstrating the values of good governance through behaviour**
    - Putting organisational values into practice
    - Individual governors behaving in ways that uphold and exemplify effective governance
4. **Good governance means taking informed, transparent decisions and managing risk**
    - Being rigorous and transparent about how decisions are taken
    - Having and using good quality information, advice and support
    - Making sure that an effective risk management system is in operation
5. **Good governance means developing the capacity and capability of the governing body to be effective**
    - Making sure that appointed and elected governors have the skills, knowledge and experience they need to perform well
    - Developing the capability of people with governance responsibilities and evaluating their performance, as individuals and as a group

- Striking a balance, in the membership of the governing body, between continuity and renewal
6. **Good governance means engaging stakeholders and making accountability real**
   - Understanding formal and informal accountability relationships
   - Taking an active and planned approach to dialogue with and accountability to the public
   - Taking an active and planned approach to responsibility to staff
   - Engaging effectively with institutional stakeholders

© OPM and CIPFA 2004. Reproduced with permission.

2.6 Good Governance: A Code for the Voluntary and Community Sector

2.6.1 Last, but not least, is *Good Governance: A Code for the Voluntary and Community Sector*, published in June 2005. The code was developed by the Charity Commission, the National Council for Voluntary Organisations (NCVO), the Association of Chief Executives of Voluntary Organisations (ACEVO), Charity Trustee Networks and the ICSA.

2.6.2 This code covers similar ground to the slightly earlier *Good Governance Standard*, but emphasises the role of the board. It also introduces the underlying principle of equality.

2.6.3 Key principles of the *Good Governance* code

- **Board leadership:** every organisation should be led and controlled by an effective board of trustees which collectively ensures delivery of its objects, sets its strategic direction and upholds its values.
- **The board in control:** the trustees as a board should collectively be responsible and accountable for ensuring and monitoring that the organisation is performing well, is solvent and complies with all its obligations.
- **The high-performance board:** the Board should have clear responsibilities and functions, and should compose and organise itself to discharge them effectively.
- **Board review and renewal:** the board should periodically review its own and the organisation's effectiveness and take any necessary steps to ensure that both continue to work well.
- **Board delegation:** the board should set out the functions of sub-committees, officers, the chief executive, other staff and agents in clear delegated authorities, and should monitor their performance.

- **Board and trustee integrity:** the board and individual trustees should act according to high ethical standards and ensure that conflicts of interest are properly dealt with.
- **The open board:** the board should be open, responsive and accountable to its users, beneficiaries, members, partners and others with an interest in its work.

2.6.4 In 2008 nfpSynergy undertook a research report into the awareness, impact and success of the code. This showed that 42 per cent of respondents were aware of the code, and had used it, but that a further 29 per cent of the respondents were aware of it, but had not used it. Amongst those respondents that were aware of the code, the most common reasons for not using it were that the boards felt that their governance was already working well (28 per cent of non-users) or a lack of time or lack of commitment on behalf of the board were cited. Certainly, the code is not mentioned in the annual reports of many major charities. The reason for this may be that charities feel that the code brought very little that was new to the field of governance, and adoption of the code, although encouraged by the Charity Commission, is not a requirement. Most well-run charities would have either been complying with the code already or at least believed they were, and so a lot of boards have tended to put the code to one side. However, consideration should also be given to the concept of proportionate governance (see below) and the possibility that the code was originally over-prescriptive in it approach for all charities.

2.6.5 The code was reviewed in 2009, and at the time of writing there is an ongoing consultation on the introduction of refashioned principles. These state that a good board will provide good leadership by:

- 'understanding their role;
- ensuring delivery of the organisational purpose;
- being effective as individuals and a team;
- exercising control;
- behaving with integrity;
- being open and accountable'.

As can been seen, these follow similar principles to the original code, but are much simpler.

3 Theories of governance

3.1 Corporate governance is most often talked about with regard to its practical application, rather than the underlying theories. However, whilst it is useful to be aware of the different models and procedures of corporate governance, it is also helpful to take a step back and think about what theories underlie those principles. There are a number of theories of governance that have influenced the charity sector. It should be acknowledged, though, that many of the theories originated in the commercial sector, and there are often a number of key differences that need to be considered. For example, many governance theories rest on the relationship between managers and shareholders, and the charity sector does not have 'owners' in the same way. There are stronger principles of wider accountability that are important in the charity sector.

3.2 Agency theory

3.2.1 Agency theory is a commonly used theory of corporate governance in the commercial sector. It has been around in a number of forms for a long time. It is concerned with the relationship between the managers of a company, and the owners, that is the shareholders. In the eighteenth century Adam Smith was among the first to raise concerns about whether employed managers would watch over other people's assets with the same vigilance as if they were their own. In the twentieth century, the theory moved forward with a statement of the potential sources of conflict that may result from a separation of ownership and control in the modern company; the owners having given their power to employed managers who exercise control on their behalf. One of the underlying assumptions of the theory is that there is a goal divergence between the owners (the principals) and the managers (the agents). This divergence of the preferences of principals and agents necessitates actions to make sure that managers who pursue their own self-interest will also pursue the collective interest. From an agency theory perspective, boards of directors are put in place to monitor managers on behalf of shareholders.

3.3 Stewardship theory

3.3.1 Agency theory does not seem to 'fit' with charitable organisations. For a start, there are no shareholders as owners in the same way as there are in commercial companies. In addition, the principle that managers will tend to act in their own self-interest does not seem applicable in the same way. This is either because those involved in charities, and in determining their governance, take a more positive approach to human nature, or it stems from the fact that the managers of a charity are often not driven by the same financial rewards as in the commercial sector. Therefore, are there other reasons for them working for the charity? Stewardship theory (Davis *et al.*, 1997) can seem more applicable. This is a theory that managers, left on their own, will indeed act as responsible stewards of the assets they control. Stewardship theory assumes that the behaviours of the management are aligned with the interests of the principals. Stewardship theory therefore favours governance mechanisms that support and empower the organisation's management and disfavours those that monitor and control it. According to stewardship theory, 'the more crucial factor influencing organisational performance is the design of the organisational structure so that managers can take effective action' (Chitayat, 1985). The key issue that the theory is concerned with is therefore not how to strengthen the control of management, or to make the board act on behalf of the 'owners' but rather how to empower management.

3.4 Policy governance

3.4.1 Policy governance (John Carver) is a model of governance that is particularly applicable to charities and seems much more designed for them. It is a theory that gives a set of principles that are designed to empower boards to fulfil their obligation of accountability for the organisations they govern. It is a much more commonly used theory in regard to charity governance, although often concepts are plucked from it rather that the theory being applied as a whole. Quite commonly organisations state that they are following policy governance, and applying it, but when you look closer at how it is being applied, there are some tenets of the theory that are not accepted. Charity boards often have an inclination to hold on to control in a much more detailed way than policy governance prescribes.

3.4.2 Although it is applicable to any boards as a generic system the theory is very applicable for charities, and this is strengthened by the fact that the theory directly refers to charities (or 'not for profits, as this is a US theory). A key point here is that it deals with the 'ownership' issue and how this is applicable within a charity with accountability to beneficiaries.

3.4.3 The theory begins with the premise that the board exists (usually on someone else's behalf) to be accountable for how its organisation works. It recognizes that in the commercial sector a board of directors is the voice of the owners (shareholders). However, it is not always apparent that charities also have owners, but the theory states that there is a moral equivalent that it refers to as the 'ownership'. Therefore, just as the commercial board exists to speak for the shareholders, the charity board exists to represent and to speak for the interests of the 'owners' in a broader sense.

3.4.4 The theory argues that traditionally, boards have developed their relationships largely inside the organisation (i.e. with staff), whereas it argues that the board's primary relationships should be outside the organisation.

3.4.5 The principles of the theory are concerned with finding ways to enable the board to focus on the larger issues and to truly lead its organisation. It argues that boards should clearly delegate and control the work of management without getting involved in the detail. Policy governance separates issues of organisational purpose (which it describes as 'ends') from all other organisational issues ('means'), placing primary importance on those ends. When applying policy governance a board should focus on the ends, and only be concerned with limiting how staff carry out the means when this breaches the board's standards of prudence and ethics.

3.4.6 Policy governance therefore places a strong emphasis on delegation and how to set the framework within which staff can operate. This should be by setting core principles for them to work within, rather than detailed policies and procedures. Policy governance recommends that the board use a single point of delegation and that all the accountability of the organisation to meet the board expectations is charged personally to the CEO. The policy therefore states that the board, in effect, has one employee. It also states that accountability in leadership requires the board to be definite about its performance expectations, to assign these expectations clearly and then to check to see that the expectations are being met.

3.4.7 Policy governance boards should also use committees only to help the board to do its own job and not to duplicate the work delegated to the CEO.

3.5 Governance as leadership

3.5.1 Modes of governance

This theory (developed by Chait, Ryan and Taylor) includes the principle that there are three modes of governance:

1. the fiduciary mode, where boards are concerned primarily with the stewardship of tangible assets;
2. the strategic mode, where boards create a strategic partnership with management; and
3. the generative mode, where boards provide a critical source of leadership for the organisation.

3.5.2 The generative mode, in contrast to the other two types, is a larger, more cognitive process that involves looking outside the usual framework of overall operations and getting at the heart of an organisation's raison d'être and purpose. Generative thinking is about the broader questions such as deciding on what to decide, probing assumptions about the organisation and identifying the underlying values that should be driving strategy and tactics.

3.5.3 The theory argues that when trustees work well in all three of these modes, the board achieves governance as leadership. Fiduciary work is vital and ensures that charities are faithful to mission, accountable for performance and compliant with relevant laws and regulations. If a board fails in this mode the charity could be damaged. In addition, the strategic work enables the board to set the charity's priorities and to deploy resources accordingly. If a board neglects strategy, the organisation could become ineffective.

3.5.4 Each mode emphasises different aspects of governance and rests on different assumptions about the nature of organisations and leadership. All three modes are equally important, but currently the fiduciary and strategic modes are the modes that dominate the work of boards. The theory states that greater importance should be placed on the generative mode.

3.6 Behavioural governance

3.6.1 In recent years the concept of behavioural governance has developed. This has been strengthened since the financial crisis of 2008/9 and the search for reasons why the governance of banks and the financial sector did not prevent the errors that were made. Whilst this theory has developed in the commercial sector, it is also applicable to the charity sector. The theory is that appropriate boardroom behaviour is an essential component of best practice corporate governance, and that there is an absence of consideration of, and guidance on, appropriate boardroom behaviours in current corporate governance models and systems. In 2009 ICSA issued a report on boardroom behaviour which stated that 'an emerging view is that the system of governance for companies is not inherently "broken", but rather that its effectiveness has been undermined by a failure to observe appropriate boardroom behaviours'.

3.6.2 Behavioural governance states that best practice in boardroom behaviour is characterised by a clear understanding of the role of the board; the appropriate deployment of knowledge, skills, experience and judgment; independent thinking; the questioning of assumptions and established views; and a supportive decision-making environment. The degree to which these behaviours can be delivered is shaped by the character and personality of the directors and the balance in the relationship between the key players in the boardroom.

3.6.3 Whilst this theory had emerged in the commercial sector, it can be seen that a shift of emphasis away from the structures of governance towards the behaviour of board members can also be applied to charities. Many charities have codes of conduct for trustees and seek to ensure that their trustees have a clear understanding of their role and are trained to fulfil it. It is interesting how the introduction of behavioural governance, if applied in the charity sector, will reapply some of the core principles that were developed in *On Trust* a number of years ago.

3.7 Proportionate governance

3.7.1 At about the same time as the commercial sector was starting to think about behavioural governance, the charity sector began to address the concept of proportionate governance. This was similar in that the emphasis was no longer placed on the adoption of formal governance procedures. However, it approached this not from the direction of board behaviour, but by focusing the

C1 PRINCIPLES OF GOVERNANCE

limited resources of many charities to concentrate on what governance was actually needed. The report, *Proportionate Governance*, was published in 2009 by the Compass Partnership. This took the view that the advice on governance to smaller charities tended to be too prescriptive. It argued that whilst the principles of the Code of Governance applied to all organisations, the way in which they were articulated was not always applicable to smaller charities, or charities in the early stage of their development.

3.7.2 Proportionate governance is about recognising the benefits of meeting requirements for organisations of different sizes in different ways. The report raised a concern that there was a danger that funders, regulators and organisations promoting good governance do not fully recognise this need for proportionate governance, and that requirements that are appropriate to the different sizes and stages of an organisations development are needed.

3.7.3 It suggested that an alternative approach be taken to governance, and the report recommended three possible approaches:

1. a simple approach based on working through six key questions relating to the key elements of governance (see below);
2. a grid-based approach, recognising that reaching thresholds in growth triggers more requirements for more sophisticated governance; and/or
3. a risk-based approach, with governance requirements being identified in proportion to the risks that a charity faces.

3.7.4 Key questions for boards

The six key questions that the report suggests that a board can work through are:

1. 'What is our organisation aiming to do or achieve in the next period of time (6 months/1 year/3 years)?
2. How will we judge how well the organisation has performed in this time – in terms of changing our aims to the standards we wish?
3. What are the key tasks to be undertaken? Who should take them on and what authority will they have?
4. What risks could threaten the organisation's success or its stakeholders' interests? What measures do we need to put in place to manage those risks?
5. How will we ensure that we are complying with the relevant laws and regulations?
6. Who needs to know about what we are doing? How will we demonstrate to them the quality and value of what we have done?'

3.7.5 This recommended approach to governance coincided with a consultation on the redrafting of the Code of Governance which also adopted a more proportionate response. The code had been reviewed the previous year and one of the conclusions of that report was that whist the principles of the code were correct, they needed to be easier to understand and more applicable to a wider range of organisations, no matter what their size. The six refashioned principles were high level and designed to be universal and applicable to all voluntary and community organisations. The consultation acknowledged that the practice and procedures would then vary according to the type and size of the organisation.

4 Legislation and regulation

4.1 A charity's legal form will also influence its governance to a great extent. For example, charities established as companies limited by guarantee will have members, directors (who are also the trustees) and a set of Memorandum and Articles. This provides a framework for a charity's governance. There is at least some degree of clarity as to what the charity is there for, who is in charge and how they are appointed or elected, what they can or cannot do and how they are accountable to the charity's members.

4.2 However, the form also raises the question of the individual accountability of trustees, and the control and influence given to members who may not be the key stakeholders. In some charities, the trustees are the only members, which may lead to a confusion of roles.

4.3 In contrast, a charitable trust can be established very simply. There are only three requirements. First, the charitable purposes must be established. Second, there must be certainty over the assets of the trust. Third, there must be certainty that a charitable trust was intended to be created. Because a trust is unincorporated, it can only interact with the outside world through its trustees. The individual trustees have a greater degree of liability and so are arguably more accountable for their collective decisions. On the other hand, it is often less clear who the trustees are accountable to. There are no members, and there is a need for great clarity in the objects to determine who the beneficiaries are.

4.4 The Charities Act 2006 has brought opportunities for both greater clarity and simplicity to the governance of charities. For example, we now have a list of charitable purposes, the public benefit requirement and the framework for the CIO (Charitable Incorporated Organisation), a new legal entity. The Companies Act 2006 has also brought changes to how charities are governed. For example, removing the legal requirement for an annual general meeting has led a number of charities to put in place more appropriate methods of electing trustees and being accountable to stakeholders. Where trustees are the only members, the AGM is not the appropriate means of accountability for a charity, and it can be advisable to seek alternative means rather than relying on this.

4.5 The Charities Act 2006 has also strengthened the Charity Commission's role in helping charities uphold the principles of good governance. Its five objectives are:

'1. The public confidence objective is to increase public trust and confidence in charities.
2. The public benefit objective is to promote awareness and understanding of the operation of the public benefit requirement.
3. The compliance objective is to promote compliance by charity trustees with their legal obligations in exercising control and management of the administration of their charities.
4. The charitable resources objective is to promote the effective use of charitable resources.
5. The accountability objective is to enhance the accountability of charities to donors, beneficiaries and the general public' (CA 2006 7(3)).

4.6 The Charity Commission's expanded register of charities now makes even more information about charities and their performance available to the public thereby increasing their accountability and making their governance more open.

5 Accountability

5.1 One of the core themes of the governance of a charity is accountability. Throughout all of the discussion above, this has come across in a number of ways – from the opening definition of governance, to the relationship with 'owners' in governance theories and the ways that the regulatory involvement has increased accountability. However, whilst accountability is so important, a core issue for a charity is accountability to whom?

5.2 In the commercial sector, accountability is mainly towards shareholders – the providers of capital. Shareholders elect directors who are responsible for running the company, and the directors' report on at least an annual basis to their shareholders via the annual report and financial statements. The Companies Act 2006 (section 172) says that 'A director of a company must act in the way he considers, in good faith, would be most likely to promote the success of the company for the benefit of its members as a whole.' This reaffirms the importance of this relationship but it goes on to say:

'and in doing so have regard (amongst other matters) to—
(a) the likely consequences of any decision in the long term;
(b) the interests of the company's employees;
(c) the need to foster the company's business relationships with suppliers, customers and others;

(d) the impact of the company's operations on the community and the environment;
(e) the desirability of the company maintaining a reputation for high standards of business conduct; and
(f) the need to act fairly as between members of the company.'

5.3 There is therefore now an explicit acknowledgement that a company's success relies on those who help produce product or services (employees and suppliers), those who purchase products or services (customers) and the community at large.

5.4 Although many charities are established under company law as companies limited by guarantee, the bond between trustees and members is of a different nature to that between directors and shareholders. The Companies Act 2006 (section 172 (2)) allows for this difference between ordinary companies and charities. It states: 'Where or to the extent that the purposes of the company consist of or include purposes other than the benefit of its members, subsection (1) has effect as if the reference to promoting the success of the company for the benefit of its members were to achieving those purposes.'

5.5 In other words, success for the trustees of a charity established as a company can be defined as achieving the charity's charitable purposes, and the range of stakeholders involved in achieving this can be very wide indeed.

5.6 The accountability of a charity is not just to its members. It must also be accountable to its beneficiaries (both present and future), its donors and the public. In addition, unlike shareholders, members normally have little financial stake in a charity and so have little to lose financially whether its trustees perform well or poorly. However, if a charity has members who are also volunteers, donors or service users the members are likely to have a have a strong interest in how well the charity is run. Many charities benefit greatly from the passion of their members for the charity's cause. But there can be conflicts between a charity's accountability to its members and its wider accountability. For example, the trustees have a duty to act in the interests of the charity and in this regard the interests of future beneficiaries must also be taken into account. How are trustees to be held accountable to a membership that may have more limited aims when they have a wider, legal obligation?

5.7 Just as a public limited company can have a wide range of stakeholders, so too can a charity. Besides those mentioned above, a charity's stakeholders may include local authorities, central government, communities in which the charity operates and other charities, particularly those with similar charitable objects.

It is important for all these stakeholders that a charity's trustees are both open and accountable, setting out clearly in advance what it is that they are aiming to achieve and reporting back on how they have performed.

5.8 The Charity Commission actively promotes accountability to stakeholders under the 'accountability objective'. In 2004 it published a research report, RS8 *Transparency and Accountability*, which reviewed the annual reports of a sample of the 200 largest charities. It concluded that 'Our evidence is that the general standard of performance against the transparency and accountability framework is not satisfactory. Whilst there are some very good examples, too many charities in our study did not meet basic requirements.'

5.9 Since then, the Charity Commission has required more detailed information from large charities in the form of the Summary Information Return (SIR), which has to be completed by all charities with an income of over £1 million. The SIR was introduced by the Charity Commission in 2005 in response to an earlier government report (*Private Action, Public Benefit*, Cabinet Office, Strategy Unit, September 2002), which identified a lack of accessible and relevant information about charities.

5.10 Whilst stakeholders may have access to more and better information, many charities still struggle with the degree to which their stakeholders should be involved in influencing the running of the charity and, in particular, shaping the services that they provide. In addition the concept of 'ownership' and who owns a charity is still a matter of wide discussion and different views. In thinking about the principles of governance and how to apply them, there have been a number of changes over time. Which theory and approach to take is a matter for the trustees to consider. However, given the importance of accountability through all aspects of corporate governance, perhaps one core principle to deal with is to be clear who the charity should be accountable to, and how.

C2
Roles and relationships

1 Introduction

1.1 This chapter looks at the roles and responsibilities of a charity's trustees, members and staff, including the role of individual trustees and the board of trustees as a whole and their relationship with staff. Although the chapter covers the legal aspects of the role of trustees, it is important to bear in mind that how trustees define their role and how they work as a board will also be influenced by the board's composition, its culture and values.

2 Role of trustees and role of the board

2.1 The main role of a charity's trustees is to govern the charity, and they do this through making decisions collectively as a board. Generally speaking, individual trustees have no powers to act on their own unless these powers are delegated to them.

2.2 As well as being trustees of a charity, where the charity is established as a company, trustees will be company directors with the duties that this entails. Although trustees act collectively as a board, for the most part the duties owed by trustees to the charity are personal to the individual trustees, and so it is the individual trustees who are each responsible for the actions of the board as a whole.

3 Trustees' responsibilities and duties

3.1 Whether a charity is constituted as a company or a trust, the trustees have the same duties under the laws relating to charities and trustees. Their responsibilities and duties derive from a number of different sources, including common law, statute law, case law, the charity's own constitution and regulatory requirements.

3.2 It is important that everyone involved in the governance of a charity is familiar with their own charity's constitution as this will vary from charity to charity.

However, care needs to be taken. In some cases legislation will override the provisions of a charity's constitution. For example, charities that are companies need to review their own constitutions as some provisions of the Companies Act 2006 override a company's own Memorandum and Articles.

3.3 The Charity Commission's publication, *The Essential Trustee: What You Need to Know* (CC3), sets out in summary the responsibilities of charity trustees.

◆ **3.4 The Essential Trustee: What You Need to Know (CC3)**

Trustees and their responsibilities

Charity trustees are the people who serve on the governing body of a charity. They may be known as trustees, directors, board members, governors or committee members. The principles and main duties are the same in all cases.

1. Trustees have and must accept ultimate responsibility for directing the affairs of a charity, and ensuring that it is solvent, well-run, and delivering the charitable outcomes for the benefit of the public for which it has been set up.

Compliance: trustees must:

2. Ensure that the charity complies with charity law, and with the requirements of the Charity Commission as regulator; in particular ensure that the charity prepares reports on what it has achieved and Annual Returns and accounts as required by law.
3. Ensure that the charity does not breach any of the requirements or rules set out in its governing document and that it remains true to the charitable purpose and objects set out there.
4. Comply with the requirements of other legislation and other regulators (if any) which govern the activities of the charity.
5. Act with integrity, and avoid any personal conflicts of interest or misuse of charity funds or assets.

Duty of prudence: trustees must:

6. Ensure that the charity is and will remain solvent.
7. Use charitable funds and assets reasonably, and only in furtherance of the charity's objects.
8. Avoid undertaking activities that might place the charity's endowment, funds, assets or reputation at undue risk.
9. Take special care when investing the funds of the charity, or borrowing funds for the charity to use.

Duty of care: trustees must:

10. Use reasonable care and skill in their work as trustees, using their personal skills and experience as needed to ensure that the charity is well-run and efficient.

11. Consider getting external professional advice on all matters where there may be material risk to the charity, or where the trustees may be in breach of their duties."

© Crown Copyright 2008. Taken from the Charity Commission website, www.charity-commission.gov.uk.

4 Trustees as directors of charitable companies

4.1 Where a charity is established as a company (normally, a company limited by guarantee) the trustees will have duties as company directors. The Companies Act 2006, ss. 171–177 sets out for the first time in legislation the duties that a company director owes to the company. These are:

- to act within powers;
- to promote the success of the company;
- to exercise independent judgement;
- to exercise reasonable care, skill and diligence;
- to avoid conflicts of interest;
- not to accept benefits from third parties; and
- to declare interest in proposed transaction or arrangement.

4.2 These requirements are largely self-explanatory, but the requirement under s. 172 'to promote the success of the company' requires a little further explanation. The section says that:

> '(1) A director of a company must act in the way he considers, in good faith, would be most likely to promote the success of the company for the benefit of its members as a whole, and in doing so have regard (amongst other matters) to—
> (a) the likely consequences of any decision in the long term;
> (b) the interests of the company's employees;
> (c) the need to foster the company's business relationships with suppliers, customers and others;
> (d) the impact of the company's operations on the community and the environment;
> (e) the desirability of the company maintaining a reputation for high standards of business conduct; and
> (f) the need to act fairly as between members of the company.
> (2) Where or to the extent that the purposes of the company consist of or include purposes other than the benefit of its members, subsection (1) has effect as if the reference to promoting the success of the company for the benefit of its members were to achieving those purposes.'

4.3 For charitable companies this means that its directors must promote the success of the charity in achieving its charitable objects, but still have regard to the list of items in subsection (1).

4.4 In addition to these core duties, the Companies Act imposes a large number of requirements on the trustees of charitable companies in their role as directors. These include keeping proper accounts, maintaining statutory books and records and filing resolutions, returns and an annual report and accounts at Companies House.

5 Trustees' powers

5.1 Charity trustees have to act within their powers, exercise their powers in the best interests of the charity and within the charity's objects and exercise their powers personally. Although trustees can delegate some of their powers, they cannot delegate their responsibilities to others.

5.2 It is important to note that the powers of individual trustees are normally very limited. The model constitution approved by the Charity Commission for a charity established as a company limited by guarantee says that the directors manage the business of the charity and may exercise all the powers of the charity unless they are subject to any restrictions imposed by the Companies Acts, the Memorandum and Articles or a special resolution passed by members. Resolutions have to be passed at a quorate meeting of trustees, although that model constitution also states that powers may be delegated to a committee of two or more trustees. The powers of individual trustees tend to be limited to matters such as calling meetings of the trustees. However, boards may delegate authority to individual trustees – for example, to sign contracts on behalf of the board.

6 Trustees' liabilities

6.1 Many people contemplating becoming a trustee of a charity are concerned that they might be held personally liable for any losses. In fact, it is very rare for a trustee to be made personally liable, as the law protects trustees who have acted reasonably.

6.2 There are three main areas of risk that may give rise to personal liability for trustees: contractual liability, liability arising from a breach of trust and legal liability. The position of the individual trustee will depend on the charity's legal form. In short, because an unincorporated charity is not a legal entity separate from its trustees, its trustees are more exposed to the liabilities of the charity than they would be if the charity were incorporated.

7 Contractual liability

7.1 Most charities will enter into contracts to supply or receive goods or services under which there will be a contractual liability. Unincorporated charities have no legal personality, and so it is the individual trustees who are party to any contract. As long as the trustees have acted properly in entering into the contract, they can draw on the charity's resources to meet their contractual obligations. However, where a charity does not have sufficient resources to fulfil the contract, the trustees remain personally liable. For incorporated charities, contracts are with the charity and not the individual trustees, so provided that there has been no breach of trust, no liability should attach to individual trustees.

7.2 There are a number of ways of reducing the trustees' risk:

- The charity itself could become incorporated, so that any contracts are with the charity and not the trustees.
- An unincorporated charity may have a corporate body as its sole trustee, with the people who would otherwise be individual trustees as its directors. In the event of a breach of its duties, only the corporate trustee would be directly liable. However, if the directors of a corporate trustee have been in breach of duty to the company, they may be liable to make good any losses suffered by it.
- Under the Charities Act 1993 Part VII (ss. 50–62), individual trustees may become an incorporated body. The benefits in terms of ease of holding assets are similar to using a corporate trustee, but individual trustees remain responsible for breaches of trust.
- Contracts may be drafted to include a term that limits the trustees' liability to the value of the charity's assets.
- Trustees may be able to take out indemnity insurance against the risk of any shortfall in the charity's assets.

8 Breach of trust

8.1 Trustees are in breach of trust when they act in a way that is contrary to the terms of their governing document, or when they fail to perform their duties as trustees. Examples of a breach of trust include using the charity's resources for a purpose that is outside the charity's objects or investing the charity's money in a type of investment not permitted under the investment rules applying to the charity. Where trustees commit a breach of trust which results in financial loss to the charity, they are liable to make good that loss.

8.2 Trustees can reduce the risk of a breach of trust by being familiar with their charity's governing document and taking professional advice or consulting with the Charity Commission on any point on which they are unsure. Under s. 61 of the Trustee Act 1925 and s. 1157 of the Companies Act 2006 the court can excuse a trustee's breach of trust if it is satisfied that the trustee acted honestly and reasonably. In addition, under s. 73D of the Charities Act 2006, the Charity Commission itself is now able to relieve a trustee from personal liability.

8.3 Trustees may be able to take out indemnity insurance to protect themselves from personal liability arising from a breach of trust. The Charity Commission leaflet CC49, *Charities and Insurance*, gives detailed advice. As trustee indemnity insurance is a benefit to trustees, it needs to be properly authorised. Where a charity does not have the necessary authority in its own constitution, following a change brought in by s. 39 of the Charities Act 2006, there is now statutory authority for charities to take out such insurance. The Charity Commission's approval is now required only if a charity's constitution explicitly prohibits the purchase of such insurance. When deciding whether indemnity insurance is appropriate, the trustees will need to take into account:

- the degree of risk to which they are exposed;
- the value of the indemnity required;
- the cost of the insurance premiums; and
- whether the insurance is in the interests of the charity.

8.4 Where indemnity insurance is taken out, the policy must contain a clause excluding:

- 'liability in respect of fines imposed in criminal proceedings, or penalties arising from regulatory action;
- liability arising from defending criminal proceedings in which the trustee is convicted of fraud, dishonesty, or wilful or reckless misconduct; and
- liability arising out of conduct which the trustee knew, or should have known, was not in the interests of the charity' (Charity Commission CSD 1279: 'Trustee Indemnity Insurance', information sheet for trustees).

8.5 As an alternative to insurance, charitable companies may indemnify their trustees, although there are restrictions. Section 234 of the Companies Act 2006 permits companies to indemnify directors for the costs of successfully defending claims from third parties, but not from the company itself.

9 Legal liability

9.1 Trustees of charitable companies need to be aware that they are subject to the provisions of the Insolvency Act 1986, which can impose personal liability on the directors for wrongful or fraudulent trading.

9.2 Directors commit fraudulent trading under s. 213 where, prior to a company's insolvent liquidation, they continue to trade and incur debts with the intent of defrauding creditors.

9.3 Under s. 214, wrongful trading is where, before the company enters into insolvent liquidation, the directors knew or should have known that there was no reasonable prospect that the company would avoid insolvent liquidation and failed to minimise the loss to creditors.

9.4 In both cases, the liquidator can apply to the court for an order to require the director to make a contribution out of his or her own assets. The liquidator will report to the DTI on the director's conduct, and this may lead to a disqualification order under the Company Directors Disqualification Act 1986.

9.5 In practice, assuming that the directors of a charity in financial difficulties have acted honestly, they are most likely to be concerned about liability for wrongful trading. The risk of this can be reduced by ensuring that management accounts are up to date and accurate and, in particular, that balance sheets and cash flow forecasts are regularly reviewed. Trustees need to remember that a charity's management accounts may show a surplus and it may have more assets than liabilities but it can still be insolvent through lack of cash. If trustees believe that their charity is in financial difficulty, legal and financial advice should be sought as soon as possible and the Charity Commission consulted.

9.6 Although there are many sections of the Companies Act which could lead to prosecution and fines or even imprisonment for directors in default of them, criminal prosecutions are rare. The usual penalty is a fine from Companies House and, for more serious offences, disqualification as a director. The risk of penalty can be reduced by ensuring that trustees receive appropriate advice.

9.7 Trustees also need to be briefed on their other statutory responsibilities, such as those for health and safety.

10 Recruitment and selection

10.1 Many charities, particularly smaller ones, struggle to find trustees, and so there may be a temptation to recruit anyone who takes an interest in the charity as a trustee. However, having the wrong person as a trustee can, at best, add nothing to the decision-making capabilities of the board and, at worst, cause immense disruption, ill-feeling and damage to the organisation. For even the smallest charity, a formal recruitment process will pay dividends.

10.2 The aim of a good trustee recruitment and selection process is to recruit trustees who:

- are eligible to act as trustees and are appointed in accordance with the charity's governing document or relevant statutory requirements;
- have the skills and experience that the charity requires and are able to apply them to benefit the charity;
- work well together; and
- are able to commit time and attention to the charity.

10.3 The recruitment and selection process can be divided into a number of phases:

- assessment of the board and charity's requirements in terms of trustee skills, knowledge and experience, also taking into account the diversity of the trustee board;
- preparation of a job description and person specification;
- advertising;
- application;
- interviewing;
- appointment/election; and
- induction and training.

10.4 As recruitment and selection is often a time-consuming business, the trustees may wish to delegate some of the work to staff, but they must retain overall control of the process. Most larger charities will do this through a nominations committee with clear terms of reference. These terms will usually include:

- reviewing and making recommendations on the composition of the board;
- making recommendations to the board on the person specification for the trustee(s) being sought and the method of recruitment;
- seeking out and making recommendations to the board on new and co-opted trustees; and
- overseeing succession planning.

10.5 The nominations committee may also have a role in making recommendations on trustees seeking re-election at the end of a term of office and the appointment of the chair and chief executive.

> **10.6 Factors for nomination committees to consider**
>
> - Should the nominations committee include members who are not current trustees – for example, representatives of the charity's beneficiaries or volunteers? The advantage of this is that it reduces the risk of the current trustees recruiting new trustees who are like themselves.

- Are the trustees on the nominations committee suitably trained?
- When recruiting for specialist roles, for example a treasurer, it may be helpful to have an external expert on the committee, such as a treasurer from another charity.
- Is the committee a vetting committee, checking that any applicants would make good trustees and are able to meet minimum requirements, but leaving the decision to an election by the membership (where applicable), or should it recommend the same number of people as there are vacancies? The former is more democratic, but may make it more difficult to achieve a well-balanced board.
- Has adequate time been allowed for the whole process? The recruitment process needs to be planned carefully, working backwards from the expected date of appointment of the new trustee. If board meetings are held quarterly, the process of assessing the board for any skills gaps may need to be carried out up to nine months in advance. This can cause problems, as trustees coming to the end of a term of office may not have yet decided whether they wish to seek to serve another term.

11 Identifying the board's requirements

11.1 When a charity is planning to recruit new trustees, the first step is to consider what skills, knowledge and experience are needed to make sure that the charity is well governed and identify any gaps amongst the present trustees. It is also important to draw up a list of other requirements for trustees – for example, the ability to attend board meetings and away days. Assessing the skills and experience of current trustees can be difficult. Normal practice is to ask trustees to complete a questionnaire, but undue modesty on the part of some trustees can sometimes lead to odd results, so it is helpful if the nominations committee can review the responses from individual trustees.

11.2 When considering skills, knowledge and experience, it is important to be as precise as possible. Do you need a property lawyer or a human rights lawyer? Also, has enough weight been given to soft skills – such as negotiating skills or the ability to speak persuasively on behalf of clients?

11.3 The Charity Commission recommends that job descriptions are prepared for each trustee. The ICSA and the National Council for Voluntary Organisations (NCVO) both produce model job descriptions for charity trustees and for chairs, secretaries and treasurers of charities. The general job description should be backed up by a person specification for each vacancy. For example, if an individual trustee is to be asked to take the lead on fundraising, this should be included in the person specification.

12 Recruiting new trustees

12.1 While traditional methods for recruiting new trustees, such as personal recommendation and word of mouth, remain popular, they are not open and transparent methods of recruitment and may not be the most effective ways of finding people with the right skills and experience. However, experience has shown that personal recommendation can play a role in identifying people who have the right skills, but might not actively be seeking to be a trustee, and encouraging them to come forward.

12.2 Advertising can be an effective way of reaching a wide group of people. However, it can also be expensive. Charities should consider alternative methods such as notices on websites and in their own and other organisations' newsletters. Sometimes an advertisement for a trustee vacancy can be included in a piece of editorial. For example, a report on a charity's successful fundraising campaign might include a note that the charity is seeking a trustee with particular experience in fundraising.

12.3 It is important to think carefully about where to place adverts and the content of the advertisement itself. If you are seeking someone with particular professional skills, it may be better to advertise in a professional journal rather than in a national newspaper. In particular the advertisement should be specific about the time commitment required, as this may be an obstacle to many people.

12.4 It may be worth running briefing sessions for potential trustees, so that they have the opportunity to find out more about the charity before deciding whether to apply. For national charities, seeking potential trustees from around the country, briefings can be held by telephone conference call, while for small charities, an open evening or even a display at the local library might work well.

12.5 Many charities find that their existing volunteers, donors or members possess suitable skills, so it is worth making sure that these groups are given early notice via newsletters or other correspondence.

12.6 Another way of finding new trustees is to make use of a trustee brokerage service or trustee register. Trustee brokers provide a matching service between potential trustees and vacancies. Some search agencies that specialise in recruiting non-executive directors for companies are also willing to advertise unpaid trustee vacancies.

12.7 The National Council for Voluntary Organisations (NCVO) operates a Trustee Brokerage Network Group and the Trustee Bank an online list of vacancies. Other organisations, such as the Institute of Chartered Secretaries and Administrators (ICSA), the Ethnic Minority Foundation (EMF), the Council of

Ethnic Minority Voluntary Sector Organisations (CEMVO) and the National Housing Federation (NHF), also provide trustee registers.

12.8 Networking with other local charities or those that work within the same field can prove useful. Where a charity has no current trustee vacancies, it may refer people who are interested in being a trustee on to other, similar charities.

13 Diversity issues

13.1 Charities will often benefit from recruiting trustees who reflect, and have a knowledge of, the communities and the area in which they operate and the people they serve. It can help provide better services to a wider range of people and may enable the charity to reach a wider range of supporters – staff, volunteers and donors. Having a diverse board can also increase accountability and the public's confidence in the charity's work.

✓ 13.2 Increasing board diversity checklist

- using more open and inclusive ways of recruitment, such as advertising or using trustee brokerage services;
- asking candidates to complete application forms rather than provide CVs as this requires the nominations committee to focus on the relevant criteria;
- organising board meetings at the most convenient times, or at different times, so that people who cannot attend at a particular time are not excluded;
- making sure that board meetings are accessible for people with disabilities and that, where needed, assistance is given in completing the application form or attending an interview;

- paying childcare expenses or providing childcare arrangements; and
- making sure that there are no cultural or religious barriers to attendance.

13.3 Some charities will be 'public authorities' and will therefore have a duty to promote equality under the Race Relations (Amendment) Act 2000, the Disability Discrimination Act 1995 and the Employment Equality (Sexual Orientation) Regulations 2003. Public authorities are, broadly speaking, bodies that carry out public functions, such as local authorities, health trusts, courts, etc. Charities are likely to be treated as public authorities where they carry out work under contract to a public authority, fulfilling a role that would otherwise have to be carried out by the public authority.

14 Beneficiaries as trustees

14.1 Many charities will have one or more of their charitable beneficiaries, or service users, as trustees. It is important to bear in mind that service users who are trustees have exactly the same duties and responsibilities as other trustees.

14.2 Boards need to ensure that there are procedures in place to manage any conflicts of interest between a trustee's personal interests and those of the charity. This is particularly important for service users, who will benefit from the activities of the charity.

14.3 Thought needs to be given as to how service users are recruited to the board. For example, there may be a certain number of places reserved for service users, who are elected by other service users. In some cases, particularly where beneficiaries do not have a long-term relationship with the charity, this may not be practicable and, in practice, the service users on the board are often those who have taken an interest in the board's work and been encouraged to put themselves forward.

14.4 Further information about user trustees is contained in the Charity Commission publication *Users on Board* (CC24).

15 Appointments

15.1 Trustees may be appointed in a number of different ways. For example:
- they may be nominated by the other trustees;
- they may be appointed by another organisation, such as a local authority;
- they may be elected by the charity's members; or
- they may become a trustee by virtue of a position which they occupy. For example, a vicar may automatically be a trustee of a church charity. These are termed 'ex officio' appointments.

15.2 The charity's governing document will set out the procedures for appointment, including any restrictions, such as any age limits. If the correct procedures are not followed, this could result in the appointment being invalid. Care should be taken, as the requirements may not be clearly spelled out. For example, governing documents sometimes require the notice of an annual general meeting to contain for each person seeking election as a trustee all the details that must be included in the register of directors. Under s. 163 of the Companies Act 2006 this will include details such as previous names.

15.3 If it is a requirement that trustees are members of the charity, check that potential new trustees are members and that any membership subscriptions are up to date. Under some constitutions, non-payment can lead to membership automatically lapsing, which might lead to a person being ineligible for appointment as a trustee.

15.4 Where trustees are nominated by an external body, such as a local authority, the charity may still be able to influence the appointment. The external body will usually respond positively to clear guidance from the charity as to any particular skills or experience the charity is looking for from its trustees.

15.5 In addition to normal appointments, the governing document may allow for the board to appoint trustees to fill casual vacancies to serve until the next annual general meeting, or there may be provision for the co-option of additional trustees for specific purposes. Again, care needs to be taken to comply with the governing document's requirements. Charities may vary as to whether co-optees count towards the quorum of a meeting and whether they have a vote in all circumstances.

15.6 The constitution of unincorporated charities will normally contain details of who is entitled to appoint new trustees. If there is no express provision, the trustees can exercise powers under s. 36 of the Trustee Act 1925 to replace outgoing trustees or appoint additional trustees.

15.7 The Charity Commission may appoint new trustees under the Charities Act 1993, s. 18(5) under certain circumstances. These are:

- to replace a trustee removed by the Charity Commission;
- where there are no trustees or because of vacancies, absence or incapacity, the current trustees cannot act;
- where there is a single charity trustee who is not a corporate trustee, and the Commission believes it is necessary to increase the number of trustees for the proper administration of the charity; and
- where the Commission is of the opinion that it is necessary for the proper administration of the charity to have an additional charity trustee because one of the existing charity trustees who ought nevertheless to remain a charity trustee either cannot be found or does not act or is outside England and Wales.

15.8 Under the Trustee Act 1925, s. 41, the High Court may appoint new trustees, but as the Charity Commission has the same powers, it would be more usual for the Charity Commission to make an appointment.

15.9 Trustees of unincorporated charities may be appointed by deed. Under s. 40 of the Trustee Act 1925, unless the deed contains a statement to the contrary, all of the charity's assets will transfer to the new trustees. This avoids the problem of having to execute transfers of titles, particularly of land, from the old trustees to the new trustees on each change of trustee. Alternatively, the same effect can be obtained by a memorandum of appointment signed by the chair of the meeting where the appointment of the new trustee took place and witnessed by two people who were present at that meeting.

16 Checks for potential new trustees

16.1 Charities must check that prospective trustees are not disqualified from being a trustee either by law or by the charity's own constitution and that prospective trustees understand the responsibilities that they are taking on. Remember that a charity's trustees are in a position of trust. This does not necessarily mean that everyone who applies to be a trustee is entirely trustworthy.

16.2 Section 72(1) of the Charities Act 1993 lists people who may not be trustees of a charity. A person will be disqualified if:

- he has an unspent conviction for any offence involving dishonesty or deception;
- he is an undischarged bankrupt;
- he has made an arrangement with his creditors and has not been discharged in respect of it;
- he has been removed from the office of trustee of charity by an order made by the Charity Commission (formerly the Charity Commissioners) or the High Court on the grounds of any misconduct or mismanagement in the administration of the charity for which he was responsible;
- he has been removed, under section 7 of the Law Reform (Miscellaneous Provisions) (Scotland) Act 1990 (powers of Court of Session to deal with management of charities), from being concerned in the management or control of any body; or
- he is subject to a disqualification order under the Company Directors Disqualification Act 1986 or to an order made under section 429(2)(b) of the Insolvency Act 1986 (failure to pay under county court administration order).

16.3 The Criminal Justice and Court Services Act 2000 disqualifies certain individuals from holding a range of positions in children's charities, which includes charity trusteeship. It is also an offence to knowingly offer either paid or voluntary work with children to someone who is disqualified from working with children or to allow them to continue doing such work.

16.4 Under the provisions of the Care Standards Act 2000, it is a criminal offence for an individual confirmed on the POVA (Protection of Vulnerable Adults) list to apply for a care position, as defined in the Act, and a provider of care, as defined in the Act, must not employ anyone in a care position who is either provisionally listed or confirmed on the POVA list.

16.5 It is important to note that people who have been disqualified as company directors are prohibited from being trustees of any charity, not just charitable companies.

16.6 In addition, charities will normally wish to check the details given on the application form and carry out the same checks that are made on new staff.

✓ 16.7 Checklist for vetting new trustees

- Take up at least two references, one from a current employer, if available.
- Check relevant academic qualifications.
- Check professional qualifications with the relevant professional body and ask if any disciplinary action has been taken against him or her.
- Ask for proof of name, address and date of birth (people under 18 cannot be trustees of a charitable trust or unincorporated association but can be a director/trustee of a charitable company, provided that they are 16 or over).
- Require potential trustees to sign a declaration that they are not disqualified from being a trustee.
- Check the Individual Insolvency Register maintained by the Insolvency Service at www.insolvency.gov.uk.
- Check the register of disqualified directors maintained by Companies House at www.companieshouse.gov.uk.
- The Charity Commission keeps a register of people removed as a trustee by the Charity Commission or by the court. Unfortunately, this is not currently available online, but a copy of the register is kept at each of the Commission's offices.
- For trustees of charities working with children or vulnerable adults, obtain a Disclosure from the Criminal Records Bureau (CRB). A CRB check is compulsory for some trustees – for example trustees of child care organisations, and may be available for trustees of charities working with vulnerable adults. The Charity Commission expects charities to take up CRB checks whenever they are available. It is important to note that CRB checks are

not available for all trustee positions. The CRB provides a range of helpful information available on its website (www.crb.gov.uk) or by calling 0870 90 90 811. Information for charities providing care services is available from the Care Quality Commission (CQC) at www.csci.org.uk, and the Department of Health has produced a guide dealing with the protection of vulnerable adults including examples of posts eligible for a CRB check, available at www.dh.gov.uk.

16.8 If a disqualified person is appointed as a trustee, the appointment will be invalid. It is normally an offence to act as a trustee while disqualified unless the Charity Commission has granted a waiver under section 72(4) of the Charities Act 1993 (as amended by s. 35 Charities Act 2006). If the governing document contains provisions which prevent certain people from acting as charity trustees, the Charity Commission cannot grant a waiver.

16.9 If existing trustees had not made proper checks before the appointment, they may be found by the Charity Commission to have acted improperly.

16.10 Checklist for the appointment of a new trustee

- Give the new trustee a letter confirming appointment (sample letters for the appointment of trustees as directors of incorporated and unincorporated charities are available from www.icsa.org.uk).
- Update the charity's details on the Register of Charities at the Charity Commission's website, www.charitycommission.gov.uk. Although there is no requirement to inform the Charity Commission immediately, an updated list has to be submitted as part of the annual return or annual information update form. If a change in trustee also involves a change in the charity's contact details, the Charity Commission should be informed as soon as possible.
- If the charity is a charitable company, ensure the details of the newly appointed director are submitted to Companies House and update the register of directors.
- Charities that are not companies may have requirements for trustees to sign their consent to act or have their name entered into a register of trustees. (It is considered best practice for all new trustees to sign a letter of consent.)
- (For unincorporated charities only.) Ensure that any property belonging to the charity which is held in the names of outgoing individual trustees is transferred into the name of the new trustee.

- Amend bank mandates if the new trustee is to be a signatory to the charity's bank account.
- Inform relevant people including staff, professional advisers and supporters and include the appointment in any newsletter.
- In particular, ensure that fundraising staff are given full details of trustees, including brief biographies, as these are often required for grant applications.
- Update details of trustees on the charity's website and in other publications.
- If a trustee must be a member of the charity, ensure that the new trustee is a member and that any membership subscription fee is paid up to date. In some charities, trustees automatically become life members, so check that new trustees are categorised correctly.

17 Induction and training

17.1 A proper induction is important to ensure that new trustees can become effective members of the board as soon as possible. Trustees should be provided with an individually tailored induction programme that is suited to the new trustee and the size and type of charity. For new trustees of smaller charities, a discussion with existing trustees may be the quickest way to learn everything they need to know to be able to make a contribution. For larger and more complex charities, a more structured induction programme is likely to be more appropriate. This may include:

- an induction pack of written material;
- assessment of any training required by the new trustee;
- attendance at staff induction training;
- meetings with other trustees, and in particular the chair and treasurer;
- meetings with senior management and staff;
- introductions to professional advisers;
- visits to see services provided by the charity; and
- meetings with beneficiaries of the charity.

17.2 As a minimum, new trustees should be given:

- a copy of the charity's constitution;
- a copy of the mission statement;
- a brief history of the charity;
- a copy of the charity's strategic plan and business plan;
- a copy of the latest report and accounts, current budget and most recent management accounts;
- a role description for trustees;

- a copy of the board's role and the terms of reference of any committees;
- copies of any policies relating to trustees, such as policies on conduct, conflicts of interest and expenses;
- details of trustee meetings;
- an organisation chart;
- contact details for the other trustees and key employees; and
- minutes and papers of recent board meetings.

17.3 An expanded recommended induction pack is available in an ICSA guidance note available free from www.icsa.org.uk.

18 Trustee appraisals and board performance review

18.1 It is considered good practice to carry out a review of the contribution of individual trustees, and the board's performance as a whole, on a regular basis. It is not enough to have skilled and experienced trustees: a charity needs to make sure that they are able to contribute and that the board as a whole is effective. Appraisals of individual trustees normally cover such things as attendance and contribution at meetings, relationships with senior staff, opportunities to promote the work of the charity and training needs.

18.2 Board performance reviews vary widely, but they will normally address such questions as whether the charity performs as well as similar charities, whether board decisions are regularly reviewed and impacts measured, whether trustees contribute effectively and whether there is effective leadership from the chair.

18.3 Board appraisal may be carried out for a number purposes and it can also be done in a number of different ways. A board appraisal may be part of the regular work of the charity, undertaken every year as a regular review of the contribution of individual board members and their function as a unit. It can be used as a means of further developing individuals and improving board performance. An increasing number of charities conduct regular board appraisal reviews in this way. At the other extreme the appraisal may be a specific task, undertaken as a part of an entire review of the governance structure.

18.4 Whatever the purpose, or the form that it takes, board appraisal inevitably involves a high level of critical inspection of individual board members, their fellow trustees and the board as a whole. Understandably this can be a difficult process and this is one of the reasons why the whole concept of board appraisal can be challenging for many trustees. Also, if not undertaken properly, the exercise can feel like a box-ticking mechanism to meet governance standards. This can lead to it being discredited, and board appraisals need to work effectively for boards to participate fully and devote the time and resources required.

18.5 Given the potential delicacy of the appraisal, it is essential that it is properly planned and executed. It can sometimes take years of persuasion before the board as a whole feels ready to undertake a full board appraisal exercise. It may be necessary to build gradually to a full appraisal – perhaps starting with an informal appraisal of how the board works as a whole and moving towards individual appraisals at a later stage. Later in this section, we will discuss the forms that an appraisal may take. For charities just starting out, it could begin with group discussions, move on to the use of questionnaires and then finally the board could begin to hold individual interviews. It is also possible that a board could decide not to conduct a full review each year, perhaps just having a group discussion or a questionnaire every year and then holding individual interviews every two years.

19 Purpose and timing

19.1 Whether the appraisal is part of a regular review or is for a specific reason, the purpose needs to be made clear. The board will also need to consider the best timing for a review. It is not advisable to undertake an appraisal during periods of crisis or conflict within the charity. The trustees are unlikely to agree a common purpose for the appraisal and the process risks deepening, rather than resolving, any conflict. It is also the case that the appraisal would distract the trustees from the primary purpose of addressing the crisis or conflict. Otherwise, if part of a regular review it should be timed to fit in well with the ongoing agenda of the board and other business to be dealt with throughout the year.

20 Method

20.1 There are a number of methods of board appraisal. The most appropriate in each case will depend on the purpose of the appraisal and, perhaps most importantly, the culture of the board. For example, a board questionnaire would be best suited to a regular review of board function, whereas a detailed examination of the performance of a board laden with strong personalities and complex histories may be better conducted by individual interviews with an independent, external facilitator. A thorough board appraisal exercise may involve a combination of different methods.

21 Do-it-yourself or independent consultant?

21.1 Once the purpose of the appraisal has been agreed the key question will be whether to conduct the appraisal internally or to draw on the resources of an external facilitator or consultant.

21.2 Internally managed board appraisals are often led by a sub-group of the trustee board. Although staff may contribute to the appraisal, they should not lead it. The advantages of this approach are that the team will know the issues, the history, the personalities and the desired outcome. It can also save costs and maintain ownership and continuity. However, such approaches may also lack objectivity and a fresh approach. Use of an independent contractor can help to ensure that board members are completely honest. They should also have expertise in conducting such reviews and may bring a fresh perspective. They can help to ensure that the necessary time and energy is devoted to the exercise. Whilst an independent consultant may be a more expensive option, it should again be noted that one would not need to be used each year, and such an approach could be combined with lower-key methods in alternate years.

21.3 As well as the issue of cost a key question to ask in this regard may be: would the board tolerate an outsider's intervention and accept the conclusions expressed or would they disregard any unpopular or difficult opinions? Much will also depend on the quality of the independent consultant.

21.4 For boards that seek objectivity in the appraisal exercise but cannot afford the expense of an external facilitator, a compromise solution may be available in the form of a trustee from another organisation undertaking the appraisal. In this way charities can enter into reciprocal appraisal arrangements with like-minded organisations.

22 Methods of board appraisal

22.1 Questionnaires

22.1.1 Questionnaires may be the first point of any appraisal process. These can provide information on areas of concern for trustees that will later form the focus for discussion. Trustees should be given adequate time to complete the questionnaires, and arrangements should be made for trustees to complete them, anonymously if necessary.

22.2 Group discussions

22.2.1 These stimulate debate as different ideas can be raised and discussed. Group discussions may involve the whole board or small groups. Although some flexibility may be desirable, discussion should be based on an agenda. Such discussions should be conducted separately from regular trustee meetings. Many charities have 'away days' or retreats in order to discuss these issues away from daily distractions.

22.3 Individual interviews

22.3.1 These can be a constructive way of identifying the feelings of individual trustees towards the board as a whole and in respect of their own role on the board.

22.4 Conclusion and implementation

22.4.1 Whatever the method of appraisal, the process should end with the preparation of a conclusion. This should include a summary of the findings, interpretation of what these findings mean and proposals for moving forward. Whether the appraisal is conducted internally or externally, the conclusion should be in written form and distributed to the whole board. In many cases, those responsible for the appraisal will also give a presentation of their conclusions. The document and presentation then serve as a starting point for the board to discuss the next course of action. Again, it may be best to have this debate at a retreat or away day, as this allows time for options to be discussed fully, free from the distractions of other board business.

22.4.2 The board may decide to implement any proposals in their entirety or to take a more selective approach. Whatever the outcome, an implementation and review plan should be developed in order to ensure that the proposals are carried through and the work is not lost. As with all plans, this should look at actions, identify those responsible for each action and set timescales. Where significant changes are being made, due consideration should be given to the impact on all those involved and reviews built into the plan to monitor the progress of implementation and the efficacy of any new systems.

22.4.3 The skills audit, individual trustee appraisals and board performance review are all likely to help shape the type of new trustee that the charity will look for.

23 Benefits and payments

23.1 The starting point when considering trustee benefits and payments is that trustees have a duty to act in the interests of the charity and not to receive any benefit unless they are authorised to do so. A benefit may include property, goods or services as well as money.

23.2 Reimbursement of legitimate expenses is not considered to be a benefit. Trustees are entitled to have their expenses met from the funds of the charity, even if there is no express power in the charity's constitution to pay expenses. These can include, for example, travel and other costs of attending meetings, telephone and internet charges and providing childcare whilst attending trustee meetings.

23.3 Note that benefits received by trustees because they are also beneficiaries of the charity are excluded from the definition of a trustee benefit. For example, a charity that provides housing may house a trustee who meets the same criteria as its other charitable beneficiaries.

23.4 Trustees may be authorised to receive payment by:

- an express power contained in the charity's constitution;
- an express power provided by the Charity Commission; or
- the statutory power introduced by the Charities Act 2006 to pay trustees for services.

23.5 The Charities Act 2006 s. 36 altered s. 73 of the 1993 Act and introduced the power for charities to pay some of their trustees for the supply of services under certain conditions. It is important to note that this power cannot be used if prohibited by the charity's governing document (and most charities include such a prohibition clause). The details are covered by the Charity Commission guidance CC11, *Trustee Expenses and Payments*. Some charity constitutions will already contain a power to pay trustees for services, but require the prior written consent of the Charity Commission. Provided that charities meet the conditions of the revised 1993 Act, the prior consent of the Charity Commission is no longer required. Briefly, all the following conditions, as set out in CC11, must be met before payment for services may be made:

(a) there is a written agreement between the charity and the trustee or connected person who is to be paid;
(b) the agreement sets out the exact or maximum amount to be paid;
(c) the trustee concerned may not take part in decisions made by the trustee board about the making of the agreement, or about the acceptability of the service provided;
(d) the payment is reasonable in relation to the service to be provided;
(e) the trustees are satisfied that the payment is in the best interests of the charity);
(f) the trustee board follows the 'duty of care' set out in the 2000 Act;
(g) the total number of trustees who are either receiving payment or who are connected to someone receiving payment are in a minority;
(h) there is no prohibition against payment of a trustee;
(i) trustees must 'have regard to' the Charity Commission's guidance on the subject, and trustees must be able to show that:
　i. they are aware of this guidance;
　ii. in making a decision where the guidance is relevant, they have taken it into account; and
　iii. if they have decided to depart from the guidance, they have a good reason for doing so.

23.6 It is important to note that the provisions for payments to trustees under the 1993 Act extend to 'connected persons'. These include close relatives such as spouses, parents and children, institutions controlled by the trustee or a close relative, and corporate bodies in which the trustee or a close relative has more than 20 per cent of the voting rights or share capital.

23.7 In contrast, there is no general power to pay a trustee for serving as a trustee. There needs to be a specific power contained in the charity's governing document, or authority must be sought from the Charity Commission or the courts. Similarly, in order for a charity to employ a trustee in some other role or compensate them for loss of earnings, the charity's constitution must contain the necessary authority or this must be sought from the Charity Commission or courts. A charity trustee may only be paid for serving as a trustee where this is clearly in the best interests of the charity and it provides a significant advantage over any other option.

23.8 In all cases, charities considering paying trustees should have clear policies and procedures for dealing with conflicts of interest and, ideally, these should be included in the charity's constitution.

23.9 Unless there is a clear power to make a payment for serving as a trustee, the charity must apply to the Charity Commission for authority before the payment is made. Otherwise, the trustees will be in breach of trust and either the board or trustee who is paid may be required to refund the payment to the charity.

23.10 Charitable companies and larger unincorporated charities are legally required to disclose payments to trustees in their accounts, and it is considered best practice for all charities of whatever size to make a similar disclosure.

23.11 Trustee payments checklist

The Charity Commission recommends that boards considering whether to make a payment to a trustee should consider six key factors:

1. Who will receive the payment – will it be a trustee, or a person or business connected with a trustee?
2. What is the payment expected to cover?
3. Is the payment clearly in the best interests of the charity?
4. Is there a legal authority for it?
5. What conditions must be met if the payment is to be made?
6. How will any conflict of interest be managed?

24 Conflicts of interest

24.1 Trustees have a duty to avoid conflicts between their duties to their charity and their own personal interests. A conflict of interest arises in any situation where a trustee's personal interests or loyalties conflict with those of the charity. This might involve a financial benefit to the trustee, such as when a trustee receives a payment directly or indirectly from the charity, or where there is no financial benefit but there is a conflict of loyalties – for example, where the trustee is also a trustee of another charity that might be competing for funding. The key issue is that a conflict of interest may compromise a trustee's ability to act in the best interests of their charity. Detailed guidance is available in the Charity Commission publication *A Guide to Conflicts of Interest for Charity Trustees*. A model conflict of interest policy and models for a Register of Interests and Declaration of Interests form are free to download under 'Guidance notes' at www.icsa.org.uk.

24.2 It is almost impossible to avoid conflicts of interest completely, so it is important to identify potential conflicts of interest as early as possible and make sure that they are addressed properly through a clear policy and procedures.

24.3 There are a number of issues that a good conflicts of interest policy should address:

- any benefits to trustees must be properly authorised (see above under 'Benefits and payments');
- actual and potential conflicts of interest should be properly disclosed to other trustees and recorded in a register; and
- trustees who have a conflict of interest do not participate in any decisions of the board of trustees relating to it.

24.4 Prospective trustees should be asked to declare potential conflicts of interest, and current trustees should be asked to update a register of interests with any significant changes and confirm actual or potential conflicts at least annually.

24.5 For charitable companies, section 175(1) of the Companies Act 2006 requires a director of a charitable company not only to disclose conflicts of interest but to 'avoid a situation in which he has, or can have, a direct or indirect interest that conflicts, or possibly may conflict, with the interests of the company'.

24.6 The Charity Commission has issued guidance on this issue as 'The Companies Act 2006' and 'Conflicts of Interest and the Companies Act 2006: Questions and Answers' (available at the Commission's website, www.charity-commission.gov.uk, under 'Publications and Guidance'). It considers that directors of charitable companies were already under a duty to avoid conflicts of interest prior to the implementation of this section and that charities do not therefore need to change their constitutions.

24.6.1 'The Companies Act duty does not apply to a conflict of interest arising in relation to a transaction or arrangement with the company if it is permitted by the company's articles of association' (section 175(3) of the Companies Act 2006 as modified for charitable companies by section 181).

Where a benefit or a transaction which may give rise to a conflict of interest is authorised by an order of the Charity Commission, the duty to avoid a conflict of interest does not apply (section 26(5)A of the Charities Act 1993).

In addition, authorisation may be given by the unconflicted directors to a conflict of interests where the company's constitution includes provision enabling them to provide such authorisation (section 175(5) as modified by section 181). Such authorisation is not necessary where the conflict arises from a transaction or arrangement with the company which is authorised by the memorandum or articles of the company' (Charity Commission, 'The Companies Act 2006).

24.6.2 'Where the existing memorandum authorises certain benefits arising from arrangements with the company, that is still sufficient to authorise the conflict of interests arising from those benefits' (Charity Commission, 'Conflicts of Interest and the Companies Act 2006: Questions and Answers).

24.7 A number of charities have raised the issue of their ability to authorise conflicts of interest arising from directors being trustees of other charities whose interests may conflict with those of the charitable company. The Charity Commission is of the opinion that such a conflict of loyalty can be avoided provided the Articles require a conflicted trustee to withdraw from discussions and take no part in the decision in which they have an interest.

25 Board composition

25.1 Key issues for board composition

- How many trustees should there be?
- What skills, knowledge and experience should they have?
- How long should they serve?
- How should the trustee body be renewed?

25.2 Most charity constitutions will set minimum and maximum numbers for trustees. A balance needs to be struck between having a board with the necessary set of skills and ensuring that it is small enough to make effective decisions. If a board is too large, individual trustees will have little opportunity to contribute at the meeting, or else meetings will become very long. There is also a greater likelihood that one or more trustees will be unable to attend any particular meeting. One solution is for the board to delegate some of their powers to committees.

25.3 The skills required by the trustees of a charity will vary from charity to charity, but need to be carefully considered. In particular, trustees should consider the level of skill required and whether there is an ongoing need for such a skill. All charities are likely to need someone with financial skills on an ongoing basis, but it is possible that in other areas it might be more appropriate for trustees to employ a consultant rather than recruit a trustee. A specimen skills register is available to download from www.icsa.org.uk under 'Guidance notes'.

25.4 There is no legal requirement that trustees should act only for a particular term or should retire at a particular age. Unless there is something to the contrary in the charity's constitution, a trustee will continue until disqualification, resignation, incapacity, removal or death intervenes. Many charities rely on the good sense of their trustees to retire at an appropriate time. However, there is a temptation for trustees to remain beyond a point when they are able to contribute significantly to the work of the charity. For this reason, many charities have introduced fixed terms of office (usually of three to five years) and a limit on the total number of terms of office (usually two or three terms).

25.5 Where there are fixed terms of office, constitutions will usually provide for a break period of one or more years after the final term of office before the trustee can seek reappointment. There may also be safeguards to ensure that key trustees, such as the chair and treasurer, do not have to retire at the same time, and that appointments or reappointments can be staggered, so that not all the trustees retire at once.

26 Resignation, retirement, disqualification and removal of trustees

26.1 A charity's constitution will normally provide for the resignation of a trustee. Care should be taken to ensure that any requirements are followed, for example, normally notice needs to be given to the charity in writing.

26.2 A trustee may retire only if there is either an express or implied power to retire. In most cases there will be an express provision in the charity's governing document. If there is not, but trustees are appointed for fixed terms of office, they will have an implied power to retire at the end of the term of office.

26.3 Under the Trustee Act 1925, s. 39, trustees of unincorporated charities have a power to retire provided that there are at least two trustees or a trust corporation will continue to hold office.

26.4 There are a number of legal grounds on which a trustee may be disqualified from being a trustee. These are covered by s. 72 of the Charities Act 1993 (see above under 'Checks for potential new trustees').

26.5 In addition, constitutions will often include other reasons for the disqualification of a trustee, including:

- for corporate charities, ceasing to be a director or a member;
- being incapable of managing his or her own affairs;
- being absent from a specified number of board meetings in a given period without leave of absence and the other trustees resolving that the trustee in question has vacated their office;
- being convicted of an offence which may not lead to statutory disqualification, but may damage the interests of the charity; or
- otherwise acting contrary to the best interests of the charity. This will usually require the unanimous agreement of all the other trustees.

26.6 A trustee of a charitable company may be removed by an ordinary resolution of its members. The requirements for this are set out in sections 168 and 169 of the Companies Act 2006.

26.7 In certain cases third parties will have the right to remove members. For example, a local-authority-appointed trustee will also be able to be removed by the local authority.

26.8 Both the High Court and the Charity Commission have powers to remove charity trustees in certain circumstances.

27 The role of members: membership charities

27.1 Not every charity has members. Charitable companies have members as do charitable unincorporated associations, but most charitable trusts do not.

27.2 There are a number of common models for charities with members, and the role of members will depend on the model used.

- In the 'flat' model, the only members are the trustees. This reflects the fact that the trustees are ultimately responsible for the running of the charity, but excludes other stakeholders from a constitutional role in how the charity is run.

- In the 'hybrid' model, members have a right to attend general meetings, receive information and elect trustees, but otherwise have little say in how the charity is run.
- In the 'membership' model, members are able to exercise a degree of control over the charity trustees. Although this may be more democratic, it is also more likely to lead to disagreements between groups of members who take different views.

27.3 The Charity Commission's Regulatory Report RS7 into membership charities says that 'the scope for problems is greater in membership charities ... because the number of people involved can make the governance arrangements more difficult to manage'.

27.4 A charity's constitution will normally state how members are appointed and prescribe their rights to call and receive notice of meetings, and to attend, speak and vote at meetings, and to bring resolutions. However, the legal duties of members to the charity remain, on the whole, unclear. Unlike trustees, there does not appear to be a clear legal duty to act in the best interests of the charity.

28 Trustees as members

28.1 Normally, trustees are required to be members. The theory behind this is that the charity is 'owned' by the members and the members elect trustees from amongst their number to run the charity on their behalf and be accountable to the rest of the members.

28.2 In some cases, however, the trustees will be the only members. This is often the case in charities that are established as charitable companies, but that do not have the intention of having a wider membership. Where this is the case care will need to be taken to distinguish between the two roles and accountability will need to be considered in a wider way.

29 Members' rights

29.1 Members' rights are governed by the charity's constitution and, for charitable companies, by the provisions of the Companies Acts. Members frequently have rights to alter the charity's constitution, elect or remove trustees, call meetings and, ultimately, wind the charity up. Members may have other, non-voting rights, such as the right to receive newsletters or the right to speak at meetings. For charitable companies, the rights of members will normally be the same as those of shareholders or guarantors of companies limited by guarantee. So the members of a charitable company will have a statutory right to remove directors;

receive the annual report and accounts; attend general meetings (and require them to be held); vote and appoint proxies; appoint the auditors and amend the Memorandum and Articles.

30 Admission and removal of members

30.1 A charity's constitution normally gives power to the charity's trustees to create different classes of membership with different rights and obligations. Trustees also normally approve individuals as members of the charity. The constitution may allow trustees to reject applications for membership at their discretion, or may require them to accept applications unless they consider that to do so is not in the best interests of the charity. People who are rejected as members may also have a right of appeal, but the trustees will usually make the final decision.

30.2 Prospective members should sign a form to show that they consent to becoming a member and, in the case of a company limited by guarantee, that they agree to the guarantee. A register of members must be kept by charitable companies and should be kept by other membership charities, showing the name, address and date of registration of each member.

30.3 Membership usually ends if the member dies, resigns, fails to pay a membership subscription within a specified period of it falling due or is removed by a resolution of the trustees. The date on which membership ceases should be entered in the membership register, as the member will still be liable under the guarantee for a year after he or she ceases to be a member.

31 Power of Charity Commission to determine members

31.1 Under Charities Act 1993, s. 29A (as inserted by the Charities Act 2006), the Charity Commission has the power to determine who a charity's members are. This is particularly important, because uncertainly surrounding a charity's members may also create uncertainty over whether trustees were validly elected. For example, a trustee may be elected at a packed AGM by a large majority voting on a show of hands; but if there is no way of telling whether the people raising their hands are actually members of the charity, the validity of the election will be open to question.

32 Honorary officers

32.1 Most charities will have a number of trustees who hold particular positions within the board. The most common are chairman, deputy or vice chairman, honorary treasurer, and honorary secretary. These are termed honorary officers ('honorary' because they are unpaid, and 'officers' because they are office holders.) The Code of Good Governance says that the board should define the roles and responsibilities of the chair and other honorary officers, in writing. This is important because it ensures clarity for the officers, for the other trustees and for senior staff, too, and reduces the risk of conflict.

33 Role of the chairman

33.1 The role of the chairman is mainly one of leadership. The chairman leads the board and makes sure that it works effectively in setting and achieving the charity's strategy; acts as an ambassador for the board in building relationships with stakeholders, for example by speaking on its behalf at the AGM; and provides a link between the board of trustees and staff through working closely with the chief executive.

33.2 The following is taken from the *ICSA Model Role Description for Chair of the Board of Charity Trustees (England & Wales)*, available from www.icsa.org.uk.

33.3 Chair role description

Main responsibilities

- Leading the trustees and members of the senior management team in the development of strategic plans for the charity.
- Providing leadership and support to the chief executive officer and ensuring that the charity is run in accordance with the decisions of the trustees, the charity's governing document, and appropriate legislation.
- Liaising with the charity secretary and chief executive officer with the drafting of agendas and supporting papers for trustee meetings and ensuring that the business is covered efficiently and effectively in those meetings.
- Undertaking a leadership role in ensuring that the board of trustees fulfils its responsibilities for the governance of the charity.
- Leading on, with the assistance of the charity secretary and chief executive where appropriate, the development and implementation of procedures for board induction, development, training, and appraisal.
- Implementing an effective communication strategy that includes the needs of staff, beneficiaries and other stakeholders.

Main duties

- Liaising with the charity secretary to lead on the planning, setting and chairing of trustee meetings and AGMs.
- Ensuring trustee decisions are acted upon.

- Supporting and appraising the performance of the chief executive officer and other appropriate members of the senior management team.
- Leading disciplinary and appointment committees, where appropriate and in line with the charity's agreed procedures.
- Representing the charity at functions, meetings and in the press and broadcasting media, in line with the charity's agreed media strategy.
- Acting between full meetings of the board in authorising action to be taken *intra vires*, e.g. banking transactions and legal documents in accordance with relevant mandates.
- Maintaining the trustees' commitment to board renewal and succession management, in line with the charity's governing document and/or current best practice.
- Ensuring that the performance of the board as a whole and the trustees individually is reviewed on an annual basis.

34 Role of the honorary treasurer

34.1 In many charities, the honorary treasurer plays a vital role in leading on all the financial aspects of the charity's work. However, there is an argument that, for larger charities, the role may come into conflict with that of the finance director and that oversight of the charity's finances is better served by a finance committee with at least one member who is an accountant or has other relevant financial experience. In this case the chair of the finance committee may take on some of the responsibilities that would otherwise fall to the honorary treasurer. Although there is no legal requirement, the charity's constitution may require the honorary treasurer to meet certain criteria in terms of qualifications, and he or she is often an accountant. It is important to remember that even where there is an honorary treasurer, all the trustees are still collectively responsible for the charity's finances and for approving its financial statements.

34.2 Where there is an honorary treasurer, he or she will normally provide advice to other trustees; act as the main point of contact on the board for the finance director and head of internal audit. The honorary treasurer may also serve on the audit committee, although in some charities this is seen as a conflict of interest.

34.3 The following is taken from the *ICSA Model Role Description for a Charity Treasurer (England & Wales)*, available from www.icsa.org.uk.

34.4 Treasurer Role Description

Main responsibilities

- To oversee and present budgets, accounts, management accounts and financial statements to the board of trustees after discussion with the finance director, where applicable.
- To ensure that proper accounts and records are kept, ensuring financial resources are spent and invested in line with the charity's policies, good governance, legal and regulatory requirements.
- To be instrumental in the development and implementation of financial, reserves and investment policies.

Main duties

- Liaising, where applicable, with the finance director or other appropriate member of staff responsible for the financial activities of the organisation.
- Chairing any finance committee in line with standing orders and terms of reference, and reporting back to the board of trustees.
- Liaising with the charity's auditors or independent examiner, where appropriate.
- Monitoring and advising on the financial viability of the charity after liaising with the charity's auditors.
- Creating, in liaison with the finance director (where there is one), sound financial instruments for the control of charity assets.
- Implementing and monitoring specific financial controls and systems are in place accordingly and adhered to.
- Advising on the financial implications of the charity's strategic plan.
- Liaising with the charity secretary and finance director, where applicable, to ensure that the charity's annual accounts are compliant with the current Charities' SORP.
- Where the charity has an internal audit function, the treasurer will be required to work closely with the internal audit team and any sub-committee of the board of trustees.
- Acting as a counter-signatory on charity cheques (including any electronic transactions) and any applications for funds.
- Maintaining sound financial management of the charity's resources, ensuring expenditure is in line with the charity's objects.
- Contributing to the fundraising strategy of the organisation.

35 Role of the honorary secretary

35.1 Under the Companies Act 2006, private companies, including companies limited by guarantee, do not have to have a company secretary, although many will choose to do so. Although, in smaller charities, the office is often held by a trustee, a charity's constitution may allow it to be held by a non-trustee. The main role of the secretary is to ensure that board and committee meetings run smoothly; that the charity complies with its legal and regulatory obligations; and to advise the board. In larger charities, the company secretary may be an employee (often, the chief executive, finance director or a dedicated company secretary), or the role is outsourced. The person is normally appointed as secretary by the board.

35.2 The following is taken from the *ICSA Model Role Description for the Charity Secretary of the Board*, available from www.icsa.org.uk.

35.3 Charity Secretary Role Description

Main responsibilities

- To liaise with the chair and chief executive officer to plan, arrange and produce agendas and supporting papers for trustee meetings and for drafting the subsequent minutes.
- To act as charity secretary and ensure that company law, charity law and regulatory requirements of reporting and public accountability are complied with.
- To ensure that all meetings comply with the requirements of the governing document.

Main duties

- Arranging and administrating trustee meetings and any sub-committees in line with legal, and other regulatory requirements, and in accordance with the governing document. If the position of charity secretary is an honorary one, this may be in partnership with a paid member of staff.
- Advise and guide the board of any legal and regulatory implications of the charity's strategic plan.
- Acting as the custodian of the governing document, in liaison with the trustees, reviewing its appropriateness and monitoring that the charity's activities reflect the objects set out in the governing document. To act also as the holder of statutory registers and books and other legal and important documents such as insurance policies.
- Supporting the trustees in fulfilling their duties and responsibilities, organising trustee induction and ongoing training.

- Ensuring that trustee decisions are implemented in accordance with the charity's governing document or other internal operational procedures.
- Being an initial point of contact for stakeholders and interested parties.
- Acting as a counter-signatory on charity cheques (including any electronic transactions) and any applications for funds.
- Ensuring the charity's stationery, including electronic communications (emails, websites, etc.), orders, invoices, cheques and other relevant documents include all the details required under company law and, if applicable, charity law and/or VAT law.
- Managing various other functions of the charity, including estates, personnel, finance, pensions, money-laundering and data protection, as delegated.

36 Constitutional position of honorary officers

36.1 The mechanism for appointing or electing the chairman will normally be specified in the charity's constitution, as will his or her terms of office and any specific powers. Other honorary officers may be covered by the charity's main constitution or standing orders. Normally, honorary officers are elected by their fellow trustees, but sometimes the constitution may specify that the chairman is elected by members or chosen in some other way. As honorary officers are often drawn from the more experienced trustees, care needs to be taken over succession planning, to avoid all the honorary officers ending their terms of office as trustees (and also as honorary officers) at the same time. It is important to remember that honorary officers are first and foremost trustees, and, with the exception of the chairman, do not usually have any additional powers under a charity's constitution.

37 Powers of the chairman

37.1 Some of the powers of the chairman will be set out in the charity's constitution. Usually these are limited to the chairman's role in chairing meetings of members and board meetings. Under the Companies Acts, the chairman's actions carry some legal weight. For example, under Companies Act 2006, s. 320, the declaration by the chairman of the result of a vote on a show of hands is conclusive evidence as to the result.

37.2 Powers that are often delegated to the chairman include:; calling board meetings, authorising payments up to a certain level, ruling on conflicts of interest and appraising the chief executive.

37.3 Incorporated charities should be aware that the Companies Act 2006, ss. 282 and 284, had the incidental effect of removing the chairman's casting vote at general meetings. However, a provision was included in the fifth CA 2006 Commencement Order stating that companies whose articles provided for a chairman's casting vote immediately before 1 October 2007 may continue to rely on the relevant article. If a company subsequently amended its articles to remove the casting vote it may reinstate the provision and continue to rely on it. Other companies, including any incorporated after 1 October 2007, cannot provide for a chairman's casting vote at general meetings in their articles. (A power of a casting vote at board meetings is unaffected.)

38 Other roles, such as patron and president

38.1 Other roles include:

- **Patron:** usually a role that has no rights or obligations attached to it. The role is often held by one or more people whose association with the charity is intended to enhance its profile with the public.
- **President:** an honorific title, usually given to the most important patron. The role may be given to a long-serving chairman on their retirement.
- **Founder:** many charities are started by an individual or a small group of people, and these are sometimes described as founder trustees.
- **Observer:** a person who attends meetings of the trustees but does not have a right to vote. An observer may be a representative of a stakeholder group, such as staff or service users. Prospective trustees are also sometimes invited to attend one or two meetings as observers, before deciding if they wish to become a trustee.
- **Portfolio trustees:** in some charities, individual trustees will be given responsibility for overseeing particular areas of the organisation's activities, such as human resources or campaigning, liaising with senior staff in between board meetings. The key advantages of this system are that it allows trustees with particular expertise to influence proposals at an early stage and gives fellow trustees confidence that one of their number is keeping a close eye on matters where they may not have particular expertise.

39 Collective responsibility and general principles of delegation

39.1 All decisions concerning a charity have to be taken by the trustees acting together, except where a power has been delegated. When the board makes a decision, even if it is not unanimous, the decision is deemed to be the responsibility of all the trustees and so all trustees are expected to support the decision, once made.

39.2 In practice, boards cannot usually take every decision that a charity needs to make. Fortunately, subject to legal constraints and the charity's own constitution, the board can delegate certain powers to others to act on their behalf. However, as a general rule, a board may delegate power but not responsibility and so the trustees will remain liable.

39.3 In order to safeguard the trustees' position, the terms of any delegation should specify:

- who is being given authority: whether it is an individual trustee, a committee (and if so, who is on the committee), or the chief executive or other staff;
- what the authority is: for example, whether it is a power to make decisions, authority to advise the trustees or authority to implement the decisions of trustees;
- whether money may be spent, and whether this must be covered by an approved budget; and
- how the trustees will monitor the exercise of delegated powers.

40 Legal and constitutional position

40.1 The Memorandum and Articles of incorporated charities will generally include an express power for the trustees to delegate powers to committees consisting of two or more people, at least one of whom must be a trustee.

40.2 If the trustees do not have a power of delegation or it is not exercised properly, the acts and decisions of those who are supposedly the agents of the trustees will be void. This may result in the trustees being liable for a breach of trust and the purported agents may potentially face personal liability.

40.3 Section 11(3) of the Trustee Act 2000 says that trustees of unincorporated charities can delegate:

- implementing a decision of the trustees;
- the investment of charity assets;
- raising funds for the trust, except by carrying out a 'primary purpose' trade; or
- any other function prescribed by an order made by the Secretary of State.

40.4 The trustees will be liable only for the acts or omissions of the delegate(s) if they have failed in their duty of care in choosing the delegate.

40.5 Under the Trustee Act 1925 an individual trustee of an unincorporated charity may delegate their powers to someone else for a period of up to 12 months through a power of attorney.

41 Sub-delegation

41.1 Unless a committee is authorised to do so by the board, it may not sub-delegate its power. However, a committee may be given authority to sub-delegate some of its work to one or more sub-committees or individuals. Where there is a power of sub-delegation, the board will always be able to over-ride or remove the sub-delegation.

42 Matters reserved to the board

42.1 As trustees are ultimately responsible for the charity, all major decisions must be taken by the board. Following the principles of good governance, boards should draw up a list of matters that require decisions to be made by the whole board, although they may be delegated for discussion and recommendation to committees. Some items on the list will legally require a board decision, such as the approval of financial statements, while others are a matter of good governance. A sample list of matters reserved for the board of trustees is available at www.icsa.org.uk.

43 Schemes of delegation and standing orders

43.1 In order to ensure that both trustees and staff understand what they may or may not approve, boards normally approve a schedule of delegations showing the delegated matters and the lowest level of committee or member of staff that can authorise action. While many matters may be financial, such as who can approve expenditure and within what limits, others may be operational, such as who can approve press releases.

43.2 Standing orders refer to the written rules that a board makes for the running of board and committee meetings under the charity's constitution. Constitutions normally focus on the running of meetings of members, and leave many decisions on how to run board meetings to the discretion of the board. Standing orders will usually cover such detailed matters as how trustees may raise items for discussion at meetings and when papers and minutes are circulated.

44 Delegation to staff: role of the CEO

44.1 Although trustees reserve the right to manage any aspect of a charity's activities, as they are ultimately responsible for its success, boards normally delegate the day-to-day management to staff, focusing on strategic matters. This is achieved by the board appointing the chief executive officer (CEO) and delegating authority to him or her, within certain boundaries (including any schemes of delegation), to appoint and manage other staff. The board will then hold the CEO accountable for achieving the goals it has set and carrying out its decisions. Normally, the chairman and one other trustee will agree the CEO's objectives and carry out appraisals.

45 Relationship between governance and management

45.1 The National Housing Federation's Code of Governance summarises the purpose of the board as being 'to determine strategy, direct, control, scrutinise, and evaluate an organisation's affairs: management of the organisation should be delegated to the organisation's staff'.

45.2 Professor Bob Tricker wrote in his book *Corporate Governance*, 'if management is about running business, governance is about seeing that it is run properly. All businesses need governing as well as managing.'

45.3 In practice, what governance entails varies between charities. For small charities, good governance may simply be about making sure that everyone knows what they are doing and that they are pulling together. For a large national charity, it may be more about public accountability. The distinction between governance and management is also not clear-cut. In many small charities, the trustees may also have a management role, and in larger charities, management and staff are likely to have a say in strategic planning, although it remains the responsibility of trustees.

45.4 In reality, the boards of most charities work in partnership with their senior managers in developing strategy and policies and making major decisions. While the board might be clear what it wants, senior managers might be better placed to know how to achieve the aims or what additional resources might be needed to bring them to fruition. In particular, goals and performance standards need to be agreed by both board and management to ensure that they are both demanding and realistic.

46 Relationship with the CEO and staff

46.1 A successful charity will have both a strong CEO and senior management team and an effective board. To ensure that the relationship works well, with openness and mutual respect, it is important that there are clear ground rules about how they interact, and also formal and informal reviews to check that board and staff are working well together. This is an area in which the chair and CEO should jointly take the lead by making sure that there is agreement on, amongst other things:

- the respective responsibilities of the chair and CEO;
- what involvement trustees should have outside board meetings;
- what authority individual trustees have;

- how complaints about the conduct of trustees or staff should be dealt with;
- how staff should communicate with trustees to keep them informed or consult with them; and
- what support trustees should expect from staff.

46.2 In addition, there must be a clear, written agreement on how the CEO's objectives are set and how he or she is appraised.

46.3 Formal reviews of the relationship between trustees and the CEO and staff should be part of board and individual trustee appraisals and also be covered in directors' appraisals. A good chair and CEO should also make sure they are aware of any problems early on so that they can be dealt with as quickly as possible.

46.4 The relationship can be a difficult one to get right, as the board needs both to support and to challenge staff. Where there is no challenge, the board is, in effect, abdicating its responsibility, either leaving important decisions to the executives or supporting them whatever they do. On the other hand, where there is challenge, but no support, the board risks coming into conflict with its senior staff.

47 Delegation to committees

47.1 Where a board delegates some of its work to committees it must ensure that it has proper control over those committees. This means that it must set clear terms of reference, including what the committee is for, how often it should meet, how its membership is determined, what authority it has and how it should report to the board.

47.2 Committees may be 'standing committees', which are a permanent part of the charity's governance or 'ad hoc' committees, set up for a specific purpose – for example, in order to oversee a major construction project.

48 Typical committees

48.1 While the boards of smaller charities may do all the work themselves, medium and large charities are likely to have a range of standing committees. These may include the following.

49 Audit committees

49.1 The main purpose of an audit committee is to provide assurance to the board that there is an effective system of internal controls. In particular, the audit committee will approve the programme of internal audits and receive all internal audit reports and liaise with the external auditors. The benefits of an effective audit committee include:

- increased confidence in the objectivity of financial reporting;
- greater emphasis on internal control and the implementation of actions following internal audits; and
- more effective challenge and review of executive management performance.

49.2 One important area that may fall within the terms of reference of the audit committee is ensuring that there is a strong framework for risk management in place. For this reasons, some charities have an audit and risk committee.

49.3 In some charities, the audit committee will also review in detail the quarterly management accounts prior to them being submitted to the board.

50 Other committees

50.1 Other committees, depending on the relative importance to the charity, may include:

(a) Finance and general purposes
   i. These are responsible for overseeing financial, property, technological and human resources.
   ii. Larger charities may have individual committees to lead on areas that might be covered by a finance and general purposes committee elsewhere. For example:
      1) investment;
      2) property; and
      3) human resources.
(b) Remuneration
   i. These are responsible for making recommendations to the board on the pay strategy and levels of pay for staff, and in particular, the remuneration of senior staff.
(c) Nominations
   i. These are responsible for recruiting new trustees.
(d) Policy and performance
   i. These are responsible for approving/making recommendations on policies and monitoring detailed performance.
(e) Governance
   i. These are responsible for making recommendations on the governance of the charity.

51 Terms of reference

51.1 All committees, whether they are standing committees or only set up for a specific purpose, must have clear, written terms of reference. These should include:

- committee name;
- purpose;
- delegated authority;
- membership and voting rights;
- committee chair;
- frequency of meetings;
- person acting as secretary or minute-taker;
- reporting procedure; and
- quorum.

51.2 Where a committee is established to help achieve a particular task, such as an office move, it may useful to include details about what the committee is expected to produce and when – for example, 'Options appraisal to be presented to the board at its meeting in May 2010'.

52 Reporting lines for committees and appointing to committees

52.1 All committees of the board should report to the board. Minutes should be circulated to all trustees. This may be done either as soon as they are available or as part of the pack of board papers. The chair of the committee should also be prepared to report to the board on any significant items or events, whether there has been a meeting of the committee since the last board meeting or not. Because of the chair's role in reporting to the board, it is usual for the committee chair to be a trustee.

52.2 In some instances, a committee may report to more than one board. For example, many charities have a trading company set up as a subsidiary. In these instances, the audit committee may report to the board of the trading company as well as the board of the parent charity.

52.3 Under the constitutions of most charities, the board normally has to approve the membership of all committees and also appoints the committee chair. In practice, committees sometimes find their own members, and elect their own chair, and they are then ratified as such by the board.

53 Sources of useful information and governance resources

53.1 There are a number of excellent books on the governance of charities and there are also plenty of resources freely available on the internet. Although the older books mentioned may be slightly out of date from a legal perspective, they are still helpful in terms of describing the role of trustees and the board and how the board may work more effectively. Where pubications are available free to download, they are listed under 'Internet resources'.

53.2 Books

- *Charity Governance*, by Con Alexander and Jos Moule (Jordans 2007)
- *The Governance and Management of Charities*, by Andrew Hind (NCVO 1995)
- *The ICSA Charity Trustee's Guide*, by Chris Priestley (ICSA 2008)
- *The Good Trustee Guide*, by Peter Dyer (NCVO 2008)
- *Excellence in Governance: Code for Members* (National Housing Federation 2009)
- *Boards that Work: A Guide for Charity Trustees*, by David Fishel (Directory of Social Change 2003)
- *Running Board Meetings*, by Patrick Dunne (Kogan Page 1997)
- *Corporate Governance and Chairmanship*, by Sir Adrian Cadbury (Oxford University Press 2002)

53.3 Internet resources

53.3.1 The Charity Commission's website at www.charity-commission.gov.uk contains a mass of publications and guidance notes, most of which are available to download. Most are also available in Welsh and in alternative formats. The most relevant publications to this chapter are:

- CC3 – *The Essential Trustee*
- CC10 – *The Hallmarks of an Effective Charity*
- CC11 – *Trustee Expenses and Payments*
- CC24 – *Users on Board: Beneficiaries Who Become Trustees?*
- CC30 – *Finding New Trustees – What Charities Need to Know*
- CC43 – *Incorporation of Charity Trustees*
- CC48 – *Charities and Meetings*
- CC49 – *Charities and Insurance*

53.3.2 The Charity Commission's website also contains model constitutions and a helpful summary of the changes brought about by the Companies Act that are most likely to affect charities.

53.3.3 The National Council for Voluntary Organisations (NCVO) has a section of its website dedicated to governance and leadership: www.ncvo-vol.org.uk. This also contains all the resources from the Governance Hub. The NCVO also runs a free-of-charge service to advertise trustee vacancies. Publications of particular relevance are:

- Good Governance: A Code for the Voluntary and Community Sector
- Trustees and Management Committee Members National Occupational Standards
- Living Values: A Pocket Guide for Trustees
- Reducing the Risks: A Guide to Trustee Liabilities

53.3.4 The full text of the Charities Act and the Companies Act are available to download from www.opsi.gov.uk.

53.3.5 The Institute of Chartered Secretaries and Administrators (ICSA) website www.icsa.org.uk contains a number of valuable guidance notes in its Knowledge Bank, including guidance and sample terms of reference for committees.

C3

Charity meetings

1 Introduction

1.1 Whilst there is no general law that requires charities to operate through meetings, the fact is that most charities do operate in this way. In fact, for the vast majority of charities, meetings are vital for the governance and administration of the charity. A core principle of a charity's work is that trustees act collectively and exercise their powers as a group. Whilst it is possible for the joint decisions of trustees to be taken in other ways than at a meeting, the most effective way of charity trustees to work together is by holding meetings. If care is taken to ensure that meetings are effective, this can make a significant difference to how the charity operates.

1.2 Whilst there is no general law that says that charities must have meetings, there will still be a number of legal and constitutional requirements regarding how such meetings are administered. A charity's constitution will often refer to meetings, how they are run and how many there should be. If the charity has members there will also be provisions regarding how the members meet together, and there will usually be a requirement for general meetings. If the charity is a company it will be subject to the detailed requirements of the Companies Act.

2 What is a meeting?

2.1 Meetings usually occur when a group of people gather together in the same place at the same time. However, there is now a range of other means of communicating collectively – principally by telephone and video conferencing. If a decision needs to be taken at a meeting, a charity will need to consider what constitutes a meeting, and if what it is proposing to do comes within that definition.

2.2 What constitutes a meeting may be stated in the constitution. Most modern model constitutions now contain wording that allow meetings to be held electronically. However, there is a common law definition of what a meeting is, and this will apply if there is no alternative provision in the constitution. This definition states that a valid meeting normally consists of people who can both see and hear each other (*Byng v London Life Association* [1989]). If the charity's constitution gives no definition to a meeting, this definition will apply.

2.3 A 'meeting' held by video conferencing or internet video facilities allows the participants to both see and hear each other. Such meetings will therefore be valid, unless the constitution prohibits them. However, as teleconferencing only allows the participants to hear each other it is the view of the Charity Commission that this does not constitute a 'meeting' within the meaning of the decision in the Byng case. For it to constitute a meeting, there would therefore need to be a specific provision in the charity's governing document stating that this was the case.

2.4 That being said it should be remembered that in the absence of a specific power to conduct business by teleconferencing, such a method may be used for preliminary discussions relating to business which could then be brought to a formal meeting for decision. It is also possible that the trustees could delegate specific decisions to be taken in this way. For example, if the trustees wanted to reach a conclusion on a matter which needed further information and did so by teleconference, they could use a formal meeting to delegate the decision to a named trustee (e.g. the chairman). All the trustees could then consider the matter by teleconference, and then take a decision which would be confirmed in writing by the specified trustee.

2.5 It should also be noted that a meeting could be held by a mixture of both physical presence and teleconferencing. If there is no provision regarding teleconferencing in the constitution, the only people who would be attending formally would be those in the meeting room. However, if they could form a quorum, the meeting would be valid. Those included by teleconferencing may of course contribute to any discussion, but they would not be able to vote on any proposal. However, as long as the trustees physically present form a quorum they will be able to validly discharge the business of the charity, so long as all of the trustees have had the opportunity to attend the 'meeting'.

2.6 None of these options is ideal, and if teleconferencing is to be used, it is preferable for the constitution to be amended to include it in the definition of meetings of the charity.

2.7 If a board is choosing to meet regularly by video or teleconferencing, it should note that there are also restrictions on how useful such meetings can be. They can work very well when there are short, individual matters to be determined. However, it can be very hard to effectively run through a whole agenda for a board meeting in such a way. If a meeting is being held by teleconference it is a good idea to focus on one or two key questions for debate. Participants should identify themselves each time they speak, and it is probably necessary for the meeting to be conducted in a more formal way than normal. The chairman should also clearly reiterate the decision taken at the end of each agenda item. If a charity is holding regular board meetings by teleconferencing or video conferencing it should also be noted that the Charity Commission recommends that at least one physical meeting of all the charity trustees takes place each year.

2.8 Charity Commission guidance also states that even where the constitution allows the charity's business to be carried out by teleconferencing there may still be circumstances where a physical or video meeting of the trustees will be necessary to validate a decision. Such circumstances could include those where legislation requires a meeting in the strict legal sense or where a third party imposes a specific condition that the act be carried out at a meeting where the participants can both see and hear each other.

3 General meetings

3.1 A meeting of the members of the charity is referred to as a general meeting. For this reason it can be seen that not all charities are required to hold general meetings, as not all charities have members. A charity established under a trust deed will therefore not usually be required to hold general meetings. That being said, the term 'general meeting' is sometimes used in a different sense, and it is therefore sometimes the case that charities without membership still hold meetings which they refer to as 'general meetings'. In some charities without a separate membership there is a mistaken assumption that the meeting each year of the trustees that approves the accounts is called the 'annual general meeting'. In addition, sometimes charities hold general meetings which are for their volunteers, or open to the public, which are called annual general meetings. Such meetings share the core purpose of accountability with a formal general meeting, but in this chapter when we discuss general meetings we will be considering the formal meetings of the members of the charity.

3.2 As general meetings are meetings of the members, they are concerned only with matters that are the members' business and not those matters that are the responsibility of the trustees. They are important in ensuring accountability but have limited application, being concerned with the reporting of the annual report and accounts, the amendment of the constitution and (often) the appointment of trustees. Although they have limited application and happen much less frequently than board meetings, they often have far more legal and constitutional requirements than board meetings.

3.3 Not all charities are required to have general meetings, but for those that are, detailed requirements for the general meetings are normally set out in the charity's constitution. Charitable companies also need to comply with the requirements of the Companies Act 2006, and in some instances these statutory requirements would override the charitable company's Articles.

3.4 Annual general meetings

3.4.1 The most common type of general meetings are annual general meetings (AGMs). However, under the Companies Act 2006, there is no longer a requirement for private companies (including charitable companies) to hold AGMs. With the ending of the requirement to hold AGMs, the Companies Act no longer uses the term and it now refers to AGMs and extraordinary general meetings (EGMs) as 'general meetings'. However, many charities still use the original terms, and they will still be applicable unless a charitable company has amended its Articles.

3.4.2 AGMs are often a requirement in the constitution of membership charities and most commonly charitable companies. Despite the Companies Act 2006, it is very likely that any charitable company registered prior to the Act's implementation will have a requirement for AGMs in its Articles. AGMs are an important means of accounting to the membership on the activities of the board, and their relevance should not be underestimated. Charities holding AGMs can maintain and develop support amongst their members and use the meetings to help ensure the transparency and accountability expected of them. It is therefore advisable for a charity with a membership to retain the requirement to hold an AGM each year. However, it is arguable that there is much less of a need where the trustees are the only members, or for the subsidiary trading companies of charities if the charity is the only member.

3.4.3 If a charitable company no longer wishes to hold AGMs, it will need to check if there is a requirement in its Articles for an AGM, and if so, amend them. The Articles will only need to be amended if it 'expressly' refers to a requirement to hold AGMs. The guidance from the Department for Business, Innovation and Skills confirms this and states, for example, that provisions commonly found in company Articles specifying that one or more directors are to retire at each AGM are not to be treated as a provision 'expressly' requiring the company to hold an AGM. However, even if there is no direct requirement in its Articles a company should also take care to ensure that any matters that would normally be dealt with at the AGM (e.g. the appointment of board members) have replacement provisions put in place to handle them.

3.4.4 It should be noted that, under the Companies Act 2006, members of private companies (including charitable companies) will no longer have a statutory right to demand that the company holds an AGM if it is not a requirement of the Articles. Only the statutory right to requisition a meeting will be available (see below). If a charitable company is considering removing the need to hold AGMs, but wants its members to easily require them to be convened, this would need to be provided for in the amended Articles.

3.4.5 The timing for AGMs will often be specified in the constitution. It used to be the case (under the Companies Act 1985) that companies were required to hold an AGM within 18 months of incorporation and to hold all further AGMs annually and in each calendar year. It was also the case that no more than 15 months could elapse between each AGM. These are therefore the usual requirements of the Articles of any charitable company created before 2006. Note that a requirement to hold an AGM in each calendar year can override the ability to have up to 15 months between AGMs. Therefore, if there is such a requirement and an AGM were held on 31 December, the following AGM must be held by the following December, to ensure that it is within the calendar year. Therefore in this case, the AGM must be held within 12 months rather than 15.

3.4.6 For charitable companies, the annual reports and accounts must be circulated to the members within nine months of the year end. The annual report and accounts are usually considered by the members at the AGM and circulated with its papers, so this will also influence the timing of the meeting.

3.5 Extraordinary general meetings

3.5.1 EGMs are usually called when the charity has special business (e.g. the amendment of the constitution) that cannot await the next AGM. The constitution will normally set out the procedural requirements for EGMs and generally the procedural requirements for both AGMs and EGMs are the same (but see below regarding notice periods).

3.6 Convening of general meetings

3.6.1 The constitution will usually specify who can convene a general meeting and this will usually be the trustees. In addition, for charitable companies, there are a number of statutory provisions regarding the convening of meetings. The Companies Act 2006 gives directors (i.e. the trustees) a general power to call a general meeting (s. 302). The directors may also be required to call the meeting by a requisition lodged under s. 303 of the Companies Act 2006 (see below). If the directors fail to call a meeting requisitioned in this way those who requisitioned the meeting (or a proportion of them) are authorised to convene the meeting (s.

305 Companies Act 2006). There is also an overall power of the court to call a general meeting under s. 306 of the Companies Act 2006.

3.6.2 A constitution may sometimes also empower one trustee or any member to convene an extraordinary general meeting when there are insufficient trustees in the United Kingdom to form a quorum. This power is useful if the number falls below the number required for a quorum of the board at any time.

3.7 Requisition of general meetings

3.7.1 The constitution of a charity that is not a company may give the members a right to requisition meetings in some way. However, there is no statutory right for them to do so. In contrast, the members of a charitable company do have a statutory right to requisition a meeting, regardless of what the Articles say. A member or members of a company holding between them not less than one tenth of the voting rights (or in the case of a share company not less than one tenth of the paid-up capital carrying voting rights) may at any time lodge a requisition requiring the directors to convene a general meeting for the purposes stated in the requisition (s. 303 Companies Act 2006). This percentage is reduced to 5 per cent if:

- more than 12 months has passed since the last general meeting; and
- that meeting had been called either in pursuance of a members' requisition or in relation to which any members of the company had rights with respect to the circulation of a resolution no less extensive than they would have had if the meeting had been so called at their request.

3.7.2 On receipt of the requisition (which may consist of several documents in similar form) the directors must, within 21 days, convene the meeting and the meeting must be held not more than 28 days after the date of the notice of the meeting. If the directors do not properly comply with this requirement, the requisitionists (or any of them representing more than one half of the voting rights of all of them) may convene the meeting at any time within three months from the date of deposit of the requisition. The requisitionists may recover their expenses from the company.

3.7.3 A general meeting of a company may also need to be convened on the requisition of an auditor who resigns. An outgoing auditor may submit a requisition calling on trustees/directors to convene a general meeting of the company to consider their explanation of the circumstances with the notice of resignation (s. 518 Companies Act 2006). They may also require the company to circulate to the members a written statement of the circumstances, but the company may apply to the court to relieve the company from this obligation if the outgoing auditor is using the procedure for securing needless publicity for defamatory matter.

3.8 Notice of general meetings

3.8.1 The notice of a general meeting will normally be sent out by the secretary, at the request of the trustees. A notice should include:

- the time, date and place of meeting;
- the business to be conducted;
- the exact wording of any resolution and if it is a special resolution;
- information on proxy voting;

and it should be signed and dated.

3.8.2 It is quite common for the constitution to specify what business will normally be conducted at an AGM. If it does not, the AGM business will commonly include:

- a presentation of the annual report and annual accounts;
- an election of trustees (if within the remit of the members under the constitution);
- appointment of auditors;
- remuneration of auditors (usually the delegation of this decision to the trustees); and
- any special business (specified in notice).

3.8.3 A general meeting can consider only business that members have been given notice of. Any resolutions to be considered must therefore be included on the notice of the meeting. Whilst there may sometimes be a general discussion and a range of issues raised, a resolution cannot be put to the members in general meeting under 'any other business'.

3.8.4 The constitution will normally specify the notice requirements for general meetings, but usually (and for charitable companies) it must to be sent to all members, trustees and auditors. Notice must be sent to all those entitled to receive it. Failure to send the notice of the meeting to all those entitled to receive it can invalidate the meeting.

3.8.5 Some constitutions contain a clause that states that 'accidental omission' to send a notice will not invalidate a meeting. The Companies Act 2006 also contains such a provision (s. 313) and so this term also applies to charitable companies whether or not it is in the constitution. Whilst this protection is helpful, care must be taken in regard to the meaning of 'accidental omission'. It will cover situations where the charity intended to send someone a notice, but accidentally did not do so. However, if there was no original intention to send the notice (e.g. if the secretary mistakenly believed that someone was not entitled to receive a notice or was not a member) it will not apply.

3.8.6 For companies, 14 clear days' notice of a general meeting is now required. However, note that Articles written prior to the implementation of the Companies Act 2006 are likely to require 21 clear days notice for an annual general meeting, as this was a requirement under the Companies Act 1985. Such Articles may also require 21 clear days' notice for special resolutions (see below). For charities that are not companies, the notice period will normally be specified in the constitution, but it is common for it to be the same as the requirements for charitable companies, that is 14 or 21 clear days. The constitution is also likely to specify when the notice is deemed to be served (i.e. how long after posting it is deemed to have been received). If this is not specified in the constitution, it should be considered to be 48 hours after being posted by first class post.

3.8.7 It is also important to note that 'clear days' does not include the day the notice is deemed to be served and the day of the meeting. This is in addition to the period between a notice being despatched and when it is deemed to be served.

3.8.8 The requirements for 'clear days' and for the period when the notice is deemed to be served therefore means that the requirement for 14 or 21 clear days in practice actually means more than 14 or 21 days' notice from the date the notice is sent out. Therefore if a notice must be served 14 clear days before the meeting and is deemed to be served (according to the charity's constitution) two days after posting, a notice sent out on the first day of the month would not be valid for a meeting held before the eighteenth day in the month.

3.8.9 We discuss below the option of giving notice electronically, and this can shorten the periods when the notice is deemed to be served, but any notice requirement, including any clear days requirements, will still be in force.

3.9 Short notice requirement

3.9.1 There may be occasions when the charity wants to hold a general meeting without meeting its full notice requirement. For example, in a charitable company where there is a requirement to present the annual accounts to the members at the AGM, if the trustees are the only members, the charity may wish to hold the AGM on the same day as the trustees approve the accounts, directly after that meeting. The notice requirements would not be met in such a case as the accounts could not be sent out before being approved and signed. In such an instance it is sometimes possible to meet provided there is agreement to shortened notice. For a charity that is not a company, there would generally need to be a provision in the constitution stating if this was allowable and how. Even without such a mechanism the signed agreement of everyone who was entitled to get notice of the meeting should suffice, so if all the members were present and in agreement this could be achieved.

3.9.2 For a charitable company, the rules regarding short notice are set out in the Companies Act 2006. A general meeting may be called by shorter notice than required under the 2006 Act provided that it is agreed by the following proportions of the members having a right to attend and vote at the meeting:

- in the case of a company not having a share capital, members who represent not less than 90 per cent of the total voting rights; and
- in the case of a company with share capital members who hold not less than 90 per cent of the share capital.

3.9.3 Whilst these provisions appear useful, in practice the proportions are so high that they will only be used by a charity that has a small number of members.

3.9.4 For a charitable company, consent to short notice does not need to be given in writing. It is also arguable that consent may even be given in person by the members just being present at the meeting. However, it is preferable to use a method that allows the company to prove that consent was given and so a written, signed consent is ideal. It should also be noted that the provisions relate to the calling of a meeting at short notice; they do not provide for the giving of notice to be completely dispensed with. A copy of the notice of the meeting should therefore still be given to the members either before or at the start of the meeting. Agreement to short notice can be given at any time up to the beginning of the meeting to which it relates.

3.9.5 There is usually also a requirement to give the auditors notice of a general meeting. Although the Companies Act does not require the agreement of the auditors of the company for a meeting to be held on short notice, it may be advisable to obtain from the auditors a letter of non-objection to the short notice.

3.10 Voting

3.10.1 Voting at general meetings is usually by a show of hands. In some instances, the constitution may permit that a poll can be demanded, and if the charity is also a company, there are provisions in the Companies Act that cover this. A poll is conducted by the use of voting papers rather than on a show of hands.

3.10.2 The Companies Act 2006 gives proxies a number of rights. A proxy is entitled to attend, to speak, to demand a poll and to vote at general meetings. More significantly, anyone appointed as a proxy will now be able to vote on a show of hands (rather than only being included on a poll vote). The Companies Act s. 284(2) states that:

- every member present in person has one vote; and

- every proxy present who has been duly appointed by a member entitled to vote on the resolution has one vote.

3.10.3 This raises a number of issues regarding the voting rights on a show of hands of a person appointed as a proxy for more than one member. How the Act will be interpreted by the courts remains to be seen. However, ICSA's guidance on Corporate Representation and Proxies at General Meetings takes the view that s. 284(2)(b) has to be interpreted as saying that where the same person has been appointed proxy by a number of members, that a person only has one vote on a show of hands (and not one vote for each member he represents). This still leaves the question of what happens when a member is also appointed as a proxy, and the interpretation would seem to be that such a person has two votes on a show of hands, one as a member and one as a proxy.

3.10.4 These sections of the Companies Act are subject to any contrary provision in the Articles (s. 284(4)) but there are limitations on reducing a member's voting rights (s. 285). Given that proxies could not previously vote on a show of hands it is extremely unlikely that any existing Articles will contain such provisions.

3.10.5 Under s. 321 of the Companies Act a provision of a company's Articles is void in so far as it would have the effect of excluding the right to demand a poll at a general meeting on any question other than:

- the election of the chairman of the meeting; or
- the adjournment of the meeting.

3.10.6 A provision of a company's Articles is also void in so far as it would have the effect of making ineffective a demand for a poll on any such question which is made:

- by not less than five members having the right to vote on the resolution; or
- by a member or members representing not less than 10 per cent of the total voting rights of all the members having the right to vote on the resolution (excluding any voting rights attached to any shares in the company held as treasury shares); or
- by a member or members holding shares in the company conferring a right to vote on the resolution, being shares on which an aggregate sum has been paid up equal to not less than 10 per cent of the total sum paid up on all the shares conferring that right (excluding shares in the company conferring a right to vote on the resolution which are held as treasury shares).

3.10.7 Given the new difficulties in regard to proxy voting rights on show of hands votes, it would seem advisable that charitable companies with a large membership take votes on significant matters on poll votes. If a person holds a number of proxy votes, there is no doubt that on a poll vote all these votes will be counted. It is the usual practice for the chairman to be the default proxy, and so the chairman will often hold a number of proxy votes. The complexity of determining who can now vote on a show of hands will make the use of poll voting attractive. In any case, it is useful to also note that there is a common law duty on the chairman of a meeting to demand a poll on a vote if she/he considers that the outcome would be different from that reached on a show of hands. Whilst you may still wish to hold a vote on a show of hands for the benefit of the members in the room, if any proxy votes have been submitted then following this vote with a poll vote may be the advisable course of action.

3.11 Chairing of general meetings

3.11.1 The election or appointment of a chairman will normally be specified in the articles. If nothing is specified, the chairman should be elected by the members at the start of the meeting.

3.11.2 The chairman has authority on the running of the meeting. For example, on a vote on a resolution at a meeting on a show of hands, a declaration by the chairman that the resolution has or has not been passed is regarded as conclusive evidence of that fact without proof of the number or proportion of the votes recorded in favour of or against the resolution.

3.11.3 It is very common for the constitution to give the chairman a casting vote. One of the effects of the Companies Act 2006 is that it abolished the right of a casting vote for the chairman at general meetings. The Department for Business, Innovation and Skills has confirmed that for any company that had a right to a casting vote in its Articles prior to 1 October 2007 this will continue to have effect, but that no company created after that date can validly include such a right in its Memorandum and Articles. (Note that this relates to general meetings – it does not affect any provisions regarding casting votes in board meeting that may be in the Articles.)

3.11.4 The constitution will also usually give the chairman the rights to call for a poll vote or to adjourn the meeting.

3.12 Proxies

3.12.1 A member of a company has a statutory right to appoint a proxy to attend the meeting in his/her place, and vote on his/her behalf (s. 324 Companies Act 2006). This right applies no matter what the Articles state. There is also a legal requirement to include a prominent statement on the right to appoint a proxy on the notice of the meeting. Also, under the Companies Act the longest period that can be specified in the Articles within which members must give notice of their wish to appoint a proxy is 48 hours prior to the meeting or a poll being demanded (excluding non-working days). For example, if your general meeting starts at 2.00 pm on a Tuesday following a Bank Holiday Monday, proxy notices can be lodged up until 2.00 pm on the previous Thursday, or even later, if permitted by the Articles.

3.12.2 There are a number of charitable companies that were established with a restriction on appointing proxies, or a restriction on who can serve as a proxy (e.g. that they must also be a member). The Companies Act 2006 overrides any such restrictions that are in the Articles. This means that a member has a statutory right to appoint a proxy, and that any person (and not just members) can be appointed to serve as a proxy.

3.12.3 For other types of charity a member can appoint a proxy if the constitution allows. Whether that proxy can be any person chosen by the member or only one of the other members (or the meeting chairman) also depends on the constitution.

3.12.4 The form of proxy document will normally be specified in the constitution together with rules on how it is to be delivered to the charity, and the deadline by which it must be received. Again, it should be noted that there are provisions in the Companies Act 2006 that relate to these matters for charitable companies:

- A proxy is a person appointed by an individual or corporate member of a company, to attend, speak and vote on behalf of his appointer at one meeting (including any adjournment thereof) of the members of the company, or a particular class of members of the company, but for no other purpose.
- A member of a company limited by guarantee is allowed to appoint only one person as his proxy, whereas a member of a company with a share capital may appoint more than one, provided that each proxy is appointed to exercise the rights attached to different shares held by that member (s. 324 (2) Companies Act 2006). It is not necessary for a proxy to be a member of the company.
- Every notice of a meeting of a company must include a statement to the effect that a member entitled to attend and vote is entitled to appoint a proxy (or proxies in the case of a company with a share capital) to attend, speak and vote on his behalf. The notice must also state that such proxy need not himself be a member of the company, and should set out any other more extensive rights conferred by the company's articles (s. 325 Companies Act 2006).
- There is no requirement to circulate proxy forms with notices of meetings. However, it is important to note that it is illegal to issue proxy forms by the company to selected members only (s. 326 (1) Companies Act 2006).

3.12.5 Electronic proxies may be specifically permitted by the constitution. In the case of a charitable company they can be used, provided the company and member agree to do so and the company provides an address for electronic lodgement of the proxy. That applies regardless of the charity's Articles.

3.12.6 Charitable companies also need to be aware that there will be some situations in which the company is deemed to have consented to receiving documents electronically. For example, if it provides an electronic address or fax number in a notice convening a general meeting, the company can be deemed to have consented to receiving documents relating to that meeting, such as proxies, using those methods. If you do not want to receive a proxy vote in this way you must ensure that such details are not included on the notice or proxy form (including the letterhead used).

3.13   Quorum

3.13.1 The quorum for a general meeting (i.e. the number of members who must be present for the meeting to be valid) will usually be specified in the constitution. If no quorum is specified, at least two members must be present.

3.13.2 Sometimes a constitution will state that the quorum needs to be present only at the start of the meeting. This means that the quorum does not need to be maintained. Therefore, if the number of members present falls below the required number of a quorum, the meeting will be able to continue.

✓ 3.13.3 Checklist: annual general meeting procedure for a charitable company

- Secretary to arrange a suitable venue for the meeting.
- Trustees to convene the AGM – deciding on the date; formally approving accounts to be considered at that meeting; agreeing the wording of any resolutions to be put to it and authorising the secretary to issue the notice.
- Notice to be issued to members within the notice period (usually either not less than 14 or 21 clear days before the meeting).
- If the AGM is to consider the accounts these should be sent with the notice.
- Notice to refer to proxies and their right to be appointed. If a proxy form is to be sent to members, it should be sent to all members.
- Copy of notice also to be sent to all trustees and to the auditors.
- Consider and prepare who will be speaking on each item, and who will answer any questions (e.g. on the accounts) that are asked.
- If the board has put resolutions to the meeting ensure that there are proposers and seconders for the resolutions.

- Before the meeting (no less than 48 hours) secretary to check and count all the proxies received.
- Prepare poll cards for any poll votes that may be held.
- At the meeting ensure that an attendee sheet is circulated or register members as they attend.
- Inform any person appointed as a proxy that they have been appointed and give then details of how they have been instructed to vote if they have been so instructed.
- If non-members are attending the meeting give all members and proxies voting cards to use on any show of hands votes.
- Have copies of the minutes of the last meeting available at the meeting. Also have extra copies of the agenda and the annual report and accounts (if being considered).

3.14 Resolutions of members

3.14.1 Most of the business conducted at a general meeting is dealt with by ordinary resolutions (i.e. a simple majority of members present and voting is required). However, sometimes the constitution may require a higher majority, and in company law some matters (such as the amendment of the Memorandum and Articles or a change of name) require a special resolution. Special resolutions under company law require a three-quarters majority of members present and voting to vote in favour for the resolution to be passed. Until the implementation of the Companies Act 2006 a special resolution also required 21 clear days' notice, and so this requirement is mirrored in many Articles. A copy of a special resolution must be filed with Companies House within 15 days of the meeting. If it has altered the Memorandum or Articles a reprinted copy of those must also be filed.

3.14.2 Constitutions commonly provide for written resolutions as an alternative to voting at a meeting. These often have a much higher requirement for a majority (either 90 per cent or 100 per cent) and therefore are of limited application, unless the charity has a very small membership.

3.14.3 However, charitable companies and trading subsidiaries can now take advantage of the Companies Act 2006 (s. 288–s. 300). This now allows written resolution to be passed with a simple majority (or a 75 per cent majority for special resolutions). Note however that the majority required is of the full voting rights in the company, not just those of the members who chose to vote (as is the case at a general meeting), and so the majority required is still likely to be higher than at a meeting.

3.14.4 The following may not be passed as a written resolution:

- a resolution under section 168 of the Companies Act removing a director before the expiration of his period of office; nor
- a resolution under section 510 of the Companies Act removing an auditor before the expiration of his term of office.

3.15 Minutes

3.15.1 Minutes of all general meetings must be kept in a minute book. In charitable companies members have the right to inspect the minutes. The minutes of each AGM should be presented to the next AGM, but this can mean a long period in which minutes are not approved. It is therefore good practice for the minutes of an AGM to be presented to the first board meeting following the AGM for approval by the board (see chapter B1).

4 Electronic communications

4.1 The traditional way of communicating with members, and of sending them the notice of meetings, is by sending a paper copy through the post. However, there is now a range of other methods of communicating, including e-mails and the use of the charity's website. There is therefore a question for the charity of how it can use such methods for formal communications. Most constitutions were written assuming that the traditional method was to be used, so they often speak of documents being 'in writing', define that in terms of paper copies and refer to the use of the post. There is therefore often an issue of whether alternative methods can be used, constitutionally and legally.

4.2 If the charity is not a company, the method of communication will be as laid down in its constitution. If this says, for example, that the notice of a meeting must be sent in the post, then this is the method that must be used, or the constitution should be amended to allow for different means of communication. If the constitution is not as explicit, then it may be possible to interpret it in such a way that the communications methods can be changed. However, it often would still be advisable for the constitution to be updated.

4.3 For companies, the Companies Act 2006 introduced a wide range of provisions regarding electronic communications. These followed, and expanded upon, the Companies Act 1985 (Electronic Communications) Order 2000. If a charity has a large number of members, the provisions under the Companies Act 2006 could provide substantial cost savings. However, it should also be noted that the use of e-communications requires the consent of the member, which may be withdrawn at any time. It is likely that not all members will agree to receiving information in this way, and both methods will therefore need to be used.

Charitable companies should consider whether reducing the number of paper copies that need to be sent out will still be an advantage. As it is likely that some members will consent to e-communication and some will not, it will lead to the company having to operate both e-communication and hard copy communication mechanisms, with the added complications and expense of keep track of two separate communication systems.

4.4 Electronic communications covers a range of options including e-mail and the use of the website (e.g. by posting a document on the website). The use of the website can be a useful option, as in this regard consent can be deemed (see below).

4.5 The 2006 Companies Act allows electronic communications to be used in relation to any document or information required or authorised to be sent or supplied under the Companies Acts. The default method of communication is still hard copy. However, a company does not need to have provisions for the use of electronic communications in its Articles or to obtain the consent of the members in general meeting unless it wishes to take advantage of the website default procedures (see below).

4.6 The general rule is that, with the exception of the website default procedures, the intended recipient must have agreed individually to accept communications in that manner. The Companies Act communications provisions can be viewed as overriding anything in a company's Articles, except where the provisions specifically allow contrary provision to be made (for example in relation to deemed delivery).

4.7 If the recipient agrees, the company may supply information and documents in electronic form. If the document or information is sent in electronic form by post or delivered by hand (e.g. on a CD or memory stick), it must be handed to the intended recipient or sent or supplied to an address to which it could be validly sent if it were in hard copy form.

4.8 If the member so requests, the company must provide a hard copy form of any document sent by electronic means or made available on a website within 21 days of receipt of the request and for no charge. If the company fails to comply with this, the company and every officer in default commits an offence and is liable to a fine and a daily fine while the contravention continues.

4.9 Deemed consent

4.9.1 The Companies Act 2006 allows companies to use their website as the default communication method instead of hard copy. The Companies Act 1985

(Electronic Communications) Order 2000 allowed for the use of electronic communication for the circulation of reports and accounts, notices of meetings and the receipt of proxy forms. However, individual consent had to be received from each recipient. The Act changes the position in regard to consent for the use of websites. There is still an obligation to seek that consent, but if no response is received from the member, consent can be deemed to have been given. In other words, the member will need to opt out of the communication method rather than opt in, as now. This makes it much more likely that a company can receive consent from sufficient members to make the use of the website worthwhile.

4.9.2 Unfortunately, the ability to deem consent in this way applies only to website communications, and not to other forms of electronic communications such as e-mail.

4.9.3 If a company wishes to use the website for formal communications with its members, either its Articles of Association must contain a provision allowing it to use the website or its membership must pass a resolution to this effect. Once this has been achieved the company must also ensure:

- A document or information on a website must be made available in a form that the company reasonably considers will enable the recipient to read it and retain a copy of it. So, the company must use an electronic form that is in common usage.
- The company must notify the intended recipient of the presence of a document or information on a website, the address of the website, the place on the website where it may be accessed and how to access the document or information. Unless the member has also consented to being contacted by electronic means, this means that this information must be provided in hard copy form (e.g. by letter).
- The company must make the document or information available on the website throughout the period specified by any relevant provision of the Companies Acts or, if no such period is specified, within the period of 28 days.
- Each member must be individually asked to consent to receive communication via a website. This consent can be either general (e.g. for all communications) or specific.
- When asking for consent, the request must state clearly that failure to respond within 28 days will mean that consent is deemed to have been received.
- The request cannot be repeated until 12 months have passed.

4.9.4 Note that the members must always be notified that the document has been posted on the website, and this extra step could mean that any cost savings of using a website could disappear, especially if members have consented to communication via the website but not via e-mail. In this case the notification that the document is available will have to be sent by post. If the document being notified is a one-page notice of a meeting, there is no cost saving if a letter has to be sent to the members saying that it is available on the website. Having said that, it is important to bear in mind that the savings will be more significant for the annual report and accounts.

4.10 Communications to the company

4.10.1 If the company agrees, documents can be sent to or served on a company by electronic means. The address is that specified by the company and so, for example, could be an e-mail address or fax number. If a document is sent in electronic form by hand or by post (for example on a CD or memory stick) then it must be sent to the company's registered office or to the address provided by the company for hard copy correspondence. The company may also agree to receive documents in a form other than hard copy or electronic.

5 Electronic voting

5.1 Electronic voting, either for proxy or other types of voting, can be very useful, particularly in charities with large membership. Done properly, it has the potential to increase members' participation in the charity.

5.2 The Companies Act 2006 permits certain communications between companies and members to be made by e-mail and other means. However, with reference to voting, the Act covers only proxy voting, and therefore other electronic voting will be permissible only if the constitution specifically allows it. Therefore, if trustees were to be elected in this way, not connected with the AGM, there would need to be specific provision.

5.3 Some charities with a large membership may find the use of electronic voting beneficial, for example for the election of trustees. If the constitution allows electronic voting, and the charity is considering introducing it, the following measures should be put into place:

- Members should have the right to submit a postal vote as an alternative to electronic voting. There will therefore need to be systems in place to ensure that there can be no duplication in the votes cast.
- There will also need to be systems in place to ensure that the voting process is sufficiently secure. For example, members could to be issued with a unique identification number.
- Voting would also need to be via a secure website, with appropriate encryption to ensure that the vote is not traceable to the member voting (if a secret ballot is required).

6 Members' statements

6.1 There is a provision under the Companies Act for members to require the circulation of their statements. This has rarely been used by the members of charitable companies, but it could be used by a minority of members as a means of lobbying the majority. However, in exercising this right, the members concerned bear the costs of doing so, which may in effect reduce its use.

6.2 The Companies Act, s. 314, gives members the power to require circulation of statements. The circulation of a statement of 1,000 words or less may be required by the members of the company to those members entitled to receive notice of a general meeting. Such statement should be concerned with:

- a matter referred to in a proposed resolution to be dealt with at that meeting; or
- other business to be dealt with at that meeting.

6.3 A company is required to circulate any such a statement once it has received such a request from:

- members representing at least 5 per cent of the total voting rights of all the members who have a relevant right to vote (excluding any voting rights attached to any shares in the company held as treasury shares); or
- for share companies, at least 100 members with a relevant right to vote and hold shares in the company for which each member has paid an average sum of at least £100.

6.4 Such a request may be in hard copy form or in electronic form, and must:

- identify the statement to be circulated;
- be authenticated by the person or persons making it; and
- be received by the company at least one week before the meeting to which it relates.

6.5 A company that is required to circulate a statement in this way must send a copy of it to each member of the company entitled to receive notice of the meeting in the same manner as the notice of the meeting, and at the same time as, or as soon as reasonably practicable after, it gives notice of the meeting.

6.6 Members of the company requesting the circulation of the statement must usually pay the company's expenses. This will not be the case if the company resolves otherwise, or if the company has previously so resolved. The company is not bound to comply with a request unless a sum reasonably sufficient to meet its expenses in doing so is deposited with or tendered to it, not later than one week before the meeting.

6.7 A company is not required to circulate a members' statement under section 315 if, on an application by the company or another person who claims to be aggrieved, the court is satisfied that the rights conferred by section 314 and that section are being abused.

7 Board meetings

7.1 The majority of charity constitutions will have far more provisions in them regarding general meetings than trustee meetings. In addition, for companies, there are a range of legislative requirements for general meetings and very few for director meetings. This can seem strange for many charities, as it is the trustee meetings that seem more important. They are held much more frequently, and it is the trustees who take the main strategic decisions of the charity. However, the emphasis legally on members' meetings is to ensure that there is accountability, and to meet the rights of members. Whilst there are some provisions regarding trustee meetings, the core duties of trustees and directors should ensure that, indirectly, they govern their own meetings effectively. However, there is still the need for clarity and guidance on how such meetings should be run.

7.2 The constitution will usually state how trustee meetings are called. It may also specify the frequency of the meetings (with a minimum requirement) and govern the chairing of such meetings. It may also (but less commonly) state the notice requirements and the numbers which will make trustee meetings quorate. Often, it will say that such matters are to be determined by rules or regulations set by the trustees.

7.3 Notice of meetings

7.3.1 The constitution may state what the notice requirement is for board meetings. If no notice is specified, trustees should always be given reasonable notice, according to the circumstances of the charity or the relevant meeting. Common practice is for those entitled to attend the meeting to be given seven days' advance notice of the event. Meetings can usually be convened by the chairman or the secretary, but again check the requirements of the constitution.

7.4 Frequency of meetings

7.4.1 This may be specified in the constitution, and will be dependent on the nature of the work of the charity. The Charity Commission recommends that a minimum of two full trustees' meetings are held in any 12-month period.

7.4.2 The practice of charities varies greatly, but common arrangements for charities include:

- monthly board meetings. This may suit a small charity with few staff and a great deal of operational work for the trustees to do. It may also be suitable in times of crisis. Sometimes boards decide to meet more frequently and remove the need for committees. Monthly meetings can be demanding on trustees and staff resources. If meeting monthly, a board may need to consider whether the board meeting themselves, and preparations for them, are generating a considerable amount of work for staff, preventing them from doing other work. It should also consider whether the frequency of board meetings is affecting the ability of some trustees to contribute;
- every two months. This practice would suit a medium-sized charity, a large charity where the board is engaged in a certain amount of operational work or where the charity is going through a period of change; and
- quarterly. This is a more common practice for the boards of large charities. It can be practical, provided there is sufficient delegation for the charity to operate effectively between meetings. Often, if a board is meeting only four times each year it can be advisable to supplement this with an away day or social functions.

7.4.3 Another factor to consider in regard to the frequency of meetings is their duration. Again, practice differs greatly, with board meetings varying from between two hours to two days. For long meetings to be effective there must be sufficient breaks.

7.5 Planning board meetings

7.5.1 The trustees should take a decision on how frequently they wish to meet and set a calendar of dates. If such matters are determined intermittently, it can affect the effectiveness of the charity. Ideally there should be a regular routine, for instance the board meets in these months, or even on these days. The secretary, or staff supporting the meetings, can then prepare a rolling agenda for the year – indicating which key items need to be considered when, and also ensure a balance across the agendas. Whilst there will be matters that arise from time to time, much of the business of the board will be of a cyclical nature and so can be planned in this way. This covers not just the core decisions to be taken by the board (such as the annual report and accounts) but the timetable of its strategic decision-making and its monitoring of work undertaken on its behalf.

7.6 Board information

7.6.1 Trustees receive a wide range of information from the charity, and much of this is dealt with at meetings. In planning the board's work programme for the year, it can also be useful to consider the information that it receives and whether this all needs to be agenda items or if some could be circulated separately for information only. This can be a helpful alternative way of dealing with regular reports and freeing up time at meetings for core decisions and deliberations. Consideration should be given to how information is presented on the agenda. Is the reason why it is on the agenda clear? If a decision is required, is this clear, and are any recommendations also clear?

7.7 Attendance at meetings

7.7.1 Charities rely on trustee attendance, and it is essential to encourage this. Attending regularly provides trustees the opportunity to use their expertise and to carry out the function of being a trustee. All trustees should therefore be encouraged to regularly attend. Regular non-attendance could be a sign that the trustee is not meeting his duties and this should be dealt with. Some constitutions will state that non attendance at a certain number of meetings, or for a certain period (e.g. six months), will potentially invalidate trusteeship. Even if the constitution has no such provision, this is something that should be discussed with the trustee. It may be that it is a matter that the charity can deal with, for example by changing the timing of the meetings, or that it is a reason for the trustee to stand down.

7.7.2 Attendance at the meetings should be clearly recorded. This will usually be in the minutes, but some charities also have a constitutional requirement for an attendance register to be kept.

7.7.3 The quorum may also be dealt with under the constitution. If not, it should be set by the trustees. If no quorum is set, the quorum for the meetings will be two. The actual quorum requirements of the charity will depend on its work and the composition of the board. However, a generally workable quorum is one third of the trustees. Sometimes a charity may want to set another requirement, for example that certain trustees should be in attendance, or have (or not have) a particular majority at a meeting. In doing this, it is important to ensure that any such provisions are workable and do not hinder the effectiveness of the board.

7.7.4 The trustees may wish to invite non-trustees to some of their meetings. For, example, it is very common for key staff to also attend. When there are non-trustees in attendance, their presence should be recorded separately in the minutes, for example stating 'Present' for the trustees and 'In attendance' for the others, to make it clear the capacity in which everyone attended. It should also always be remembered that whilst the trustees may choose to invite observers to any, or part of, its meetings, the only people with a right to attend and to vote are the trustee members themselves. There is also no general right for observers to speak at a meeting, unless invited to do so by the chair. In determining who the trustees of a charity are, the courts will look at function, rather than title. It is therefore important that there is absolute clarity about who is participating in decision-making at board meetings. Boards usually accept comments and contributions from observers during meetings. However, they should also be aware that the priority at any meeting is for trustees to ask questions and contribute to the debate. When invited to participate in discussion and debate, observers should do so in an advisory capacity only.

7.8 Chairman of the trustees

7.8.1 The election of the chairman will usually be covered by the constitution, and the chairman of the trustees will usually be the same person as the trustee who chairs general meetings. The role of the chairman is covered (see chapter C2). However, it should be noted that the requirements of the Companies Act 2006 regarding the chairman's casting vote at general meetings do not apply to meetings of the board.

7.9 Alternatives to board meetings: written resolutions

7.9.1 The Companies Act 2006 requirements apply to written resolutions of members, not of trustees. Therefore requirements need to be included in the Articles or the constitution for non-company charities. If there is nothing in the constitution the charity can rely on the common law principle of assent – but this requires all trustees to agree. Written resolutions often require a higher level of consent than for vote at meeting, for example 75 per cent, as there is no opportunity for debate.

8 Committees

8.1 A charity may delegate some of its work to committees, and the powers to do so and examples of the key committees are set out (see chapter C2). How the meetings of the committees are run will be governed predominately by their terms of reference. A constitution may sometimes place some regulations on committees, for example it is fairly common of the constitution to specify that there must be a minimum number of trustees on the committee. However, in all other regards the way in which the meetings of the committees are run will be in the hands of the board in setting its terms of reference.

◆ 8.2 Sample terms of reference for a committee

X committee: terms of reference

Purpose	The X Committee is established in accordance with Article X. Its purpose is …
Membership and proceedings	1. The members of the committee shall be appointed by the board and the profile of the committee is formally reviewed every … year. 2. Members shall include: 3. The (*name support staff*) may be invited to attend all or part of particular meetings. 4. The secretary shall act as secretary to the committee. 5. The quorum shall be *x* members. 6. The committee shall meet not less than *x* times a year.
Function	The committee is responsible for: 1. 2. 3.
Powers	1. The committee is authorised by the board to … 2. The committee may establish sub-committees and delegate to them. 3. In all other matters the role of the committee is advisory, unless a specific delegation power is made by the board.
Reporting	1. The secretary shall circulate minutes of the committee's meetings to all trustees. 2. A report of the committee's deliberations shall be made to the next board meeting. Papers shall be presented to the board as and when required.

9 Guidelines for effective meetings

9.1 Effective meetings are effectively chaired. There is a wide variety of guidance on how to chair meetings well. Here are some suggested pointers:

- In general a chairman should spend their time listening, moving the discussion on, summarising and being firm but sensitive.
- The chairman is under an obligation to know and understand the charity's constitution and any rules or regulations governing how the board or committee operates. S/he should also have at least a basic understanding of the matter under discussion, and should be briefed on this in advance if necessary.
- The chairman should ensure that a proper agenda is drawn up, even if this is done by a staff member. S/he should discuss the agenda with the relevant staff before the meeting and be clear about the action that is required for each agenda item.
- The chairman should summarise the discussion periodically, especially if the item under discussion is complex. At the end of each agenda item the chairman should ensure that all present are clear about the outcome reached.
- A good chairman will ensure that all members are able to participate; that all points of view are heard in a debate, including dissenting voices; and that one voice cannot dominate the meeting. The chairman should encourage all members to have some input.
- If the chairman offers their own opinion it should be made clear that this is a personal view, rather than a summary of the meeting's position.
- The chairman needs to manage each agenda item. It can sometimes be helpful to think about the discussion progressing in the following order – facts; opinions; decisions; action.

9.2 Ensuring that the meeting is chaired effectively is the responsibility of all those present, not just the chairman and the chairman needs support in order to fulfil their role. Many charities have codes of conduct for trustees. They can often include how to behave at meetings, and there should be some mechanisms of ensuring that trustees:

- respect the chairman and his or her decisions about the conduct of the meeting; and
- address the meeting through the chairman. This essentially means getting the attention of the chairman and awaiting his or her permission to speak, rather than making the point directly. It is the chairman's role to ensure that everyone is heard.

9.3 Whilst it is important that charity meetings are conducted in an orderly way, care should be taken to ensure that meetings do not get bogged down in overly formal procedures. In board and committee meetings it is not usually necessary for every issue under discussion to be proposed and seconded. However, the fact that there are no formal meeting procedures does not mean that there should not be some level of formality in the proceedings or that the conduct of the meetings is unimportant. Charities should be clear to their trustees about what behaviour is, and is not, acceptable in meetings. Examples of unacceptable behaviour could include:

- participating in side conversations during the meeting;
- performing other tasks during the meeting (e.g. catching up on other paperwork);
- any aggressive or rude behaviour;
- not listening, or dominating the discussion; and
- 'caucusing', that is agreeing to a particular approach amongst a small group of members in advance of the meeting.

9.4 Even if well conducted and with a good chairman, meetings can become ineffective. Typically this can happen when a board or committee is insufficiently focused on its role. Such meetings will be characterised by a long agenda, sometimes with little or no clear reasons why some agenda items have been brought to the meeting. Sometimes there will be a standard agenda, for example with a list of reports from officers, with no indication on the agenda itself of what the core subject matter actually is.

9.5 The first steps towards effective meetings is to identify the significant issues that require attention and then focus on them. These can be categorised in a number of ways. One way may be to categorise board items as:

- governance;
- key decisions;
- monitoring; and
- strategy.

9.6 There are a number of different ways of keeping the focus on the core business:

- **Using a 'business agenda':** grouping together items that require formal decisions only and dealing with these first. The meeting then agrees that everything in this section will be dealt with without any discussion unless a trustee asks in advance for an item to be discussed. If such a request is made, that item is taken out of the business agenda and put into the main agenda. The business agenda is therefore still dealt with, with no discussion, and the discussion item is dealt with elsewhere on the agenda.
- **Avoiding standard agenda:** review the work programme for the year and consider in advance what you need to agree and when. Then draft the agenda so that each item to be discussed is described, along with the action needed. Be careful of the overuse of 'matters arising' and 'any other business'. If a matter arising from the last meeting needs to be discussed it should be an agenda item in its own right. 'Any other business' should be restricted to urgent matters or short matters for information only.

- **Having timed agenda:** Chairmen sometimes set timings, but do not inform the rest of the meeting. However, being open about the timings helps everyone to keep to them – and it establishes the relative importance of items in advance. If a participant wants more time allocated to an item, they can request this at the start of the meeting.
- **Keeping the agenda short:** ideally no more than eight substantive items. This does not necessarily mean shorter meetings, but should give more focus on the key issues.
- **Removing information items:** often, agenda are taken up with items that are for information only. If you have a lot of these, think about having a separate information pack which you send out to the trustees/committee.

9.7 It can help a board or committee to work more effectively if the members also have the opportunity to meet socially, even if just during the refreshment breaks at the meeting itself. This not only helps address conflicts, but also ensures that there are opportunities for matters to be discussed appropriately outside the meeting. Without this type of discussion trustees or committee members may raise inappropriate issues at meetings or begin to caucus privately.

9.8 It may also be useful to provide opportunities to think aloud and for creative thinking. This can be done by varying the format of meetings. For example, there could be some informal sessions mixed in with the standard meeting or the meeting could break into smaller groups for brainstorming.

SECTION D

The charity's business

D1
Employment

1 Volunteers

Many charitable and voluntary organisations could not function without the services of their volunteers, who give of their time and talents expecting nothing in return. However, it is possible for a volunteer to undergo a change in status and become an employee without the organisation or the volunteer necessarily being aware of it at the time. Employees have rights to the national minimum wage, paid holidays, statutory sick pay and redundancy pay to name but a few, whereas volunteers have none of these rights. It is therefore essential to be clear on the status of volunteers when they join the organisation but also to regularly revisit the volunteers' roles to ascertain whether there has been any change in status. In this section we look at the pitfalls to be avoided when taking on volunteers in order to ensure employee status is not acquired

1.1 What is a volunteer?

1.1.1 There may be differing opinions as to what constitutes a volunteer but it is generally agreed that a volunteer is someone who gives their time to a particular cause whilst expecting nothing in return. For national minimum wage purposes a volunteer is a worker who is employed by a charity, a voluntary organisation, an associated fund-raising body or a statutory body and who receives no monetary payments of any description except in respect of expenses actually incurred in the performance of his duties or a reasonable estimate of these expenses, and receives no benefits in kind.

1.1.2 In recent years we have seen substantial changes to the way in which volunteers are recruited. The recruitment process has become more professional, with many organisations having their pick from a substantial pool of applicants. The roles volunteers play can form an integral part of an organisation's structure, and more and more often we see organisations trying to introduce measures to better enable them to plan their activities and control their volunteers. This change in approach may have contributed to the blurring of lines between employee and volunteer status.

1.1.3 Volunteers do not owe the same obligations to an organisation as do its employees. To a certain extent volunteers may come and go as they please, although many organisations ask their volunteers to commit a certain amount of their time for a specific period. Volunteers are unpaid, but they can claim genuine out-of-pocket expenses.

1.1.4 The lines between volunteer and employee become blurred when the organization seeks to bind volunteers to work particular hours, etc. and/or pay more than genuine expenses. Should a volunteer inadvertently acquire employee status it is important that the organisation is aware of this, as employees have many rights which an organisation could easily infringe if it does not appreciate that the volunteer's status has changed.

1.1.5 There is very little case law on the subject, and, as each case turns on its own facts, it is difficult to draw up a list of the dos and don'ts for those recruiting and using volunteers. The cases we do have involved fairly unusual arrangements but we can use them to highlight potential pitfalls, as they provide guidance on a number of things that can be done to make the status of volunteers clearer, as detailed below.

1.2 Contract

1.2.1 It is important for any organisation taking on employees or volunteers to define the nature of the relationship between them at the outset.

1.3 Offer and acceptance

Given that volunteering involves an offer and an acceptance by the parties involved it is not surprising that contractual questions may arise. After all, is that not the basis of most contracts? It is indeed possible for a contract to exist, but in the case of a genuine volunteer it will not be a contract of employment.

1.3.1 In the Employment Appeal Tribunal (EAT) case *South East Sheffield Citizen Advice Bureau v Grayson* [2004] IRLR 353 which grappled with the question of the status of volunteers under employment legislation, the question in point was whether the agreement/contract imposed an obligation on the organisation to offer work to the volunteer and whether the volunteer was personally obliged to do that work. The decision in that case was that no such obligation existed and that the volunteer could not obtain rights under employment legislation.

1.4 Consideration

1.4.1 An employment contract does not have to be in writing, and the consideration need not necessarily be money. Under volunteers' contracts the consideration is the exchange of something of value between the volunteer and the charity.

In an employment contract, consideration is usually salary; however, it could be other things such as rewards, training or regular payments that are more than out-of-pocket expenses. For example, in the case of *Migrant Advisory Services v Choudray* 1198 EAT, the claimant was paid £25, ostensibly for expenses incurred, although none had actually been incurred. Furthermore, payments were also made to the volunteer when she was sick or on holiday. The tribunal therefore held that such payments should be regarded as salary and were supportive of an employment relationship.

1.5 Expenses

1.5.1 It would be unfair to expect volunteers to be out of pocket for expenses incurred in the course of their volunteering work, and it important to reimburse them in a timely fashion. Best practice for dealing with expenses is to make payments only where receipts are available and then to keep receipts and records of money paid for future reference and for the purpose of financial reporting.

1.5.2 One-off payments, presents and rewards can be problematic in keeping the distinction between volunteer and employee clear unless it can be shown that there was no expectation on the part of the volunteer to receive these things in return for their work and that making such payments was not accepted practice. If this were not the case, not only would the volunteer be deemed an employee, but he would be liable to pay National Insurance Contributions (NIC), as would the charity. As such, officers of the charity might find themselves personally liable if the employer's liability insurance has not been maintained.

1.5.3 As a charity's most valuable asset, it is important to support volunteers and to make them feel valued. So whilst it is important to avoid 'consideration', a 'thank you' such as the occasional social event, Christmas lunch or extra resources would not jeopardize the volunteer status.

1.5.4 Many volunteers view their work for charities as providing an opportunity to extend their skills through some form of training related to their volunteering. However, care must be taken to ensure that the training provided relates directly to their volunteering work, as it can be deemed 'consideration' by a tribunal. For instance, paying for IT training where this is not relevant for the work done, in, say, a charity shop, can amount to consideration and confer employee status. However, training can be legitimately provided to volunteers, as was shown in *Gradwell v. Council for Voluntary Service Blackpool, Wyre & Fylde*. Conversely, in *Armitage v. Relate*, training was deemed to be consideration, partly because the volunteer had to repay the costs of training if they left.

1.6 Mutuality of obligation

1.6.1 In a true volunteering situation there is no legal obligation on the part of the volunteer to do the work, nor is there an obligation on the organisation to offer work. Neither has an obligation to the other in this respect and there is not a legally enforceable contract of employment. No mutuality of obligation exists.

1.7 Intention to create a legal relationship

1.7.1 The onus is on the party trying to avoid an employment contract to demonstrate that there is no intention to create one. Issues which might infer an intention to create an employment contract might be:

- Similarity of work and overlap with the work of the organisation's employees. It is possible for employment status to be inferred, if, on comparison, there is a high degree of overlap.
- The degree of similarity in the wording and formality between volunteering agreements and staff contracts.
- Implications or statements to the effect that the voluntary work is intended to lead on to paid work.

1.8 Personal service

1.8.1 The one thing that can distinguish a volunteer from an employee is that an employee is contractually obliged to carry out work whereas a volunteer is not.

1.9 Volunteer agreement

1.9.1 Many volunteers will be issued with a volunteer agreement. This document normally sets out the nature of the voluntary work to be undertaken and what he/she can expect in terms of support from the organisation. It can also cover insurance provisions covering his/her activities for the organisation. It may also contain a procedure for dealing with disputes. Some volunteer agreements do constitute binding contracts on the organisation to pay expenses or to indemnify the volunteer against actions resulting from the volunteer work. These agreements can be enforced by the volunteers. However, it will take more than that to change the status of a volunteer to that of an employee.

1.10 Consider all the facts

1.10.1 By looking at the whole picture you can consider ways to make clearer distinctions between your employees and volunteers. These distinctions will help to clearly define the two roles in order to protect an organisation from employment tribunal claims by volunteers seeking to obtain employee status. A useful exercise is to place your volunteers on a spectrum that has paid employees at one end and unpaid volunteers at the other. Consider where your volunteers sit on that spectrum.

1.11 Supporting volunteer status

1.11.1 Volunteers have far fewer rights than employees (see below) and have no rights to bring employment claims before an Employment Tribunal (ET).

1.11.2 The following recommendations, if followed, will assist in supporting volunteer status in the event of a claim:

- The agreement between the organisation and the volunteer should be clearly defined under a Volunteer Agreement. It should be couched in appropriate language to explain what is expected of volunteers rather than obliging volunteers to behave in a particular way. There should be no requirement that the agreement is signed.
- A volunteer agreement should state that there is no intention to create a legal relationship.
- Volunteer task lists, Equal Opportunities Policy and Complaints Procedures should be provided.
- Performance reviews and penalties for poor performance should be avoided.
- Provision for volunteers to work specific hours can be included but there should be no penalty in the event that a volunteer refuses or fails to work that shift. It is essential to avoid creating any mutuality of obligation. A volunteer should never be contractually obliged to do work.
- Pay expenses only.
- Termination arrangements are unnecessary and should be avoided.
- Training given should be specific to the work to be undertaken by the volunteer.
- Allow volunteers where appropriate to find a replacement on occasions when they are unable to attend a previously agreed volunteer session.

1.12 Changes in status: the risks

1.12.1 Employees have many rights and it would be easy for an organisation to infringe those rights inadvertently. The likely claims would be as follows:

- National Minimum Wage for the hours worked;
- paid holidays based on the time worked by the volunteer/employee;
- unfair dismissal rights (after one year's service except in excluded categories where there is no service requirement, e.g. discrimination);
- discrimination claims;
- redundancy entitlements for employees with over two years' service; and
- tax and National Insurance contributions.

1.13 The National Minimum Wage

1.13.1 The National Minimum Wage Act 1998 (as amended) excludes 'voluntary workers' (section 44). To ensure volunteers are kept outside the scope of the Act, the key points to remember are:

- pay expenses on receipts;
- relate training given to the job done; and
- prior to giving benefits or rewards to volunteers think carefully as to how such benefits or rewards may affect the volunteer's status.

1.14 Health and safety

1.14.1 Under health and safety law, an organisation only has to have one paid employee to be an employer, and as such, the organization must assess risks to the health and safety of employees and volunteers alike, and take steps to minimise any hazards. Further information health and safety can be found in paragraph 5.

2 Recruitment and the employment contract

2.1 Introduction

2.1.1 The recruitment process is circumscribed by many of the legal requirements which must be taken into account in an application form. Discrimination in all its forms must be avoided not only during employment, but also during recruitment. A claim of discrimination can be made to an ET by an applicant for a job even though they have never been employed by the prospective employer.

2.1.2 To ensure that recruitment is conducted fairly and to be able to evidence this in the event of an allegation of discrimination, strict adherence to a procedure that enables the process to be monitored should be maintained.

✓ **2.1.3 Objective selection checklist**
- Details of all applicants should be kept with an analysis of which (objective) criteria were used to select those called for interview.
- Details of the progress of the interview should be held in a central file.
- From an analysis of the candidates, a shortlist should be compiled and the criteria for such selection retained.
- Item 2 should be repeated for the shortlist interview stage.
- The ultimate selection process and criteria used should be noted.
- Interviewers need to ensure that they do not ask questions which breach the anti-discrimination laws – no matter how idle or casual the enquiry may be – unless similar questions are asked of all candidates, regardless of sex, race, ethnic origin, sexual orientation, religion and age. In addition, it is customary during an interview for the interviewer to make notes. There needs to be some caution even here, since the Information Commissioner (who polices the Data Protection Act (DPA)) has indicated that such notes may be subject to the access requirements of applicants. It may be advisable immediately after the interview for any notes to be transcribed into a wording/format that would not cause any problem if made subject to such access and for the original to be shredded.

2.2 Job offers

2.2.1 An offer of a job, no matter how informally made, and an acceptance by an applicant, no matter how informally indicated, creates a contract.

2.3 Right to work in the UK

2.3.1 Since 2004 employers have been required to check that those applying for jobs have the right to work in the UK. This applies to all applicants, including those born in the UK. Failure to effect adequate checks can generate sanctions. The penalty for employing a person lacking the right to work in the UK is £10,000 (since March 2008), with imprisonment and an unlimited fine for anyone employing an unauthorised person intentionally.

2.4 Contract

2.4.1 Provision of contract. Unlike the arrangements for volunteers discussed in section 1, employment legislation requires employees to be given a contract of employment within eight weeks of their start date, and it may be that this could be a convenient space for a probationary period, although the period more commonly used is three months. As explained in section 1 this does not apply to volunteers.

2.4.2 Using a probationary period is not a legal requirement and is purely a matter of contract between the parties. This provides flexibility to the employer to terminate employment earlier than the expected expiry date of the period or to extend the period if they are unsure about performance. Conversely, if the employer is confident the employee can do the job, any probationary period can be brought to an end before the term stipulated. When the employment is to be made permanent this should be confirmed in writing, with the date of the start of the probationary period (not the date permanent employment is confirmed as starting) used as the employment start date.

2.4.3 In addition to the contract of employment, it is not uncommon for employers to provide staff with a handbook detailing other more operational issues, such as: internet use policy, sickness reporting, confidentiality, etc. It is important to note that not everything in such handbooks need form part of the contract of employment. Quite often employers will include a section of rules and procedures that form part of the contract of employment and another section of rules and procedures that do not form part of the contract of employment. Changes to the contract of employment, other than very minor changes, should not be made by an employer without the employee's consent, whereas changes to the non-contractual rules and procedures can be made by the employer without consent simply by giving reasonable notice to the employee.

2.4.4 Items employers are legally obliged to include in the contract are:

(a) names of both parties (employer and employee);
(b) date employment began and date continuous employment began. 'Continuous employment' is referred to in order to cover the position where, for instance, employer Z acquires employer B and B's employees. Z must give B's employees contracts, but the date they began employment is the date they started with B and NOT the date Z took them over. (See 'Transfer of Undertakings (Protection of Employment) (TUPE)' below.);
(c) job title or brief description of job;
(d) pay, scale of pay and details of payment arrangements;
(e) place of work;
(f) hours of work;
(g) holiday entitlement and arrangements regarding holiday pay;
(h) data which must be given to employees, but not necessarily in the contract:
   i. details of occupational sickness leave and payment. It is usual to recite the arrangements regarding the entitlement to Statutory Sick Pay (SSP) for which the employer is responsible for provision and payment on behalf of the state;
   ii. details of occupational/stakeholder pension schemes available to employees;
   iii. notice period and/or termination date if fixed term (see below);
   iv. particulars of **collective agreements**; and
   v. disciplinary arrangements.

2.5 Changing the contract

2.5.1 It is possible to change material terms of the contract, but only after a process of consultation. What constitutes a 'material term' may vary from employee to employee and from contract to contract, but pay and hours are normally regarded as material terms. Consultation can take place only if both parties are willing to consult and try to find a compromise. If there is a real need to change either pay or hours (or both) and the employee is not prepared to compromise or even discuss the matter, the employer can take the option of bringing the contract to an end, giving the required notice under the contract or statutory notice (one week per year of service to a maximum of 12 weeks – whichever is longer) and offering a new contract on the revised terms, recognising the past service. This is a dismissal, but should be a fair one provided every effort was made to negotiate.

2.5.2 Contracts can be used to provide someone to work on a specific project which is finite in time. The arrangements are now subject to the requirements of the Fixed Term Employees (Prevention of Less Favourable Treatment) Regulations (FTE (PLFT) R) (see below).

2.6 Transfer of Undertakings (Protection of Employment) (TUPE)

2.6.1 Under the UK version of the EU Acquired Rights Directive – TUPE – where an economic entity is transferred from one organisation to another, the employees involved in such an entity have the right to be transferred on the same terms to the new owners (or to choose not to transfer, in which case they are regarded as having resigned and gain no compensation). The transfer must, however, be on the basis of the same terms of employment as existed before the transfer. If there are changes to the terms 'by reason of the transfer', then such a change is illegal and the employees may be able to take action against the employer(s). EU rules are strict despite some confusion from the European Court of Justice (ECJ), whose rulings on cases under the directive have sometimes seemed confusing and even contradictory.

2.6.2 The TUPE Regulations were revised on 1 April 2006. Whilst the original principle (that employees working for an economic entity have the right to transfer to the new ownership of that entity on their existing terms and conditions) remains, the 2006 amendments:

(a) extend coverage of the principle to 'service provision changes';
(b) require the transferring employer to provide employment details of transferring employees;
(c) clarify the situation with regard to transfer-related dismissals and changes to terms and conditions of transferring employees;
(d) provide greater flexibility where the transferring employer is insolvent;
(e) service provision changes occur when an acquiring employer brings into their organisation work previously performed by a third party on their behalf, or where they contract such work out to a third party. In these cases there will be a transfer if:
 i. there is an economic entity (an organised grouping of employees/resources) of a business (or part thereof) that immediately before the transfer was situated in the UK; and/or
 ii. there is a change to the provision of such services – i.e. a transfer in or out of the organisation or a transfer from one contractor to another
 iii. one-off contracts (and contracts for supply of goods) are not covered.

3 Benefits

3.1 Working hours

3.1.1 The Working Time Regulations (WTR) make provisions on daily and weekly rest breaks and annual leave to ensure that employees and workers do not work for periods of time that may adversely impact on their health. There are very specific restrictions concerning young workers and night workers.

3.1.2 Under the WTR, most employers are not permitted to force their employees to work more than 48 hours a week averaged over a 17-week period (a period which can by agreement be increased up to 52 weeks).

3.1.3 Under UK opt-outs, employees are permitted to work more than 48 hours a week on a regular basis, provided each individual signs a personal opt-out. Such an opt-out is subject to three months' notice. Hence if, during recruitment, an employer forced an applicant to agree to work more than 48 hours (which is permitted), on the first day of service, the employee could give the employer three months' notice to terminate the opt-out. If the employer applied sanctions to the employee as a result, that would be a breach of a statutory right and the employee would be able to have such complaint heard at a tribunal.

3.2 National Minimum Wage

3.2.1 A rate of pay at least equivalent to the National Minimum Wage (NMW) must be paid in respect of all hours for which an employee is at work or on call for work. Although simple in concept, the regulations contain many exclusions. In principle, employers should ensure that all hours during which an employee is at work, travelling on their employer's business to a place which is not their own place of work or on call for the purposes of the employer's work are paid at least the minimum rate (which is usually reviewed annually). There are criminal penalties for failing to pay at least the NMW in respect of all qualifying hours. Anyone underpaid can claim all back-pay (even from a previous employer), a form of claim which is not statute-barred.

3.3 Holidays

3.3.1 As a result of the EU commitment to the principle that all workers should have an annual break from work, employees are entitled to 5.6 weeks' paid holiday (inclusive of bank or public holidays) within their employer's holiday year. Such statutory holiday must:

- be taken within the employer's holiday year;
- not be carried forward to a following year; and
- not be paid in lieu (except where the person is leaving with an unused accrued entitlement).

3.3.2 If a person has not taken their holiday within the holiday year, the employer can compulsorily allocate days of holiday that they must take. However, if a woman has been unable to take holiday as a result of her taking maternity leave, she is allowed to carry it forward to a following holiday year (the effect of the decision in the ECJ *Merino Gomez* case).

3.3.3 In a recent case heard by the ECJ it was held that workers on long-term sick leave are entitled to accrue holidays during their absence and to carry these accrued holidays forward into the next holiday year.

3.3.4 There is a practice favoured by some employers, especially employers who employ high numbers of part-time and casual workers, involving rolled-up holiday pay. This means that an amount is added to the employee's hourly rate which counts as holiday pay, e.g. an hourly rate of £6.00 plus £0.70 holiday pay. As a result the employee does not get paid holiday when he/she actually takes holiday leave as the holiday pay has already been paid in respect of every hour worked. This practice was challenged and was finally decided by the ECJ, which held that the practice was unlawful. However, there is no penalty for employers who choose to follow this practice and it is therefore still widely used in certain sectors. In practice this has meant that employers seeking to use the rolled-up holiday pay method must explain the process at the recruitment stage and set out the details in the contract of employment. The part of the employee's pay attributed to holiday pay must be specified in the employee's pay slip, records of all holidays taken must be kept and reasonably practical steps must be taken to encourage employees to take their holiday entitlement.

3.4 Pensions

3.4.1 Employers (other than those with fewer than five eligible employees) are now required to offer an occupational scheme or a stakeholder pension. Failing to offer membership of a stakeholder pension scheme where there is no occupational pension scheme is punishable by a fine of £50,000.

3.5 'Family-friendly' rights

3.5.1 With an ageing population, the government has adopted a policy of legislating to encourage childbirth and caring by a range of protections for workers who have parental and/or caring responsibilities.

3.6 Maternity

3.6.1 The important date for the calculation of maternity rights, etc. is a woman's expected week of childbirth (EWC).

3.6.2 All women are entitled to 26 weeks' ordinary maternity leave (OML) and 26 weeks' additional maternity leave (AML) (a total of 52 weeks). There is no obligation on the woman to take all the leave or even part of it, subject to the prohibition on a woman returning to work within two weeks of having given birth (four weeks if she works in a factory).

3.6.3 Women who have 40 weeks' service with their employer by the EWC will qualify for Statutory Maternity Pay (SMP) provided their earnings exceed the Lower Earnings Limit. This is paid by the employer, who can then recover it from the government. Women who earn below the Lower Earnings Limit will be entitled to Maternity Allowance (MA), which is paid to them by the government.

3.6.4 The first six weeks of SMP are paid at the rate of 90 per cent of the woman's average weekly earnings and the following 33 weeks are paid at the rate of £ 123.06 (April 2009) or 90 per cent of the woman's average weekly earnings whichever is the lower.

3.6.5 MA is paid for 39 weeks at the standard rate of £123.06 or 90 per cent of the woman's average weekly earnings, whichever is the lower. To qualify for MA the woman must have been registered as self-employed or have been employed in at least 26 weeks of the 66-week period running into the week before the EWC.

- A woman must give 28 days' notice of the date that she wishes her maternity leave to start. Her employer must (within 28 days of that notification) state the latest date by which she must return to work. She may change the leave start date, and, if so, within 28 days of the notification of the change the employer must advise a new return date.
- A woman can return before the end of her leave on giving 56 days' notice. Her employer can postpone her return to the end of the 56-day period if the full notice was not given, but not to any date later than the end of her leave.

Note: In the case of *Alabaster v Woolwich Building Society*, the ECJ stated that *all* pay rises before the end of the maternity leave (i.e. a full year in some cases) must be reflected and related back to the first day on which SMP was due. This means the average for the six weeks must be recalculated and arrears paid. If a woman is still employed, she has six years to make a claim for any arrears. However, if she has left that employment, she must lodge any claim within six months of leaving.

3.6.6 Keeping in touch

During her maternity leave a woman is entitled to work (and be paid for) up to 10 'in-touch' days without this affecting her leave or maternity pay. If she works during a time when she is in receipt of maternity pay, it would be logical to 'top up' her maternity pay to her normal day's pay (adjusted by any increase effected during her leave). If she works during the unpaid portion of her leave a full day's pay should be given.

3.6.7 Job on return

A woman taking only OML has a right to return to the job she was doing before her leave. But a woman taking both OML and AML has a right to return to that job or to a similar job (on no less favourable terms). Some women may wish to work part-time on return. Women with children up to the age of six (18 if the child is disabled) can ask their employer to consider a request to work flexibly. Such a request must be considered objectively.

3.7 Paternity

3.7.1 If they have a minimum of 26 weeks' service leading into the fifteenth week before due date, by their partner's EWC, fathers /civil partners/adopters are entitled to Statutory Paternity Leave (SPL) and (subject to earnings) to pay. Statutory Paternity Pay (SPP) is paid at the rate of 90 per cent of the father's average earnings for the eight weeks ending at the fifteenth week before the mother's EWC or £123.06 (April 2009), whichever is less. A father is entitled to SPP per week of leave, which can either be one week or two weeks, but must be taken within eight weeks of the birth. Only one leave and payment is due in respect of each pregnancy. Thus for a multiple birth the father is entitled to only one term of leave and payment. An employer has no right to ask for proof that the baby is expected or has been born. However, before there can be any payment or leave, a father needs to complete and sign a Declaration SC3 (available from HMRC).

3.8 Adoption

3.8.1 Employees who adopt are, subject to service, entitled to statutory adoption leave (SAL) and, subject to earnings, to statutory adoption pay (SAP). Adoptive parents are the 'main' parent (the person named in the Adoption Matching Certificate) and the 'other' parent. Married couples, male and female couples, single-sex partners and single persons can adopt and become eligible for benefit. Adopting employees need to have worked for their employer for 26 weeks by the end of the Matching Week to qualify for the rights. These are:

- **Leave:** the 'main' parent is entitled to two leaves – ordinary and additional (equivalent to the maternity leave rights), making a total absence of 52 weeks. If (s)he wishes to return before the end of either leave, 56 days' notice must be given. The 'other' parent is entitled to the equivalent of 'paternity pay/leave', that is one or two weeks' leave (which must be taken within 56 days of the adoption). The contract of employment continues during the leave(s).
- **Pay:** payment for the first 39 weeks leave for the main parent is at the rate of 90 per cent of the person's average earnings or £123.06 (April 2009), whichever is less. There is no payment for the last period of 13 weeks. Payment for the other parent's paternity leave is at the rate of 90 per cent of average earnings or £123.06 (April 2009), whichever is less. Adoptive leave is available only on a single basis – if two or more children are adopted, only one set of leaves/pay is available for each parent.

3.9 Emergency leave

3.9.1 Employees are entitled to take a 'reasonable' amount of unpaid leave to deal with 'family emergencies'. Such a leave entitlement is not subject to any service requirement and is aimed to cover the following purposes:

- to help when a dependant is ill, gives birth, is injured or assaulted;
- to arrange for an ill or injured dependant to be cared for because a dependant's care arrangements are unexpectedly changed;
- as a result of the death of a dependant; and
- to deal with an incident involving a child which occurs unexpectedly in school time.

3.10 Parental leave

3.10.1 All those who have parental responsibility for children aged up to five years (18 if the child is disabled) and who have a year's service with their employer are entitled to parental leave of up to a maximum of four weeks' leave in any year in respect of any individual child.

3.10.2 Those wishing to take the leave must give at least three weeks' notice. The employer has the right to postpone the leave (for no more than six months). Fathers who give three weeks' notice of the birth of their child have the right to take this leave immediately after the birth and the employer has no right of postponement in this instance.

3.10.3 Employers are under no obligation to keep records, but it is difficult to see how this can be avoided simply to keep track of the entitlements and avoid disputes. Employees have the right to the leave in respect of each child for whom they have parental responsibility. Parental leave is unpaid.

3.11 Flexibility of working arrangements

3.11.1 It seems that a majority of employees would prefer greater control over their own hours to additional salary. There are many ways to provide flexibility of working (e.g. allowing employees to surrender pay in exchange for additional time off) and many employers who allow flexibility of hours claim it improves productivity. Employees with parental responsibilities for children up to the age of 16 (18 if disabled) as well as those with caring requirements have the right to lodge a formal request with their employer to work flexibly. A set procedure must be followed:

(a) The employer is required to acknowledge the request within 14 days and make a practical business assessment of the request and its impact, which should be in writing.

(b) Within four weeks of the request, a meeting must be held with the employee to discuss the request and its implications. The employee has a right to be accompanied at that meeting by a workplace colleague.
(c) Within two weeks of the meeting the employer must write to the employee setting out either:
   i   any required action on which the decision to agree the flexibility is to be based and setting a date for commencement; or
   ii   any compromise offer (which should include a date by which a response is expected; or
   iii a rejection of the request giving explanations of the business reasons for such decision and setting out the appeal procedure.

3.11.2 Business reasons for rejecting the request could include:

- the burden of costs on the employer;
- problems meeting customer demand;
- an inability to reorganise the work;
- problems meeting quality requirements;
- problems meeting performance output;
- an inability to find other employees to cover the hours not now to be worked; and/or
- other reasons specific to the employer.

3.11.3 Employees can appeal a decision they believe to be unfair. An appeal must be lodged within 14 days and held within another 14 days. An employee has the right to be accompanied by a workplace colleague. Within a further 14 days the employer must give the employee the decision.

Only if all internal procedures have been exhausted does the employee have a right of access to an Employment Tribunal, which can award eight weeks' pay up to the maximum 'weeks' pay' allowed (a figure which is revised each year on 1 February). A Tribunal will have to examine the procedural aspects of the case (referring it to the employer if these are faulty) or facts claimed have been found to be incorrect. In such a case the employee may be entitled to compensation. After a rejected request, an employee (assuming they are eligible) can make another request each year.

4 Discipline and dismissal

4.1 Disciplinary rationale

4.1.1 Under the Employment Rights Act 1996 (ERA), employers are required to provide their employees with details of a disciplinary procedure within eight weeks of appointment. Many employers incorporate the procedure in the contract of employment which, if a copy is given to the employee, should avoid the possibility of the employee denying receipt of it.

4.1.2 Every disciplinary procedure can be regarded as having two distinct purposes:

1. A 'positive purpose': attempting to display, to the 'offending' employee, the nature of their transgression, with the aim of converting that behaviour – which is unacceptable in the eyes of the employer – to that which is acceptable.
2. A 'negative purpose': this assumes the breakdown of the partnership between employer and employee, and seeks to provide evidence that may ultimately support a dismissal and help successfully defend any subsequent Tribunal case.

4.2 Disciplinary procedure

4.2.1 All disciplinary procedures must be recognisable, fair, accepted and adhered to. It is the charity management's right to formulate a policy; it is management's responsibility to make certain that everyone knows the procedure and to ensure that it is adhered to at all times. Whereas ETs rarely criticise the wording of disciplinary procedures, they can be highly critical of employers failing to abide by their own procedures. Indeed, this has on many occasions created 'a procedurally unfair dismissal'.

4.2.2 If an employee has, or is reported to have, infringed the methods or rules of work or behaviour, the problem (the facts having been established) needs to be discussed with them to ensure the report is accurate and to discover any reasons for such action, and then (if applicable) to provide guidance as to the correct behaviour.

4.2.3 Many disciplinary matters can be dealt with informally by the immediate superior by way of few words to put the employee straight on their transgression – in short, an 'informal nudge'. Such an approach can be far more effective in terms of creating awareness of the required behaviour than the formal disciplinary proceedings If, however, such informal 'nudges' need constant repeating, a note of such verbal warnings should be made in the employee's personnel file, with a copy given to the employee.

4.2.4 For serious offences or where there has been repetition of minor transgressions (probably already the subject of informal warnings, with an indication of a sanction) there will be a need to use the formal warning procedure. The form this procedure might take should be outlined in a formal disciplinary policy.

4.2.5 The ACAS Code of Practice is the standard against which employers' disciplinary and dismissal procedures are measured. The Code provides that disciplinary procedures should:

- be in writing;
- be non-discriminatory;
- provide for matters to be dealt with speedily;
- allow for information to be kept confidential;
- tell employees what disciplinary action might be taken;
- say what levels of management have the authority to take the various forms of disciplinary action;
- require employees to be informed of the complaints against them, and supporting evidence, before a disciplinary meeting;
- give employees a chance to have their say before management reaches a decision;
- provide employees with the right to be accompanied;
- provide that no employee is dismissed for a first breach of discipline, except in cases of gross misconduct;
- require management to investigate fully before any disciplinary action is taken;
- ensure that employees are given an explanation for any sanction and allow employees to appeal against a decision; and
- apply to all employees, irrespective of their length of service, status or, say, if there are different rules for different groups.

4.3 Hearings

4.3.1 Regardless of the severity of the offence or potential sanction, a meeting to discuss it must be conducted in an open and positive manner, and in accordance with the rules of natural justice. Even if the employee has admitted the offence, a hearing must be held. Hearings should be held at a mutually convenient time, preferably in the subject's working hours, and should ideally be conducted by an impartial 'adjudicator' listening to both sides of the argument and to any witnesses, giving both parties every opportunity to ask questions of the other and of any witnesses, and to make any points in support or rebuttal. It may be preferable (other than in the smallest organisation) that the person chairing the hearing is not the person making the employer's case.

4.3.2 Once both parties have finished, the adjudicator will need to come to a decision. This does not necessarily need to be announced immediately; it may be preferable with complicated complaints to allow time for reflection, and/or possible further independent investigation by the adjudicator. If the complaint is serious, it may be preferable to suspend the employee on full pay pending the decision, which, irrespective of the seriousness, should be made known as swiftly as possible.

4.4 Record

4.4.1 Full notes of the hearing should be made by an independent person, with transcripts made available to both employee and supervisor/manager, and an opportunity for anyone disagreeing with the transcript to challenge and, with the agreement of the adjudicator and the other party, correct the record. In the event of disagreement, the adjudicator will need to decide the correct content. The notes or tape recording of the hearing should state the approval/objection/correction process in their conclusion. The original notes (even if transcribed) should be preserved carefully.

4.5 Right to be accompanied

4.5.1 The Employment Relations Act (ERelA) grants a right to representation 'where [the hearing] could result in the employer administering a formal warning to a worker or taking some other action in respect of him or her'. Good industrial practice suggests that to ensure that justice is seen to be done as well as being done, the employee should have the opportunity of being accompanied by a representative. The ERelA also requires representation at a grievance hearing which 'concerns the performance of a duty by the employer to a worker' – although again it may be safer (and easier to administer) if such representation is allowed on all occasions. Finally, an employee has a right to be accompanied at an interview at which an employee is made redundant even though this is not a disciplinary interview.

4.6 Procedure

4.6.1 If any challenge to the fairness of the hearing is to be defeated, it is essential that it is run in accordance with the principles of natural justice. A full record should be made. It is vital that a comprehensive and accurate record is taken – verbatim if possible – so that this exists in the event of a subsequent challenge to the fairness of the procedure and that any decision is capable of being shown to be 'reasonable'. A comprehensive 'fair version' of the notes made should be typed up immediately after the hearing. Use of a synopsis is to be avoided since its composition will almost certainly entail a certain degree of subjectivity. The original notes should be preserved safely in case of challenge.

4.7 Sanctions

4.7.1 Warnings: assuming the case has been proved, the adjudicator needs not only to record this, but also to decide on and initiate appropriate sanctions. This will normally take the form of a written warning, usually requiring the employee to desist from unacceptable behaviour, or to comply with rules and procedures previously transgressed. If the employee has already been given a warning for the same offence this may (depending on the organisation's procedure) be classified as a final warning.

4.7.2 Warnings may specify a requirement of action (or inaction) within a certain time – for example, a persistent latecomer (already in receipt of a first warning, which seems to have had no effect) might be given a final warning specifying that if he is late a further twice in the next month, he will be dismissed. Any penalties specified should be commensurate with the offence.

4.7.3 Demotion: as an alternative to dismissal (see below), demotion is an option, but caution needs to be exercised, particularly where this will involve a reduction in pay or benefits. If demotion is to be considered, then the choice between demotion and dismissal must be given to the employee and a note of this made in the written record of the interview unless demotion is allowed as a sanction in the organisation's procedure. If this is not the case, the employee should be asked to sign a statement agreeing to the demotion and to a reduction in pay from a future date.

4.7.4 Suspension: during investigation of an alleged offence it may be helpful to suspend the subject employee on pay. Only if the right to suspend without pay is included in the contract documentation should this be used as a sanction unless specifically agreed to by the employee without any duress.

4.7.5 Dismissal: it is often overlooked that recruiting, inducting and coaching an employee in the principles and practices of a particular employer are extremely costly and the dismissal of any employee effectively means that all such costs of their time and those involved are written off. The current regime of employee rights is such that many reasons for dismissal can be challenged and, if found wanting, prove very costly to the employer, in terms of the awards made to past employees and the loss of time spent defending actions.

4.7.6 The decision to dismiss should therefore only be taken after four checks:
(1) as a last resort;
(2) after calm consideration, and reconsideration, of the events which led to the decision;
(3) after checking that the whole process is in accordance with the procedure laid down; and
(4) (if in any doubt) after taking legal advice.

4.7.7 There are now six fair reasons for dismissing an employee:
(1) redundancy;
(2) lack of capability or qualifications;
(3) unacceptable conduct;
(4) where continued employment would breach legislation;
(5) some other substantial reason (SOSR), which could include (for example) the refusal by an employee to accept a necessary change in shift pattern; and

(6) enforcing retirement at 65 or later provided the statutory procedure has been followed.

4.7.8 In addition to clearly identifying under which heading a proposed dismissal should be classified, the employer must also follow four principles:

(1) follow procedure;
(2) act reasonably;
(3) give the employee a chance to explain and (if a question of capability) improve; and
(4) provide an opportunity to appeal.

4.7.9 Except where summary dismissal seems to be warranted, the occasions for which are relatively rare, most dismissals tend to follow the exhaustion of the process of the disciplinary procedure, i.e. all the steps have been taken and the last option reached. It is important when considering dismissal as a sanction that the person required to make the decision reviews what has gone before to ensure this is the case.

4.8 Summary dismissal

4.8.1 Since even in the most extreme situation employees should be given a chance to explain themselves, in the true sense of the words there should be no such thing as 'instant' dismissal. If the circumstances of the offence or incident go to the heart of the contract and make the continuation of the employer/employee relationship impossible:

- the employee should be asked for an explanation; and
- representation should be offered for a hearing; which
- could take place reasonably quickly and, if the accusations are sound, and there is no defence;
- a decision to dismiss without notice could be taken.

4.8.2 However, rather than making such an instant decision, particularly in the heat of the moment, it may be safer to suspend the employee (with pay) for 24 hours to provide time for reconsideration of the circumstances, make investigations and take account of any background, etc.

4.9 Appeals

4.9.1 Regardless of the circumstances, everyone should have a right of appeal. As already noted, it may be advisable to use a very simple and unconditional appeal clause or even to use the employer's grievance procedure (the provision of which is also a requirement of the EA). Making the appeal clause unconditional may result in the employer hearing a number of worthless appeals, but a rejection of a request for an appeal may create a procedurally unfair dismissal.

4.10 Grievance procedure

4.10.1 An essential part of the disciplinary procedure should be a means by which the employee can request someone other than those previously involved to review the decision taken. Whilst such an appeal may be made by using a dedicated dismissal procedure, employees may be referred to the grievance procedure. This should be made available for every instance when an employee feels aggrieved that their point of view or interest has not at least been listened to by someone – particularly by their immediate superior. In this way not only can the employee's voice be heard, but also it can provide a defence against harassment, victimisation and bullying, prejudicial behaviour, favouritism and bias, and be seen as an important aspect of the employer's commitment to equal opportunities.

4.10.2 The requirement for a statutory grievance procedure that was introduced in 2004 was repealed in April 2009. Nonetheless it is very important for an employer to have a grievance procedure to enable employees' grievances to be heard within a structured framework.

4.10.3 The principles of a grievance procedure are that it should provide details of:

- how to notify the concern, or, if it arises from the application of the disciplinary procedure, the appeal;
- whom to appeal to and, should the appeal be rejected, details of the next and any further stages;
- time limits that apply regarding each decision; and
- how decisions are to be communicated.

4.10.4 It is usual to introduce the grievance policy with words such as those shown below:

◆ 4.10.5 Sample wording grievance policy

Grievance policy

[The organisation] believes that grievances should be settled as quickly as possible. If you have a grievance, you should discuss it first with your immediate superior. Every effort should be made to resolve the grievance at this stage.

Your superior will deal with the matter within three working days (either verbally or in writing).

If you are not satisfied with your superior's decision, you may make an appeal to the next tier of manager. Again, a decision will be given within three working days.

Finally, you have a right of appeal to [a Trustee or the Chairman], whose decision will be final and will be given as soon as practically possible.

At all meetings you have the right (if you wish) to be accompanied by a colleague or trade union representative.

> If the subject of the grievance is discrimination or harassment which involves the employee's own superior, then application for a hearing under this policy may be made to [name – for example, Personnel Manager] who will then conduct the matter on behalf of the employee. As far as possible in these circumstances the anonymity of the employee should be protected.

4.11 Constructive dismissal

4.11.1 This is the action by which an employee brings the employment relationship to an end because the employer has carried out an act (or failed to carry out a promised act) which is fundamental to the continuance of the contract, or carries out a series of acts or inactions, the cumulative effect of which makes it untenable for the employee to remain. Although the employee resigns, this is regarded as a 'dismissal' forced by the employer's act (or inactions).

4.11.1 In a constructive dismissal situation, an employee 'dismisses himself' on the grounds that:

- certain behaviour or an action on the part of his employer makes it impossible for him to continue in employment. That is, such a one-off action on the part of the employer goes to the heart of the contract and is thus a fundamental breach of it; or
- one particular act, the last in a series of such acts, is the 'last straw' and makes continued working for the employer untenable. If the action(s) complained of is (are) unfair, it will be an unfair constructive dismissal and the employee will be entitled to compensation in exactly the same way as an employee who has been unfairly dismissed by their employer; and
- all organisations are constantly changing and decisions need to be taken which alter the status quo. Not everyone will like the changes but just because an employee does not like the changes which affect him does not give him the right to resign and claim constructive dismissal.

4.12 Redundancy

4.12.1 Redundancy is circumscribed by a number of legal requirements. Making an employee redundant is a 'dismissal' and if the decision is improper in any way, the dismissal is covered by the 'unfair dismissal' penalties.

4.12.2 Dismissal for redundancy is unlike any other because it results from an occurrence that is entirely beyond the control of the employee – a facet of redundancy which should not be forgotten by those responsible for administering the process.

4.13 Proving a genuine redundancy

4.13.1 If challenged in a tribunal, an employer will need to prove that there was a genuine redundancy. Thus figures drawn from management accounts, order book, etc. demonstrating the downturn will be required. Copies may be provided, but the originals should be available. The employer must also be able show that during consultation the reasons for the redundancy were discussed.

4.13.2 The ERA defines redundancy as:

(a) the employer ceasing or intending to cease:
  i. to carry on the business for the purposes of which the employee was employed by him;
  ii. to carry on that business in the place where the employee was so employed; or
(b) the requirements of the business:
  i. for employees to carry out work of a particular kind; or
  ii. for employees to carry out work of a particular kind in the place where the employee was employed by the employer have ceased or diminished or are expected to cease or diminish.

4.14 Determining the correct staffing levels

4.14.1 When management becomes aware of a reduction in funding or a reduced need for its services, they need to assess how that reduction will impact on the number of hours worked by affected employees and to establish whether they require to reduce the hours worked by employees or reduce the number of employees they have.

4.15 The procedure

4.15.1 Making an employee redundant is a dismissal and, as with all dismissals, following the correct procedure is essential if a fair dismissal is to be created and the penalties for an unfair dismissal avoided. The following checklist should provide such a procedure provided the steps are taken in the order shown.

> ✓ **4.15.2 Redundancy procedure checklist**
>
> 1. Explain the reasons for the potential redundancies.
> 2. Determine the (provable) excess of working hours/employees (see above).
> 3. Consult about the situation:
>   a. ask for comments/alternatives/suggestions, or make a presentation identifying the alternatives, showing why these cannot be used; and
>   b. ask for suggestions on selection criteria if terminations are needed.

4. Consider these suggestions and alternatives.
5. If some of these suggestions or alternatives can be used, say so and reassess the organisation's requirements after these have been taken into account.
6. If the suggestions or alternatives are not feasible, give reasons for not using them.
7. Decide on the hours/days/numbers to be lost.
8. Identify the pool (the particular area or the whole organisation) from which the number to be made redundant is to be drawn.
9. Ask for volunteers.
10. Identify those to be made redundant, ideally using totally objective criteria.
11. Inform those affected (allowing them to be accompanied if requested) giving notice under contract, details of redundancy payments and right of appeal.
12. Advise any vacancies and oversee trial periods.
13. Consider outplacement.
14. Deal with queries and appeals.
15. Check the calculations again (particularly those undertaking trial periods).
16. Arrange for the provision of references.

4.15.3 The dismissal of the employee on the grounds of redundancy should take place after meaningful consultation. The employee should be invited to the dismissal hearing and given the right to be accompanied by a work colleague or trade union representative. Where the employee has been selected from a pool of employees his/her score under the selection procedure should have been discussed prior to the final dismissal meeting.

4.16 Consultation

4.16.1 Current legislation requires employers to consult with elected representatives of their workforce if 20 or more are to be declared redundant within a period of 90 days. If fewer redundancies are expected, consultation should take place with individuals and, even where there has been consultation with elected representatives, there should also be consultation on an individual basis as well. Ideally, consultation should take place before 'bodies required to be lost' have been identified. Representatives should be told the situation and asked if they have any suggestions. Tribunals repeatedly stress how important it is for employers to consult with their employees. Several employers have lost unfair dismissal cases when making employees redundant, not because the redundancy decision was flawed, but because they failed to consult with elected representatives of employees when the question of redundancies was first considered.

4.16.2 When consulting, those involved should be given a short period (e.g. four or five days) to consider the situation and make any suggestions. There is no need for management to accept any suggestions, they are simply required to consult (not negotiate). Obviously, sensible suggestions should be considered, but even then may have to be rejected for business reasons.

4.17 Selection for redundancy

4.17.1 The manner of selection of those to be made redundant should be another facet of consultation. The basis of selection should be objective rather than subjective, and be based on facts available at the time of assessment.

4.17.2 Individuals selected should be told and given the opportunity for further consultation – for example, if they have had any alternative ideas or possibly wish to be considered for another job if there are any vacancies.

4.17.3 No one should be made redundant without being given the opportunity to ask to be considered for vacancies in the organisation. If they do wish to be considered and are thought potentially suitable, they should be given (say) a month's trial period. If successful, a new (continuous) contract should be issued. If unsuccessful, the original redundancy situation must be resumed.

4.18 Notice

4.18.1 Once the selection has been made, a notice of termination of employment on grounds of redundancy should be issued. This should state the leaving date and give the amount of notice required under the contract or one week for each year of service to a maximum of 12 weeks as required by law, whichever is the longer.

4.18.2 If the required period of notice cannot be given (because the period to the required termination date is too short) then a payment in lieu of notice (PILON) must be paid in respect of the amount of notice required that has not been given.

4.18.3 During the notice period an employee is entitled to all benefits under the contract. If a PILON is made then the cash equivalent of the benefits should be agreed between the parties and paid.

4.19 State redundancy pay

4.19.1 Where an employee has worked for an employer for more than two years, the employee becomes eligible for state redundancy pay in the event of redundancy. The statutory redundancy rate is currently capped at £380 (October 2009).

This is reviewed annually. The statutory redundancy scheme works on the basis of the employee's age and length of service.

- Employees up to and including the age of 21 receive 0.5 week's pay for each completed year of service.
- Employees aged 22 to 40 receive 1.0 week's pay for each completed year of service.
- Employees aged 41 and above receive 1.5 weeks' pay for each year of service.

4.19.2 The maximum number of weeks payable under the statutory redundancy scheme is 30.

5 Health and safety

5.1 Charities, like other organisations, are required to take reasonable precautions to ensure the safety of those for whom they are responsible: their employees, volunteers and visitors to their premises. Thus, the charity can be held liable for compensation to those injured at work, or as a result of their work or activities.

5.2 Although a considerable number of later regulations exist covering, for example, display screens, manual handling, etc., the current legal framework derives from the implementation of the Health and Safety at Work, etc. Act 1974 (HASAWA), which, despite its age, has stood the test of time.

5.3 Two of the prime responsibilities under the Act are:

- For employers to provide a safe place of work for their employees. These days this is taken to mean the provision, as far as reasonably practical, of safety from harassment, bullying and discrimination as much as safety from physical harm.
- For employees to take reasonable care of themselves and their colleagues.

5.4 The legislation places a wide-ranging and onerous responsibility on every employer, and implementation needs to be made the responsibility of a senior, even board-level, manager in the organisation. A competent person from within the charity (or an outside consultant) could be given responsibility for carrying out safety and risk assessments. Competency is judged on training, experience and knowledge of the workplace/process. Since such assessments are individual to each location, brief reference only has been made to this part of the requirements. However, it must be noted that the legislation requires detailed and ongoing assessments of risk to be made at each location. In addition, all organisations with five or more employees are required to prepare and display their policy statement regarding health and safety matters. A number of initiatives (see below) suggest that HASAWA may well be extensively revised and re-enacted soon. Anticipating such a move, the Health and Safety Commission (HSC) Executive published a consultative document, which is intended to lead to a Code on Health and Safety Responsibilities of Directors. This suggests that trustees should:

5.4.1 Ensure they understand their personal legal liability and responsibility. Every organisation must have a defined safety management plan as set out in the HSC's 'Successful Health and Safety Management' and also in the British Standard BS8 800. In addition, the high-level responsibilities of trustees and senior executives should be stated in the safety policy, as suggested in the Code. Boards of trustees should consider the requirements to report publicly on their organisation's record on health and safety, including accident and enforcement data. They should also consider if there are breaches of the requirements and, if so, identify action to be taken – and ensure it is taken.

5.4.2 Collectively and individually accept 'publicly' their collective role in providing health and safety leadership in their charity. This entails the trustees and senior executives undergoing training in safety management and risk prevention.

5.4.3 Ensure board of trustees decisions reflect these health and safety intentions as set out in their charity's health and safety policy. This may include not simply analysing the effect of and eradication of occurrences that caused accidents, but also identifying and recording details of near-misses, learning from them and making adjustments to try to prevent a repetition.

5.4.4 Consult employees and volunteers on matters of health and safety. Engaging them in the identification of hazards (see below) should not only assist in eradicating or minimising such hazards, but also comply with this requirement – at least in part.

5.4.5 Appoint one of their number to be responsible for health and safety and the promotion of such matters. Currently, successful cases usually result in fines but may increasingly result in the imprisonment of those responsible. A board appointment (with the personal responsibility that entails) may be the real way in which safety in the workplace is given the priority it needs.

5.5 Risk assessments

5.5.1 Safety
Inherent in the guidance set out above and in the increasing legislative requirements is a duty on the employer to carry out assessment in the workplace. A risk assessment:

- seeks to identify all the hazards posed in a particular situation;
- considers ways in which, if possible, hazards can be minimised or eradicated;
- identifies who it is that is at risk;
- evaluates the risk, the likelihood of occurrence and the number exposed to the risk, the severity of injury and the existing control measures;
- decides on any necessary new control measures to reduce or eliminate the risk;
- implements the controls and monitors their effectiveness;
- records the assessment and brings it to the attention of those affected; and
- sets a timetable within which the situation will be re-assessed or reviewed.

5.5.2 Some risks cannot be removed or even minimised, and the requirement to construct assessments recognises this. What is required is that risks are identified, and where possible removed or restricted. Where this is impossible they must be brought to the attention of all likely to use the area and suitable advice provided. In addition, employers should consider the competency of those likely to be at risk and take note where skills, experience, etc. are not felt sufficient to deal with the risk and make suitable arrangements to protect those at risk. Risk assessments should be prepared throughout the operation and made available in written form, although this would not prevent an employer being held liable if a risk could have been minimised or removed and was not, or suitable preventative measures which could easily have been implemented were not present.

5.6 Pregnancy

5.6.1 Risk assessments are required in all situations where there could be risk to an employee (or any other person using the workplace). One area where there is particular concern relates to pregnant women in the workplace where there is a duty of care not just to the employee but also to her unborn child. Since 1999 employers have been required to conduct a risk assessment detailing the dangers to pregnant women and their unborn babies, and to new mothers (those who have given birth within the previous six months) caused by the workplace (requirement of the Management of Health and Safety at Work Regulations 1999 (MoH & SaWR). The Equal Opportunities Commission noted that in 2001 there were 1,387 maternity-related discrimination claims regarding breaches of health and safety legislation (96 per cent of the discrimination claims). The average compensation claim paid was £9,871. Failure to have a risk assessment available to employees who are pregnant and/or new mothers breaches the above regulations (and the employer is liable) and is tantamount to sex discrimination, as the EAT commented in its ruling in the *Day v T Pickles Farms* case.

5.6.2 The dangers

The HSE identifies a number of main and general risks to pregnant women in the workplace. These should be taken as guidance only since the risk assessment of each workplace will be different. In addition, each employer should identify the particular risks related to their own operation. The risks include:

- working with dangerous substances;
- violent or stressful environments;
- lifting;
- confined working space; and
- using an unsuitable workstation.

During the time she continues working, a pregnant woman has a right to:

- have the risks removed, or, if this is impossible;
- have her work location moved, or, if this is impossible;
- work on other tasks (without any detriment regarding salient features of her contract – hours, pay, benefits, etc.), or, if this is impossible;
- be suspended on full pay until such time as her maternity leave commences.

5.7 Safety policy

5.7.1 Although the requirement on employers to have and maintain a safety policy is an obligation under HASAWA, a surprising number of employers do not have one. Should there be an accident, such an omission could lead to personal fines on or imprisonment of those responsible.

5.7.2 Employers must report accidents as required under the Reporting of Injuries, Deaths and Dangerous Occurrences Regulations (RIDDOR) using the HSC Incident Contact Centre (HSCICC). The obligation is to report deaths, major injuries (that is, where an accident results in the employee being away from work for three days or more) and work-related diseases and dangerous occurrences which could have resulted in a reportable injury.

5.8 On-site data

5.8.1 Safety folder. A copy of the safety policy should be given to every employee. It provides a prompt for action and a criterion for guidance. It may also be feasible and advisable to post in every place of work (and on every floor where there is multi-floor occupation) a readily identifiable and visible folder in which a number of forms are kept, including hazard reporting forms. The visible sheet of such a folder could include a checklist of items demonstrating when each was last checked (e.g. fire evacuation, equipment inspection dates, etc.) so that employees' views can operate as a reminder if it is too long, for example, since the last time there was a fire drill.

5.8.2 Hazard reporting. A supply of hazard reporting forms can be included in the safety folder. The principle behind this is that the sooner the organisation knows of a hazard, the better the chance of avoiding injury by being able to effect remedial work.

5.9 The Health and Safety Executive (HSE)

5.9.1 The Health and Safety Executive (HSE) is the government body charged with promoting and policing safety in the workplace. It provides details of the criteria to be used to decide which injury or other complaints should be investigated and detailed guidelines regarding initiating prosecutions where:

- death resulted from a legislative breach;
- the situation is grave or the general record of the offender requires it;
- there has been a repetition of breaches;
- non-compliant work has been carried out without a licence;
- there has been a failure to comply with an improvement or prohibition order;
- a breach subject to a caution has been repeated;
- false information has been provided and/or there has been an intent to deceive; and
- inspectors have been deliberately obstructed.

5.9.2 In future prosecutions are to be recommended *inter alia* where:

- it is appropriate in order to draw attention to the need for legal compliance;
- a breach has continued despite repeated warnings.

5.10 First aid

5.10.1 First aid can be defined as instant action carried out by (normally) untrained persons in order to preserve life, pending attendance by a trained medical practitioner. As well as a need to provide instant assistance in the event of injury, etc., under Reporting of Injuries, Diseases and Dangerous Occurrences Regulations 1995 (RIDDOR), employers are also required to notify the appropriate authorities of all reportable incidents affecting everyone on their sites, whether employed or visiting. These regulations require employers to report acts of non-consensual physical violence (e.g. so-called 'skylarking' or pranks of a physical nature) done to a person at work.

5.10.2 The Health & Safety (First Aid at Work) Regulations 1981 (and the approved code of practice and guidance issued in 1997) sets out detailed requirements placed on an employer regarding the provision of first aid facilities, as follows:

- Provide suitable first aid staff and services in accordance with the nature of the business, the degree of danger or hazard in the operations, the number of employees and the proximity to medical assistance. A first aider is defined as someone who holds a current certificate in first aid.

- If there are 400 or more employed at a single site, an employer will normally be required to provide a first aid room, but again its provision will depend on the assessment of the hazards.
- Provide properly stocked first aid boxes.

5.10.3 It may help if the organisation adopts a first aid policy that reflects its commitment to and administration of first aid. Legally, employers are required to enter details of all accidents at work in an accident book. Since this means that personal details of employees are included in the record, the provisions of the DPA must be observed and revised editions of such a book which conceal such personal data are now available.

5.11 Fire precautions

5.11.1 Unless they have been involved in a fire, most people on hearing a fire alarm seem overcome by inertia. To ensure prompt evacuation this must be overcome. This can be achieved by means of constant practice, so that on hearing the alarm the automatic response is to move rather than freeze. Such movement may need to be hastened by specially appointed employees acting as fire marshals (with deputies, to cover absences). Regular fire alarm tests and even fire drills (which are now mandatory in some cases) should be held.

5.11.2 The Regulatory Reform (Fire Safety) Order 2005 came into effect in October 2006. Although it revokes the 1997 Regulations (see below), most of the requirements are restated, with the important change that no longer will Fire Certificates be issued.

5.11.3 The previous requirement to react to the advice of the fire officer, and obtaining guidance and clearance by the issue of such a certificate, has now been replaced by a requirement to be completely proactive particularly regarding the preparation of (and regularly updating of) risk assessments.

5.11.4 Such assessments must be carried out by a 'responsible person' (RP). If the workplace is under the control of the employer the RP is the employer; but if the workplace is under another person's control, the RP could be the owner. Thus where a property is in a multi-occupation, in each of the 'suites' or areas occupied by individual employers, they are the RP for their own area. However, the RP for the 'common areas' would probably be the landlord.

5.11.5 Enforcement is carried out by Fire Safety Inspectors (appointed by the local fire and rescue authority), although in some circumstances (e.g. where the subject location is a construction site) enforcement is under the control of the HSE, or (where the location is a sports centre) the local authority. Failure to comply with requirements issued by an enforcement authority can lead to a fine of £20,000 or, on conviction, to an unlimited fine and/or two years imprisonment.

5.12 Stress

5.12.1 Stress in the workplace is a very real problem as it can lead to long-term illness and absence and subsequent employment claims against employers who are believed responsible for placing employees in unacceptably stressful situations. The 2007 Psychosocial Working Conditions (PWC) survey indicated that around 13.6 per cent of all working individuals thought their job was very or extremely stressful. Charities should therefore take the following precautions try to ensure that they avoid stress claims:

(a) Stay aware of the developing situation (see below).
(b) Have a policy and procedure in place.
(c) Ensure all managers are proactive in watching for signs of stress.
(d) Emphasise that if there is a suspicion of stress, action must be taken.
(e) Inform all employees that the organisation wishes to know if and when any employee is subject to stress.
(f) Investigate fully all claims of stress, referring cases to expert advice and counselling.
(g) Ensure that a person who has suffered stress is not, on recovery, placed in a similarly stressful position.
(h) To be able to hold the employer liable for stress an employee must be able to prove:
   i. there was a breach of the employer's common law obligation to provide a safe working environment; and
   ii. there was medical evidence demonstrating that the condition was stress-related and the stress was linked to the working environment; and
   iii. the employer was in some way negligent in that the condition was foreseeable and yet the employer did nothing about it.

5.12.2 To some extent the exposure of employers has been alleviated as a result of a ground-breaking decision in which the Court of Appeal reversed the bias in favour of employees who claim to be suffering from work-induced stress. The Court listed 12 items of advice, of which three are given here.

(1) Employers are entitled to take at face value what they are told by their employees and do not need to make searching enquiries. Presumably, therefore, if the employer suspected an employee was under stress but the employee stated they were not, the employer would be able to accept that answer without further enquiry, although even then it might be advisable to take medical advice on the matter.

(2) Employers are entitled to assume that an employee will be able to withstand the normal pressures of the job unless they know of a particular problem. Again it might be advisable to investigate further, with medical advice if appropriate, if there is any suspicion that the employee is under stress.
(3) Any employer who offers a confidential counselling service with access to treatment is unlikely to be held liable in the event of a stress claim.

5.12.3 The adverse decision of the Court of Appeal in one case was overturned by the House of Lords and thus the above advice should be used with caution.

5.12.4 The new HSE 'Management Standards for Stress', developed after a consultation process with public and private sector organisations, states that there are six main areas of investigation and an employer should be able to resist a stress claim if 85 per cent or more employees state that Demands, Control and Support criteria are met, and 65 per cent or more state Relationships, Role and Change criteria are met.

(1) **Demands:** employees should be given adequate and achievable demands related to hours worked. Skills and abilities should be matched to job demands and the latter should be within an employee's capability.
(2) **Control:** employees should be permitted control over their pace of work and when they can take breaks. Employers should encourage employees to develop their skills and to undertake new challenges. Employees should be consulted concerning working patterns.
(3) **Support:** there should be clear policies and procedures to support employees adequately. Managers must support their team members and every employee should support each of their colleagues. Employees should know what support is available and how to access it.
(4) **Role:** employers should provide employees with clear information so that they can understand their role and responsibilities. There should be systems allowing employees to raise concerns about uncertainties and conflicts.
(5) **Relationships:** positive behaviour should be promoted in the working environment to avoid conflict and ensure fairness. There should be procedures to outlaw and prevent unacceptable behaviour. Employees should be encouraged to share information about their work.
(6) **Change:** the employer should provide information to employees concerning all change likely to affect them. There should be adequate consultation and a process whereby employees can influence proposals. Timetables for change should be published and employees should have access to support during the change process.

5.12.5 As in all areas where safety and health are at risk, risk assessment is advisable.

5.13 Driving requirements

5.13.1 The Corporate Manslaughter Act makes it easier for the authorities to prosecute for death caused by negligence, which could include requiring employees to drive for too long a time without a break. It is estimated that around 300 people are killed each year as a result of drivers falling asleep at the wheel or driving a car with defects.

5.13.2 Charities should therefore carry out basic checks – ensuring there is an MOT certificate, that the vehicle is insured for business use and that the driver has a valid driving licence and take steps to ensure that their staff are not asked to drive for unreasonably long periods of time.

5.13.3 The use of Vehicle Folders (required to be carried at all times on cars used for a charity's business) may become essential as a means of proving that the employer took their responsibilities seriously and took 'reasonable' precautions to ensure that vehicles being driven on their behalf (and the drivers) were legally compliant in all respects.

5.13.4 The question of using mobile phones in cars should be considered – forcing employees to have a phone switched on when driving could result in some liability being placed on an employer even if it is a 'hands-free' system. In addition, driving licences should be required on appointment and inspected yearly thereafter (since it is possible for an employee to lose the right to drive and not to have declared this to his/her employer). Employees should also be required to confirm that the licence displayed is the only UK licence they have. Insurers could refuse to indemnify the company for damage, etc. if an unlicensed driver has an accident.

5.14 Bullying

5.14.1 Charities have an obligation to provide a safe place of work. This obligation is not only restricted to ensuring that procedures, processes and buildings are safe, but also to ensuring safe interaction between employees and between employees and third parties. If bullying does take place in the workplace it must be stopped swiftly.

5.15 Corporate killing

5.15.1 Since 1980 over 3,000 people have been killed in work-based accidents in the UK. Many more people have been seriously injured and/or permanently incapacitated as a result of accidents at work. In all that time despite 'corporate manslaughter' legislation being available, there have only been a few successful prosecutions under this legislation. Ironically, it is claimed to be easier to bring a successful charge against directors and managers of small companies (which tend to have less serious accidents) than those responsible in large companies, as a result of whose operations most of the high-profile accidents – which tend to involve large numbers of people – occur.

5.15.1 The Corporate Manslaughter (Corporate Homicide in Scotland) Act came into effect in April 2008. In the event of a death, a company/employer will be held to be guilty if:

- the way in which its activities were organised amounted to a gross breach of a duty of care owed by it to the deceased; and
- it causes the death of the deceased; and/or
- the way in which its activities are managed or organised by its senior management is a substantial element in the breach.

5.15.2 Sanctions include unlimited fines (and even imprisonment), a requirement to remedy a failing and a requirement for the company to publicise the offence (i.e. to name and shame).

5.15.3 The government is on record as saying that employers have no fear of prosecution under the new Act where they have 'conscientiously':

- ensured safe working practices (i.e. employees are trained and equipment is safely maintained);
- maintained premises safely (e.g. taken adequate fire precautions); and
- complied with health and safety legislation.

5.15.4 Prudently one might add: and provided also that the employer can *prove* that they have 'ensured ..., maintained ..., and complied ...'! (Using safety folders displayed in every workplace may be one way of assisting in the provision of safe working practices, whilst also protecting the personal position of those in charge.)

5.15.5 The thrust of this anticipated legislation is to make those ultimately responsible for death and/or injury accountable for their actions (or inactions). This summarises the requirement in safety matters that have been developing since the early 1990s, i.e. that employers must take positive steps to create as safe as possible an environment within which they require their employees to work.

D2
Fundraising and trading

1 Fundraising

1.1 Introduction

1.1.1 Some organisations, such as grant-making trusts with extensive endowments, are in the fortunate position of not having to raise funds to continue their work, but for most charities fundraising is crucial to their ongoing viability. Trustees and staff with responsibility for the financial health of their charity must ensure that it has adequate resources to deliver its objectives while also ensuring that it complies with the law and must consider the effect of the fundraising activity on the reputation of the charity.

1.1.2 In this chapter, we will look at important aspects of fundraising, including developing the charity's strategy and ensuring that its fundraising activities stay within the law. However, this chapter will not include advice on how to raise money or on different fundraising approaches.

1.2 Recent changes

1.2.1 It is important that everyone involved in fundraising keeps up to date with the most recent legislation and best practice.

1.2.2 The Charities Act 2006 brought in new requirements for professional fundraisers and commercial participators (see below) and contains provisions that will, when they come into force, which may be in the next few years, change the way public collections are regulated.

1.2.3 The Charities Act 2006 also gave Parliament the power to regulate fundraising if self-regulation by charities was not effective. The Fundraising Standards Board (FRSB) was established by a number of third-sector organisations in 2006 to promote the self-regulation of fundraising by charities. Charities are recommended to join FRSB to demonstrate their commitment to good fundraising practice.

1.2.4 The Gambling Act 2005 changed the rules governing how lotteries must be run. More information on lotteries is set out below but any charities wishing to run lotteries should consult the Gambling Commission guidance for detailed information.

1.3 Developing the fundraising strategy

1.3.1 Fundraising is an integral part of the overall strategy of a charity and is closely connected with business planning, budget setting and investment. Trustees and key staff must determine how much money they need to run the charity's existing activities and to establish new ones. Within this global figure, the different sources of income should be identified and this information will form the foundation of the fundraising strategy. In this section, we will consider the areas to cover when developing a fundraising strategy. An action plan that can be used to draft a charity's strategy is included at the end of this section.

1.4 Where is the money coming from?

1.4.1 Relying on a single source of income tends to make an organisation vulnerable and could compromise its independence. For example, historically many local charities have been largely or entirely financed by local authority grants and so have been highly vulnerable to funding cuts. In 2007 many charities suffered following cuts in EU funding. Charities should be aware of provisions in funding agreements that allow funders to terminate the contract earlier than anticipated and should bear in mind the possibility that an annual agreement that has been renewed for many years may be terminated in the future. Diversifying income sources offers charities a degree of protection, or at least some breathing space, should a particular income stream run dry.

1.4.2 Different areas of work may lend themselves naturally to certain sources of income, and some income streams may already be secure. For example, charities may already have a number of contracts or grants in place. Ongoing projects, such as the employment of a worker dedicated to a particular aspect of the charity's work (e.g. supporting a particular element of its client group), require continuing funding and are frequently funded by renewable grants or contracts. In contrast, activities that require expenditure over a relatively short period, such as extending a building or commissioning a piece of research, may be funded by one-off or short-term funding such as a specific grant or from the proceeds of an appeal. Fundraising events and street collections can be useful ways of raising unrestricted funds that can be used for any purpose within the organisation.

1.4.3 Ethical issues relating to fundraising should be considered. This may be covered by the charity's ethical investment policy. If the charity would not invest in tobacco companies, should it accept donations from them? Trustees may agree on wider restrictions, for example not to raise money through gambling or not to encourage events involving dangerous sports.

1.4.4 As always with ethical issues, trustees should ensure that any self-imposed restrictions on sources of fundraising income are in the best interests of the charity, either because of the risk of direct conflict with charitable objects or because of a likely negative impact on other funding streams.

1.4.5 The fundraising strategy may be divided into raising money for specific purposes and raising money for the general purposes of the charity. Many charities find it easier to raise funds for specific purposes, as corporate sponsors, grant makers and the public like to feel that they are supporting a specific project. As discussed below, such appeals should include a statement that funds raised from the appeal that cannot be spent on the purpose that was the subject of the appeal will be used for the general purposes of the charity. Where an appeal is held for a specific activity, charities should consider opening a separate bank account to hold funds raised through that appeal. Funds to finance the general activities and overheads of the charity may be raised through a variety of approaches, including general appeals, fundraising events, trading activities and legacy appeals.

1.5 Timescale

1.5.1 As well as identifying the amount of income required and potential sources of income, the fundraising strategy should include details of when funding is required, as it is no good raising money in two years' time for a project that is currently only funded for the next six months. By identifying what money is needed and when, trustees can prioritise the different elements of the fundraising strategy and create an action plan. In this way, the charity's fundraising strategy will be closely linked to its business plan. Timescales should also be set for individual appeals, indicating when the appeal will end. This makes for better appeal planning and facilitates clearer accounting of appeal funds.

1.6 'Joined-up thinking'

1.6.1 As well as linking into business planning, budgeting and the investment policy, the fundraising strategy should be consistent with any public relations approach agreed by the organisation, be complementary to operational work and be sympathetic with the organisation's objectives. For example, it may be considered inappropriate for a charity working to alleviate family poverty to raise funds through events involving gambling, such as race nights. Similarly, the message of a charity promoting the independence of its beneficiaries would be undermined by a fundraising campaign that sought to evoke pity for its beneficiaries from the public.

1.6.2 Studies have indicated that some members of the public resent street collections carried out by fundraisers known colloquially as 'chuggers', and trustees should balance the potential for triggering resentment among the public against the funds that might be raised through such methods. Charities should also ensure that any advertising campaign they carry out complies with the relevant advertising regulations.

1.7 Is it worth it?

1.7.1 The strategy should also consider the 'effort:reward' ratio. Will the anticipated benefit of the fundraising activity including the income raised and the publicity generated justify the resources, including time and money invested in carrying out the activity? By the use of innovative or particularly well-targeted fundraising methods, a relatively small investment of resources can reap great rewards. In contrast if a charity's fundraising strategy is not well planned or followed, the amount to be spent on major fundraising campaigns or the employment of specialist fundraising staff or consultants may not be justified by the benefits to the charity, such as the amount of money raised or publicity generated. For local charities, fundraising events can be a labour-intensive option but may only generate small financial rewards, although the collateral benefits of increased profile or user involvement may make such events worthwhile.

1.7.2 It is for the trustees to decide in each case whether the reward is sufficient to make the effort worthwhile. For example, is expenditure of £1,000 generating a total income of £1,500 and a net gain of £500 justifiable, or would the activity have to generate a net gain of £1,000 to be worthwhile?

1.7.3 Fundraisers should also question whether the anticipated outcome is a realistic prediction. Are estimated returns for a street collection, legacy appeal or other fundraising event based on guesswork, previous experience or some other factor? Are grant applications likely to be successful – for example, have the applications been targeted at those grant makers most likely to fund your type of organisation or project?

1.8 Reporting the costs

1.8.1 The amount of money spent on fundraising should be reported in the charity's annual accounts and in the Summary Information Report that charities with an annual income exceeding £1 million are required to submit to the Charity Commission each year. Some fundraising activities also serve as a means of promoting charitable objectives, for example by raising awareness of the charity's work and message.

1.9 Who is responsible?

1.9.1 The respective roles of trustees, staff and supporters should be considered as part of the fundraising strategy and reflected in the job descriptions of staff and trustees as fundraising is one of those areas of charity work that can easily fall through the gaps in clearly defined responsibilities of staff and trustees, particularly in small charities.

1.9.2 It should be clear who will take responsibility for the day-to-day tasks involved in fundraising, from rattling tins through to negotiating with grant-making bodies. If these tasks are to be delegated to a member of staff, the scope of the role should be explicitly described in the employee's job description, the skills and experience required should be an integral part of the person specification and everyone involved in the recruitment process should be conscious of the blend of skills that they are looking for and the balance between fundraising and other activities. For instance, it might be unrealistic to expect a worker who had been employed for their social care and counselling skills also to be an experienced fundraiser. It might also be unrealistic to expect the same worker to take a lead role in securing ongoing funding, without compromising an already full workload of providing client services. In such circumstances, the trustees have a clear responsibility to seek ongoing funding in order to sustain the charity, and they should take the lead in any relevant negotiations.

1.10 Fundraising strategy: action plan

1.10.1 Who is responsible?

Task	Who is responsible
Identify the most appropriate sources of funding.	Trustees and senior staff, including any fundraising staff.
Check that the proposed fundraising approach is consistent with the organisation's public image and operational concerns.	Trustees and senior staff, in consultation with operational staff and any PR personnel.
Agree a baseline in terms of the ratio of fundraising costs to fundraising income.	Trustees (particularly the treasurer), senior officer and senior finance officer.
Consider any legal restrictions or best practice issues relating to your preferred methods of fundraising.	Trustees with the advice and support of senior staff.

1.10.2 Even where fundraising is delegated to employees of the charity, the trustees continue to have the ultimate responsibility for the financial viability of the organisation. The appointment of professional fundraising staff does not absolve them of this responsibility; it merely allows them to delegate the fundraising task to people with appropriate skills and experience.

1.10.3 The fundraising of many local charities is led by volunteers. Whilst such volunteers are often extremely successful and hugely valuable to the charity, trustees have the overall responsibility for fundraising and must exercise authority over the actions of volunteers. This is frequently achieved through a fundraising sub-committee involving trustees and volunteers.

1.11 Rules and good practice

1.11.1 Trustees and fundraisers also need to be aware of the regulatory framework that surrounds fundraising activities. In addition to the information given below, the application of other legal requirements should also be considered. For example, information held on donors is subject to the provisions of the Data Protection Act 1998, and health and safety requirements should be complied with in relation to any fundraising events.

1.11.2 The focus of this section is on those fundraising activities that are most commonly used by small to medium-sized charities.

1.11.3 The regulation of fundraising activities has been reviewed and many changes will come into effect in the next few years. This section will set out current rules and outline future changes.

1.12 Street collections

1.12.1 A permit or licence is normally required for charity collections or sales taking place in the street or other public places. Under the current scheme, licences and permits can be obtained from the relevant local authority or, for collections in London, from the police or the City of London authorities.

1.12.2 Permits and licences are granted under local regulations. Issues that will be considered include obstructions to both human and vehicular traffic, financial controls and accounting arrangements for any funds raised through the collection and the frequency of collections (some high streets have street collections booked throughout the year, whilst other local authorities prefer to keep the number of collections down). Contact your local authority for information about the regulations in your area.

1.12.3 Pay particular attention to arrangements for public places that are privately owned, e.g. shopping centres and railway stations. Under provisions of the Charities Act 2006 that may come into force in the next few years, charities wishing to carry out collections in public places, including street collections, would, unless an exemption applied, require a public collections certificate issued by the Charity Commission and a permit granted by the relevant local authority.

1.13 Door-to-door collections

1.13.1 Door-to-door collections are also subject to licensing arrangements, again controlled by the local authority or, in London, the police or the City of London. The arrangements apply to charity sales and collections of money and goods from residential and business premises (including public houses). Exemptions from the licensing requirements are available from the Home Secretary for collections covering a wide area (i.e. a substantial part of the country). Exemptions are available from the police for local collections taking place over a short period of time.

1.13.2 It is good practice to collect cash donations from street and door-to-door collections in sealed collecting tins. This not only helps reduce the risk of theft from the collection, but also reassures donors that the risk of theft has been reduced.

1.13.3 Those collecting public donations should always wear visible identity cards establishing their connection with the charity and the legality of the collection.

1.13.4 Under provisions of the Charities Act 2006 that may come into force in the next few years charities wishing to carry out door-to-door collections will, unless an exemption applied, require a public collections certificate and must notify the local authority before the collection.

1.14 Events

1.14.1 Charities raise funds through a wide variety of events, from jumble sales and raffles through to high-profile auctions and expensive balls. Trustees need to research carefully any legal requirements relating to the events planned. The tax exemptions available for fundraising and trading are discussed in paragraph 6. Other issues include health and safety requirements (e.g. maximum capacity for venues used), insurance and specific regulations relating to the nature of the event, such as any licences required for gambling or the sale of alcohol.

1.15 Lotteries (including raffles)

1.15.1 Charities and their subsidiary companies may run lotteries to raise money for their charitable purposes. These are regulated by the Gambling Commission under the Gambling Act 2005. Charity lotteries fall into two categories:

(1) **Incidental lotteries:** there is no requirement to register a lottery that is incidental to an exempt entertainment that is not held for private gain, for example a charity fête or concert. The classic example of a small lottery is a raffle. Such lotteries must comply with certain requirements, for example, tickets must be sold and issued, the results announced during the event and on the premises where it is held and no more than £500 of the takings may be spent on prizes and no more than £100 of the takings may be spent on expenses.

(2) **Society lotteries:** other charity lotteries must be registered with the local authority or the Gambling Commission. Gambling Commission registration is required where ticket sales exceed £20,000 for a single lottery or £250,000 for lotteries organised by a charity in a one-year period. Trustees undertaking society lotteries should contact their local authority or (if necessary) the Gambling Commission for information on the detailed requirements relating to issues such as the price of tickets, prize money, deduction of costs, age restrictions and accounting requirements.

1.15.2 Further information about the regulation of lotteries may be found on the Gambling Commission website: www.gamblingcommisison.gov.uk. Lottery profits are tax exempt as long as they are used solely for the charity's objects and all regulatory requirements are complied with. The tax exemption does not apply to lotteries run by subsidiary companies, although the company can donate all pre-tax profits to the charity under the gift aid scheme.

1.16 Telephone and broadcast media fundraising

1.16.1 Codes of conduct are available for both telephone fundraising and broadcast appeals. Even trustees of small charities may find opportunities for broadcast appeals, for example on local radio and television. Trustees have a duty to ensure clarity in terms of identifying the charity (not just the cause) that will receive the funds and the proportion of the donation that will be spent on the charity's objects. Funds raised must be transferred directly to the charity.

1.17 Legacies

1.17.1 Legacy fundraising is a sensitive and complex area of fundraising, and trustees looking to raise resources through legacies should plan their approach carefully. It is particularly important to develop a code for fundraisers, be they volunteers, employees or external fundraisers, that covers legal requirements and best practice. Such a code should also consider wider issues, such as the marketing of a legacy campaign. An insensitive campaign runs the risk of offending people and alienating potential donors. The Institute of Fundraising has produced a code of practice for legacy fundraising. Trustees should also bear in mind the length of time that is likely to pass between the appeal being made and the funds coming to the charity when considering the resources used on legacy fundraising and the reliance placed on legacies.

1.17.2 When seeking legacies, it is important to follow the basic principles of fundraising, including communicating clear information on the organisation's charitable status and the way in which the donation will be used.

1.17.3 Given the sensitivity of legacy fundraising, it is critical that donors are not pressurised into making a donation. Particular care should be taken when dealing with vulnerable people, e.g. those who are terminally ill, elderly or recently bereaved. If it can be proved that the legacy was made under undue influence, the will could be held to be invalid and the gift will fail.

1.17.4 It is clearly in the charity's best interests that wills are made with legal advice, and fundraisers should recommend to donors that they consult an appropriate professional although fundraisers should not recommend or comment on the competence of individual solicitors. In addition, wills must not be witnessed by a representative of the charity. When a donor decides to make a donation to a charity, they should be encouraged to include the charity's registered number as well as its name to avoid confusion with other organisations, as the name of the charity may change before the supporter dies or the supporter may confuse the charity with a similarly named organisation.

1.17.5 It is not unusual for donors to want their legacy to be used for a particular purpose. If a charity decides to make an appeal encouraging donors to make legacies to be used for a particular purpose, the charity should make it clear that if the legacy cannot be used for that purpose it will be used for the general purposes of the charity.

1.18 Declaration of charitable status

1.18.1 Registered charities with a gross annual income of £10,000 or more are required to declare their charitable status on all media that solicit funds. It is good practice for all charities to do so. Similarly, although charities are not required to state their Charity Commission registration number, it is good practice to do so. Further information may be found on the Charity Commission website, and details of the requirements for charities registered in Scotland may be found on the website of the Office of the Scottish Charity Regulator (OSCR).

1.19 Restricted funds

1.19.1 If funds have been raised for a particular purpose, they may only be spent on that purpose. This principle of restricted funds applies to public appeals as well as grant applications and can create difficulties if a specific fundraising appeal is more, or less, successful than anticipated. In such circumstances any unspent funds cannot be applied to other causes within the charity without the express permission of the donor.

1.19.2 Many charities prefer to base fundraising campaigns and street collections on a specific issue, partly because they need money for that particular cause but also because, as has already been said, people like to give on this basis rather than just contributing to the general funds of the charity. If more funds are raised than required, the charity will have to seek advice from the Charity Commission on whether a Commission Scheme will be necessary to enable the funds to be used for other purposes within the charity's objects. If the funds raised are insufficient, trustees must try to return any funds given by identifiable donors. If donors do not wish to take their money back, they must sign a disclaimer to this effect. Funds raised through collecting tins, competitions and lotteries are presumed to be from unidentifiable donors. The Charity Commission can make a Scheme to apply any remaining funds to other similar purposes within the charity. These funds must be kept in reserve for six months in order to meet any outstanding claims from donors. Trustees facing either situation should contact the Commission for advice. Charities may avoid this problem by ensuring that every request for funds for a specified purpose is accompanied by a statement that funds that cannot be used for that purpose will be used for the general purposes of the charity.

1.20 Audit trail

1.20.1 Organisations that receive cash donations or undertake any form of public collection must have clear and effective cash-handling procedures. Procedures should cover issues such as the use of sealed collecting tins and envelopes, joint counting of donated cash and careful recording of donations. Funds given for a specific appeal should be treated as restricted funds, subject to the points made above, and so should be recorded as such on receipt.

2 Institute of Fundraising: Code of Conduct and codes of fundraising practice

2.1 In response to public concerns about charity fundraising techniques, the Institute of Fundraising has developed a Code of Conduct for fundraisers and codes of conduct with which all members of the Institute are expected to comply. Copies of the code of conduct and the codes of practice are available on the Institute's website (www.institute-of-fundraising.org.uk).

2.2 The Institute encourages charities to sign up to the scheme established by the Fundraising Standards Board, an independent body established to promote the self-regulation of fundraising by charities. Member charities are entitled to display the FRSB logo on their fundraising materials and are required to comply with the FRSB Fundraising Promise (formerly known as the 'Donors' Charter'), which is a commitment made to the public to comply with key principles including:

- honesty, transparency and legal compliance by the charity;
- respect for the donor, including consideration of the donor's wishes, privacy, confidentiality and data protection concerns; and
- responsible handling of the donation, covering the use of the donation for the purposes given and for the greatest advantage of the beneficiaries, whilst preserving the dignity of beneficiaries.

2.3 The charter also covers arrangements for handling complaints made by donors.

2.4 Members of the public who believe that a charity has not complied with the promise can make a complaint to FRSB if the charity concerned is a member of FRSB.

2.5 Unauthorised fundraising

2.5.1 Unfortunately, some charities encounter problems with over-zealous supporters who raise funds on behalf of the charity without the organisation's consent and unscrupulous people who raise money fraudulently by claiming that it will be given to charity. This may lead to regulatory problems, clashes with the charity's fundraising policy and alienation of the organisation's existing or potential supporters. Problems may also occur if a professional fundraiser with whom the charity has an agreement acts outside that agreement. Of course, the first approach is for charities to seek to persuade the fundraiser to stop the unauthorised activity. However, a legal remedy is also available in the form of an injunction to prevent unauthorised fundraising. Trustees wishing to take this course of action will need to obtain appropriate legal advice.

2.6 Instructing professional fundraisers

2.6.1 Many charities choose to engage professional fundraisers instead of, or in addition to, employing fundraising staff. As with all fundraising approaches, trustees need to ensure that the reward justifies the resources used, so if professional fundraisers are to be used, the trustees must be confident that this will represent good value for money.

2.7 Selecting consultants

2.7.1 Charities should first determine the role of the professional fundraiser, for example, whether the fundraiser will be developing or implementing strategy or both and whether the consultant will be responsible for a complete campaign or elements within the campaign (e.g. events, donor development or grant applications). The charity will then need to identify a number of appropriate individuals, perhaps through names provided by an umbrella body such as NCVO (the National Council for Voluntary Organisations) or the Institute of Fundraising. They should consider the following issues in relation to each professional fundraiser:

- relevant qualifications;
- experience, including experience of similar campaigns in comparable organisations;
- success record;
- sympathy with the charity and its culture; and
- arrangements for monitoring activities and reporting to the trustees;
- costs.

2.7.2 Fundraisers' fees may be determined in a number of ways, including flat fees and commission based on a percentage of the total amount of money raised.

2.8 Professional Fundraising Statement

2.8.1 When a professional fundraiser solicits money for a charity they must make a 'solicitation statement' giving the potential donor the following information:

- the name of the charity or charities for which they are raising money;
- the proportions the charities (if there is more than one) will receive;
- the way the fundraiser's remuneration will be paid; and
- the amount (or the most accurate estimate of the amount that may reasonably be calculated at the time the statement is made) that the fundraiser will receive in connection with the appeal

2.8.2 These requirements came into force under the Charities Act 2006 and the last in particular is more extensive than the previous requirement to state in general terms how the remuneration of the fundraiser was determined. The Office of the Third Sector has published guidance to help charities comply with the new rules.

2.9 Fundraising with businesses

2.9.1 Long-term relationships with corporate sponsors can offer charities a degree of financial stability. When working with businesses on fundraising promotions and activities, the trustees will need to consider additional wider issues, such as whether the charity wishes to be associated with the company or product sold and whether the perceived business practices of the company and the product sold are compatible with the charity's objectives. Is the company seeking to use the relationship to promote sales or to target a specific market and, if so, is the charity comfortable with this?

2.9.2 Where a company or individual represents that part of the price paid for goods or services provided in the course of their business will be donated to charity they are known as a 'commercial participator'. Charity law requires commercial participators to comply with certain requirements. For example, where a commercial participator represents that a donation will be made to charity, they must state the amount that will be donated to the charity and they must enter into an agreement with the charity, as set out below.

2.10 Commercial Participator Statements

2.10.1 When representing that donations will be made to a charity in connection with the sale of a product or service, commercial participators must make a statement informing potential customers of:

- the name of the charity or charities that will benefit; and
- the amount (or the most accurate estimate of the amount that may reasonably be calculated at the time the statement is made) that will be received by the charity in connection with the purchase.

2.10.2 These requirements came into force under the Charities Act 2006 and the second in particular is more extensive than the previous requirement to state in general terms how the amount the charity would receive would be determined. The Office of the Third Sector has published guidance to help charities comply with the new rules.

2.11 Agreements with professional fundraisers and commercial participators

2.11.1 The requirements for agreements between charities and professional fundraisers and commercial participators are laid down by law. All such agreements must be made in writing and be signed by both parties. The agreement, whether with a professional fundraiser or commercial participator, must contain the following information:

- the name and address of each party;
- the date and period of the agreement;
- terms regarding the variation or early termination of the agreement;
- the objectives of the agreement and the methods to be used in achieving those objectives;
- if more than one charity is involved in the agreement, the proportion of benefit to each charity (e.g. will the funds raised be equally divided or will there be a weighted split?); and
- provision for the amount of remuneration or expenses to be paid to the fundraiser or participator under the agreement and the method for calculating the amount (e.g. a percentage of funds raised or a flat amount).

2.11.2 In addition, for commercial participators, the agreement should cover the following:

- the proportion of the sale price that will be given to the charity or the donations that will be made; and
- a description of the type of contributions which will be made and of the circumstances in which they will be made.

2.11.3 Fundraisers' and commercial participators' documents and other records relating to the agreement should be available to the charity. Funds raised under the agreement should be paid to the charity within an agreed period, often 28 days of receipt.

2.11.4 The Institute of Fundraising has developed model agreements for relationships between charities and commercial participators and between charities and professional fundraisers.

3 Trading

3.1 Charities, unlike commercial organisations, are established to promote particular charitable purposes and to act in the public interest rather than to carry out a trade with a view to making a profit. However, many charities carry out some trading activities and this chapter will set out the factors that should be considered when a charity is considering undertaking trading.

3.2 Trustees of charities that carry out trading improperly may be found to have acted either *ultra vires* and/or in breach of trust. They may also find that they are required to pay tax on any profits from trading. It may be held to be inappropriate to claim these liabilities from charitable funds and that the trustees should pay, so trustees should consider carefully the issues involved before deciding to carry out trading activities.

3.3 More detailed information may be found in the Charity Commission publication *Trustees, Trading and Tax*.

3.4 Governing documents

3.4.1 The governing documents of some charities, particularly older charities, prohibit any sort of trading. However, many permit trading, provided that it is not taxable trading. Before carrying out any trading activities, charities should check their governing documents and, if they prohibit trading, charities should consider amending them. This would require the consent of the Charity Commission.

3.5 Financial risk

3.5.1 Before carrying out any trading activity, the charity (or its trading subsidiary) should consider the level of risk involved and the commercial factors that might affect that risk, just as it would for any fundraising activity.

3.6 Types of trading that may be undertaken by charities

3.6.1 Primary purpose trading: this involves the sale of goods or services that further the charitable objects of the charity. For example, a charity that runs a theatre charity may charge for tickets to see a play. Ancillary trading that is related to the primary purpose is regarded as primary purpose trading. For example, a theatre charity may charge audience members for programmes and refreshments. Income generated by a charity from primary purpose trading is exempt from income and corporation tax.

3.6.2 There is no limit to the amount of primary purpose trading a charity may carry out. Many charities obtain the bulk of their funding from such primary purpose activities – schools charge school fees to cover their costs, social care charities provide services under contracts to local authorities and historic buildings charge admission fees.

3.6.3 Under the Charities Act 2006, charities are required to demonstrate that they are carrying out their activities for the public benefit, and charities that charge fees for their services must demonstrate that those fees do not prevent the charity benefiting a sufficient section of the public. The Charity Commission has published detailed guidance on this issue.

3.6.4 Trade carried out by the beneficiaries: trading by charities in goods that have been manufactured by their beneficiaries and in services provided by the beneficiaries is also exempt from income and corporation tax. The involvement of non-beneficiaries in the trade (e.g. in a management or advisory capacity) will not present problems as long as the majority of the work is carried out by beneficiaries.

3.6.5 Small-scale exemption: a tax exemption applies to trading by charities that is not primary purpose trading or a trade carried out by beneficiaries. This small-scale applies where a charity's total annual turnover from such trading is less £5,000 or, if greater than £5,000, is less than 25 per cent of the charity's annual income, subject to a maximum of £50,000. This exemption may still apply if these limits are exceeded if the charity had a reasonable expectation that their turnover from such trading would be within the limits.

3.6.6 Fundraising events: profits from fundraising events are exempt from Corporation and income tax if the events comply with certain requirements.

3.6.7 Sale of donated goods: the sale of donated goods by charities (provided the goods have not been significantly modified) is exempt from income and corporation tax. Common examples include charity shops and auctions of donated goods.

3.6.8 Lotteries: these are considered to be trading but profits from charity lotteries are exempt from corporation and income tax.

3.6.9 Income from the sale and leasing of land: this is generally exempt from tax, but complex rules govern this exemption, for example if a charity provides services such as catering to the organisations to which it leases its premises it may be regarded as carrying on a trade that is not exempt. Charities considering leasing or selling land should seek detailed guidance.

3.6.10 Business sponsorship: a business's payment for the use of a charity's logo, or the display by a charity of a business's logo, may be considered trading and may, therefore, be taxable. This will depend on the details of the agreement between the parties. In addition, VAT may be payable on fees for such services.

3.6.11 Even tax-exempt trading may be subject to VAT. See the VAT section below for further information.

4 Trading companies

4.1 Many charities set up trading subsidiaries to carry out trading activities that the charity cannot carry out itself and other activities that the charity could carry out but where it would be in the interests of the charity for the activity to be carried out by a separate entity, for example where the activity carries a risk of loss or other liability.

4.2 Trading companies operate as normal commercial companies, unrestricted by the limitations on charity trading. They may seek investment from a number of sources but are usually established by charities as a wholly owned subsidiary, i.e. the charity is the sole share-holder or a number of charities each hold a share.

4.3 Trading subsidiaries are subject to the same taxes as regular commercial companies. However, under the Gift Aid scheme they may donate their profits, prior to the deduction of taxes, to the charity. The charity does not need to reclaim any tax and the company will receive a deduction in corporation tax in respect of the gift aid donation, thereby avoiding some or all of its corporation tax liability. The scheme allows for gift aid payments relating to a particular accounting period to be made up to nine months after the end of that accounting period.

4.4 The company will probably need to keep a proportion of its profits in order to maintain adequate cash balances to continue trading. Alternatively the charity can establish the company with sufficient capital to allow it to gift all of its profits to the charity.

4.5 However the charity's financial investment in setting up and maintaining the company must be made for charitable purposes only and for the benefit of the charity, not the trading subsidiary. A loan by a charity to its trading subsidiary should be secured (for example by a charge over the property of the trading subsidiary) and should be recorded in a document that sets out when the loan will be repaid and the interest payable on the loan.

4.6 On a practical level, a number of the trustees of the charity should serve as directors of the subsidiary trading company in order to ensure that the company is operating in accordance with the interests of the charity, including consistency between the charity and the company in areas such as public relations. However, the board of the charity should also include individuals that are not on the board of the trading subsidiary and vice versa in order to ensure that some board members may have an independent perspective on the relations between the entities.

When to set up a trading company		
1 Do you want to trade on a regular, significant basis (i.e. not small-scale trading)?	*No – trading company not necessary.*	*Yes – go to 2.*
2 Do you want to trade outside the primary objects of the charity or enter into trading that is not carried out by your beneficiaries?	*No – trading company not necessary, go to 3.*	*Yes – trading company necessary.*
3 Is the level or type of trading or the capital investment required such that it is necessary to protect the charity from business risks?	*No – trading company not required.*	*Yes – trading company necessary.*

5 Donations

5.1 One of the tax concessions available to charities is the ability to receive tax-efficient donations, either through donations made before tax has been deducted (payroll giving) or through reclaiming tax on donations under the Gift Aid system.

5.2 Payroll giving: a system whereby individuals make donations to charity that are deducted directly from their pay or occupational pension. The donations are taken by the employer from the employee's gross pay, before tax deductions are made, and thus no income tax is paid on the donation element of the salary. Donations are passed to an agency charity which distributes the funds to the charities nominated by the employees. There is no limit on the value of an individual employee's donations.

5.3 Trustees of charities receiving donations under payroll giving should be wary of offering benefits to donors as this may disqualify the donation from relief under the scheme. Benefits of negligible financial value, such as stickers or newsletters, are normally acceptable within the scheme.

5.4 Gift Aid: the Gift Aid scheme provides for flexible tax-efficient donations to charities. Gift Aid is available in respect of monetary donations (rather than gifts in kind) from tax-paying individuals and from companies.

5.4.1 The Gift Aid scheme applies to gifts of cash by individual UK tax payers to UK charities. Where it applies, the sum of cash which the donor gives is deemed to be a larger sum from which tax at the basic rate (20 per cent) has been deducted. So, if a donor gives a charity a cheque for £800, they are deemed to have made a donation of £1,000, from which £200 has been deducted. This means that the charity can reclaim the basic rate income tax that is deemed to have been deducted from that gift from HMCR (in the example, £200).

5.5 For Gift Aid donations made between 6 April 2008 and 5 April 2011 an additional government supplement of approximately 3p will be given to the charity for every pound donated. In the example, the charity would receive an additional £24 from HMRC. If the donor is a higher-rate taxpayer, they will be entitled to recover the higher-rate tax (the additional 20 per cent) paid on the gross amount of the gift. In the example, the donor would receive £200. This means that if a higher-rate tax payer gives £800 to charity under the Gift Aid scheme the net cost of doing so to the donor will be £600 and the charity will receive £1,024.

5.6 Provided the donor has paid enough tax, their Gift Aid Declaration can allow the charity to claim Gift Aid on all donations that they made in the preceding six years.

5.6.1 Gift Aid donations from companies are paid without deduction of income tax. Unlike the requirements for individual donors, no declaration is required and the charity only needs to keep the accounting records necessary to record donations. Company donors should retain any correspondence as evidence of the donation.

5.7 There are no limits on the size or number of Gift Aid donations although there is a requirement for charities to maintain an audit trail, documenting the source and value of the donations. More information is given on this below, when the Gift Aid declaration is considered. However, trustees should consider the administrative costs of reclaiming the tax on donations and may want to introduce a self-imposed minimum level below which donations will be accepted, but the tax will not be reclaimed.

5.8 Gift Aid declaration: in order to reclaim tax on a donation, charities must obtain a Gift Aid declaration from the individual donor. Although HMRC have produced a model form, there is no prescribed format for the declaration. Declarations may be made before, at the time of or after the donation, and may cover single or multiple donations. The declaration may be given in writing (including fax and e-mail) or orally and should contain the following information:

- name and home address of the donor;
- the name of the charity;
- a description of the donations covered by the declaration, e.g. a single donation or all donations from a certain date onwards; and
- a declaration that donations are to be treated as Gift Aid donations. Written declarations should also contain a note explaining that the donor must pay income tax and/or capital gains tax equivalent to the tax deducted from donations.

5.9 Although there is no requirement for the declaration to be signed and dated it is good practice to do so, and a date will be essential if it defines the donations made under the scheme. If the charity receives an oral Gift Aid declaration it should follow this up in writing by sending the donor a record of the declaration. This should include the details provided by the donor in the declaration, the date of the donation and of the charity's written confirmation, together with notes relating to the tax requirements and the donor's right to cancel the declaration within 30 days. Oral declarations should not be regarded as effective until the written record has been sent.

5.10 For sponsored events, forms can be designed that serve as a Gift Aid declaration for each sponsor. The declaration can be placed at the top of each sheet, with an opt-in box for sponsors to tick if they want their donation to be treated as Gift Aid. The form should include each sponsor's full name and home address, the amount pledged and paid, confirmation that the donor is a UK tax payer, the date each donation was made and the total handed over to the charity. A model form is available from HMRC.

5.11 Donors may cancel their declarations through any means. Cancellations will be effective from the date of notification or some future date identified by the donor. Retrospective cancellations are only effective during the 30-day 'cooling off' period after written confirmation has been sent in respect of an oral declaration.

5.12 Charities need to keep documentary evidence to support their tax claims. In particular they must be able to show how much has been received from each donor. There is no set format for storing this information, and charities will need to develop procedures that are compatible with their other administrative systems.

5.13 Funds given to charities for the provision of services or some other form of significant benefit will not qualify under the Gift Aid scheme, although limited benefits to Gift Aid donors are acceptable. A Gift Aid toolkit is available from HMRC.

5.14 Shares: there is provision for those who donate certain shares to charities to reclaim some tax in relation to those shares.

6 Taxation issues

6.1 Claiming tax refunds

6.1.1 Charities must reclaim tax on the prescribed forms provided by HMRC. In addition to the reclaimed tax, HMRC will calculate and refund any interest payable. Claims must be made no later than six years after the end of the accounting period to which the claim relates.

6.2 VAT

6.2.1 Value added tax (VAT) is a tax on the supply of goods and services (other than exempt goods or services) in the UK and the Isle of Man. VAT is charged at either:

- standard rate (this applies to most goods and services);
- reduced rate (e.g. on fuel and power); or
- zero rate (e.g. food and books).

6.2.2 The supply of goods and services that are subject to these rates of VAT are the taxable supplies. There are also exempt supplies, which are not subject to VAT. Organisations are required to register for VAT if the total financial value of their 'business' activities which are subject to VAT reaches the registration threshold. In this context 'business' is not restricted to those activities which are profit-making, but includes:

- activities involving the supply of goods or services for consideration (i.e. payment in either money or kind);

- frequent or significant activities; and
- activities that continue over a period of time.

6.2.3 Charitable activities may, therefore, be counted as business activities or supplies. (The table below describes the charitable activities that are subject to VAT.) Those business supplies that are subject to VAT at any of the three rates are the organisation's taxable supplies, and it is the measurement of the turnover of the taxable supplies against the registration threshold that determines whether the organisation should register for VAT. The registration threshold increases each year, and from April 2010 is £70,000.

6.2.4 The amount of VAT paid to HMRC is determined by the difference between input tax and output tax.

- **Output tax:** this is the VAT charged on standard and reduced rate supplies.
- **Input tax:** this is the VAT paid on purchases in relation to the VATable supplies.

6.2.5 If the output tax is greater than the input tax, the charity must pay the difference to HMRC. If the charity has paid more input tax than it has charged as output tax, then it may claim the difference back. The amounts are submitted to HMRC on a VAT return. Input tax paid by charities in relation to goods and services connected to the charity's non-business and exempt activities cannot be offset against output tax or reclaimed.

6.2.6 Clearly, extensive documentation is required to account for input and output tax and to support the VAT return. The VAT paid on input supplies can only be claimed back if the charity is VAT registered. It is possible for organisations falling below the threshold to register voluntarily, but trustees will need to consider whether the charity will be able to reclaim any tax and balance the financial benefit against the corresponding administrative burden.

6.3 Business or non-business?

6.3.1 As can be seen from the discussion above, it is essential for trustees to assess the services offered by their charity and to consider which elements represent business activities and whether the value of these activities crosses the registration threshold, requiring the charity to register. Unfortunately, some of the distinctions between business and non-business activity are very fine. In addition, although some charitable activity is considered business, the supplies in question may be either zero-rated or exempt from VAT. The table below gives an overview of the provisions. Trustees who believe that their charity may be required to be VAT registered should seek further advice, for example by contacting their local HMRC office.

Activity	Business	Non-business
Donations, bequests and grants	A funding agreement where the funder directly receives a benefit from the service provided will be subject to VAT. This is a very grey area and professional advice is usually required.	Voluntary contributions and grants which are freely given and which are not a purchase of services are non-business and outside the scope of VAT. Grants subsidising a service which would be provided by the charity anyway are also non-business.
Voluntary services provided without charge		Free services are non-business activities, e.g. first aid, sea rescue and worship. Any genuine donations freely given by the recipients of these services are outside the scope of VAT.
Sale of goods (including charity shops)	The sale of goods is a business activity. The sale of donated goods is zero-rated whether the sale is through a shop or not. The sale of bought-in goods is standard-rated unless they are covered by another zero-rating, e.g. books.	
Hire of charity-run buildings (for example village halls)	The hire of a charity-run building for a fee is business. This includes village halls and other community buildings. The fee is normally exempt from VAT unless the charity chooses to waive the exemption, allowing it to register and recover input tax. The exemption cannot be waived for lets to another charity for non-business use.	

Activity	Business	Non-business
Welfare services (including spiritual welfare)	Welfare services supplied by charities, together with any related goods, are business but are exempt provided the supplies are not made for profit, i.e. any surplus made is reinvested in the same service. If the surplus was used for a different charitable activity, the supply of welfare would be standard-rated.	The same services are non-business when they are consistently supplied below cost (i.e. subsidised by at least 15% from the charity's funds) to relieve the distress of beneficiaries.
Education	The provision of education in exchange for consideration (i.e. a fee) is a business activity, but it is exempt from VAT provided any surplus made is reinvested in the same service. If the surplus was used for a different charitable activity, the provision of education would be standard-rated.	The same provision is non-business if it is provided for free (e.g. in a state school).
Cultural services (e.g. admission to museums, galleries, zoos and theatres)	Admission charges are exempt from VAT provided any surplus made is reinvested in the same activity and the organisation is managed and administered on a voluntary basis.	Admission is non-business if provided for free.
Membership subscriptions	If members receive benefits in return for their subscriptions e.g. publications, advice services or events, then the subscriptions will be considered to be business and subject to VAT.	Subscriptions are non-business if the members are entitled to nothing more than copies of statutory documents (i.e. annual reports and accounts) and voting rights at general meetings.
Corporate sponsorship	Sponsorship from companies and other bodies is subject to the standard rate of VAT if the funds are conditional on some benefit, such as the publication of the organisation's logo. The fundraising exemption (see opposite) will apply to sponsorship in relation to one-off events.	Corporate donations are outside the scope of VAT if there is no reciprocal benefit. A small acknowledgement in an annual report will not change a donation into a sponsorship.

Activity	Business	Non-business
Sales of advertising in charity publications	If less than 50% of the advertisements in the publication are from private individuals, the income from all the adverts will be subject to standard rate VAT. The supply of advertising to a charity may be zero-rated and the publication may be exempt if it is part of a one-off fundraising event.	If 50% or more of the advertisements in the publication are clearly from private individuals, the income may be treated as donations and outside the scope of VAT
Interest payments		Interest earned on funds kept in bank and building society accounts is non-business.

6.4 Zero-rated supplies to charities

6.4.1 A number of supplies made to charities are zero-rated, meaning the charity does not have to pay any VAT on the goods and services in question. In these circumstances, the onus is on the charity to provide the supplier with a written declaration of its eligibility for zero-rating on the supplies in question. Zero-rating is available on the following:

- advertising in all types of media and all preparation work (e.g. design and artwork);
- recording and playback equipment for the production of talking books and newspapers for people with visual impairments (cassette tapes are standard-rated);
- supply, repair, maintenance and importation of sea rescue equipment;
- construction of new self-contained buildings and annexes, excluding professional services, which are standard-rated; and
- the purchase of a freehold or leasehold (exceeding 21 years) where the property will be used for a relevant charitable or residential purpose.

6.5 Fundraising events

6.5.1 As has been mentioned above, fundraising events may be exempt from VAT. The exemption applies to events that meet the following criteria:

- The event must be organised and promoted primarily to raise money for the benefit of the charity.
- The people attending the event must be aware of the fundraising purpose.

- The event must not be part of continuous or semi-regular activities (frequent events would represent trading and not qualify for the exemption). In effect, this means that charities are limited to holding 15 events of the same kind in the same location in each financial year, although more frequent small-scale events (where gross weekly income does not exceed £1,000) are acceptable.

6.5.2 Trustees should be aware that small-scale events taking place, for example, once or twice weekly, may be considered as trading.

6.5.3 The exemption applies to a wide range of events, including quizzes, dances, concerts, fêtes and jumble sales.

6.5.4 The VAT exemption is mandatory for events that fulfil all the conditions and all the charity's income in connection with the event will be exempt, although the sale of commemorative goods for a period after the event will not enjoy VAT exemption. Goods and services purchased for the event are subject to the normal VAT treatment. However, charities can make zero-rated supplies at an event, for example through the sale of programmes and donated goods, and can claim back their input tax in relation to those supplies.

6.5.5 If charities exceed the 15-event limit, none of the fundraising events will qualify for the VAT exemption.

6.5.6 Charities can hold joint fundraising events with other charities, but care should be taken when holding joint events in partnership with non-charities as the exemption may not apply.

6.6 VAT and branches

6.6.1 Where branches are part of the parent charity, the obligation to register for VAT is determined by the total taxable supplies of the branches and main charity combined. Where the branch is independent and legally separate from the parent, the requirement for the branch to register will be dependent on its own turnover of taxable supplies. In this situation, any donation made by the branch to the parent body which is a genuine donation (i.e. not a subscription for services) will be treated as non-business.

D3

Data protection and e-commerce

1 Introduction

1.1 This chapter gives an overview of UK data protection law with reference to current interpretation and guidance where this is available and helpful to an understanding of the law. It also covers e-commerce issues such as the required content for commercial websites and how to market by direct mail, fax, telephone, email or SMS (text messaging) in a compliant way to meet the current regulatory environment.

1.2 Combined data protection and e-commerce topics cover key issues for charities such as when consent is required to process personal information for marketing or other purposes, the importance of confidentiality and how to communicate this core value to staff, as well as other key business and HR issues.

2 Data protection

2.1 The background

2.1.1 The EU Data Protection Directive 95/46 harmonised the law on data protection throughout EU Member States. The Directive was implemented in the UK in the form of the Data Protection Act 1998.

2.1.2 The Data Protection Act 1998 (DPA) came into force on 1 March 2000. It replaced the 1984 Data Protection Act, which was more restricted in its scope, notably if an organisation was not registered under the 1984 Act it need not comply with any of the Data Protection Principles. This limitation was removed by the 1998 Act, but the commercial myth that data protection law does not apply to all organisations still persists.

2.1.3 The Directive requires all European Union Member States to operate a central registry. In the UK those who process personal data must notify (formerly called 'registration') with the Information Commissioner. A few organisations are exempt from notification; in particular there are specific exemptions for certain non-profit-making activities, but even so all organisations must comply with the other provisions of the legislation.

2.1.4 The DPA sets out eight Data Protection Principles that must be followed by those holding personal data. Individuals are given specific rights to access information relating to them and to object to the processing of their personal information in certain circumstances.

2.1.5 The DPA created the role of Commissioner to enforce compliance with the Act and provide guidance on interpretation to businesses and individuals alike. The Act is backed by criminal sanctions for non-compliance in key areas. The Information Commissioner reports annually to Parliament and takes an active role in promoting privacy when there are initiatives, including government initiatives, which have the potential to intrude upon private life. There is an association between data protection, privacy and the right to respect for family life in the Human Rights Act 1998.

2.1.6 The Information Commissioner is supported by Assistant Commissioners in Northern Ireland, Scotland and in Wales. The Commissioners have responsibility for Freedom of Information and the Environmental Information Regulations as well as data protection.

3 The Data Protection Principles

3.1 The Principles form the backbone of UK data protection law and their wording is taken from the EU Data Protection Directive. They are set out in Schedule 1 to the DPA, and there are interpretative provisions in Part 2 of Schedule 1 to further regulate and guide organisations when implementing the Principles.

3.2   Principle 1: Personal data shall be processed fairly and lawfully

3.2.1 There are three main strands to the First Principle.

(1) The normal meaning of 'fair and lawful'.
(2) In the interpretative provisions there is a requirement to give data subjects specified information about the identity of the party collecting the information, the purposes for which personal data will be processed and any other information relevant in the circumstances. The fair processing information requirements are key to data protection compliance, as they are the organisation's authority to process personal information. The impact of this provision is considered in more detail in the section entitled 'Key business impacts' below.

(3) The interpretative provisions also set out the requirement to meet one or more of the conditions for fair processing in Schedule 2 to the DPA or if sensitive data is being processed, one or more of the conditions in Schedule 3 to the Act as well. These are technical requirements and generally compliance with Schedule 2 conditions is not difficult. However the Schedule 3 conditions are restrictive and are considered further under 'Key HR impacts' below.

3.2.2 What is personal data?

Information relating to a living individual who can be identified from the information or by cross-referring other details in your possession is personal data. The information must be biographical with the individual as the main focus of it. Examples include name and contact details, records of personal information such as health records, employment records, banking history and tax records.

3.3 Principle 2: Personal data shall be obtained only for one or more specified and lawful purposes and shall not be processed in any manner incompatible with that purpose or those purposes

3.3.1 This Principle works in conjunction with the First Principle. Having provided fair processing information (identity, processing purposes, other relevant information) future processing of personal data is restricted to those activities.

3.3.2 In practice this means that data obtained for one purpose must not be used for a different purpose unless the data subject was informed at the time of obtaining the data of that other or those other purposes.

3.3.3 What is meant by processing?

The term is widely defined to include every potential activity involving personal data. It means obtaining, holding, processing, transferring and transmitting, deleting and destroying.

3.4 Principle 3: Personal data shall be adequate, relevant and not excessive in relation to the purpose or purposes for which they are processed

3.4.1 When obtaining information consideration should be given to what is relevant and appropriate for the stated purposes for which it will be processed. During the lifecycle of information held on a database, these issues should be considered again. What is appropriate information for handling an enquiry will not be adequate if the enquirer becomes a regular customer or supplier for example.

3.5 Principle 4: Personal data shall be accurate and, where necessary, kept up to date

3.5.1 Charities should be able to show that they have taken steps to ensure the accuracy of personal information obtained, for example confirming details like spellings and house numbers when obtaining information face-to-face or by telephone. When gathering information online the system can provide drop-down lists to help with accurate data entry and fields can be restricted to prevent alphabetical entries in a field collecting telephone numbers, for example.

3.5.2 The interpretative provisions allow that accuracy is not compromised if the organisation obtained the data from a third party rather than direct from the individual who is the subject of the data so long as reasonable steps were taken to ensure accuracy.

3.5.3 If the subject of the personal data informs the organisation that the data is inaccurate, it can choose either to amend it or to simply record the data subject's comments without amendment.

3.6 Principle 5: Personal data processed for any purpose or purposes shall not be kept for longer than is necessary for that purpose or those purposes

3.6.1 Data protection law does not specify how long information should be kept, simply that it shall not be kept longer than is required. There are many legal requirements relating to the retention of data, for example accounting records should be kept for seven years for tax purposes, documents relating to a contract should be retained for six years from termination of the contract or 12 years if it was a contract under seal.

3.6.2 To meet the requirements of the Fifth Principle charities should consider what information they process and decide on appropriate retention periods based on legal requirements and reasonable business needs. The longer information is held the more likely it is to become inaccurate, out of date or inappropriate for the purposes for which it was obtained.

3.7 Principle 6: Personal data shall be processed in accordance with the rights of data subjects under this Act

3.7.1 Individuals have a number of rights under the DPA. The most widely recognised is the right to access personal information relating to them. Requests must be made in writing and supported by such information as is reasonably required to prove identity and to locate the information required. Charities may charge up to £10 for each subject access request and once the fee is paid, 40 days are allowed in which to comply with the request.

3.7.2 There are limited exceptions to the obligation to respond to a request, which are considered in more detail in the section 'Key HR impacts' below.

3.7.3 Other rights set out in the DPA are the right to object to processing of personal data in certain circumstances, for example processing for purposes of direct marketing and processing likely to cause damage or distress to someone.

3.7.4 The DPA requires that such requests be made in writing and gives organisations a 'reasonable' period in which to comply. It is important therefore that such requests are identified and dealt with quickly. It is advisable to keep a record, with dates, of the request and actions taken to comply with it.

3.7.5 Where an individual objects to processing on the grounds that it causes damage or distress to someone the organisation should consider the circumstances and make a reasonable decision either to cease processing or to continue as before. Such a finding is open to appeal to the courts.

3.7.6 A data subject has the right to object to decisions taken by automated means in circumstances where the decision:

- is taken by or on behalf of the charity;
- significantly affects that individual;
- is based solely on the processing by automatic means of the individual's personal data; and
- is taken for the purpose of evaluating matters relating to him.

3.7.7 Examples of areas likely to be affected are:

- HR, where automated decisions may be taken, for example in respect of absence from work due to illness or accident or an individual's performance at work; and
- credit scoring, where an automated decision may be taken regarding the data subject's creditworthiness.

3.7.8 There is a right to compensation for any individual who suffers damage or distress by reason of contravention of any of the requirements of the DPA. Where the complaint involves inaccurate data, the individual concerned has the right to apply to the court for rectification, blocking, erasure or destruction of the inaccurate data. The court may also order the organisation to pay compensation for any damage or distress suffered.

3.8 Principle 7: Appropriate technological and organisational measures shall be taken against unauthorised or unlawful processing of personal data and against accidental loss or destruction of, or damage to, personal data

3.8.1 This is a key requirement of the DPA, the duty to keep personal data secure and it is considered below under 'Key business impacts'.

3.8.2 There is a less obvious implication also for organisations that outsource personal data processing. The interpretative provisions relating to the Seventh Principle require that organisations carry out compliance checks on the security of service providers and put in place written contracts incorporating specific contract terms. This issue is also covered under 'Key business impacts' below.

3.8.3 The interpretative provisions also require organisations to ensure the reliability of staff whose work involves processing personal data. This is achieved by training and monitoring, especially in high-risk areas, for example where temporary or new staff are working.

3.9 Principle 8: Personal data shall not be transferred to a country or territory outside the European Economic Area unless that country or territory ensures an adequate level of protection for the rights and freedoms of data subjects in relation to the processing of personal data

3.9.1 This principle prohibits the export of data outside the European Economic Area (EU member states, Liechtenstein, Norway and Iceland) unless further steps are taken to authorise the transfer.

3.9.2 Further countries have been designated by the European Council as providing adequate security for personal data. They are Argentina, Canada, Isle of Man, Guernsey, Jersey, Faroe Islands and Switzerland. Also, US companies that subscribe to the 'safe harbor' protocol provide adequate security.

3.9.3 An alternative method to ensure the security of personal data transferred outside the EEA is put a contract in place between transferor and transferee. The terms must be in the form approved by the European Council.

3.9.4 There are other derogations from the Eighth Principle including the informed consent of the subject of the data and transfers necessary for the performance of a contract.

3.9.5 Failing all other methods of authorising transfers outside the EEA, organisations should undertake the 'adequacy test', making an assessment on the state of privacy law in the territory where the transferee is located, the access to rights for EU citizens in that territory and the controls and security measures in place at the transferee organisation.

4 Data Protection Act offences

4.1 There are a number of offences under the DPA.

4.2 Notification offences: it is an offence to process personal data without notifying the Data Protection Registrar if required to do so (DPA s. 21). This is a strict liability offence; there is no defence if the organisation is processing without a notification if one is required. It is also an offence to fail to keep a notification entry up to date.

4.3 Unfair obtaining or disclosure: Section 55 of the Act makes it a criminal offence to knowingly or recklessly obtain or disclose personal information without the consent of the data controller. This offence is frequently reported in relation to police officers using their access to DVLA and other records for personal reasons. The offence is also reported in relation to private investigators and tracing agents who falsely represent themselves as data subjects to gain access to personal information held on government agency files.

4.4 Enforced subject access: since the introduction of the Criminal Records Bureau, which allows certain categories of employer to apply for details of an individual's criminal record, if any, it has been an offence under s. 56 of the Act to require candidates for employment to apply to the police for a copy of their criminal record using the right of subject access. The Criminal Records Bureau (CRB) is now the only legal way to check whether or not an individual has a criminal record and checks may only be carried out in respect of people who work with children and certain other vulnerable groups. There are plans to introduce a basic check facility at CRB for all employers.

4.5 Failure to comply with a notice issued by the Information Commissioner under the DPA: it is an offence under s. 47 to fail to comply with the terms of an enforcement notice, an information notice or a special information notice issued by the Information Commissioner. This is an important investigative and enforcement tool for the Commissioner.

4.5.1 It is a defence under s. 47(3) to show that all due diligence was exercised to comply with the notice in question.

4.5.2 An enforcement notice is a notice requiring a data controller to take, or to refrain from, specified processing of personal data. It might specify that a particular process is to be discontinued generally or simply in relation to a specific data subject. The notice will specify a period of time.

4.6 False statements: it is also an offence (s. 47(2)) for a person to make a false statement when complying with an information notice or special information notice. The necessary intent is either that the person knows the statement to be false in a material respect or that they make the statement recklessly and it is false in a material respect.

4.7 Liability for data protection offences: organisations can be guilty of the offences in the Act, such as failure to notify and the failure to keep a notification up to date.

4.7.1 A trustee, manager or officer of a charity can be liable for Data Protection Act offences pursuant to s. 61 of the DPA if he or she consents to or connives at the commission of the offence or if the offence can be shown to be attributable to any neglect on their part.

4.7.2 Data protection law is unusual in that there are criminal sanctions against individual employees too, not just against the organisation and its directors. Offences under the DPA may be committed by individuals, for example the s. 51 offences of unauthorised disclosure or obtaining of personal information.

4.7.3 The Employment Practices Data Protection Code emphasises that employers should undertake staff training to highlight data protection issues and the risk of personal liability to those staff whose work involves handling personal information. Where an individual employee is found guilty of an offence, the employer will need to show that employees had been trained about unauthorised disclosures and other misuse of personal information if it is to avoid a charge that it has been negligent.

5 Key business impacts

5.1 Notification

5.1.1 All organisations and persons that process personal data must register with the Data Protection Register (part of the Information Commissioner's Office) unless their processing activities are exempt.

5.1.2 There are few exemptions and the most widely applicable is the 'core business exemption' which exempts organisations whose activities do not involve personal data processing other than to administer its own employees, produce accounts and records for its own customers and undertake limited marketing of its own goods or services to its own customers only.

5.1.3 There is also an exemption for not-for-profit organisations. It applies to personal data processing which is only for the purpose of:

- establishing or maintaining membership;
- supporting a not-for-profit body or association; or
- providing or administering activities for either the members or those who have regular contact with it.

5.1.4 The exemption will not apply to all charities and in particular larger organisations will find that their activities exceed the bounds of the exemption.

5.1.5 Notification (also known as registration, the terms mean the same) can be commenced online at the Information Commissioner's website or by telephone. Hard-copy forms are then sent to the Office with the filing fee, currently £35 for registered charities. The registration is renewable annually.

5.2 Fair processing information

5.2.1 In order to meet the fair processing requirements in the First Principle data subjects should be advised of the identity of the data controller, the purposes for which personal data will be processed and any other information relevant in the circumstances. What is considered 'relevant in the circumstances' is a matter of fact. Guidance from the Information Commissioner suggests that other sources of personal data and likely disclosures of the data would be relevant.

5.2.2 A useful test is to consider whether there is any information relating to the intended processing which, if revealed to the data subject, could affect that individual's decision to provide the data. For example if your organisation routinely retains personal data for an especially long period or if it shares data for purposes of national security or fraud prevention measures. These would be circumstances that should be disclosed to an individual before they provide any personal data.

5.2.3 So long as the fair processing information requirements are met, future processing of the data for the purposes outlined is authorised. There is no general need for consent.

5.2.4 The ideal location for fair processing information is at the point of collection of personal data, for example if an application form is used to gather information about prospective job candidates or prospective members, customers, clients, etc. the form is the appropriate location for fair processing information.

5.2.5 The size and prominence of subject information has been debated by the Data Protection Tribunal in the Linguaphone case, where it stated that:

> '... the position, size of print and wording of the opt-out box does not amount to a sufficient explanation to an enquirer that the company intends or may wish to hold, use or disclose that personal data ...'

5.2.6 The Information Commissioner has said that the term 'fair processing information' is unhelpful to the public and is trying to promote the use of 'Privacy Policy' instead.

5.3 Security of personal data

5.3.1 The Seventh Principle requires organisations to use appropriate organisational and technical measures to ensure the security of personal data, keeping it free from unauthorised access, damage or destruction. Organisations are required to use reasonable care and skill to ensure that computer systems are secure, although the 'state of the art' is recognised and the interpretative provisions allow organisations to balance the harm that could result from unlawful disclosure against the cost and complexity of systems to prevent such disclosure.

5.3.2 Organisational security measures means building security, CCTV, locking filing cabinets, policies and procedures to regulate the processing environment as appropriate to the type of data and the risk of unlawful disclosure or loss. Many professions and businesses promote a duty of confidentiality regarding information in the workplace. This can be a key element in staff training and procedures to evidence that the organisation operates a system of control for information in its custody and control. Important information in its control might include trade or business secrets, skills and know-how as well as customer and marketing databases and donor lists.

5.3.3 The level of confidentiality offered will depend on the circumstances; some information is inherently more sensitive and confidential than other information, for example records of individual donations subject to a duty of confidentiality are more sensitive than information already in the public domain such as names and addresses. The level of confidentiality that is appropriate will also depend on the expectations of the individual who is the subject of the data. What was he led to believe when he provided his personal data? The key to managing expectations is clear and comprehensive fair processing information.

5.3.4 Technical security measures means IT security: firewalls, virus protection, back-up procedures, restricted access to data on a 'need to know' basis, restricted download facilities and passwords, for example.

5.4 Outsourcing

5.4.1 Who is the data controller? A person who (either alone or jointly or in common with other persons) determines the purposes for which and the manner in which any personal data are, or are to be, processed. When processing information about donors, the data controller is the charity.

5.4.2 Who is a data processor? Any person (other than an employee of the data controller) who processes the data on behalf of the data controller. A mailing house is a data processor when it addresses and posts brochures on behalf of the charity.

5.4.3 The interpretative provisions of the Seventh Principle require data controllers to take steps to ensure the reliability of their data processors both in the selection criteria for choosing a service provider and in subsequent monitoring of the provider's performance.

5.4.4 In addition, the data controller must have a written contract with its data processor(s) which commit the data processor to act only on the instructions of the data controller and to adhere to the requirements of the Seventh principle when processing personal data on behalf of the data controller.

5.4.5 Identifying those relationships involving a data processor is not always straightforward. The test is whether or not the outsource service provider makes decisions about the personal data. A simple example would be a payroll bureau.

5.4.6 A payroll bureau has no interest in processing personal data relating to the employees of its clients except that it is remunerated for so doing. The data controller, in this example the employer, is outsourcing its data processing activity in relation to the payroll. The payroll bureau is a data processor, it makes no decisions about the personal data, it processes purely on instructions from the employer.

5.4.7 As data protection law does not recognise 'groups' of companies, where there is a group of two or more legal entities consideration should be given to identifying which ones might be acting as an outsource service provider to the others. For example, which entity is the employing company? Is there a service company responsible for security issues or which 'owns' computer equipment for financial accounting purposes? Some of these companies will be data controllers, others will be data processors and some will be both. Appropriate contract terms should be put in place between group companies.

6 Key HR impacts

6.1 For many charitable bodies, the personal data relating to their own staff is the most confidential and complex personal data being processed. Therefore the DPA will impact on HR activities to a significant extent. The Information Commissioner has issued guidance for HR professionals in the form of the Employment Practices Data Protection Code, which considers the impact of data protection law on HR activities in particular. This section does not seek to replicate the Employment Code but picks up some data protection issues which impact on HR and therefore provide good illustrations of key issues in practice.

6.2 What is sensitive data? Information relating to physical or mental health, race or ethnic origin, religion, political beliefs, philosophical beliefs, TU membership, criminal convictions and allegations of criminal conduct.

6.3 Processing sensitive data

6.3.1 Certain categories of sensitive data are likely to be relevant to the operation of an HR department. When processing sensitive data organisations should consider the conditions for fair processing set out in schedule 3 to the DPA and ensure that they can meet one or more of the conditions. The fair processing conditions must be met otherwise the data processing is unfair.

6.3.2 The key conditions in schedule 3 are:

- Processing to meet a legal obligation in connection with employment. This covers routine HR administration when employees are absent due to illness or injury.
- Processing to establish, exercise or defend legal rights. This applies for example when taking legal advice on terminating employment due to absence caused by ill health.
- Equal opportunities monitoring allows HR departments to monitor the effectiveness of equal opportunities policies and practices but only in so far as they are promoting equal opportunities.
- Processing with the explicit consent of the data subject. This is very common in practice, although there can be difficulties relying on consent. Consent between an employee and employer is subject to the inherent duress of the relationship which impairs its validity.

6.4 Handling the exercise of subject rights

6.4.1 When an employee exercises rights under the DPA the technical requirements are identical to those applying to other data subjects. However, the type of data held on a personnel file provides a useful illustration of the main exceptions to the obligation to provide information in response to a subject access request.

6.4.2 The organisation is not obliged to comply with a request for subject access unless he is supplied with such information as he may reasonably require in order to:
- satisfy himself as to the identity of the person making the request; and
- locate the information which that person seeks.

6.4.3 This is the only circumstance that enables the organisation to refuse to comply with the request in its entirety. All other exceptions apply to exempt pieces of information, and other relevant information should still be provided.

6.4.4 Where compliance with a request involves the disclosure of information relating to another individual (a third party) who can be identified from that information, there is no obligation to comply with the request unless:

- the third party has consented to the disclosure of the information; or
- it is reasonable in all the circumstances to comply with the request without the consent of the third party.

6.4.5 This includes the fact that information has been provided by the third party. What is reasonable will depend on any duty of confidentiality owed, any steps taken by the data controller to obtain the consent of the third party, whether the third party is capable of giving consent and whether consent has been refused.

6.4.6 Personal data are exempt from a subject access request if they consist of a reference given or to be given in confidence by the data controller for the purposes of education, training or employment. But the exemption does not apply in the hands of the recipient of the reference, so it will only apply to draft references before they are sent.

6.4.7 Personal data processed for the purposes of management forecasting or management planning to assist the data controller in the conduct of any business or other activity are exempt from subject access in any case to the extent to which the application of those provisions would be likely to prejudice the conduct of that business or other activity. There is a corporate finance exemption which will apply to listed companies whose share price could be affected by the information.

6.4.8 Personal data are exempt from subject access if the data consist of information in respect of which a claim to legal professional privilege could be maintained in legal proceedings.

6.4.9 A person need not comply with any request or order regarding subject access to the extent that compliance would, by revealing evidence of the commission of any offence other than an offence under this Act, expose him to proceedings for that offence.

6.5 Monitoring at work

6.5.1 Monitoring employees in the workplace may involve creating records of activity or behaviour, for example CCTV images. It is also an invasion of privacy when it involves e-mail interception and scrutiny of websites visited by an employee during working hours. Monitoring potentially conflicts with Article 8 of the Human Rights Act 1998 which provides for the right to respect for the privacy of family life, home and correspondence.

◆ 6.5.2 Principles for monitoring

The Information Commissioner has issued guidance on monitoring in the Employment Code and recommends the following principles.

(a) Identify who has authority to instigate monitoring activity. The introduction and use of monitoring should be controlled. Line managers should not be authorised to introduce new monitoring activities but should follow agreed practices and make suggestions if they have any improvements to make.

(b) Consider also which is the appropriate department to undertake monitoring. In some cases, for example performance monitoring, it will be appropriate for line management or compliance personnel to monitor. In others, such as crime prevention and detection, it will be more appropriate for security personnel to undertake monitoring.

(c) Keep a sense of perspective. Monitoring should only be undertaken after an assessment of the impact on employees. Balance the likely harm to staff relations and the impact on individual freedom with the perceived benefit of monitoring.

(d) Identify the business need and target monitoring appropriately. Monitoring is by its nature intrusive should be undertaken in such a way that the privacy and autonomy of individual employees is respected. Targeted monitoring is more likely to achieve this than a wholesale approach. For example:
    i. If prevention of pilfering from cash tills is the objective, then CCTV cameras should be targeted on cash tills.

ii. If the objective is policing a policy forbidding the downloading of undesirable material such as pornography from the internet, then an automated check on flesh tint pixels in images might be the first step. Further investigation can made if it appears that much of the images being stored or downloaded features flesh tints.
(e) Be open about monitoring. The organisation should be open about its monitoring policy and practices. Covert monitoring will only be justifiable in limited circumstances, usually on the advice of or with the involvement of the police.
(f) Train monitors about their data protection obligations. Senior HR personnel and those who are authorised to introduce monitoring activity should be familiar with the Employment Code. Employees who monitor should be trained in the data protection obligations relating to employee rights, the processing of sensitive data and the importance of following monitoring policies.

6.6 Regulation of Investigatory Powers Act 2000

6.6.1 The interception of electronic communications (i.e. intercepting e-mail) is a criminal offence under RIPA but can usually be justified under the Telecommunications (Lawful Business Practice) (Interception of Communications) Regulations 2000 so long as the charity can evidence a reasonable system of control which compliance with the Employment Code will achieve.

7 E-commerce law

7.1 Website compliance

7.1.1 Privacy policies. The DPA First Principle requires fair processing information to be provided where individuals are invited to submit any personal information. In guidance entitled 'Websites: Frequently Asked Questions' issued June 2001 the Information Commissioner said that a privacy statement will not always suffice to meet subject information requirements if it is in the form of 'click here to view our privacy statement'. Instead key fair processing information should be provided at any point where personal information is collected online.

7.1.2 In its 'Email Marketing Best Practice' consultation document of 2004, the Direct Marketing Association advised that an online privacy policy should be accessible by one click of the mouse via a prominently flagged link. It should not be one link amongst many nor should it refer the user to general terms and conditions. The link should be easy to locate and on the top part of the page visible on screen, preferably not in a side-panel list of links nor visible only when the user has scrolled to the bottom of the page.

7.2 Other information requirements

7.2.1 Websites are subject to the Electronic Commerce (EC Directive) Regulations 2002. The regulations apply to any organisation (or person) which advertises goods or services online or sell goods or services to businesses or consumers online. The main requirements relate to information that must be provided on the website, and failure to comply with the Regulations gives consumers and business consumers the right to cancel any orders placed online and to seek compensation for any losses incurred as a result of the non-compliance.

7.2.2 The information required is:

- Clear contact details for the website owner, including a geographical address.
- An explanation of any cookies used on or by the website, their function and purpose.
- A facility for individuals to opt-out of the use of cookies.
- Clear price indications for products available to purchase over the internet.
- The advertiser's VAT number where products are available to purchase over the internet.
- Details of how contracts will be made online.
- Details of any relevant trade organisations to which the advertiser belongs or any authority to conduct business. This will include the charity's registered number and a statement that it is regulated by the Charities Commission.

7.2.3 Charities that are limited companies must also disclose limited status and provide registration details to meet the Companies (Registrar, Languages and Trading Disclosures) Regulations 2006 and the Companies Act 2006.

7.2.4 Check that all information is clear, simple to understand and given due prominence.

8 Compliant direct marketing

8.1 The DPA refers to direct marketing as 'the communication (by whatever means) of any advertising or marketing material which is directed to particular individuals'. There are various forms of direct marketing and slightly different rules apply to each. However, it is a standard requirement that the use of personal data for marketing purposes requires a form of consent. For direct mail, telephone and fax marketing the standard is the opt-out: 'please tick this box if you do not wish to receive marketing material from us'. To market by e-mail or text message the higher standard of the opt-in is required: 'please tick this box if you do want to receive marketing material from us'.

8.2 Direct mail

8.2.1 Best practice when marketing by direct mail is to clean the mailing list prior to use. This involves checking standard abbreviations for titles and correct decoration suffixes as well as correcting common misspellings, omissions and transpositions.

8.2.2 Mailing lists should be deduplicated, matching names and addresses to remove duplicate records as well as screening for validation and suppression markers. Lists should also be checked against the Mailing Preference Service (MPS). This is a list of surnames and addresses of people who want to opt out of receiving marketing material. Once screened the list may be used for up to 28 days, after which it will require rescreening.

8.2.3 If a consumer has had dealings with the charity in the past then it will be entitled to make direct marketing approaches from time to time regardless of the MPS suppression list as there is an existing relationship between the parties. So mailings are not unsolicited unless and until the individual writes to request that it cease using his or her personal data for direct marketing.

8.3 Telephone marketing

8.3.1 As with the MPS there is a register of persons who do not want to receive marketing telephone calls or faxes, the Telephone Preference Service and Fax Preference Service respectively.

8.3.2 The sending of unsolicited faxes and making unsolicited telephone calls for purposes of direct marketing are regulated under the Privacy and Electronic Communications (EC Directive) Regulations 2003 ('the Regulations') and the Amendment Regulations 2004. They apply to both consumers and corporate telephone subscribers, making it unlawful to make unsolicited telephone calls for purposes of direct marketing if the subscriber has either registered with the relevant preference service or has previously told the advertiser not to make marketing calls on that telephone number.

8.3.3 The Regulations apply to a wide range of marketing activities including corporate advertising, the promotion of the organisation's aims and ideals. They only apply to 'unsolicited calls'. So, if a coupon has been completed and returned asking for further information about a product or service and has asked for the information to be sent to a particular fax or telephone number, then a call to that number to provide the information requested is not unsolicited.

8.4 Texting and e-mail marketing

8.4.1 When marketing by means of e-mail or text messaging to mobile telephones the Regulations apply again. They regulate the use of electronic messaging for purposes of unsolicited direct marketing to individual subscribers; they do not apply to businesses or to e-mail addresses of individuals at work.

8.4.2 Marketing by text or e-mail is only lawful if undertaken with the express consent of the individual or in circumstances where the individual has purchased similar goods or services from the charity previously (known as the 'soft opt-in').

8.4.3 The Regulations also specify information to be included in marketing messages sent by electronic means, including a prominent reference to the fact that it is an advertisement.

8.4.4 The Companies (Registrar, Languages and Trading Disclosures) Regulations 2006 specify that limited companies must disclose their full registration details on all e-mails, as does the Companies Act 2006.

8.5 For more information on compliant marketing, see the 'Good Practice Note – Charities and Marketing' at www.ico.gov.uk/upload/documents/library/data_protection/practical_application/charities_and_marketing_12_06.pdf.

SECTION E

The charity's assets

E1
Use of charitable assets

1 Introduction

1.1 Charity trustees have a general duty to use charitable funds and assets reasonably and only in furtherance of the charity's objects. They should also avoid undertaking activities that might place the charity's funds, assets or reputation at risk. Their primary concern must always be the interests of the charity. There are also special considerations for charity trustees when they wish to invest charity funds, buy or sell land or borrow money.

1.2 This chapter reviews the types of assets which may be owned by a charity, and explains the various options that the trustees have when using these assets.

2 Funds

2.1 The Statement of Recommended Practice for Charities (SORP, Charity Commission, revised 2005) defines a fund as 'a pool of resources, held and maintained separately from other pools because of the circumstances in which the resources were originally received or the way in which they have subsequently been treated'.

2.2 The diagram below shows the different types of funds of charities:

```
                    Funds of a Charity
                   /                  \
         Unrestricted Funds      Restricted Funds
          /          \            /            \
       General   Designated    Income       Endowment
                                             /        \
                                      Expendable   Permanent
```

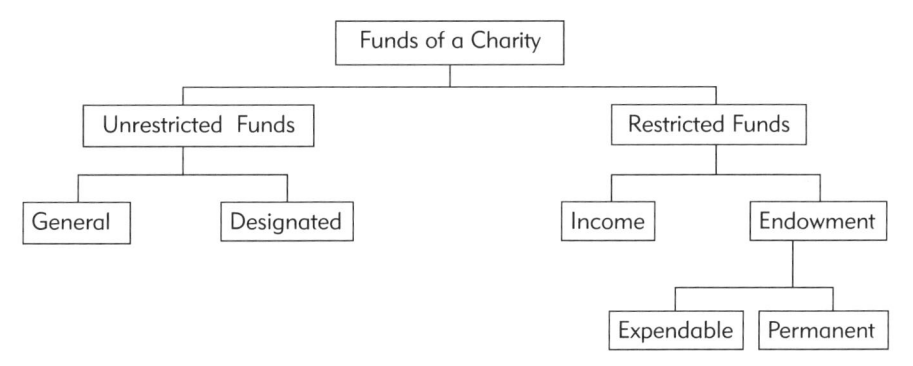

Figure 1.1: Different types of funds for a charity

2.3 Charity funds are either unrestricted or restricted funds.

2.3.1 Unrestricted funds: have no restrictions placed on them by funders or donors and so may be spent at the discretion of the trustees in furtherance of the charity's objects. Any funds applied for purposes other than those set out in the governing document will be in breach of trust.

2.3.2 Trustees may decide to earmark part of the charity's unrestricted funds for a particular purpose (for example to purchase a property or to provide for redundancy costs). These funds are known as *designated funds*. Although designated funds are set aside for a specific purpose, the trustees have complete power to redesignate or to remove the designation altogether. For this reason designated funds continue to be accounted for as part of the charity's unrestricted funds.

2.3.3 Non-designated unrestricted funds are usually placed in one general fund and may be used for any purpose allowed by the governing document.

2.3.4 Restricted funds: may only be used for certain purposes as specified by the original funder or donor. This may include funds raised for a particular purpose via a public appeal (i.e. the donor has given money on the assumption that it will be used for a particular purpose). The purposes for which restricted funds are to be used must still be within the wider objects of the charity.

2.3.5 Restricted funds may be restricted income funds or endowment (capital) funds.

2.3.6 Restricted income funds: spent at the discretion of the trustees within the terms of the fund. Charity trustees will be in breach of trust if they spend restricted income funds otherwise than in accordance with the terms of the fund. This may also result in the funder or donor requesting that the income be returned to them.

2.3.7 Where a fixed asset is purchased with restricted funds, the treatment of the fixed asset will depend on the terms of the fund. In most cases, once the fixed asset is purchased the restrictions cease and the fixed asset may be used for any purpose within the charity's objects. The fixed asset therefore becomes part of unrestricted funds. It is important to note that the initial purchase of the asset must be within the terms of the restricted fund.

2.3.8 A separate designated fund is often created for capital assets to separate unrestricted income funds from unrestricted fixed assets. In other cases the terms of the restricted fund may indicate that once purchased the fixed asset may only be used for specific purposes and so it will remain in a restricted fund. Again it makes sense to create a separate restricted fund for capital assets to separate them from restricted income funds. When a fixed asset is sold, the proceeds will form part of the fund in which the asset was held.

2.3.9 Endowment funds: capital funds which are required to be invested, or retained for actual use, rather than expended. They are always regarded as restricted funds as by their very nature there is some kind of restriction over the use of the capital. The income from the capital fund may or may not be restricted depending on the terms of the fund.

2.3.10 Permanent endowment funds: must be held indefinitely under the terms of the fund and may not be sold or otherwise converted into income. In some cases there may be the ability to exchange an asset in a permanent endowment fund for another similar asset (e.g. investments in stocks and shares). In other cases (e.g. historic property) the terms of the fund relate to a specific asset. Any expenses relating directly to the endowment should be taken out of the fund (e.g. investment management costs or valuation fees). However, costs relating to the generation of income from any land or property held in an endowment fund (e.g. rent collection or property repairs) would be charged against the relevant income fund. Usually any income generated from permanent endowment funds (e.g. rent or dividend income) may be treated as unrestricted income unless the terms of the endowment fund specify otherwise. Note that any income (from whatever source) that is spent on the maintenance or improvement of land or property held in a permanent endowment fund will become part of that fund.

2.3.11 It may be possible to spend the permanent endowment (i.e. convert it to income) if the trustees consider that it is in the best interests of the charity to do so. More details can be found in the next section on Orders and Schemes.

2.3.12 Expendable endowment funds: may be converted into income at the discretion of the trustees. An example would include long-term investments held for the purpose of meeting property maintenance costs. In this case the trustees would need to manage the investments to ensure that sufficient income is generated at the right time and that the income is spent in accordance with the terms of the fund (which may mean that the income is placed into a restricted income fund). Note that unlike income funds, the trustees are under no obligation to spend an expendable endowment fund.

2.3.13 Trustees may wish to consider using a *Total Return on Investment* approach for permanent endowment funds. This allows trustees to manage investments without the need to take account of whether the return is income (e.g. interest or dividends) or capital gains or losses. The entire return on investment may be spent at the discretion of the trustees, subject to certain accounting and reporting disclosures and subject to a duty to treat present and future beneficiaries fairly. Normally this approach is not allowed for permanent endowment funds, but the Charity Commission will give the power for existing charities to adopt this approach by Order under section 26 of the Charities Act 1993. New charities may include the power to adopt this approach in their governing document.

3 Powers of the Charity Commission: Orders and Schemes

3.1 Trustees should regularly review their charity's governing document and ensure that the objects continue to be practical and relevant to their beneficiaries' needs, and that the charity's assets are being effectively applied. It is likely that over time circumstances and needs will change and that the governing document will need updating to reflect these changes.

3.2 Trustees have a number of options for making changes to their governing documents. The method used will depend on the type and size of charity, the changes they wish to make and any powers of amendment given to the trustees in the governing document.

3.3 If the power to amend the governing document is not available to the trustees, they may apply to the Charity Commission for a Scheme or an Order which authorises the trustees to make the changes.

3.4 All new model governing documents for charities should include a power of amendment and of dissolution.

3.5 Trustees' existing powers

3.5.1 Small unincorporated charities with income of £10,000 or less may change their objects and purposes by resolution even if there is no express power in the governing document allowing them to do this. The power to do this comes from the Charities Act 1993. Trustees must pass a resolution by at least two-thirds of those who vote, and send a copy to the Charity Commission with the reasons for making the change. Unless the Charity Commission object, request further information or require publicity to be given, the resolution will automatically take effect 60 days after the Charity Commission have received it.

3.5.2 If the charity's governing document contains a specific power to change the purposes and objects that is quicker and simpler than that described above, the trustees are free to use that power instead.

3.5.3 Larger unincorporated charities with income of more than £10,000 can only change their objects and purposes if their governing document gives them power to do so. If that power is available, the procedure to be followed will be laid out in the governing document. In all cases, a copy of the resolution making the change must be sent to the Charity Commission together with a copy of the revised governing document.

3.5.4 If the governing document does not give the trustees power to change the objects of the charity, they must apply to the Charity Commission for a Scheme.

3.5.5 All unincorporated charities have a statutory power to change the administrative procedures and powers of their charity. A resolution is required using whatever method is specified in the governing document for such resolutions, and a copy must be sent to the Charity Commission. Note that trustees cannot use this power to alter their charity's purposes, spend capital held as permanent endowment or to authorise payments to themselves or to related parties. It should also not be used to amend powers which the trustees can only exercise with the consent of a third party unless the charity trustees have the agreement of the third party or the third party has ceased to exist.

3.5.6 Charitable Companies have the power to amend their memorandum and articles of association under company law, but prior written consent from the Charity Commission is required if the change is a "regulated alteration". Prior consent will also be required if the memorandum and articles of association demands it.

3.5.7 Regulated alterations are changes to areas of fundamental importance as follows:

- Any change to the objects clause;
- Any change to what happens to the charity's property on winding up;
- Any change which authorises the directors or members to benefit from the charity's assets.

3.5.8 Once written consent has been obtained from the Charity Commission, the charity will need to pass a special resolution making the alteration. The charity must then send a signed copy of the resolution and a copy of the amended memorandum and/or articles of association to both the Charity Commission and to Companies House within 15 days of the resolution being made.

3.5.9 Trustees of all registered charities must keep the Charity Commission informed of all changes to their governing document.

3.6 Charity Commission Orders

3.6.1 The Charity Commission may make an Order under section 26 of the Charities Act 1993 to authorise trustees to carry out an act that they otherwise have no power to do. An Order is discretionary (i.e. trustees may choose whether or not to follow it) and will only be made if the Charity Commission believe it is in the best interests of the charity.

3.6.2 An Order is easier and quicker to put in place than a Scheme and so should usually be applied for in preference to a Scheme. However an Order cannot be used to:

- Authorise the trustees to amend the purposes and objects of the Charity;
- Authorise the trustees to do anything that overrides an express prohibition in either an Act of Parliament or in the governing document (e.g. if the governing document prohibits trustees from being paid); or
- Impose duties or directions on the trustees that do not relate to the Powers given in the Order.

3.6.3 Examples of situations when Orders may be used include:

- Obtaining the power to use a total return on investment approach for permanent endowment funds;
- Authorising a specific transaction when trustees are faced with a conflict of interest (e.g. payment of trustees as long as it is not expressly prohibited);
- Authorising a specific borrowing where there is no power to borrow in the governing document;
- Obtaining the power to spend certain permanent endowments when the statutory power is not available (see the section on permanent endowments later in this chapter).

3.6.4 There is no formal application process for an Order. A request for it can be made from any person suitably authorised to apply on behalf of the charity's trustees. There is also no right of appeal and the Charity Commission may prefer to make a Scheme where it is important to preserve this right.

3.7 Charity Commission Schemes

3.7.1 A scheme is a legal document made by the Charity Commission that amends, replaces or extends the governing document of a charity. It may affect the objects and purposes of a charity, the constitutional arrangements or the powers of trustees. The Charity Commission will only offer a Scheme where no other method of changing a charity's governing document is available. Like an Order, a Scheme will only be made if it is in the best interests of the charity.

3.7.2 A Scheme is most likely to be used where:

- A larger unincorporated charity with income over £10,000 has no power to change the objects and purposes in their governing document;
- An unincorporated charity wishes to make changes that are expressly prohibited in their governing document;
- An unincorporated charity wishes to amend a power that can only be exercised with the consent of a third party and the third party is either not willing or is unable to consent to such a change;
- The Charity Commission wish to impose duties or directions on trustees.

3.7.3 Section 13(1) of the Charities Act 1993, as amended by section 15 of the Charities Act 2006 sets out the circumstances when the Charity Commission can make a Scheme to change the objects of a charity. These are where:

(a) The original objects, in whole or in part:
  i. Have, as far as possible, been fulfilled;
  ii. Cannot be carried out, or not in the way laid down in the governing document;
(b) The original objects provide a use for only part of the charity's property;
(c) Two or more charities with similar objects want to merge but do not have the legal power to do so.
(d) The original purposes use outdated definitions of areas, places or classes of people;
(e) The original objects, in whole or in part:
  i. Have subsequently been adequately provided for in other ways (e.g. out of public funds);
  ii. Are no longer charitable in law; or no longer provide a suitable and effective method of using the charity's assets.

3.7.4 The Charity Commission will apply the legal doctrine of "cy-pres" (Norman French for "close to") in agreeing new purposes. This means that they will take into consideration the spirit of the original objects and also current social and economic circumstances when considering cases that fall within s.13 (1)c), (d) and (e).

3.7.5 The spirit of the original objects means the basic intention underlying the original objects as a whole. In deciding this, records from when the time the charity was established may be relevant, as may the way in which the charity has been administered and managed over the years.

3.7.6 The purpose of reviewing the current social and economic circumstances is to evaluate the ongoing usefulness of the charity and its current objects. The definition of social and economic circumstances is broad and could also include environmental, legal, scientific or technological considerations.

3.8 Applying for a Scheme

3.8.1 The most usual route is for the trustees of the charity to apply for a scheme. Initially, the trustees should discuss their proposed changes with the Charity Commission and their own professional advisors. In potentially contentious cases, trustees should also consult on the changes with beneficiaries and other stakeholders.

3.8.2 The Charity Commission will then agree a broad outline of the Scheme before inviting the trustees to make a formal application.

3.8.3 The application should be made on one of the Charity Commission forms (CHY-ST1 (A) or CHY-ST1 (B)) by the trustees acting as a body. This means that either:

(a) The trustees resolve to authorise one or more people, who do not have to be trustees, to sign on their behalf; or
(b) All trustees (or a sufficient number of them to indicate that the decision has been properly taken) sign the application.

3.8.4 Option (a) is the most common approach and the Charity Commission will normally give advice on the precise wording of the resolution.

3.8.5 If trustees are unable to achieve a quorum, the Charity Commission may accept an application from whatever number of trustees they consider to be appropriate in the circumstances. This may occur if there are insufficient trustees in office or if one or more trustees are absent or incapacitated. If there are no trustees the Charity Commission will appoint one.

3.8.6 In some circumstances the Charity Commission may make a Scheme for the administration of a charity "of their own motion" and no application from the trustees is needed. This would only usually happen where there is (or has been) misconduct or mismanagement in the administration of the charity and the Charity Commission wish to protect the charity's property.

3.8.7 Alternatively, the Charity Commission may proceed with a Scheme if they deem it necessary but the charity trustees fail or refuse to apply. For this to happen, the charity must not be exempt and it must have been established for over 40 years.

3.8.8 The Charity Commission may also invite an application for a Scheme from the Attorney General when there is substantial public interest and no other method of obtaining jurisdiction is practicable. In exceptional circumstances the Court may order a Scheme to be established.

3.9 The Process for Establishing a Scheme

3.9.1 The Charity Commission is responsible for the legal and practical effect of a Scheme and for deciding its final content. Once they have received a formal application, they will prepare a detailed draft of the Scheme and send it to trustees for their comments and agreement.

3.9.2 Where the scheme is likely to be non-controversial, publicity will not be required. However in some circumstances the Charity Commission may decide that publicity is necessary. In this case the Charity Commission will give public notice of the proposals, and invite representations about them to be made within a period specified in the notice. Any comments and objections will be given due consideration and changes made to the Scheme as required. This stage can be avoided by trustees carrying out and evidencing adequate consultation at the start of the process.

3.9.3 The Scheme will then be brought into effect by sealing it.
The Charity Commission publishes guidance on Orders and Schemes in the form of CC36 – Changing you Charity's Governing Document. The Commission's internal operational guidance is also available on its website and this contains a multitude of guidance on Orders and Schemes.

✓ 3.9.4 Checklist: Applying for a Scheme

Planning

1. Have the trustees identified what change is to be made?
2. Are the trustees aware of the contents of CC36 (Changing your governing document)?
3. Can the charity use alternative machinery to make the change (e.g. the Small Charities provisions, an existing power of amendment)?
4. Have the trustees discussed the change with professional advisors (e.g. solicitors and accountants)?
5. If the change is controversial, have beneficiaries and other stakeholders been consulted?
6. Have the proposed changes been discussed with the Charity Commission?
7. Has a broad outline of the Scheme been agreed with the Charity Commission?

Applying

8. Have the Charity Commission invited a formal application?
9. Is the charity quorate? If no, go to question 13.

10. Has a resolution been passed to authorize one or more people to sign the application on behalf of the trustees? If no, go to question 12.
11. Has the application form been completed and certified by the authorized applicant(s)? If yes, go to question 14
12. Has the application form been completed and certified by a quorum of trustees? If yes, go to question 14. If no, application cannot go ahead.
13. If the charity cannot apply for a scheme because there are insufficient trustees, will the Charity Commission accept an application from fewer trustees? (a No answer is rare, unless there are no trustees)
14. Send the completed application form to the Charity Commission.

Establishing the scheme

15. Have the Charity Commission sent a draft of the Scheme to the Trustees to be reviewed?
16. Have the Trustees reviewed the draft and notified the Charity Commission of their approval (or any comments)?
17. Is the Charity Commission satisfied that publicity requirements have been met?
18. Has the Scheme been sealed and sent to the Trustees for safekeeping?
19. Have any public notice requirements from the Charity Commission been met?

3.10 Spending permanent endowments

3.10.1 As mentioned earlier in this chapter, permanent endowment funds must be held indefinitely under the terms of the fund and may not be sold or otherwise converted into income. However, there will be cases where it is in the best interests of the charity to convert permanent endowments into income. A statutory power exists to do this where the trustees decide that by using their charity's permanent endowment as well as any income it will be able to carry out its purposes more effectively.

3.10.2 The availability of the statutory power depends to a certain extent on the type of permanent endowment:

- **investment permanent endowment:** capital which is to be used to provide an income for the charity. The restriction on spending the capital is considered to be an administrative restriction; or
- **functional permanent endowment:** capital used for a specific purpose for the charity (e.g. historic buildings or village halls). Here the sale of the endowment and the use of the proceeds for a purpose other than the replacement of the endowment in question may involve a change of purpose.

3.10.3 The Charity Commission considers it unlikely that trustees will be able to use the statutory power for functional permanent endowments as trustees are unlikely to be able to prove that the charity can carry out its purposes more effectively by disposing of the asset. In addition, the Charity Commission considers that the power does not apply to assets that do not generate an income as the capital must be used 'as well as any income'.

3.10.4 The way in which the statutory power is used depends on the size of the charity and the characteristics of the permanent endowment.

3.10.5 A type 1 charity must have:

- annual gross income of more than £1,000; and
- permanent endowment consisting entirely of property that (a) was entirely given (i.e. not created by the trustees) and (b) has a market value of more than £10,000.

3.10.6 If any of the above conditions are not met, the charity will be a type 2 charity.

3.10.7 Type 1 charities must get the approval of the Charity Commission before spending the permanent endowment. To do this, the trustees must pass a formal resolution that the permanent endowment restrictions should be removed from all or part of the fund concerned. A copy of the resolution and a statement of the reasons for passing it should then be sent to the Charity Commission, who has three months to make a decision. The decision will be based upon whether the proposal is in keeping with the spirit of the gift (i.e. the application of the legal doctrine of cy-pres). The Charity Commission may request further information and/or public notice before making a decision.

3.10.8 Type 2 charities do not need the approval of the Charity Commission before spending the permanent endowment. The trustees are still required to pass a formal resolution that the permanent endowment restrictions should be removed from all or part of the fund concerned, but the endowment can be spent as soon as the resolution is in place.

3.10.9 Where the statutory power is not available, or the trustees choose not to use it, the Charity Commission may be able to authorise the trustees to spend the permanent endowment. If the Charity Commission is satisfied that it is in the best interests of the charity, they can remove an administrative restriction by making an Order under section 26 of the Charities Act 1993. However, where there is a change of purpose, and there is no power that allows the property to be used for the new purpose, the change can only be made by a Scheme.

3.10.10 The Charity Commission may decide that the permanent endowment can be spent, but that it must be replaced out of future income. This is usual when a charity needs to find extra money for, say, repairs or renovation costs.

3.11 Financial management

3.11.1 Charity trustees must ensure that the charity's funds and assets are used appropriately, prudently, lawfully and in accordance with its objects. Proper financial management is key to achieving this. Proper financial management will also ensure that the charity continues to be effective and remains solvent.

3.11.2 The core principles of financial management are as follows:

- creating an appropriate financial environment;
- understanding the current financial position; and
- looking forward: financial strategy and planning.

3.11.3 If an appropriate financial environment is created, the process of understanding the current financial position and planning for the future become easier. Similarly it is very difficult to look forward without understanding the current financial position.

3.11.4 Creating an appropriate financial environment. Key aspects to consider when creating an appropriate financial environment will include:

- **Trustees:** the board of trustees should possess appropriate financial skills and be able to devote sufficient time to the financial management of the charity. All trustees, not just the treasurer (if there is one), are responsible for the financial stewardship of the charity. There should also be a clear delegation of responsibilities, whether to the treasurer, finance committee or staff.
- **Staff:** finance staff should possess the appropriate skills, capabilities and knowledge to carry out their responsibilities and duties. Any gaps may need to be addressed through recruitment and training.
- **Accounting systems:** trustees are under a duty to ensure that the charity keeps proper books and records. Any accounting system must enable the trustees to understand the current financial position of the charity. For anything other than the smallest charity this will involve the use of IT and specialist accounting software.
- **Internal financial controls:** must be established to protect the assets of the charity and to apply them properly. This is discussed in more detail in the next chapter.
- **Risk management:** the trustees need to assess and understand the risks associated with the charity's financial management and manage them appropriately. Indeed the trustees' annual report should include a statement 'confirming that the major risks to which the charity is exposed, as identified by

the trustees, have been reviewed and systems or procedures have been established to manage those risks' (SORP 2005, paragraph 45).

3.11.5 Understanding the current financial position. Financial reports should be presented and considered by the trustees at regular trustee meetings. But what needs to go into a financial report, and how should it be presented?

3.11.6 Many trustees and non-finance staff find charity accounts difficult to understand (and may be embarrassed to say so). It is therefore important to ensure that financial reports are clear, easy to understand and presented with a narrative. Alternative means of presenting the information should be considered (e.g. graphs or a face-to-face presentation).

3.11.7 There is often no need for detailed financial information to be presented to trustees. Headline figures may be appropriate, as may the use of key performance indicators. Non-financial indicators should also be included (e.g. the number of beneficiaries helped).

3.11.8 It is important that the information is presented in context, i.e. it is compared to something. For example the actual results of the charity for a particular month may be compared to:

- the results for the month before;
- the results for the same month last year (or for the last two years);
- the budgeted results; or
- the performance of other charities in the same sector.

3.11.9 All financial reports should be up to date and accurate. Here the creation of an appropriate financial environment is crucial. Competent staff and appropriate financial controls will reduce the risk of errors. An efficient accounting system and a culture of up-to-date reporting will ensure a timely report.

3.11.10 Finally, and a point that is often overlooked, trustees need to receive the financial reports sufficiently in advance of the meeting to give them time to read and digest the contents.

3.11.11 Looking forward: financial strategy and planning. A financial strategy defines how a charity will get from its current financial position to the position it wishes to be in the future.

3.11.12 The desired future position will be determined by the charity's overall mission, objectives and strategy. It must also take account of any external or internal factors affecting the charity (i.e. loss of key staff, availability of future funding).

3.11.13 The strategy will include:

- whether the funds and assets of the charity are to be spent or retained for future use;
- what the funds and assets are to be spent on; and
- how any additional income is to be raised;

3.11.14 A financial strategy should include budgets and cash flow forecasts. The detail of the strategy will vary depending on how far forward it is forecasting. One might see detailed plans for the next 12 months, less detailed for years two and three and an overview for year four onwards. It should be updated on at least an annual basis.

3.11.15 Actual results should be monitored against budget to identify any potential problems or budget inaccuracies. Future budgets and forecasts may be updated on an ongoing basis to take account of changes in operating conditions. A tight cash situation may necessitate more detailed short-term planning than would otherwise be the case.

3.12 Investments

3.12.1 Trustees should look to invest any money not needed for immediate expenditure. There is a wide range of investments available to charities, but first trustees need to ensure that they have the power to invest the charity's funds.

3.12.2 Section 3 of the Trustee Act 2000 gives trustees of unincorporated charities the power to invest charity funds in any kind of investment, excluding land, in which they could invest if they were the absolute owner of those funds. Section 8 of the same Act gives trustees the power to acquire as an investment freehold or leasehold land in the United Kingdom on the same basis as the power in section 3. This is known as a general power of investment. In some cases a charity's governing document may restrict or exclude this power.

3.12.3 Note that the Trustee Act 2000 does not authorise the purchase of land outside the United Kingdom. If charities wish to do this they will need to seek some other kind of power.

3.12.4 Charitable companies usually have a similar power of investment in their governing document. A provision in a charitable company's Articles of Association to the effect that the powers of investment are those prescribed by law would normally give the general power of investment to the directors of the company.

3.12.5 As mentioned in paragraph 10 above, charitable companies have the power to amend their Articles of Association under company law, with the prior consent of the Charity Commission required only if the change is a 'regulated alteration'.

Therefore it will always be possible for a charitable company to add a power of investment to the governing document should one not already be there.

3.12.6 Trustees' duties: trustees must take a prudent approach when managing a charity's investments. They also have a general duty of care, which means that they must use reasonable skill and care appropriate to their personal knowledge and experience. Therefore a trustee who is experienced in investments or who is being paid would be expected to exercise a higher level of skill and care.

3.12.7 Trustees also have specific duties in relation to investments:

- **Suitability:** trustees must ensure that the investment is suitable for the charity's needs. This would include a consideration of the length of the investment, the exposure to risk, the balance of income versus capital as well as any ethical considerations.
- **Diversification:** trustees must ensure that the investment portfolio is suitably diversified to reduce the risk of losses.
- **Periodic review:** trustees must review the suitability and diversification of the investments on a regular basis (at least once a year).
- **Proper advice:** trustees must obtain proper advice from a suitably qualified adviser (who may be one of the trustees) before making any investments and when reviewing the investments. This advice is not required if the investment is so small that the advice would not be cost effective.

3.12.8 The Charity Commission recommends that in adopting a prudent approach trustees are particularly wary of speculative investments and invest only in markets where financial services are closely regulated and compensation schemes are in place.

3.12.9 Investment policy: charity trustees are encouraged to create an investment policy which should specify the charity's attitude to risk and its approach to ethical investment. This policy should be recorded in writing and reviewed regularly. It should also be disclosed in the charity's annual report. Larger charities (income over £500,000) are also required to report on their investment performance in their annual report.

3.12.10 A charity's approach to ethical investment needs to be carefully thought out. Trustees have a duty to further the purposes of the charity, and it is generally considered that those purposes will be best served by obtaining the maximum return on investments. This duty is not always compatible with ethical investment. However, there are certain circumstances when a charity is justified in allowing their investment strategy to be governed by ethical considerations:

- where the investment would for practical (not moral) reasons conflict with the aims of the charity (e.g. an environmental charity may not support a business known to pollute the environment);
- where the investment might hamper the charity's work, either by making potential beneficiaries less willing to be helped or by alienating supporters;
- if the investment is morally unacceptable a charity may reject it as long as this will not result in significant financial detriment due to underperformance as a result of the exclusion.

3.12.11 Any decision regarding ethical investments should be recorded in writing, after taking appropriate advice.

3.12.12 Incorporated charities may own investments in their own name as they have a legal identity. Unincorporated charities do not, however, have a legal identity and so cannot hold investments in their own name. Any investments owned by such charities will have to be held in the names of individuals, sometimes selected from the trustees, who are known as nominees or holding trustees. The charity may also select a custodian who looks after the title documents to the investments.

3.12.13 Common types of investments include stocks and shares, unit trusts, bank deposits and land let with the intention of producing rental income. Any assets purchased with a view to sale will be treated as trading and so will not receive the usual tax relief offered to charities (examples include land or commodities).

3.12.14 Land may be a suitable investment for some charities, but it generally requires more active management and cannot be turned into cash as readily as other investments. It is also difficult to diversify investment in land unless the charity has a sufficiently wide and varied portfolio of other investments.

3.12.15 Charities have the option of investing in Common Investment Funds (CIFs) and Common Deposit Funds (CDFs) which are collective investment funds only available to charities. They comprise funds from many different charities pooled together and then spread across a variety of deposit takers (for CDFs) or stocks and shares (for CIFs). The investment return can be higher and the risk lower than if an individual charity had made its own investments. Both CIFs and CDFs are charities themselves and investment returns are therefore tax free. This is an attractive option for smaller charities for which it is not cost effective to appoint their own investment manager.

3.12.16 The discussion of investments so far has assumed that the trustees' main reason for making an investment is to maximise their financial return. The primary aim of Programme Related Investments (or Social Investments) is to further the charitable objectives of the organisation and any financial return is a secondary consideration. Examples would include loans to beneficiaries or to other charities.

3.12.17 Larger charities may wish to delegate their investment management decisions to a delegated investment manager. Under trust law trustees need an explicit authority to delegate these decisions which for unincorporated charities will generally come from the Trustees Act 2000. Again, an incorporated charity will usually have the required powers in its governing document. All charities' governing documents should be checked for restrictions or exclusions.

3.12.18 The process of selecting an investment manager may not be delegated, and trustees have a general duty of care when making this decision. They also have a number of specific duties when appointing an investment manager:

(a) There must be an agreement with the investment manager in writing or evidenced in writing.
(b) The trustees must prepare a policy statement which gives guidance to the investment manager as to how to manage the investments. This statement should again be in writing or evidenced in writing and its preparation cannot be delegated (but trustees may and should take proper advice regarding its preparation). The statement may include the following:
    i. the charity's aims in investing its funds, including its position on risk;
    ii. asset allocation strategy;
    iii. benchmarks and targets by which the investment manager will be judged;
    iv. the charity's stance on ethical investment;
    v. the balance between capital growth and income generation; and/or
    vi. the scope of investment powers.
(c) Trustees have a duty to regularly review the performance of the investment manager and the terms under which he is appointed.

3.12.19 Charities will generally be exempt from tax on all investment income. However, certain types of investment may be considered to be 'non-charitable expenditure' by HMRC, which may result in a restriction in tax relief. Charities need to be able to satisfy HMRC that any such investments are made for the financial benefit of the charity and not for the avoidance of tax, whether by the charity or another person.

3.12.20 The Charity Commission has published guidance on investments in the form of CC14, 'Investment of Charitable Funds: Basic Principles' and gives more detailed guidance on its website.

3.13 Land and property

3.13.1 Acquiring land and property: Section 8 of the Trustee Act 2000 gives trustees of unincorporated charities the power to acquire freehold or leasehold land in the United Kingdom to carry out the purposes of the charity or for investment. In some cases a charity's governing document may restrict or exclude this power. Charitable companies usually have a similar power of investment in their governing document.

3.13.2 Note that the Trustee Act 2000 does not authorise the purchase of land or property outside the United Kingdom as an investment. If charities wish to do this they will need to seek some other kind of power.

3.13.3 The trustees will need to obtain a section 26 Order from the Charity Commission if they wish to acquire land or property when they have no power to do so. This will also be necessary if they intend to use money held as permanent endowment or acquire land or property from a connected party.

3.13.4 Trustees have a statutory duty of care when acquiring land and property. This means that they must exercise such care and skill as is reasonable in the circumstances. A higher level of care and skill is expected when a trustee either has special knowledge and experience or is being paid for giving advice in this area.

3.13.5 Trustees also have a number of specific duties when acquiring land and property and need to ensure that:

- the charity has the necessary power or authority to acquire the land or property;
- the property is suitable for its intended use;
- the price or rent is fair and reasonable and represents best value for the charity;
- the terms of any lease are fair and reasonable;
- the charity can afford the purchase or rent; and
- any necessary planning permission is obtained.

3.13.6 If the land or property is to be an investment, the specific duties outlined in the last section also apply.

3.13.7 The Charity Commission recommends that the trustees engage a qualified surveyor to prepare a report which includes the following:

- a description of the land or property;
- details of any planning permission needed;
- a valuation of the land or property;

- advice on the price the trustees ought to offer to pay, or on the maximum bid they should make at an auction;
- a description of any repairs or alterations needed and the estimated cost;
- a positive recommendation (with reasons) that it is in the interests of the charity to purchase the land or property; and
- anything else the surveyor thinks relevant, including a description of any restrictive or other covenants to which the land is subject.

3.13.8 It is expected that the trustees also engage the services of a solicitor.

3.13.9 Trustees may in certain circumstances acquire land and property with a mortgage. Further guidance on this is given in paragraph 3.7 on borrowing.

3.13.10 As with investments, unincorporated charities cannot hold land or property in their own name. The land or property will need to be held in the names of holding trustees or nominees. It is also sometimes held in the name of all the trustees. Alternatively, charities may request the Official Custodian for Charities to hold the land or property on their behalf. This is a free service provided by the Charity Commission which simplifies the ownership of the land or property and removes the need to make new deeds when the trustees change. It also removes the risk that the land or property is owned by trustees who are no longer connected to the charity and may be difficult to trace. The Official Custodian for Charities will not normally hold investments on behalf of charities.

3.13.11 Trustees have a number of general duties in relation to the management of land and property. These include:

- Trustees are individually and jointly responsible for the protection, management and supervision of land and property. This means they should retain control as a board rather than leaving matters to an individual.
- In managing land and property, trustees must act *only* in the interests of the charity and its beneficiaries.
- Trustees must act honestly and prudently and seek advice where necessary from independent professional advisors acting exclusively for the charity.

3.13.12 Disposing of land and property: the term 'disposal' covers all sales, leases, grants of rights, exchanges of land, and all other transactions in which trustees part with or grant and interest in their land *except* for the release of a rent charge and the granting of a mortgage. More details on the release of a rent charge can be found in Charity Commission publication CC228, 'Disposing of Charity Land'. The granting of a mortgage is covered in the section on borrowing below.

3.13.13 There are four issues to be considered when trustees dispose of charity land or property:

(1) Do the trustees have the power to make the disposal?
(2) Is the disposal beneficial to the charity? Trustees need to be able to show why the disposal is in the best interest of the charity.
(3) Are the terms of the disposal the best that can be obtained for the charity?
(4) Is consent from the Charity Commission required?

3.13.14 The Charity Commission expects any decisions regarding the disposal of land and property to be made by the board and not delegated.

3.13.15 The governing document of most charities will usually give the trustees the power to dispose of land and property. The trustees should pay attention to any conditions in their governing document relating to the power. If there is no such power, trustees may rely on the powers given in section 6(1) of the Trusts of Land and Appointment of Trustees Act 1996.

3.13.16 The following circumstances may not be covered by existing powers:

- converting permanent endowment into income (see details earlier in this chapter); and
- the sale of designated land (i.e. land held on trust for the purposes of the charity) where the proceeds are not to be used to acquire land for a similar purpose. A Charity Commission Scheme will usually be required to do this.

3.13.17 Trustees must always secure the best terms reasonably obtainable when they dispose of land and property. This usually means that they must accept the highest price offered, even if they find the purchaser objectionable. However, the trustees are not expected to accept an offer where they believe the purchaser will use the land in such a way that will either be directly contrary to the purposes of the charity or will affect other land that the charity holds.

3.13.18 There may sometimes be other non-monetary reasons why a lower price will be more beneficial to the charity. This includes the case when land or property is being sold at less than market value to another charity with similar purposes. As long as the trustees have the power to make such a disposal, and the disposal is furthering the objects of the charity, Charity Commission consent is not required.

3.13.19 Charity Commission consent is not required to dispose of land or property if the statutory requirements in section 36 of the Charities Act 1993 are met. These are as follows:

- Trustees must obtain and consider a written report on the proposed disposal from a qualified (RICS) surveyor instructed by the trustees and acting exclusively for the charity. This report must include amongst other things

a valuation and advice on how best to sell the land or property. The exact contents of the report are laid down in the Charities (Qualified Surveyors' Reports) Regulations 1992.
- Trustees must advertise the property in accordance with the surveyor's advice.
- The trustees must satisfy themselves that the terms of the disposal are the best that can be reasonably obtained.
- The person to whom the trustees are disposing the land is not a connected person.
- These requirements are met before the trustees enter into an agreement for disposal.

3.13.20 The statutory requirements are slightly less onerous if the charity is granting a lease for seven years or less and does not receive a premium. Instead of appointing a qualified surveyor, the trustees may consider the advice of a person they 'reasonably believe to have the ability and experience to advise them competently on the granting of the lease'. They must still meet the last three requirements detailed above.

3.13.21 Charity Commission consent will therefore be required if any of the above requirements are not met. The most common reason for consent being needed is that a disposal is to a connected person (i.e. a trustee or employee, or a close relative thereof).

3.13.22 Consent will also be required for designated land if there is a change in the trust purposes on which the land is held. This will be the case if replacement land is not purchased with the proceeds or retention of that specific piece of land is part of the trust. In addition, trustees are required to give public notice of their intention to dispose of designated land where no replacement land is being purchased. Further details of disposing of designated land can be found in Charity Commission publication CC228, 'Disposing of Charity Land'.

3.13.23 Section 27 of the Charities Act 1993 requires trustees to include certain statements and certificates in the contract or deed for the disposal of the land or property. These statements make it clear to the purchaser that:
- they are acquiring land or property from a charity;
- the trustees have the power to make the disposal; and
- the trustees have either met the appropriate statutory requirements or that the necessary consent has been obtained from the Charity Commission.

3.13.24 The last statement above has the effect of protecting the purchaser's title to the land if it later becomes clear that the trustees made the disposal without following the statutory requirements.

3.6.25 Any custodian or holding trustees (including the Official Custodian for Charities) must be party to the contract or deed for the disposal of the land or property. It is not necessary for all the trustees to sign the deed. Under section 82 of the Charities Act 1993 two or more trustees can execute a document on behalf of the trustees if the trustees have resolved that this can be done. The trustees should appoint a solicitor to ensure that the contract or deed is technically correct.

✓ 3.13.26 Sale of land checklist

- Has the decision to dispose of land been taken by the trustees acting together?
- Do the trustees have the power to dispose of land?
- Are the trustees able to justify why the disposal is in the best interests of the charity?
- Are the terms of the disposal the best that can be obtained for the charity? (N/A if disposing to another charity.)
- Is consent from the Charity Commission required? (See below.)
- Are the required statements under s. 27 of the Charities Act 1993 included in the contract or deed of disposal?
- Are any custodian or holding trustees party to the contract or deed of disposal?

Charity Commission consent is required if:

- The disposal is to a connected person; or
- the surveyor is unable to recommend the terms of the transaction; or
- the trustees do not wish to use a surveyor; or
- the surveyor used is not qualified (as defined in the Charities Act 1993); or
- the trustees fail to follow the statutory requirements before they enter into an agreement to dispose; or
- the land is designated land or held on permanent endowment, and replacement land is not purchased with the proceeds or retention of that specific piece of land is part of the trust.

3.14 Borrowing

3.14.1 Trustees may borrow money only if they have the power to do so. Normally this power would be expressly given in the charity's governing document. If the governing document does not contain such a power, there are a number of alternatives:

- unincorporated charities may use the statutory power contained in the Trusts of Land and Appointment of Trustees Act 1996 (TLAT 1996) and the Trustee

Act 2000 (TA 2000). This allows trustees to raise money by mortgage for the purposes of acquiring land and property or for the repair, maintenance and improvement of the land and property; or
- trustees may use the power of amendment in section 74D of the Charities Act 1993 (as inserted by the Charities Act 2006) or the relevant power in the Companies Act to confer on the charity a power to borrow (with the consent of the Charity Commission); or
- trustees may apply to the Charity Commission for a section 26 Order to authorise the borrowing.

3.14.2 If the governing document expressly prohibits borrowing, the trustees will need to apply to the Charity Commission for a Scheme.

3.14.3 Trustees do not require the consent of the Charity Commission to grant a mortgage over charity land as security for any purpose (including a loan, overdraft or grant) provided they have express power to do so and they meet two requirements laid down in section 38 of the Charities Act 1993. These requirements are as follows:

(a) Trustees must obtain and consider the advice of someone who they reasonably believe has sufficient ability in, and practical experience of, financial matters to give them sound advice. This person may be a trustee or employee of the charity, but must not have any financial interest in the loan or grant.
(b) The advisor must provide the trustees with advice in writing on three matters:
 i. whether the loan or grant is necessary in order for the trustees to be able to pursue the particular course of action in connection with which the loan or grant is sought;
 ii. whether the terms of the loan or grant are reasonable; and
 iii. the charity's ability to repay the loan or grant on the terms agreed with the lender.

3.14.4 If the above requirements cannot be met, the trustees will need the consent of the Charity Commission before they create the mortgage.

3.14.5 The above requirements do not need to be followed where the express authority for the mortgage is contained in an Act of Parliament, a statutory instrument or a Charity Commission Scheme.

3.14.6 There are no longer any statutory controls over the mortgaging or charging of charity property other than land.

3.14.7 Trustees may also consider unsecured borrowing. The Charity Commission recommends that trustees always seek professional advice before taking out any substantial unsecured loans. It is also recommended that the trustees ensure that the charity has sufficient assets to repay the loan should the charity suffer a sudden loss of income.

3.14.8 For unincorporated charities, unsecured loans pose an additional risk to trustees, who are effectively borrowing the money in their own name. They will expect to be indemnified out of the charity's assets rather than having to repay the money personally. This indemnity will be secured by a charge on the whole of the charity's assets (under s. 30 (2) of the Trustee Act 1925), but does not require compliance with section 38 of the Charities Act 1993 for it to be valid. Note that trustees will only be indemnified if they have acted properly in the administration of the charity, both when taking the loan out and when spending the money.

E2
Risk management and internal controls

2.1 Introduction

2.1.1 If a charity is to maximise its charitable impact, it must manage the underlying risks which may prevent it from operating in an effective and efficient manner. The risks facing every charity are different and so trustees must first identify the risks facing their own organisation before they can put in place measures to minimise their impact.

2.1.2 Although it has always been considered good practice for trustees to formally manage risk, the Charities (Accounts and Reports) Regulations 2005 place a legal requirement on charities subject to a statutory audit to make a statement in the trustees' annual report confirming that 'the major risks to which the charity is exposed, as identified by the trustees, have been reviewed and systems or procedures have been established to manage those risks' (SORP 2005, paragraph 45). Charities not subject to a statutory audit are encouraged to make the statement as best practice.

2.1.3 It is therefore recommended that all charities have in place procedures to formally manage risk. In addition to ensuring compliance with the SORP and preventing disaster, an effective risk management strategy can help ensure:

- the charity's aims are achieved more effectively;
- significant risks are known and monitored, enabling trustees to make a more effective contribution;
- new opportunities can be identified, assessed and seized;
- there is a healthy self criticism within the charity;
- projects and initiatives are better managed;
- unnecessary opportunistic risks are avoided;
- there is a greater awareness of activities and initiatives across the charity; and
- improved forward planning.

2.1.4 Sound risk management may also provide some protection for the charity and trustees in the event of adverse outcomes. First, the adverse outcome may not be as severe as it might otherwise as been, and second, those accountable can demonstrate that they have exercised a proper level of diligence.

2.2 The role of the board

2.2.1 The responsibility for the management and control of a charity rests firmly with the trustee body and as such their involvement in the key aspects of the risk management process is essential. This does not mean that they must undertake every aspect of the process themselves, but they do need to ensure that they are involved in the key aspects. In all but the smallest charities trustees are likely to delegate parts of the risk management process to managers. The level of involvement should be such that trustees can make the required statement on risk management with reasonable confidence.

2.2.2 Typically the trustees will:
- initiate and plan the process of risk management;
- influence the culture of risk management and ensure that it is embedded in the operation of the organisation;
- determine the appropriate risk appetite or level of exposure for the charity;
- approve major decisions affecting the charity's risk profile or exposure;
- ensure that the process is linked to the achievement of the charity's aims and objectives;
- monitor the management of significant risks to reduce the likelihood of unwelcome surprises;
- satisfy themselves that the less significant risks are being actively managed, with appropriate controls in place and working effectively; and
- annually review the charity's approach to risk management and approve changes or improvements to key elements of its processes and procedures.

2.2.3 Charities may wish to use a risk management policy to define the role of the trustees and the role of the senior management team and so draw a clear distinction between the two. Typically the role of the senior management team is to:
- implement policies on risk management and internal control;
- identify and evaluate the significant risks faced by the charity for consideration by the trustees;
- provide adequate information in a timely manner to the trustees on the status of risks and controls; and
- undertake an annual review of effectiveness of the system of internal control and provide a report to the trustees.

2.3 Risk management

2.3.1 For charities, risk can be defined as 'any event or action that may adversely affect an organisation's ability to achieve its charitable objects and execute its strategies'. This means that risk is not just confined to the financial affairs of the charity or to health and safety issues, but extends to all areas of the charity's operations.

2.3.2 Risk management involves identifying risks and devising a strategy to deal with them. A successful risk management framework will have the following characteristics:

- aligned to the charity's objectives;
- supported by trustees, staff and volunteers;
- communicated effectively throughout the charity;
- adaptable to environmental change; and
- simple yet structured.

2.3.3 The Charity Commission recommends that any risk management process includes the following key elements:

- establishing a risk appetite;
- identifying risks;
- assessing risk;
- evaluating what action needs to be taken; and
- periodic monitoring and assessment.

2.3.4 The process should be seen as an ongoing cycle and not just a one-off event to enable trustees to make the required statement in their annual report. A good risk management process can improve the operations of the charity, enabling it to work more efficiently and effectively.

2.3.5 The first step for any charity in a risk management process is to formally define the amount and type of risk that is acceptable in the pursuit of its charitable objectives. This is the charity's risk appetite. Once defined, the risk appetite needs to be communicated to staff to ensure there is a clear understanding on the boundaries and limits.

2.3.6 Charities will have different exposures to risk and different capacities to tolerate or absorb risk. A charity with sound reserves and diversified sources of income could accept a higher risk profile on a new project than a charity with a low level of reserves and few other sources of income. In addition, a charity may need to tolerate a higher level of risk as a result of its specific objectives (e.g. a charity operating in a war zone). A charity should also seek to understand the risk tolerances of stakeholders before deciding on its risk appetite.

2.3.7 There are a number of ways of defining risk appetite:

- **Score limit:** Risk appetite may be defined as any risk with a score of greater than x being unacceptable.
- **Defining statement:** In the case of a charity in financial difficulties, the trustees may decide that the charity cannot afford to take risks until the position has improved;

2.3.8 A charity may accept different risk levels in different area, e.g. a charity may be very risk adverse regarding their reputation but less risk adverse with new ventures.

2.3.9 A charity's risk appetite will change as activities and financial health changes. It should therefore be regularly reviewed and updated.

2.3.10 For example:

'The organisation's general approach is to minimise its exposure to risk. It will seek to recognise risk and mitigate the adverse consequences.

However, the organisation recognises that in pursuit of its objectives it may choose to accept an increased level of risk. It will do so, subject always to ensuring that the potential benefits and risks are fully understood before developments are authorised, and that sensible measures to mitigate risk are established.' (Source: *Risk Management in Higher Education* – PricewaterhouseCoopers, 2005)

2.3.11 The whole charity should be involved in the identification of risks and the process should be led from the top. How this process is carried out will depend on the size of the charity and the resources available, but charities do need to ensure that the responsibility for risk management is clearly defined. Some charities may decide to identify a lead trustee or to ensure that the responsibility is within the terms of reference of a committee.

2.3.12 Charities need to be clear about what are their key objectives before they can identify the risks associated with achieving those objectives. The risks that a charity faces depend very much on the size, nature and complexity of the activities undertaken and on the finances of the charity itself. As a general rule, the larger and more complex or diverse a charity's activities, the more difficult it will be to identify the major risks faced.

2.3.13 Risks may be external (e.g. economic or social changes) or internal to the charity (e.g. loss of a key member of staff).

2.3.14 Although there are various tools and checklists available, the identification of risks is often best done by a brainstorming session involving the trustees and senior staff. Charities may also wish to consult other stakeholders (e.g. staff, volunteers, beneficiaries or supporters).

2.3.15 It is important that all areas of risk are considered, and the following headings may help to achieve that:

- **Governance and management risk:** this includes the objectives of the charity, the commitment and skills of the trustee board, conflicts of interest, loss of key staff or trustees and the organisational structure.
- **Operational risk:** this includes contracts and service provision, use of resources, staffing, volunteers, IT, health and safety and safeguarding assets.
- **Financial risks:** this includes diversity of income, budgetary control, adequacy of reserves and cash flow, financial reporting, borrowing, financial commitments, trading, investments, fraud and error.
- **Environmental/external factors:** this includes public perception, relationship with funders, government policy and social, demographic and economic factors.
- **Compliance with laws and regulations:** this includes charity and company law, taxation, the charity's constitution, health and safety, employment law, Data Protection Act and other laws and regulations specific to the activities of the charity.

2.3.16 The Charity Commission produces a useful document in Appendix III of 'Charities and Risk Management' guidance available on their website. This gives detailed examples of potential risk areas, their potential impact and mitigation.

2.3.17 Bear in mind that no list of examples can cover all the risks that any charity faces and each charity needs to develop their own individual list of the risks that apply specifically to them.

2.3.18 Identified risks need to be put into perspective in terms of the potential severity of impact and the likelihood of their occurrence. For instance there is a small risk that a charity's buildings will burn down, but the impact of such an event is large enough that the trustees will wish to insure against such an event.

2.3.19 Initially risks need to be assessed as though there were no controls in place. For the above example this means assessing the risk of fire without taking into account whether there is any insurance in place. This is called the 'gross' risk. There are a number of reasons for assessing risk in this way. First, trustees need to focus their attention on those risks that pose the most danger to the charity (the major risks). They also need to ensure that controls are in place to mitigate the effect of these major risks and that these controls actually work. Trustees do not need to spend as much time and effort reviewing controls that mitigate minor risks.

2.3.20 Once major risks have been identified, the adequacy of the existing controls needs to be reviewed. The resulting risk after the effect of the controls is called the 'net' risk and this is the actual risk retained and accepted by the charity.

2.3.21 For example, the trustees of a charity may have identified two risks, risk A and risk B – risk A is the risk of the Chief Executive leaving and risk B the risk of the building burning down. The trustees consider that risk A is a minor risk which requires no further action except regular monitoring. However they consider risk B to be a major risk that requires action to mitigate the effect (i.e. insurance). Once adequate insurance is in place, the two risks have the same 'net' risk and the trustees are happy to accept this level of risk. Had the trustees considered only the effect of the risks after the insurance had been put in place, they would have failed to identify that they rely heavily on the insurance policy to mitigate a major risk. They may not therefore have made sufficient effort to ensure that the insurance policy was up to date and adequate.

2.3.22 There are two main ways of assessing risk. The first is to plot the risks on a risk map. The second is to use a scoring system to identify those risks posing the most danger to the charity.

Using a risk map

At the simplest level, assessing risks means deciding whether there is (a) a high or low likelihood of the event occurring and (b) whether the impact on the charity would be major or minor. All risks identified can then be inserted into one of the four boxes on the risk map shown in Figure 2.1.

Major risks are those in the top right-hand box (i.e. those which have a high chance of happening and would have a major impact on the charity). The trustees would focus their time and effort on those risks classed as major risks.

Using a scoring system

This method allows significant risks to be easily identified, but the risk map will become difficult to read, with too much detail or too many risks plotted. It does, however, provide a useful tool for presenting the information to others.

Each of the risks identified should be given a score for the likelihood of occurrence and another score for their impact using the following guidelines:

E2 RISK MANAGEMENT AND INTERNAL CONTROLS 361

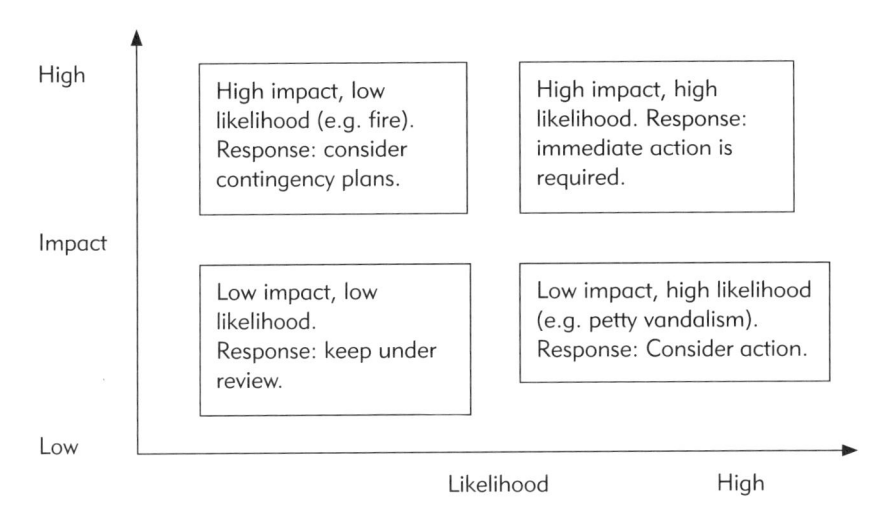

```
High │
     │  ┌──────────────────┐      ┌──────────────────┐
     │  │ High impact, low │      │ High impact, high│
     │  │ likelihood (e.g. │      │ likelihood.      │
     │  │ fire).           │      │ Response:        │
     │  │ Response:        │      │ immediate action │
     │  │ consider         │      │ is required.     │
     │  │ contingency plans│      │                  │
     │  └──────────────────┘      └──────────────────┘
Impact
     │  ┌──────────────────┐      ┌──────────────────┐
     │  │ Low impact, low  │      │ Low impact, high │
     │  │ likelihood.      │      │ likelihood (e.g. │
     │  │ Response: keep   │      │ petty vandalism).│
     │  │ under review.    │      │ Response:        │
     │  │                  │      │ Consider action. │
     │  └──────────────────┘      └──────────────────┘
Low  └──────────────────────────────────────────────────→
                 Likelihood              High
```

Figure 2.1: A sample risk map

Likelihood

1. extremely unlikely, rare occurrence;
2. unlikely;
3. moderately likely;
4. regular occurrence;
5. highly likely;
6. extremely likely, frequent occurrence;

Impact

1. not critical to continued operation;
2. minor impact in some areas;
3. minor impact in many areas;
4. significant impact – would not affect continued operations in short term but might in long term;
5. significant impact in medium term;
6. fundamental to continued operations.
    i. The risks should then be recorded on a risk register. There is a sample risk register pro forma below. Again, initially the 'gross risks' only should be recorded (i.e. as if the charity did not have any system of controls in place). The two scores should then be multiplied together to arrive at the overall 'gross' risk. Obviously the higher the score, the greater the risk.
    ii. The trustees will need to determine which risks to examine further, for example the top 10 risks or those with a score over 15. This decision will depend on the charity's tolerance to risk.

iii. For example, a charity has a significant contract to provide a care service and there is a recent history of complaints from beneficiaries that has led to concerns being raised by the contract funder. The loss of the contract would have a severe impact on the charity's finances and also on its ability to obtain further contract work, which is a key priority to the charity. The severity of the impact is likely to score five, and the likelihood (given recent history) scores six. The overall risk score of 30 indicates a major risk and highlights an urgent need for the risk to be mitigated.

That is not to say that other risks should be ignored. Those with a high potential impact but low likelihood of occurrence need to be kept under review, possibly annually, and will need some arrangements to be in place to ensure that they can be addressed should they arise. Similarly, events with low severity but with a high likelihood of occurrence may become gradual drains on a charity's finances or reputation. Those risks with both low severity and low likelihood of occurrence are unlikely to merit significant attention and effort might be better focused elsewhere.

2.3.23 Once the trustees have identified the major risks they have a number of options available to them:

- reduce or eliminate the risk by establishing or improving internal controls;
- avoiding the risk by ceasing the operations causing the risk;
- transferring risk by, e.g., taking out insurance or outsourcing activities;
- sharing the risk by, e.g., a joint venture; or
- accepting the risk.

2.3.24 Trustees should consider the controls already in place and should test whether they actually work. This may involve reviewing insurance policies, watching people at work or discussing the controls with those affected. Any control weaknesses may need to be addressed by reviewing the design of the systems and processes. The next section of this chapter covers these internal controls in more detail. For any charity there will be a trade off between the level of risks and the cost of reducing them to an acceptable level.

2.3.25 The sample risk register on the previous page includes space to list the controls already in place and then to detail whether any further action is required.

2.3.26 Some organisations give a value to the net risk to indicate the level of risk remaining after the internal controls have been applied. This requires a certain degree of judgement as to how the effect of the internal controls is valued, but it does enable the charity to evaluate whether the net risk is acceptable. An extra column could be added to the risk register for this purpose

E2 RISK MANAGEMENT AND INTERNAL CONTROLS

Sample risk register pro-forma

	Risk	Likelihood (L) (1–6)	Impact (I) (1–6)	Overall gross risk (L × I)	Existing control procedures	Action required	Monitoring process
(1)	Theft of assets	5	6	30	Insurance. Physical security procedures	Review insurance and security procedures. Ensure asset register is up to date	Annual review of insurance, asset register and security procedures
(2)	Computer system failure	2	6	12	Data backup procedures and precautions	Test backup procedures. Create disaster recovery plan	Review disaster recovery plan annually
(3)	Dependency on income sources. Cash flow and budget impact of loss of income source	4	6	24	Adequate reserves policy	Diversification plans	Annual review of reserves policy and diversification plans
(4)	Public perception. Impact on voluntary income and ability to access grants	3	5	15	Communication with supporters and beneficiaries	Review communication policy. Consider PR training	Annual review of communication policy
(5)	Trustee body lacks commitment	4	6	24	Recruitment processes. Trustee training	Review trustee recruitment process and trustee training	Review situation on a regular basis

2.3.27 Trustees should remember the mnemonic SMART when formulating an action plan. That is, actions should be Smart, Measurable, Achievable, Realistic and Timely.

2.3.28 Risk management extends beyond simply setting out systems and procedures. The process needs to be dynamic to ensure new risks are addressed as they arise, and cyclical to establish how previously identified risks may have changed. Risk management is not a one-off event and should be seen as a process that will require monitoring and assessment.

2.3.29 The risk register will need reviewing at least once a year, and also when the charity faces any significant changes. Risk aspects of significant new projects should be considered as part of project appraisals. Control systems need reviewing and testing to ensure that they operate as expected and that they do actually mitigate the relevant risks (see the section on internal audit later in this chapter).

2.3.30 A key element to the success of risk management is to make sure that the process is embedded into the culture of the charity. Staff and managers need to take responsibility for implementation and there needs to be communication with staff at all levels to ensure responsibilities are understood.

2.3.31 The trustees can monitor risk by:

- ensuring that the identification, assessment and mitigation of risk is linked to the achievement of the charity's operational objectives;
- ensuring that the assessment process reflects the trustees' view of acceptable risk;
- reviewing and considering the principal results of risk identification, evaluation and management;
- reviewing and considering update reports where the need for further action is identified;
- considering any significant new activities or opportunities as they arise to ensure any risks are identified and managed; and
- considering periodically external factors such as new legislation or new requirements from funders.

✓ 2.3.32 Self-assessment risk management checklist

Involvement of the governing body
(1) Do the trustees have sufficient involvement in the risk management process?
(2) Do the trustees provide direction in the risk management process?
(3) Do trustees know that the risk management processes are operating effectively?

Risk appetite
(4) Has risk appetite been clearly defined?
(5) Have all relevant criteria been taken into account when defining risk appetite? This should include the charity's strategy, the interests of stakeholders and financial performance.
(6) Is risk appetite consistently applied across the charity?
(7) Is risk appetite reviewed periodically to see whether it is still appropriate?

Resourcing
(8) Have sufficient resources been allocated to effectively implement the risk management process?
(9) Are all areas of the charity sufficiently involved in risk management?

Assessing risks and mitigating controls
(10) Have risks initially been scored 'gross' of mitigating controls?
(11) Are mitigating controls adequate to reduce the net (residual) risk to an acceptable level?
(12) Is the cost of operating these controls efficient and commensurate with the risk?
(13) Are the mitigating controls being carried out on a regular basis?
(14) Are mitigating controls monitored and occasionally tested?

Actions for improvement
(15) Has consideration been given to options for treating risk?
(16) Where actions for improvement have been identified, are these allocated to individuals and given implementation timescales?
(17) Are actions for improvement tracked?
(18) Are actions for improvement reported on periodically?

Risk reporting
(19) Has consideration been given to reporting on risk management to stakeholders?
(20) Have risks been prioritised for reporting purposes?

Embedding risk management
(21) Have steps been taken to build a culture where everyone is a 'risk manager'?

(22) Do risk management objectives complement the charity's existing vision and goals?
(23) Is risk explicitly considered as part of existing reports and in respect of key decisions?
(24) Is risk management used to understand performance shortcomings?
(25) Is risk management built into HR practices, such as training, induction and performance appraisals?
(26) Is information about risk management shared?

2.4 Internal controls

2.4.1 Internal controls exist to mitigate the risks that threaten the achievement of a charity's objectives. Other benefits arising from having an effective internal control framework include:

- safeguarding assets and ensuring their proper application under charity law;
- preventing and detecting fraud;
- ensuring reliability of internal and external reporting;
- promoting economy, efficiency and effectiveness; and
- ensuring compliance with laws and regulations.

2.4.2 Guidance on developing an effective internal control framework is given in the Turnbull Review Group's 'Internal Control: Revised Guidance for Directors of the Combined Code', published by the Financial Reporting Council in October 2005 (also known as the Revised Turnbull Report). Although this report was developed primarily for directors of listed companies, it is of interest to charities and other organisations operating in the public domain.

2.4.3 The Turnbull Report defines an internal control system as a system that 'encompasses the policies, processes, tasks, behaviours and other aspects of a company that, taken together:

(a) Facilitate its effective and efficient operation by enabling it to respond appropriately to significant business, operational, financial, compliance and other risks to achieving the company's objectives. This includes the safeguarding of assets from inappropriate use or from loss and fraud and ensuring that liabilities are identified and managed;
(b) Help ensure the quality of internal and external reporting. This requires the maintenance of proper records and processes that generate a flow of timely, relevant and reliable information from within and outside the organisation;
(c) Help ensure compliance with applicable laws and regulations, and also with internal policies with respect to the conduct of business.'

2.4.4 The Turnbull Report states that a 'system of internal control should:

(a) Be embedded in the operations of the organisation and form part of its culture;
(b) Be capable of responding quickly to evolving risks to the business arising from factors within the organisation and to changes in the business environment; and
(c) Include procedures for reporting immediately to appropriate levels of management any significant control failings or weaknesses that are identified together with details of corrective action being undertaken.'

Source: Internal Control: Revised Guidance for Directors on the Combined Code (Financial report Council, October 2005).

2.4.5 Any internal control system should consist of the following components:

- the control environment;
- the charity's risk assessment process;
- information systems relevant to financial reporting and communication;
- control activities; and
- monitoring of controls.

2.4.6 The control environment includes the attitudes, awareness and actions of management and those charged with governance concerning the charity's internal control and its importance in the entity. It sets the tone of an organisation, influencing the control consciousness of its people. It is the foundation for effective internal control, providing discipline and structure.

2.4.7 The following elements make up the control environment:

- **Communication and enforcement of integrity and ethical values:** integrity and ethical values are essential elements of the control environment which influence the effectiveness of the design, operation and evaluation of other control activities.
- **Commitment to competence:** this involves ensuring that staff have the required knowledge and skills to carry out their tasks.
- **Participation by the trustees:** the involvement of the trustees in the internal controls will significantly influence their effectiveness.
- **Management's philosophy and operating style:** this includes management's attitudes towards risk and financial reporting.
- **Organisational structure:** all internal control systems need to be based on a recognised plan of the charity's structure which clearly shows areas of responsibility, lines of authority and lines of reporting.
- **Assignment of authority and responsibility:** this includes policies and communications directed at ensuring that staff understand the charity's objectives,

know how their individual actions interrelate and contribute to these objectives, and recognise how and for what they will be held accountable.
- **Human resource policies and practices:** this includes recruitment, training, evaluating, counselling, promoting and paying staff.

2.4.8 The charity's risk assessment process: the process for identifying and responding to risks that will prevent the charity from achieving its objectives. This has been discussed in detail earlier in this chapter.

2.4.9 The quality of an information system will affect management's ability to make appropriate decisions in managing and controlling the charity's activities and to prepare reliable financial reports. It is important that information provided to management is timely, relevant and reliable.

2.4.10 An information system comprises infrastructure (e.g. computer hardware), software, people, processes and data. It may be completely manual or it may be heavily reliant on computers.

2.4.11 The financial reporting system is obviously an important information system in any charity, but in addition there will be systems to identify problems with the charity's reputation, to collect information on beneficiaries or to report staff performance.

2.4.12 The information systems of a charity also include the process for communicating information from trustees to staff which may take the form of policies, procedures, manuals or memoranda.

2.4.13 Control activities: are the policies and procedures that help ensure that necessary actions are taken to address the identified risks. There are a number of types of activities:
- **Segregation of duties:** the scope for fraud and error can be reduced by ensuring that no one person is responsible for a single process from beginning to end. For example different people may be assigned the duties of recording a transaction, authorising the transaction and maintaining custody of the asset. However, the possibility of collaboration between staff members can never be completely eliminated. It may be more difficult to segregate duties in smaller charities with fewer staff members. Here the trustees will need to be more closely involved in the day-to-day operations of the charity and in the authorisation of transactions.
- **Physical controls:** these ensure the physical security of assets and will include restricting access to IT software and data as well as the safekeeping of stock and cash.

- **Information processing:** these controls ensure the accuracy, completeness and authorisation of transactions (whether financial or otherwise). They may include general IT controls such as restricting access to data or keeping virus definitions up to date. They will also include controls such as reconciling the bank account or reviewing exception reports.
- **Performance reviews:** this includes reviewing reports and analyses of actual performance against budget, forecast or prior year performance. The presence of unexpected fluctuations will help to identify errors, fraud or other causes for concern.

2.4.14 An internal control framework is not just about designing adequate controls. It should also ensure that the controls are effective (i.e. do they actually control the risk) and that the controls are actually being complied with. These procedures are ongoing and may form part of the role of internal audit (see the next section).

2.4.15 Reviewing the effectiveness of the internal controls is an essential part of the trustees' responsibilities, and trustees should therefore regularly receive and review reports on internal control. Any significant control failings or weaknesses should be reviewed by the trustees with a view to determining how the failing or weakness arose and ensuring that suitable remedies are put in place.

2.4.16 Charities will have differing internal control systems depending on their size, nature, culture and management philosophy. There are many options when deciding on the nature and extent of controls, for example whether the controls are manual or computerised, and whether they are preventative or detective. There is also a balance to be achieved between the cost of implementing the control and the perceived benefits arising from the control.

2.4.17 Prevention controls are controls designed to avoid an unintended event or result from occurring (e.g. increased security to prevent theft). Detection controls are designed to discover that an unintended event or result has occurred (e.g. bank reconciliations performed monthly). Most internal control systems will involve both types of controls, but the nature and extent of each will depend on factors such as the degree of risk, the quality of staff and the reliability of information.

2.4.18 Smaller charities may use less formal means and simpler processes and procedures in their internal control system. The trustees of smaller charities may be involved in the day-to-day running of the organisation and will provide an important control in doing this.

2.4.19 Internal controls can only be designed once applicable risks have been identified and assessed. Management should then consider:

- the desired balance between prevention and detection controls;
- the cost versus the benefits of the proposed controls; and
- specific control objectives (i.e. what do the controls need to achieve?).

2.4.20 Considerations for specific risk areas consist of:

(a) **Financial assets:** Charities should obtain a copy of the Charity Commission's publication CC8, 'Internal Financial Controls for Charities'. This gives lists of suggested controls for the key transaction cycles and asset categories. It also includes a checklist in a questionnaire format that is a recommended tool for all charities. It should be remembered, however, that the checklist is designed for a 'typical' charity. Given that all charities are different, no charity should simply adopt the recommendations in the guide and consider their internal controls complete. Charities will need to design controls for any specialist areas and also consider whether the guidelines in the checklist would be effective in their particular circumstances.

All internal financial controls should include controls over:
  i. **Incoming resources:** controls should ensure that the charity receives all the income that it is entitled to. Typical controls include physical controls to ensure no money is misplaced and reconciliations to ensure all money has been paid into the bank account. Controls should also be in place to ensure that all reclaimable tax on Gift Aid donations from individuals has been reclaimed.
  ii. **Expenditure:** controls should ensure that money is only spent on authorised items that represent value for the purpose of the charity. Typical controls include authorisation of expenditure and rigorous cheque signing procedures.
  iii. **Fixed assets:** controls should ensure that fixed assets can be effectively used to promote the charity's objects. Typical controls include maintaining an up-to-date fixed asset register and checking the condition of fixed assets.
  iv. **Investments:** controls should ensure that trustees comply with their duties and powers (see previous chapter) and that any investments are safeguarded. Typical controls include maintaining an up-to-date list of investments and formulating an investment policy.

Although the Charity Commission's checklist forms an excellent base, there are a number of areas that it does not cover:
  i. **Internet banking:** most charities have in place rigorous cheque-signing procedures, but may be lacking similar controls over internet banking. It makes little sense to insist on all cheques being signed by two trustees and then allow one member of staff to authorise the payment of the monthly wages bill over the internet. Unfortunately most internet

banking systems do not have the option of requiring two 'signatories' to authorise a transaction. In this situation it is up to the individual charity to put in place procedures to reduce the risk of fraud or error. For example the member of staff processing the wages should not then be responsible for inputting the transaction details into the internet banking system.

ii. **Grant applications:** these should always be reviewed by a senior manager or trustee before being submitted to the funder. Copies should be maintained in case the funder has questions about the application.

iii. **Insurance:** all charities should ensure that they hold sufficient insurance cover. See later in this chapter for more detail.

iv. **Budgetary controls:** in order to achieve full control of the charity's finances it is necessary to work within an agreed budget and to undertake full financial planning. Annual income and expenditure forecasts should be prepared prior to the start of each financial year and updated on a regular basis. Ideally the forecasts should be prepared on a rolling basis, i.e. they always cover the next 12 months, and as one month passes another month is added to the end of the forecast. Trustees should approve the annual budgets, although they may not necessarily prepare the detail themselves.

Trustees should then monitor the charity's performance against the budget on a regular basis (i.e. monthly or quarterly). Any variances should be investigated, and any errors in the assumptions made in the forecasts should be corrected in future forecasts. This comparison of actual results to budget helps identify any unusual transactions and hence areas where fraud or error may have occurred. It will also give an early warning of potential risk areas (e.g. if income is unexpectedly declining).

Some charities use key performance indicators (KPIs) to highlight financial and non-financial performance against budgets and plans, for example the number of beneficiaries helped in the last month or the number of complaints.

(b) **Physical assets:** the security threat to all organisations is perceived as increasing, and charities need to ensure that premises security and insurance is adequate.

(c) **Human assets:** charities usually make considerable investment in attracting and recruiting the right quality of managers and staff, yet the same degree of rigour is often not applied in the recruitment of trustees. Good recruitment processes cost money, but the cost is small compared to the impact of recruiting the wrong person or operating with gaps in skills or knowledge.

Strategies should be employed to reduce the risk of high staff turnover, including a review of the attractiveness of the work and the working environment.

(d) Data and technology assets: Most charities protect their computer systems with passwords. It is also important to ensure that virus definitions and firewalls are up to date, and that there is an adequate backup procedure. Ideally a copy of the backup should be stored off the premises in case of fire or flood. Charities should also test their backups regularly to ensure that data can actually be recovered from them.

All charities should have a disaster recovery plan which ideally should be tested to ensure that it actually works.

(e) Reputational assets: Many charities take no active measures to protect their reputation. Although it is usually external parties, such as the media or disgruntled stakeholders, who seize upon inappropriate actions and cause resultant damage, there are relatively few cases of reputation being damaged by entirely fictional allegations.

Controls therefore need to ensure that internal actions and external communications are appropriate. It may also be wise to have an action plan for dealing with any adverse publicity.

2.5 The role of internal audit

2.5.1 Internal auditing is defined by the Institute of Internal Auditors (IIA) as:

'an independent, objective assurance and consulting activity designed to add value and improve an organisation's operations. It helps an organisation accomplish its objectives by bringing a systematic, disciplined approach to evaluate and improve the effectiveness of risk management, control and governance processes.'

2.5.2 Broadly speaking, an internal auditor will review the charity's risk management system, internal controls and governance process with a view to assessing their adequacy. A report will then be made to the trustees detailing any weaknesses and making recommendations for improvements.

2.5.3 An internal audit is not a statutory requirement for charities as it is for public authorities. However, it is a very useful tool for reviewing, improving and ensuring that a charity has effective internal controls. It also helps to assure the general public that a charity is being properly governed.

2.5.4 An internal auditor will monitor and evaluate the effectiveness of the charity's risk management processes. This involves identifying and evaluating significant risk exposures relating to the charity's governance, operations and information systems regarding the:

- reliability and integrity of financial and operational information;
- effectiveness and efficiency of operations;

- safeguarding of assets; and
- compliance with laws, regulation and contracts.

2.5.5 An internal audit assists the charity in maintaining effective controls internal by evaluating their effectiveness and efficiency and by promoting continual improvement.

2.5.6 It is important to remember that it remains the responsibility of the trustees to establish and maintain the systems of internal control used in the charity. The role of internal audit is to assess whether those controls and systems designed by management are adequate, being complied with as intended and are operating effectively, and to make recommendations for improvements where weaknesses are identified.

2.5.7 The role of the internal auditor in the governance of a charity is generally more informal and may be accomplished through participation in meetings and discussions with trustees. The internal auditor is often considered one of the 'four pillars' of governance, the other pillars being the trustees, management and the external auditor.

2.5.8 Professional internal auditing standards require the internal auditor to 'assess and make appropriate recommendations for improving the governance process in its accomplishment of the following objectives:

- promoting appropriate ethics and values within the organisation;
- ensuring effective organisational performance management and accountability;
- effectively communicating risk and control information to appropriate areas of the organisation; and
- effectively coordinating the activities of, and communicating information among, the board, external and internal auditors and management.' (Source: Institute of Internal Auditors, 'International Standards for the Professional Practice of Internal Auditing'.)

2.5.9 There is no statutory requirement for an internal audit function in a charity to follow these standards; however, they represent best practice in internal auditing and should be considered.

2.5.10 Some of the benefits of an internal audit are that it:

- demonstrates a thorough and resilient management;
- tests the charity's control systems and suggests ways to improve them;
- monitors whether the recommended improvements have been made;
- demonstrates to funders and stakeholders that the charity has taken steps to control assets and activities;

- establishes the trustees' responsibility for risk management and control;
- contributes to risk management;
- assists people within the charity to reach a better understanding of the purpose and effectiveness of risk management and controls;
- improves the quality and quantity of information;
- improves communication and motivation; and
- links risk to objectives and strategies.

2.5.11 An effective internal audit function may help to reduce or modify the scope and timing of external audit procedures but it cannot eliminate the requirement for external audit. The effectiveness of internal audit can have a significant impact on how the external auditors assess the internal control system and audit risk. It is therefore important that the internal auditor liaises with the external auditor at as early a stage as possible.

2.5.12 The main difference between internal and external audit relates to their objectives. The objectives of internal auditors are set by the trustees or senior management, who will often decide what parts of the charity or which systems are to be reviewed. In contrast, the objectives of external auditors are defined by statute and in certain circumstances by other regulatory codes. The report produced by external auditors states whether the published financial statements show a true and fair view and adhere to accounting standards and the Charities/Companies Acts. Also, an internal auditor's role can be more varied and wide-ranging than an external auditor's and cover both financial and non-financial controls.

2.5.13 There is also a difference in the independence of internal and external auditors. Both require independence from the charity and its managers and trustees to be able to perform their roles effectively. However, internal auditors are often employees of the charity, which will restrict their independence. External auditors, however, must be independent of the charity and its trustees and may not be employees.

2.5.14 *Possible structures for internal audit:* Many charities, particularly smaller ones, have no internal audit function. This may be on the grounds of cost, or because the trustees consider the activities to be relatively straightforward. There is often a misconception that internal audit is for larger organisations only. However, trustees would be well advised to consider how they know that the risks within their charity are being properly managed and that the internal controls operate effectively.

2.5.15 An external auditor will usually review the systems and controls of a charity and make recommendations for improvement where weaknesses are identified. However, this is primarily aimed at financial systems and controls and not at the non-financial areas.

2.5.16 A larger charity may set up their own internal audit function and employ a part-time or even full-time member of staff. This will not be possible for smaller charities, who may wish to consider the following alternatives:

- Many firms of accountants and auditors offer an internal audit function. This may involve, for example, an auditor visiting the charity for one day a month to review and test the systems and controls and then reporting back to the trustees. It is good practice for the internal and external auditors to be different firms, or at least employees from different departments.
- A volunteer may be found with the relevant skills and experience to independently review the controls and report back to the trustees.
- A number of charities may decide to share internal audit resources through a consortium arrangement.

2.5.17 The internal audit process: internal auditors, trustees and management determine where to focus internal auditing efforts based on a risk assessment of the charity. A typical internal audit involves the following steps:

- Establish and communicate the scope and objectives for the audit to appropriate management.
- Develop an understanding of the area under review including objectives, measurements and key transaction types. This will involve a review of documents and interviews, and may involve creating flowcharts and narrative notes.
- Identify control procedures used to ensure each key transaction type is properly controlled and monitored.
- Develop and execute a risk-based sampling and testing approach to determine whether the most important controls are operating as intended.
- Report problems identified and negotiate action plans with management to address the problems.
- Follow up on reported findings at appropriate intervals.

2.5.18 Model job description: charity internal auditor

Responsible to: audit committee or chief executive. Some internal auditors report to the finance director but it is preferable that internal audit remains independent of the finance function.

Job purpose: to carry out an independent appraisal of the effectiveness of the policies, procedures and standards by which the charity's financial, physical and information resources are managed. To add value by acting as a facilitator in business risk management and carrying out value for money reviews, thereby assisting the management and the trustees of the charity in the effective discharge of their responsibilities.

Definition: 'Internal auditing is an independent, objective assurance and consulting activity designed to add value and improve an organisation's operations. It helps an organisation accomplish its objectives by bringing a systematic, disciplined approach to evaluate and improve the effectiveness of risk management, control and governance processes.' (Source: Institute of Internal Auditors – UK and Ireland Ltd)

Principal duties and responsibilities

(1) To work with trustees and management to ensure a system is in place which ensures that all major risks of the charity are identified and analysed, on an annual basis.
(2) To review the effectiveness of the charity's risk management and governance processes.
(3) To plan, organise and carry out the internal audit function including the preparation of an audit plan which fulfils the responsibility of the department, scheduling and assigning work and estimating resource needs.
(4) To report to both the audit committee and management on the policies, programmes and activities of the department.
(5) To coordinate coverage with the external auditors and ensure that each party is not only aware of the other's work but also well briefed on areas of concern.
(6) To make recommendations on the systems and procedures being reviewed, report on the findings and recommendations and monitor management's response and implementation.
(7) To review and report on the accuracy, timeliness and relevance of the financial and other information that is provided for management.
(8) To report on the value for money that the charity obtains in all its activities with special regard to economy, efficiency and effectiveness.
(9) To conduct any reviews or tasks requested by trustees, the audit committee, chief executive or finance director, provided such reviews and tasks do not compromise the independence or objectivity of the internal audit function.
(10) To provide both management and the audit committee with an opinion on the internal controls in the charity.
(11) To work at all times in compliance with the IIA's Standards for the Professional Practice of Internal Auditing.

Person specification

(12) A recognised professional qualification, e.g.:
　　i.　CIMA (Chartered Institute of Management Accountants);
　　ii.　ACA (Association of Chartered Accountants);
　　iii.　ACCA (Certified Chartered Accountant);

iv. CIPFA (Public Finance Accountant); or
v. IIA (Institute of Internal Auditors)

which implies a thorough knowledge of the principles, procedures and practices of accounting and financial records and transactions.

(13) A knowledge of audit procedures, including planning, techniques, tests and sampling methods involved in conducting audits.
(14) A commitment to continuing personal development and continuous improvement in delivery of the internal audit activity.
(15) A knowledge of computerised accounting and auditing record keeping systems.
(16) An ability to gather, analyse and evaluate facts and to prepare and present concise oral and written reports.
(17) An ability to maintain current knowledge of developments related to business matters of interest to internal audit, particularly legislation changes and developments as they affect charities, and new auditing techniques and practices.
(18) An ability to establish and retain effective working relationships with other charity staff and to communicate clearly and effectively, both orally and in writing.
(19) An understanding of and empathy with the charitable sector.
(20) An ability to work unsupervised.

(Source: *Charity Finance Yearbook 2008*)

2.6 Insurance

2.6.1 The trustees of a charity have a duty to safeguard the property of the charity not only from direct loss or damage but also from third-party liabilities which would otherwise have to be satisfied out of the property of the charity. If trustees unreasonably fail to discharge this duty they may be personally liable to make good the charity's losses. Insurance is a common way of discharging this duty and reducing the impact of major risks.

2.6.2 The Trustee Act 2000 gives trustees of an unincorporated charity the power to insure any property which is subject to trust against risks of loss or damage as a result of any event and to pay the premiums out of the charity funds. Incorporated charities usually have sufficient power in the company's Articles of Association to purchase such insurance.

2.6.3 The Charities Act 1993 (as affected by the 2006 Act) gives trustees a power to purchase indemnity insurance against their own personal liability, and to pay the premiums out of charity funds.

2.6.4 Although there is no general power for types of insurance other than those mentioned above, trustees may be given the specific power in their charity's constitution. Even where there is no specific power, it would usually be appropriate to imply such a power where the nature of the charity's business warrants it.

2.6.5 As with all ways to mitigate risk, the trustees should weigh up the cost of the insurance against the perceived benefit. Insurance premiums have been rising for some years and there are no indications that this trend will cease. In addition, some insurers are refusing to insure high-risk areas and this may result in them refusing the business altogether or adding exclusions to the policy.

2.6.6 Trustees should always consider whether anything can be done to reduce the cost of an insurance premium. This may include reducing the likelihood of a claim by improving controls and systems (e.g. security) or it may mean contacting a number of different insurance companies until a competitive quote is found. It may also be possible to collaborate with other charities and purchase insurance 'in bulk'.

2.6.7 It may be acceptable for the charity to carry part or all of the risk itself. It is usually possible to reduce insurance premiums by accepting a higher excess. Larger charities with diversified sources of income and adequate reserves might accept the consequences of their exposure to risk without taking out insurance. Obviously there is greater need for insurance where the charity risks losing all or most of its assets at once. Where insurance is compulsory (e.g. employer's liability insurance) there is no option for the charity to carry the risk.

2.6.8 Finally, the trustees may decide to reduce or abandon altogether a high-risk activity that is difficult or costly to insure.

2.6.9 Types of insurance: there are a number of forms of insurance available to trustees, some of which are mandatory. The most common types include the following:

(a) **Buildings insurance:** recommended where the charity is the freehold owner of a building and insurance is not the responsibility of the lessee or tenant (if any). The policy should provide cover for the full reinstatement value of the building (i.e. the cost of replacing the building in the same style as the original). This is important as the trustees may personally be liable for any shortfall in cover should it be found that they were negligent in purchasing inadequate insurance. Trustees are advised to seek advice on the level of insurance cover required from a professionally qualified building surveyor.

Where a charity leases property it is essential to check the terms of the lease to see who is responsible for insuring the building.

(b) **Contents insurance:** advisable for all charities owning furniture, equipment or cash. There are usually a number of options to consider, including cover for accidental damage, cover on a 'new for old' basis and cover for specific items, e.g. computers. Trustees should ensure that any cash held on the premises does not exceed the insured limit in their insurance policy.

(c) **Public liability insurance:** may be appropriate for charities owning or occupying land or buildings. It covers claims from members of the public for injury, loss or damage incurred on the charity's premises. It also covers claims arising under the Occupier's Liability Acts 1957 and 1984. These Acts place on the occupier of the property a duty of care in respect of visitors to and trespassers on their property. There is no statutory minimum level of cover.

(d) **Employers' liability insurance:** is compulsory for charities with employees. All employers are required to have a minimum insurance cover of £5 million for injury or disease suffered or contracted by employees whilst carrying out their duties. A certificate showing that a valid policy is in force must be prominently displayed by the employer.

(e) **Motor insurance:** against third-party injury and property damage is compulsory where a charity owns or operates motor vehicles. If trustees, employees or volunteers use their own vehicle for charity purposes, their vehicle insurance must extend to such use.

(f) **Fidelity insurance:** covers losses to the charity arising from fraud or dishonesty on the part of charity employees where they are handling the charity's cash or other valuables. It should not be seen as an alternative to sound personnel and financial risk management.

(g) **Insurance for fundraising events:** may cover losses arising from cancellation on account of bad weather, misappropriation of cash raised (where large amounts are on hand), or losses where the response to an appeal does not cover the costs of administration.

(h) **Legal expenses insurance:** may be purchased to cover the cost of certain legal expenses which may arise if the charity has to bring or defend legal proceedings. These costs would usually be payable by the charity out of its own assets unless recoverable from the opponent. In an employment dispute, this insurance may also cover the costs of any compensation awarded to the employee.

(i) **Loss of revenue:** insurance can be arranged to cover the loss of revenue or increased costs sustained as a result of disruption from, e.g., fire or flood.

(j) **Professional indemnity insurance (PII):** is recommended for all charities providing any form of advice or professional service (e.g. counselling) whether free of charge or otherwise. The insurance will cover the charity against claims for losses or damages sustained by clients as a result of a negligent service.

2.6.10 Trustee indemnity insurance (TII): trustee indemnity insurance covers trustees from having to personally pay out when legal claims are made against them (by their charity or by a third party) for a breach of trust, or a breach of duty or negligence, committed by them in their capacity as trustees.

2.6.11 The main difference between TII and other types of insurance taken out for the benefit of the charity is that TII directly benefits an individual trustee rather than the charity itself. For that reason TII is regarded as a form of personal benefit needing a proper legal authority before the charity can purchase it. Many charities have the express authority to purchase TII in their governing document, and where they do not, the Charities Act 2006 now provides a general power to purchase TII using charity funds.

2.6.12 The only time Charity Commission consent is required is where the charity's governing document expressly prohibits the purchase of TII. Any general prohibitions on trustee benefits are overridden by the general legal power to purchase TII without the consent of the Charity Commission.

2.6.13 TII will only insure trustees against claims that may arise as a result of their legitimate actions as trustees. It cannot provide cover for:

- criminal fines, or penalties imposed by public authorities;
- costs of criminal proceedings where a trustee is convicted of fraud, dishonesty or reckless conduct; or
- liability arising out of conduct which a trustee knew, or should reasonably have known, was not in the interest of the charity.

E3
Accounting and audit

1 Introduction

1.1 Charities have always needed to be accountable and transparent to the public, and the annual report and accounts is one way of achieving this. All trustees should use their annual reports and accounts to communicate with stakeholders and the wider public about their work – explaining the work their charities do and the achievements that result.

1.2 The accounting and auditing regulations for charities have never been straightforward and appear to be in a constant state of flux. The Charities Act 2006 made changes to the auditing requirements, and these have been implemented in stages throughout 2007, 2008 and 2009. At the time of writing, the last of the changes have been implemented and we can hopefully look forward to a period with relatively few changes to the auditing and accounting requirements of charities.

2 Annual report and accounts

2.1 All charities must prepare accounts and an annual report and make them available on request. For registered charities with income above £25,000 per annum, the accounts and annual report must also be sent to the Charity Commission within 10 months of the financial year end.

2.2 The annual report (or trustees' annual report) is an opportunity for the trustees to explain to funders, beneficiaries and other stakeholders what the charity is achieving. The accounts themselves are often not fully understood by stakeholders, which places more importance on the contents of the annual report. In addition, figures cannot show the impact of the charity's activities.

2.3 The basic contents of the trustees' annual report are the same for all charities. Charities not requiring a statutory audit are exempt from some of the more detailed requirements. The exact content of the trustees' annual report is given below:

Content of the trustees' annual report

1 Reference and administrative details
The following details should be given:

(a) the name of the charity;
(b) the charity registration number;
(c) the company registration number (if applicable);
(d) the address of the principal office of the charity and, if a company, the registered office;
(e) the names of all charity trustees on the date the report was approved;
(f) the name of any other person who was a trustee during the financial year in question;
(g) the name of the chief executive officer or other senior staff member; and
(h) the name and address of any advisers (e.g. bankers, solicitors, accountants/auditor).

Charities not subject to a statutory audit may omit (g) and (h).

2 Structure, governance and management
This should include:

(a) the nature of the governing document and how the charity is constituted (e.g. limited company);
(b) the methods adopted for the recruitment and appointment of new trustees;
(c) the policies and procedures adopted for the induction and training of trustees;
(d) the organisational structure of the charity and how decisions are made;
(e) details of any wider networks;
(f) details of any related parties or connected charities, including subsidiaries; and
(g) a statement confirming that the major risks to which the charity is exposed, as identified by the trustees, have been reviewed and systems or procedures have been established to manage those risks.

Charities not subject to a statutory audit may omit (c) to (g).

3 Objectives and activities
This should include:

(a) a summary of the charity's objects;
(b) an explanation of the charity's aims including the changes or differences it seeks to make through its activities;
(c) an explanation of the charity's main objectives for the year;
(d) an explanation of the charity's strategies for achieving the stated objectives;
(e) details of significant activities that contribute to the achievement of the stated objectives;

(f) where the charity conducts a significant amount of its activities through grant making, a statement should be provided setting out its grant making policies;
(g) where social or programme-related investment activities are material in the context of the charitable activities undertaken, the investment policies should be explained; and
(h) where a charity uses volunteers to a significant extent in its charitable or income-generating activities, this should be noted and details may be given.

Charities not subject to a statutory audit may omit (b) to (d) and (f) to (h)

4 Achievements and performance

This should include:

(a) a review of the charitable activities undertaken that explains the performance achieved against objectives set;
(b) where material fundraising activities are undertaken, details of performance achieved against fundraising objectives set;
(c) where material investments are held, details of performance achieved against investment objectives set; and
(d) comment on the factors within and outside the charity's control which are relevant to the achievement of its objectives.

Charities not subject to a statutory audit may provide a summary of the achievements of the charity during the year instead of (a) to (d).

5 Financial review

This should include:

(a) a review of the financial position of the charity and its subsidiaries;
(b) a statement of the principal financial management policies adopted in the year;
(c) reserves policy;
(d) details of any funds materially in deficit and steps taken to eliminate the deficit;
(e) details of principal funding sources and how expenditure in the year has supported the objectives of the charity; and
(f) where material investments are held, the investment policy and objectives.

Charities not subject to a statutory audit may omit (e) and (f).

6 Plans for future periods

This should include the charity's plans for the future and any aims, objectives and planned activities. Charities not subject to a statutory audit may omit this disclosure.

7 Funds held as custodian trustee

Where a charity (or its trustees) holds funds on behalf of others, the following should be disclosed:

(a) a description of the assets held;
(b) the name and objects of the charity on whose behalf assets are held and how this activity falls within their own objects; and
(c) details of the arrangements for safe custody and segregation of such assets from the charity's own assets.

8 Public benefit statement

A statement confirming whether the charity trustees have complied with their duty to have due regard to the guidance on public benefit published by the Charity Commission in exercising their powers or duties.

(Sources: 'Statement of Recommended Practice – Accounting and Reporting by Charities' (revised 2005) and CC15b, 'Charity Reporting and Accounting: The Essentials' (Charity Commission, April 2009))

2.4 Although charities not subject to a statutory audit may omit a lot of the more detailed disclosures, full disclosure is encouraged as a matter of good practice.

2.5 Some areas of the trustees' annual report are worth further discussion.

2.6 *Public benefit statement*: This new requirement is a direct result of the Charities Act 2006. The statement is required in all annual reports for accounting periods starting on or after 1 April 2008.

2.7 Trustees are required to give details in the annual report of how the charity is meeting the public benefit requirements. A lot of charities will find that this is being done already in the 'Objectives and Activities' and 'Achievements and Performance' sections of the annual report, but it will be worth checking that it is clear how the aims of the charity are carried out, through the activities, for the public benefit.

2.8 Smaller charities (i.e. those not requiring a statutory audit) are required to give a brief summary of the main activities undertaken in order to carry out the charity's aims for the public benefit.

2.9 Larger charities (i.e. those requiring a statutory audit) are required to provide a more detailed explanation of the significant activities undertaken in order to carry out the charity's aims for the public benefit.

2.10 When considering how to report on public benefit, trustees may wish to ask themselves the following questions:

- What are the identifiable benefits that arise from the charity's aims?
- How does the charity benefit the public or a section of the public?
- Are there any restrictions on who can benefit and are these restrictions reasonable (e.g. geographical restrictions or fee charging)?
- Are people in poverty excluded from the opportunity to benefit?
- Do the charity's aims cause any detriment or harm? If so, are these outweighed by the benefits?

2.11 Further guidance on reporting public benefit can be found on the Charity Commission website (www.charity-commission.gov.uk).

2.12 Reserves policy: the Charity Commission has been stressing the importance of reserves policies for a number of years. Their concern stemmed from the notion that charities raise money by fundraising for specific causes but then do not spend the money on the advertised cause. Instead, the money is kept in reserve for times of hardship or when unexpected costs arise. It is perfectly acceptable for charities to keep some money in reserve – the question is, how much?

2.13 Trustees are required to set a reserves policy which includes the following:

- the reasons why the charity needs reserves;
- what level (or range) of reserves the trustees believe the charity needs;
- what steps the charity is going to take to establish or maintain reserves at the agreed level (or range); and
- arrangements for monitoring and reviewing the policy.

2.14 In theory the trustees may set target reserves at whatever level they feel is appropriate. In the writer's experience, some funders may reject funding applications from charities with more than 12 months' working capital in reserve and also those with reserves of under two months' working capital. Those charities with large levels of reserves may be deemed not to require additional funding, while those with too little in reserve may be seen to be at risk of closing before the funding has had any impact.

2.15 An example of an acceptable reserves policy may include three to six months' working capital plus redundancy costs.

2.16 The definition of reserves (per SORP 2005) is 'that part of a charity's income funds that is freely available'. This excludes:

- endowment funds;
- restricted funds; and
- funds which can only be realized by disposing of fixed assets.

2.17 Designated funds would not normally be included in reserves, but trustees should ensure that the designated fund is created for a specific future need rather than for the purpose of reducing reserves to an acceptable level.

2.18 Trustees are required to do the following in the financial review section of the annual report:

- describe their charity's reserves policy;
- explain why they hold or do not hold reserves;
- quantify and explain the purpose of any material designated funds, and where set aside for future expenditure, the likely timing of that expenditure; and
- give the level of reserves at the last day of the financial year to which the report relates

2.19 Plenty of guidance has been published on the subject including the Charity Commission publications CC19, 'Charities' Reserves' and RS3, 'Charity Reserves'.

3 Accounting requirements for charities

3.1 In England and Wales the Charities Act 1993 as amended by the Charities Act 2006 provides the basic framework for charity accounting requirements. For financial years ending on or after 1 April 2009, unincorporated charities with gross annual income of less than £250,000 may prepare receipts and payments accounts. Prior to that, the threshold for receipts and payments accounts was a gross annual income of £100,000. All other charities, including *all* charitable companies, must prepare accruals accounts.

3.2 In Scotland the equivalent legislation is the Charities and Trustee Investment (Scotland) Act 2005. Unincorporated charities with gross income of less than £100,000 may prepare receipts and payments accounts. All other Scottish charities must prepare accruals accounts. Further details on the accounting requirements for Scottish charities can be found on the website of the Office of the Scottish Charity Regulator (www.oscr.org.uk).

3.3 The primary legislation in Northern Ireland is the Charities Act (Northern Ireland) 1964. Unincorporated charities may choose to prepare either a receipts and payments account or an income and expenditure account. Further details on the accounting requirements for Northern Ireland charities can be obtained from the Northern Ireland Department for Social Development – Charities Branch Voluntary Activity Unit.

3.4 Exempt charities are not required to submit accounts and annual returns to the Charity Commission. The accounting requirements will be dependent on how such charities are constituted and any specific statutes or regulations applying to them. For example, an exempt charity constituted as an Industrial and Provident Society will need to apply legislation applicable to such societies.

3.5 Excepted charities do not usually have to submit accounts to the Charity Commission (except on request). They are, however, required to prepare accounts and are subject to the same audit and examination requirements as they would be if registered. They can be required under s. 46 of the Charities Act 1993 to prepare an annual report and submit it together with the accounts for the year.

3.6 All UK charitable companies are subject to the requirements of the Companies Act 2006 and are required to prepare accruals accounts showing a true and fair view.

3.7 Gross income is defined by the Charities Act 1993 as being the total income received from all sources excluding gains from disposal or revaluation of fixed assets and investments, and excluding endowment income. It does, however, include amounts transferred from endowment funds to income funds.

3.8 Receipts and payments accounts comprise a simple statement of money received and money paid out during the year and a short assets and liabilities statement. There are not required to show a true and fair view. The Charity Commission provides a useful template in Microsoft Excel (CC16, 'Receipts and Payments Accounts Pack'). Note that charitable companies may not prepare receipts and payments accounts.

3.9 Accruals accounts are by definition prepared on the accruals basis (i.e. income is recognised in the accounts when it is earned, rather than when it is received). The accounts comprise a Statement of Financial Activities (SOFA), a balance sheet and supporting notes.

3.10 The exact contents and format of accruals accounts are governed by the latest 'Statement of Recommended Practice – Accounting and Reporting by Charities' (SORP). This is currently updated every five years, with the latest version dating from March 2005. The next version is expected in 2010. The Charities (Accounts and Reports) Regulations 2008 requires the SORP to be followed whenever accounts are prepared under the Charities Act 1993 unless a more specific SORP applies (e.g. Registered Social Landlords or Higher and Further Education establishments).

4 SORP requirements

4.1 As mentioned above the SORP stipulates the contents and format of all charity accounts prepared under the accruals basis in the United Kingdom (i.e. including Scotland and Northern Ireland).

5 Accounts structure

5.1 The SORP states that charity accruals accounts should comprise:

- A SOFA for the year that shows all incoming resources and all resources expended and reconciles all changes in funds. The statement should consist of a single set of accounting statements and be presented in columnar form if the charity operates more than one class of fund.
- An income and expenditure account where this is a legal requirement. This applies to unincorporated charities in Scotland, and to certain charitable companies. In certain circumstances the SOFA will also meet the legal requirements for an income and expenditure account.
- A balance sheet that shows the recognised assets, the liabilities and the different categories of fund of the charity;
- A cash flow statement, where required (*).
- Notes explaining the accounting policies adopted and other notes which explain or expand upon the information contained in the accounting statements referred to above or which provide further useful information.

(Source: 'Statement of Recommended Practice – Accounting and Reporting by Charities' (revised 2005) (paragraph 30))

(*) A cash flow statement is required for all charities above the small company thresholds. More details on the thresholds for small companies are given later in this chapter.

6 Statement of Financial Activities (SOFA)

6.1 A sample SOFA is shown on page 394. The main requirements are as follows:

- If a charity has more than one fund, the SOFA should show, in columns, the incoming resources and resources expended for each different type of funds (i.e. unrestricted, restricted and endowment funds) as well as the total.
- Comparatives should be given for the previous period, but only the totals are required, not the analysis across the different funds.
- Category headings may be omitted where there are no figures for the current or previous accounting period.

6.2 Note that incoming resources and resources expended are analysed by activity and not by function (e.g. 'Costs of charitable activities' and 'Costs of generating voluntary income' rather than wages and rent). In addition, there is a clear link between the activities raising the income and the activities spending it.

6.3 Smaller charities (those not requiring a statutory audit) do not have to analyse their income and expenditure by activity, but may choose their own headings which may be on a functional basis. However, the Charity Commission encourages an activity-based approach wherever possible.

6.4 The activity headings should be analysed in more detail in the notes to the accounts so that the reader can understand the components making up the totals.

7 Incoming resources

7.1 Incoming resources should be analysed according to the activity that generated the income.

7.2 Voluntary income: includes all income given without expectation of a return. This includes donations, legacies, gifts and also grants which provide core funding. It may also include membership subscriptions where these amount to donations.

7.3 Activities for generating funds: include all income from fundraising activities, including charity shops.

7.4 Investment income: includes all income from investment assets, e.g. bank interest, rental income and dividend income. It will also include donations from subsidiary undertakings.

7.5 Incoming resources from charitable activities: includes all income which is payment for goods and services provided in furtherance of the charity's aims. This includes performance related grants and service level agreements. The notes to the accounts should analyse this total figure into the income receivable from each material charitable activity.

8 Recognition of income

8.1 One area which often causes confusion is the decision about when income should be recognised in the accounts. The SORP (paragraph 94) states that income should be recognised when the following three conditions are met:

(1) **Entitlement:** is the charity entitled to the income and does it have control over its application?
(2) **Certainty:** is the charity virtually certain that the income will be received?
(3) **Measurement:** can the value of the income be measured with sufficient reliability?

8.2 In practice, charities are normally entitled to grant income when it is receivable, and at this point the other two conditions are usually also met. It is therefore at this point that the grant income should be recognised in full in the accounts. There is a common misconception amongst charities that grant income can be deferred at the end of an accounting period if it has not been spent. This is not the case, unless the funder has specified a time period in which the expenditure of the resources can take place. The following examples illustrate this point.

Example 1
Partnership North East receives a grant from Northern Rock Foundation of £60,000 in January 2008 to be spent at the charity's discretion by 31 December 2008. The charity has a financial year end of 31 March 2008 at which point none of the grant income has been spent. How much of the grant income should be recognised in the accounts for the year ending 31 March 2008?

The charity has entitlement to the income in January 2008 and the timing of the expenditure is at the discretion of the charity. Therefore the full £60,000 should be shown as income in the year ending 31 March 2008.

Example 2
Northshire County Council gives core funding to Partnership North East every year. On 28 March 2008 the Council gives the charity £45,000 and stipulates that this is the core funding for the 2008/09 financial year (i.e. the money is to be spent in the period 1 April 2008 to 31 March 2009). How much of the grant income should be recognised in the accounts for the year ending 31 March 2008?

The charity is not entitled to the income until 1 April 2008 and therefore the income should be deferred until that date. The receipt should be shown as a liability in the accounts for the year ending 31 March 2008 and no income should be recognised.

8.3 Contractual income (e.g. the provision of goods and services) and performance-related grants should be recognised in the accounts to the extent that the charity has provided the goods and services.

8.4 Where income is given to acquire a fixed asset, or a fixed asset is donated, the charity will usually be entitled to the income when it is receivable. This means that the income should be recognised in full at that point and not deferred over the life of the asset.

9 Resources expended

9.1 Similarly resources expended should be analysed according to the activity that generated the income.

- **Costs of generating voluntary income:** includes the costs of fundraising, advertising, marketing and any associated staff costs.
- **Fundraising trading – cost of goods sold and other costs:** include associated staff costs, premises costs and an appropriate proportion of support costs.
- **Investment management costs:** includes the cost of obtaining investment advice and managing and maintaining any investment properties.
- **Charitable activities:** includes all costs spent on furthering the aims of the charity.
- **Governance costs:** include all costs relating the general running of the charity, e.g. audit, accountancy, strategic planning and trustees' meeting.

9.2 Expenditure should be allocated to activities on a reasonable, justifiable and consistent basis.

9.3 Expenditure is recognised in the accounts on an accruals basis as a liability is incurred, i.e. when there is a legal or constructive obligation committing the charity to the expenditure.

9.4 The notes to the accounts should provide a more detailed analysis of the costs incurred, with the costs of charitable activities being broken down into the different activities carried out by the charity as follows:

Activity	Direct costs £	Grant funding of activities £	Support costs £	Total £
Running Community Centre	95,000	–	20,000	115,000
Youth work	40,000	3,000	10,000	53,000
Town heritage project	20,000	–	10,000	30,000
Total	155,000	3,000	40,000	198,000

10 Grant funding

10.1 Grant payments are voluntary payments to a person or institution made by a charity in furtherance of its objects. Where grant funding is material, the notes to the accounts should give further information about the nature of the activities or projects that are being supported and whether the grants are given to individuals or to institutions. Institutions should be named where the grant given to them is material, unless such disclosure would 'seriously prejudice either the grant maker or the recipient' (SORP 2005, paragraph 200(d)).

10.2 Care should be taken to ensure that grant payments are recognised in the accounts where there is a legal or constructive obligation committing the charity to the expenditure. For example, if a charity makes a specific unconditional commitment to pay a grant of £1,000 per year for four years, the liability for the full four years of funding should be recognised immediately. If, however, the grant payment is conditional on, for example, an annual review of progress and the charity has some discretion over future payments of the grant, only the first year of funding should be recognised as a liability in the first instance.

11 Support costs

11.1 Most charities will incur support costs. These are costs necessary to deliver an activity, but which do not directly produce the output of the charitable activity, e.g. administration, management, IT and accounting. Support costs should be allocated to charitable activities on a reasonable, justifiable and consistent basis. Examples of bases for apportionment include:

- usage, i.e. on the same basis as expenditure incurred directly in undertaking an activity;
- per capita, i.e. based on the number of people employed within an activity;
- floor area occupied by an activity; and
- time spent on an activity.

11.2 Where support costs are material, the notes to the accounts should explain how the costs have been allocated to the charitable activities.

12 Transfers

12.1 The transfer row of the SOFA should show the total funds transferred between the different types of funds. The notes to the accounts should give details of each material transfer between funds.

12.2 Other recognized gains and losses

12.3 This section of the SOFA will include:

- unrealised (i.e. revaluation) gains and losses on fixed assets for the charity's own use;
- all (i.e. unrealised and realised) gains or losses on investment assets; and
- actuarial gains or losses on defined benefit pension schemes.

12.4 Note that gains or losses on disposal of fixed assets for the charity's own use should be included in incoming resources or resources expended as appropriate.

13 Balance sheet

13.1 A sample balance sheet is shown on page 396. In practice a charity's balance sheet is very similar to that for any other entity. It gives a snapshot of the charity's assets and liabilities at the end of the charity's financial year and how the net assets (or liabilities) are split between the different types of funds.

13.2 Assets and liabilities are generally shown in the accounts at the lower of cost and market value, but there are some important exceptions to this:

- fixed assets used by the charity will be shown in the accounts at either cost less depreciation or at current market value;
- investment assets must be shown in the accounts at market value; and
- heritage assets and contingent liabilities may not be shown in the balance sheet at all.

13.3 The balance sheet cannot therefore be used to give an up-to-date value of the charity's assets and liabilities. Instead it is meant to show the resources available to the charity and whether these are freely available or have restricted use.

13.4 As with the SOFA, the balance sheet headings should be analysed in more detail in the notes to the accounts so that the reader can understand the components making up the totals.

13.5 Many of the items in a charity's balance sheet are accounted for in accordance with the UK accounting standards (known as Financial Reporting Standards or FRSs) rather than under specific charity guidance. Where this is the case, the reader will be directed to the relevant FRS.

PARTNERSHIP NORTH EAST
STATEMENT OF FINANCIAL ACTIVITIES (INCORPORATING THE INCOME AND EXPENDITURE ACCOUNT)
YEAR ENDED 31 MARCH 2009

	Note	Unrestricted Funds £	Restricted Funds £	Total Funds 2009 £	Total Funds 2008 £
Incoming Resources					
Incoming resources from generating funds:					
Voluntary income	2	700	8,436	9,136	20,505
Activities for generating funds	3	10,562	–	10,562	8,934
Investment income	4	2,789	–	2,789	1,553
Incoming resources from charitable activities	5	229,066	82,586	311,652	346,274
Total incoming resources		243,117	91,022	334,139	377,266
Resources Expended					
Costs of generating funds:					
Costs of generating voluntary income	6	–	(1,396)	(1,396)	(2,731)
Fundraising trading: cost of goods sold and other costs	7	(4,296)	–	(4,296)	(3,051)
Investment management costs	8	(530)	–	(530)	(437)
Charitable activities	9	(219,510)	(97,571)	(317,081)	(351,162)
Governance costs	10	(2,957)	(891)	(3,848)	(3,126)
Total resources expended		(227,293)	(99,858)	(327,151)	(360,507)

Net (outgoing)/incoming resources before transfers	11	15,824	(8,836)	6,988	16,759
Transfers					
Transfer between funds	12	1,832	(1,832)	–	–
Net (outgoing)/incoming resources before other recognised gains and losses		17,656	(10,668)	6,988	16,759
Other recognised gains/losses					
Gains on revaluation of fixed assets for charity's own use	13	35,000	–	35,000	–
Net movement in funds		52,656	(10,668)	41,988	16,759
Reconciliation of funds					
Total funds brought forward		11,624	31,409	43,033	26,274
Total funds carried forward		64,280	20,741	85,021	43,033

PARTNERSHIP NORTH EAST
BALANCE SHEET AS AT
31 MARCH 2009

	Note	£	2009 £	£	2008 £
Fixed Assets					
Intangible assets	11			45000	50000
Tangible assets	12			12691	10169
Heritage assets	13			30686	21693
Investments	14			5724	5928
				94101	87790
Current Assets					
Stocks	15		5000		4500
Debtors	16		12953		3159
Cash at bank			55707		64774
			73660		72433
Liabilities					
Creditors: Amounts falling due within one year	17		(32006)		(35049)
Net Current Assets				41654	37384
Total Assets less Current Liabilities				135755	125174
Creditors: Amounts falling due after more than one year	18			(26310)	(35719)
Provisions for liabilities and charges	19			(4592)	(3829)
Net Assets				104853	85626
Funds of the charity					
Endowment funds	20			5724	5928
Restricted income funds	21			5448	3465
Unrestricted income funds	22			5304	(5629)
Unrestricted capital funds	22			88377	81862
Total Funds				104853	85626

13.6 Intangible fixed assets

13.6.1 Intangible fixed assets are defined in FRS 10, 'Goodwill and Intangible Assets' as 'Non-financial fixed assets that do not have physical substance but are identifiable and controlled by the entity through custody or legal rights.' Examples include goodwill, licences, franchises and quotas.

13.6.2 FRS 10 requires purchased goodwill and intangible fixed assets to be capitalised on the balance sheet and amortised over their life (usually 20 years).

13.7 Tangible fixed assets

13.7.1 FRS 15, 'Tangible Fixed Assets' requires all tangible fixed assets (except investments) to be capitalised at either (a) cost less depreciation or (b) valuation.

13.7.2 If a fixed asset is donated to a charity, it should be included on the balance sheet at the value at the date of the gift.

13.7.3 Depreciation is the measure of wearing out or consuming an asset through use or the passage of time. All fixed assets (except freehold land) should be depreciated at rates appropriate to their useful economic life and the annual depreciation charge included as an expense in the SOFA. The only exceptions to this rule are freehold land, which need not be depreciated, and cases where the depreciation is not material.

13.7.4 Where a charity chooses to include fixed assets at a valuation, the value must be updated on a regular basis (at least every five years) by a 'suitably qualified person', who may be a trustee or employee. Details of the valuer and the basis of the valuation must be disclosed in the accounts.

13.7.5 Note that if a charity includes one fixed asset in its accounts at a valuation, it must also revalue all the other fixed assets within that class of assets. The charity may define classes of fixed assets as it see fit, within reason.

13.7.6 If the current value of a fixed asset is less than the cost less depreciation, it must be included in the balance sheet at the lower value (i.e. the current value). This process is known as impairment. The impairment loss should be included in the SOFA as additional depreciation.

13.8 Heritage assets

13.8.1 Heritage assets are defined as 'assets of historical, artistic or scientific importance that are held to advance preservation, conservation and educational objectives of charities and through public access contribute to the nation's culture and education either at a national or local level' (SORP 2005 GL32). Examples include historic buildings, museums and areas of natural beauty or scientific interest.

13.8.2 Heritage assets are often difficult to value and reliable cost information may not be available. In these situations the assets may be excluded from the balance sheet although details of the assets must be given in the notes to the accounts.

13.8.3 Where reliable cost information is available (e.g. if the charity has recently purchased the asset), the heritage asset should capitalised at cost and depreciated as appropriate.

13.8.4 Note that the assets are only classed as heritage assets if they are held to 'advance preservation, conservation and educational objectives of charities'. Where they are used for another purpose (e.g. used as offices or rented out as an investment), they should be shown on the balance sheet as tangible fixed assets or investments.

13.9 Investments

13.9.1 Investment assets may be split into two categories:

(1) Assets held for the sole purpose of generating income and capital appreciation. They may include investment properties rented out at market rent or a share portfolio.
(2) Programme Related Investments which are made primarily to further the charity's objectives and not to generate the best financial return. These may include loans to beneficiaries at low interest rates, or social housing rented out at below market rent.

13.9.2 The first category should be included in the balance sheet at market value. Programme Related Investments should be included in the balance sheet at the amount invested less any impairment (e.g. bad debts).

13.10 Current assets

13.10.1 Current assets are usually shown in the balance sheet at the lower of cost and net realisable value.

13.11 Liabilities

13.11.1 Liabilities are usually shown in the balance sheet at their settlement value. They are split into those due within 12 months of the balance sheet dated and those due after more than 12 months.

13.11.2 A provision is 'a liability of uncertain timing or amount. It is recognised when a charity has a present obligation as a result of a past event, it is probable that a transfer of economic benefits will be required to settle to obligation and the amount can be reliably estimated' (SORP 2005 GL48). The amount recognised in the balance sheet should be the best estimate of the expenditure required to settle the obligation at the balance sheet date. Where the expenditure is expected to be far enough into the future, the expected cost should be discounted to its present value.

13.11.3 If the expenditure is possible but not probable, or the amount cannot be reliably estimated, or the probability of the expenditure is unknown, the liability is classed as a 'contingent liability'. Contingent liabilities should not be shown on the balance sheet but should be disclosed in the notes to the accounts.

13.12 Notes to the accounts

13.12.1 In addition to a breakdown of the material items in the SOFA and the balance sheet, the notes to the accounts should disclose the following:

- **Accounting policies** chosen by the charity: specific policies that are required include the policy for including each type of material incoming resource, the policy for recognition of liabilities, the method of allocating costs between different activities, details of whether fixed assets are included at cost or valuation and the depreciation rates used and a description of the different types of funds.
- **Trustee remuneration and benefits:** detailed disclosures are required including the amount paid to each trustee. If no such payments have been made a statement is required to that effect.
- **Trustees' expenses:** the aggregate amount reimbursed to trustees should be disclosed, also the nature of the expenses and the number of trustees involved.
- **Staff costs and emoluments:** including the total staff costs (split into gross wages, employer's National Insurance and pension costs), number of employees and the number of staff earning more than £60,000 per year in bands of £10,000 from £60,000 upwards. If there are no staff earning more than £60,000 a statement is required to that effect.
- **Related party transactions:** disclosure is required of any transaction between the charity and a related party. Two parties are deemed to be related if one has direct or indirect control over the other, or they are subject to common control or one influences the other such that their own separate interests are inhibited. Related parties include all trustees, senior employees, charities under common control and those connected with them (e.g. members of the same household). Contracts of employment between the charity and employees do not need to be disclosed (unless the employee is also a trustee), nor do unconditional donations from related parties. Examples of transactions which do need to be disclosed include the payment of trustees for the supply of any services, sale/purchase of assets to/from trustees and donations or grants made by the charity to trustees.
- **Particulars of individual funds:** including a description of the purpose of each fund and any restrictions imposed. Each fund should be analysed into component assets and liabilities (e.g. investments, fixed assets and net current liabilities), and funds in deficit should be separately disclosed.

13.12.2 Accounts for charitable companies: charitable companies are required to prepare accounts which comply with both the SORP and company law. By following the SORP, most of the company law reporting requirements will normally be met, but there are a few areas that require further consideration.

13.12.3 Strictly, the directors of charitable companies in England and Wales have to prepare both a directors' report and a trustees' annual report, but the Charity Commission is prepared to accept a directors' report instead of a trustees annual report if it contains all the required information.

13.12.4 Under company law all companies must include an income and expenditure account in their financial statements. The charities' SOFA is designed to include many of the items that would usually be found in an income and expenditure account, and so a separate statement is not always required. Circumstances where a separate income and expenditure account is required includes unrealised gains and losses arising during the year (e.g. revaluation of investments) or movement on endowment funds.

13.12.5 Charitable companies must also separately disclose any revaluation reserve within the relevant funds section on the face of the balance sheet. A revaluation reserve will arise when fixed assets are revalued upwards and the reserve represents 'unrealised gains'.

13.13 Accounting timetables: it is sensible to draw up an accounting timetable in consultation with your finance staff, external auditor or examiner and the trustees. This will ensure that the accounts are completed on a timely basis and everyone involved knows when their contribution is required. Below is an example of a fairly leisurely accounting timetable for a charity with a year-end of 31 March.

13.13.1 Sample accounting timetable

Partnership North East

Accounting Timetable for the year ending 31 March 2010

February/March 2010 – Discussions with auditor about forthcoming audit and timetable.

31 March 2010 – Charity's financial year end. Stock take and cash count to be performed if applicable.

30 April 2010 – Accounting data is complete up to the year end and all reconciliations have been carried out. Management accounts produced for the trustees if applicable.

20 May 2010 – Trustees' annual report to be completed.

31 May 2010 – Statutory accounts completed.

June 2010 – Audit work commences.

31 July 2010 – Audit work is complete. The trustees and/or senior finance staff meet with auditor to discuss the audit and to agree any adjustments to the accounts.

August 2010 – Final accounts approved by trustees and sent to members prior to AGM if applicable.

> September 2010 – AGM.
> 31 December 2010 – Accounts to be submitted to Companies House by this date. (See note below about the changes in the Companies House filing deadlines.)
> 31 January 2011 – Accounts to be submitted to Charity Commission by this date.

13.13.2 In practice it will be difficult to progress the accounts during August and so they are unlikely to be approved until September, pushing the AGM back to October. This is a full six months after the year end and many charities do not wish to wait that long for their final accounts.

13.13.3 A common approach is to have the statutory accounts completed by mid-May and the audit complete by the end of June, giving the potential for an AGM in July. A faster timetable is of course possible with co-operation from the finance staff and auditor.

13.13.4 Timing for submission of reports and accounts

13.13.4.1 Accounts have to be submitted to the Charity Commission within 10 months of the charity's year end. For a charity with a year end of 31 March, this means submitting accounts by the following 31 January. The Charity Commission do encourage charities to file earlier for reasons of public accountability and transparency.

13.13.4.2 Until recently charitable companies have also had to submit accounts to Companies House within 10 months of the year end. However, for accounting periods starting on or after 6 April 2008, accounts need to be filed with Companies House within nine months of the year end (i.e. 31 December for a year end of 31 March).

13.14 Accounting reference date

13.14.1 The accounting reference date (ARD) is the financial year end (i.e. the date to which accounts are prepared). Charities may choose their own accounting reference date. The most common ARDs are 31 December or 31 March. An ARD of 31 March ties in with most funders' reporting periods, making funding reports easier to compile.

13.14.2 Charitable companies will initially be allocated an accounting reference date by Companies House. This will be the first month end after the company was incorporated (e.g. if the company is incorporated on 2 April the initial accounting reference date will be 30 April). Companies may change their accounting reference date once in any five-year period and the change must not result in an accounting period of longer than 18 months. The change must be registered at Companies House using Form AA01 available from the Companies House website (www.companieshouse.gov.uk).

13.15 Requirement to keep accounting records

13.15.1 Charities are legally required to keep adequate accounting records.

13.15.2 For unincorporated charities the legal requirements are laid out in section 41 of the 1993 Charities Act. Charity trustees are required to maintain accounting records which show and explain all the charity's transactions and which are sufficient to disclose at any time, with reasonable accuracy, the financial position of the charity at that time.

13.15.3 In particular, the accounting records should contain:

- entries showing from day to day all sums of money received and expended by the charity, and the matters in respect of which the receipt and expenditure takes place; and
- a record of the assets and liabilities of the charity.

13.15.4 The accounting records should be kept for at least six years from the end of the financial year to which they relate.

13.15.5 Company law requires charitable companies to keep accounting records which are 'sufficient to show and explain a company's transactions and to disclose (with reasonable accuracy) its financial position at any time'.

13.15.6 Company accounting records must contain:

- entries showing all money received and expended by the company; and
- a record of the assets and liabilities.

13.15.7 The requirements for charitable companies are therefore very similar to those for unincorporated charities.

14 Group accounts

14.1 Charities which have either charitable or non-charitable subsidiaries must prepare group accounts if the net annual income of the group is greater than £500,000.

14.2 The net income is the total income of the group less any intra-group transactions and other consolidation adjustments.

14.3 Group accounts do not need to be prepared by a charity that is itself the subsidiary of a charity. In addition, group accounts do not need to be prepared if:

- The results of the subsidiary undertaking(s) are not material to the group.
- The subsidiary is not a company and, by virtue of being a special trust or a charity subject to a uniting direction under s. 96 (5) or (6) of the Charities Act 1993, has had its accounts aggregated with those of the parent charity.
- There are severe long-term restrictions which substantially hinder the exercise of the parent undertakings rights over the subsidiary undertaking's assets or management.
- The subsidiary is held only for sale.
- The subsidiary undertaking is a registered company which is insolvent and is being wound up.

14.4 The purpose of consolidated accounts is to present a true and fair view of the state of the financial affairs of all the group interest of the reporting charity including its subsidiary undertakings. The principles and methods of consolidation are covered by FRS2, 'Subsidiary Undertakings'. These principles should be applied irrespective of whether the parent charity and its subsidiaries are companies or otherwise constituted.

14.5 The basic principles of preparing group accounts are as follows:

- The consolidation should be carried out on a line-by-line basis.
- All intra-group transactions should be removed.
- Uniform group accounting policies should generally be used.
- The financial statements of the subsidiaries to be used in preparing the group accounts should have the same financial year end as those for the parent charity.
- A subsidiary that is a charity with objects narrower than its parent will need to be accounted for by the use of one or more restricted funds in the group accounts.

14.6 Care should be taken to ensure that only subsidiary undertakings are consolidated in the group accounts. The definition of a subsidiary undertaking (as per SORP 2005) is as follows:

► 14.7 Definition of a subsidiary and parent undertaking

In relation to a charity, an undertaking is the parent of another undertaking, called a subsidiary undertaking, where the charity controls the subsidiary. Control requires that the parent can both direct and derive benefit from the subsidiary.

Direction is achieved if the charity or its trustees:

- hold or control the majority of the voting rights; or
- have the right to appoint or remove a majority of the board of directors or trustees of the subsidiary undertaking; or
- have the power to exercise, or actually exercise, a dominant influence over the subsidiary undertaking; or
- manage the charity and the subsidiary on a unified basis.

Benefit derived can either be economic benefit that results in a net cash inflow to the charity or can arise through the provision of goods or services to the benefit of the charity or its beneficiaries.

14.8 Further guidance on the consolidation of subsidiary undertakings is given in paragraphs 381 to 406 of SORP 2005.

14.9 The SORP also gives guidance on accounting for associates, joint ventures and joint arrangements. An associate is defined as an undertaking in which a charity has a long-term participating interest and where the charity exercises significant influence over its operating and financial policy. For the avoidance of doubt, a charity holding 20 per cent or more of the voting rights in another undertaking will be presumed to have a participating interest.

14.10 In a joint venture situation, a separate entity is jointly controlled by two or more undertakings, all of which have a say in the operations of the joint venture, so that no single investing undertaking controls the joint venture but all together can do so.

14.11 Charities may also undertake joint arrangements where they may carry out activities in partnership with other bodies but without establishing a separate legal entity.

14.12 Guidance on accounting for associates, joint ventures and joint arrangements can be found in paragraphs 407 to 418 of SORP 2005.

15 Thresholds for small companies

15.1 A number of charity accounting and auditing requirements are determined by whether the charity meets the small company criteria (e.g. inclusion of a cash flow statement in the accounts).

15.2 A company must meet two of the following three criteria in order to be classed as small. The corresponding amounts for periods starting before 6 April 2008 are in brackets:

- annual turnover not exceeding £6.5 million (5.6 million);
- balance sheet total not exceeding £3.26 million (£2.8 million); and/or
- average number of employees not exceeding 50 (50).

16 Audit requirements by size and type of charity

16.1 As mentioned in the introduction to this chapter, the Charities Act 2006 made substantial changes to the audit requirements for charities. The changes have been implemented in stages, meaning that some accounting periods will be affected by some but not all of the changes. These complications should reduce in time and leave a much simpler set of auditing requirements for charities.

16.2 The main changes have been as follows:

- The audit threshold for all charities increased to £500,000 for accounting periods beginning on or after 27 February 2007.
- The accountant's report (audit exemption report) for incorporated charities has been scrapped for periods starting on or after 1 April 2008. An independent examination report is now required for all charities with annual income between £10,000 and £500,000.

16.3 The detailed provisions for charities registered in England and Wales are as follows:

For accounting periods starting before 27 February 2007

Annual income	Charitable companies	Unincorporated charities
< £10,000	No requirement	No requirement. Annual expenditure must also be below £10,000.
> £10,000 and < £90,000	No requirement	Independent Examination
> £90,000 and < £250,000	Accountant's report	Independent Examination. Annual expenditure must also be below £250,000.
> £250,000	Statutory audit. Also required if gross assets are over £1.4m.	Statutory audit

16.4 A statutory audit must be carried out by a registered auditor.

16.5 For incorporated charities the limits are based on the current year's income only. For unincorporated charities the limits must be met for the current year and the two preceding years.

For accounting periods starting on or after 27 February 2007 but before 1 April 2008

Annual income	Incorporated	Unincorporated
<£10,000	No requirement	No requirement
>£10,000 and <£90,000	No requirement	Independent examination
>£90,000 and <£250,000	Accountant's report	Independent examination
>£250,000 and <£500,000	Accountant's report	Independent examination by an eligible person*
>£500,000	Statutory audit. Also required if gross assets >£2.8m.	Statutory audit. Also required if gross assets >£2.8m. and annual income >£100,000

* = As defined by the Charities Act 2006. See paragraph 18.3.2 for a detailed list of eligible people.
Note that the limits are based on the current year's income only and the reference to annual expenditure for unincorporated charities has been removed.

For accounting periods starting on or after 1 April 2008 and ending before 1 April 2009

Annual income	Incorporated	Unincorporated
<£10,000	No requirement	No requirement
>£10,000 and <£250,000	Independent examination	Independent examination
>£250,000 and <£500,000	Independent examination by an eligible person*	Independent examination by an eligible person *
>£500,000 or gross assets > £2.8m and income £100,000	Statutory audit	Statutory audit

Note that the scrutiny requirements for charitable companies have now been brought in line with those for unincorporated charities.

For accounting periods ending on or after 1 April 2009

Annual income	Incorporated	Unincorporated
<£25,000	No requirement	No requirement
> £25,000 and <£250,000	Independent examination	Independent examination
>£250,000 and <£500,000	Independent examination by an eligible person*	Independent examination by an eligible person*
>£500,000 or gross assets >£3.26m. and income £250,000	Statutory audit	Statutory audit

16.6 For all accounting periods, a charity's governing document may require an audit even if the regulations give the charity the option of an independent examination. In such cases the trustees may wish to amend their governing document to bring the requirement for external scrutiny in line with statutory requirements.

17 Scottish audit requirements

17.1 Scottish charitable companies are subject to similar audit requirements as charities registered in England and Wales, i.e. an audit is required if gross income is over £500,000 or if gross assets are over £2.8million. An independent examination is, however, required for all charitable companies that do not require an audit and the examiner must belong to a specified body.

17.2 Unincorporated charities also require an audit if their gross income is over £500,000 or gross assets are over £2.8million. Again an independent examination is required for all charities that do not require an audit. The independent examiner must be qualified unless receipts and payments accounts are being prepared.

17.3 There are no statutory requirements specific to charities in Northern Ireland.

18 Audit versus independent examination

18.1 An *audit* is a detailed review of a charity's activities, accounting systems, financial controls and financial statements with the aim of issuing an audit report stating that the financial statements show a 'true and fair' view and have been 'properly prepared' in accordance with the relevant accounting legislation.

18.2 The term 'true and fair' is often misunderstood, and the actual definition is that the accounts are not 'materially misstated'. An item is material if its inclusion or exclusion from the accounts would be likely to change a reader's view about the accounts. The auditor will set a materiality level at the start of each audit based on the size of the charity (usually approximately 2 per cent of total income). This means that for a charity with total income of £500,000, materiality will be approximately £10,000. The audit report for this particular charity therefore states that the financial statements are correct to the nearest £10,000. This is not quite the assurance that a lot of trustees think they are paying for! Some transactions are of course material whatever their size – examples include transactions with trustees and breaches of trust which require a higher degree of accountability.

18.3 A statutory audit must be carried out by a registered auditor.

18.3.1 An *independent examination* is a less onerous review of the charity's financial statements with the aim of issuing a report stating that nothing has come to the examiner's attention to make him/her believe that proper accounting records have not been kept or that the accounts have not been prepared in accordance with the relevant accounting legislation. This is known as negative assurance (i.e. 'nothing has come to my attention') rather than the positive assurance given by the audit report ('these accounts show a true and fair view'). None the less, an independent examination is a worthy alternative to an audit, especially given the cost savings involved.

18.3.2 An independent examination must be carried out by 'an independent person who is reasonably believed by the charity trustees to have the requisite ability and practical experience to carry out a competent examination of the accounts' (CC31/32, 'Independent Examination of Charity Accounts'). For charities with gross income above £250,000, the Charities Act 2006 requires the independent examiner to be a member of one of the following accountancy bodies:

- Institute of Chartered Accountants in England and Wales;
- Institute of Chartered Accountants of Scotland;
- Institute of Chartered Accountants in Ireland;
- Association of Chartered Certified Accountants;

- Association of Authorised Public Accountants;
- Association of Accounting Technicians;
- Association of International Accountants;
- Chartered Institute of Management Accountants;
- Institute of Chartered Secretaries and Administrators;
- Chartered Institute of Public Finance and Accountancy; or
- A Fellow of the Association of Charity Independent Examiners.

19 Role of external auditors

19.1 The audit of a charity is an audit of stewardship. The emphasis is on transparency and accountability to all stakeholders including beneficiaries, funders and employees, who will wish to be reassured that the charity is using its resources efficiently and effectively.

19.2 The role of the auditor is therefore more than just issuing an audit report to state that the accounts show a true and fair view. Typically a charity audit will include the following:

(a) A pre-audit meeting to discuss any significant changes to the charity during the year (e.g. changes in activities, accounting systems, finance staff or legislation) and the audit/accounting timetable. It is important to agree at this stage such things as the expected audit fee and whether the auditor or the charity's finance staff will prepare the statutory accounts.

(b) Obtaining an understanding of the charity, its activities and the environment in which it operates.

(c) A detailed review of the accounting system and internal financial controls. The auditor will identify any weaknesses in the system and should recommend improvements via the management letter (see below).

(d) A consideration of the risks facing the charity including the risk of fraud. The auditor will ask management and trustees whether they have any knowledge of suspected or actual fraud affecting the charity.

(e) A consideration of the laws and regulations facing the charity where non-compliance may materially affect the financial statements. Any instances of non-compliance should be reported to trustees as soon as practicable. The auditor is required to report any knowledge or suspicion of money-laundering offences to the Serious Organised Crime Agency (SOCA). The auditor also has a statutory duty to report to the Charity Commission (or the OSCR in Scotland) any matters which may be of material significance to the regulator.

(f) A review of management's assessment of whether the charity is a 'going concern'. The management of a charity are expected to consider at least the next 12 months and ideally further into the future when considering the viability of the charity.

(g) An assessment of the risks of material misstatement from the above information and then planning the audit so as to reduce this risk to an acceptably low level. Detailed audit work will then be performed in accordance with this plan.

(h) Obtaining written confirmations (Management Representations) from trustees where oral statements made cannot be verified by other audit evidence. This usually includes confirmation that the trustees believe the charity to be a going concern, that there are no undisclosed instances of non-compliance with laws and regulations and that all information has been made available to the auditors.

(i) Communicating audit matters of governance interest arising from the audit to the trustees of the charity. This would usually take the form of a written management letter and a post-audit meeting. The management letter would usually contain matters such as any weaknesses identified in the accounting system and financial controls, any errors identified in the financial statements, non-compliance with laws and regulations and any suspicion of fraud.

(j) Issuing an audit report which contains a clear expression of opinion on the financial statements. An 'unqualified' or 'clean' audit report will state that:
   i. the financial statements give a true and fair view of the state of the charity's affairs as at — and of its incoming resources and application of resources, including its income and expenditure, for the year then ending;
   ii. the financial statements have been properly prepared in accordance with United Kingdom Generally Acceptable Accounting Practice; and
   iii. the financial statements have been prepared in accordance with the Charities Act 1993/Companies Act 2006.

(Source: The Auditing Practices Board, 'Practice Note 11 – The Audit of Charities in the United Kingdom')

19.3 A 'qualified' audit report may state that the financial statements do not show a true and fair view (disagreement) or that the auditor is unable to tell whether the financial statements show a true and fair view (limitation in audit scope). These qualifications may refer to the financial statements as a whole or, more usually, to a particular area of the financial statements.

19.4 The auditor is also required to state in the audit report if:

- the charity has failed to keep accounting records in accordance with the relevant Act; or
- the financial statements are not in agreement with the accounting records; or
- necessary information and explanations have not been made available to them.

19.5 To get the most out of an audit, a charity should seek an auditor who not only is independent, but also shows empathy with and knowledge of the charity sector. A charity audit is very different from a commercial audit and experience in one does not also imply experience in the other. Ideally there should be informal communication between the auditor and charity trustees or management throughout the year and also throughout the audit, rather than just the formal meetings at the start and finish of the audit work.

19.6 It is good practice to review auditors every three to five years to ensure the best possible service is being provided.

20 Appointment of auditors

20.1 To be eligible as appointment for auditor, a potential auditor must be a member of a recognised supervisory body and eligible for appointment under the rules of that body. This basically means that the auditor is regulated by the appropriate institute, has standards that they must follow, has fit and proper status, professional integrity, independence, up-to-date technical standards and procedures for maintaining competence.

20.2 Generally an auditor must be appointed or reappointed each financial year. In an unincorporated charity this is done by the trustees of the charity, but in a charitable company the annual reappointment must be made by a resolution of the members. This resolution may be passed at the meeting at which the immediately preceding years accounts are laid before the members or by written resolution. The trustees of a charitable company are, however, able to appoint the first auditor of the charity.

20.3 If the auditor is not reappointed by a resolution of the members, the auditor remains in office until the members pass a resolution to reappoint him or to remove him as auditor (5 per cent of members, or fewer if the articles say so, can force the consideration of a resolution to remove an auditor). This provision about remaining in office, however, does not apply if the auditor's most recent appointment was by the trustees or the charity's articles require annual appointment.

21 Removal and resignation of auditors

21.1 An auditor may resign by giving notice to the charity trustees. An auditor may also be removed from office at any time during their term of office, or may not be reappointed for a further term. Usually most auditors will resign and a new auditor will be appointed and this will be reported to the AGM. The auditors of unincorporated charities may be removed by the trustees, but an auditor of a charitable company will need to be removed by a resolution of the members. The charitable company must send a copy of the notice of the intended resolution to the auditor, who then has the right to make a written response and require that the charity sends it to its members and to speak at the meeting where the resolution is to be considered.

21.2 When an auditor ceases to hold office (for whatever reason), he must deposit at the charity's registered office a statement of the circumstances connected with his ceasing to hold office, unless he considers that there are no such circumstances that need to be brought to the attention of the members and trustees. If there are no circumstances that need to be brought to the attention of the members and trustees, the auditor must deposit a statement to that effect.

21.3 When the auditor deposits a statement of circumstances connected with his ceasing to hold office, the charity must within 14 days either (a) send a copy of the statement to every member who is entitled to receive a copy of the accounts or (b) apply to the court for relief from having to send the statement to all members. The court will only grant relief if it is satisfied that the auditor is trying to secure needless publicity for defamatory matter.

21.4 The auditor is also obliged to notify the appropriate audit authority if (a) the audit is a 'major' audit or (b) the auditor ceases to hold office before the end of his term of office. A major audit is defined as the audit of a charity in which there is a major public interest. The audit of a charitable company with income exceeding £100 million is deemed to be a major audit.

22 Procedures on change of auditor

22.1 Under ethical guidelines an auditor cannot accept nomination to replace an existing auditor without first communicating with that auditor. The charity should inform the existing auditor about the proposed change, and will need to give permission to both firms to discuss the relevant issues. The proposed auditor will write to the existing auditor and enquire about the following matters:

- the reasons for the change in the appointment;
- any significant differences of principle or practice which have arisen between the auditor and client;
- whether the client, its trustees or employees are guilty of an unlawful act which is relevant to the audit and should be investigated by the appropriate authority;
- any serious doubts the existing auditor has regarding the integrity of the trustees and or senior management; and

- whether the client, its trustees or employees have deliberately withheld information or limited the scope of the audit.

22.2 The prospective auditor will give due weight to the existing auditor's reply, along with any other information he has obtained in order to make his decision.

Appendix A

Directory

Advisory, Conciliation and Arbitration Service (ACAS)
Acas National (Head Office)
Euston Tower
286 Euston Road
London NW1 3JJ
Tel: 08457 474 747
www.acas.org.uk

Association of Chief Executives of Voluntary Organisations (ACEVO)
1 New Oxford Street
London WC1A 1NU
Tel: 020 7280 4960
Fax: 020 7280 4989
www.acevo.org.uk

Association of Chief Executives of Scottish Voluntary Organisations (ACOSVO)
Thorn House
5 Rose Street
Edinburgh EH2 2PR
Tel: 0131 243 2755
Email: office@acosvo.org.uk
www.acosvo.org.uk

BACS Payment Systems Limited
BACS Payment Schemes Limited
3rd Floor, Livingstone House
12 Finsbury Square
London EC2A 1AS
Tel: 020 7711 6370
www.bacs.co.uk

Big Lottery Fund
1 Plough Place
London EC4A 1DE
Tel: 0207 211 1800
Fax: 020 7211 1750
Email: general.enquiries@biglotteryfund.org.uk
www.biglotteryfund.org.uk

British Standards Institute (BSI)
BSI British Standards
389 Chiswick High Road
London W4 4AL
Tel: 020 8996 9001
Fax: 020 8996 7001
Email: cservices@bsigroup.com
www.bsigroup.co.uk

Business in the Community (BITC)
Business in the Community
137 Shepherdess Walk
London N1 7RQ
Tel: 020 7566 8650
Email: information@bitc.org.uk
www.bitc.org.uk

Care Quality Commission (CQC)
Care Quality Commission National Correspondence
Citygate
Gallowgate
Newcastle upon Tyne NE1 4PA
Tel: 03000 616 161
Email: enquiries@cqc.org.uk
www.cqc.org.uk

Charities Aid Foundation (CAF)
Head office
25 Kings Hill Avenue
Kings Hill
West Malling
Kent ME19 4TA
Tel: 03000 123 000
Fax: 03000 123 001
Email: enquiries@cafonline.org
www.cafonline.org

Charities Evaluation Services (CES)
4 Coldbath Square
London EC1R 5HL
Tel: 020 7713 5722
Fax: 020 7713 5692
Email: enquiries@ces-vol.org.uk
www.ces-vol.org.uk

Charity Commission
PO Box 1227
Liverpool L69 3UG
Tel: 0845 3000 218
Fax: 0151 7031 555
www.charity-commission.gov.uk

Charity Finance Director's Group (CFDG)
3rd Floor, Downstream Building
1 London Bridge
London SE1 9BG
Tel: 0845 345 3192
Fax: 0845 345 3193
Email: info@cfdg.org.uk
www.cfdg.org.uk

Charity Learning Consortium
Vine House
Selsley Road
North Woodchester
Stroud GL5 5NN
Tel: 08451 707 702
www.charitylearning.org

Charity Tribunal
The First-tier Tribunal (Charity) Manager
Tribunals Operational Support Centre
PO Box 6987
Leicester LE1 6ZX

CIC Regulator
Room 3.68
Companies House
Crown Way
Maindy
Cardiff CF14 3UZ
Tel: 029 2034 6228 (24hr voicemail service)
Fax: 029 2034 6229
Email: cicregulator@companieshouse.gov.uk
www.cicregulator.gov.uk

Commission for Equality and Human Rights
www.equalityhumanrights.com

England
Freepost RRLL-GHUX-CTRX
Arndale House
Arndale Centre
Manchester M4 3AQ
Tel: 0845 604 6610
Email: englandhelpline@equalityhumanrights.com

Scotland
Tel: 0845 604 5510
Email: scotlandhelpline@equalityhumanrights.com

Wales
Tel: 0845 604 8810
Email: waleshelpline@equalityhumanrights.com

Companies House
England and Wales
Companies House
Crown Way
Cardiff CF14 3UZ
Tel: 0303 1234 500
email: enquiries@companies-house.gov.uk
www.companieshouse.gov.uk

London Office
Companies House Executive Agency
21 Bloomsbury Street
London WC1B 3XD
Tel: 0303 1234 500

Scotland Office
Companies House
37 Castle Terrace
Edinburgh EH1 2EB
Tel: 0303 1234 500

Northern Ireland Office
Companies Registry
1st Floor, Waterfront Plaza
8 Laganbank Road
Belfast BT1 3BS
Tel: 0845 604 8888

Co-Operatives UK
Holyoake House
Hanover Street
Manchester M60 0AS
Tel: 0161 246 2900
Fax: 0161 831 7684
Email: info@cooperatives-uk.coop
www.cooperatives-uk.coop

Council of Ethnic Minority Voluntary
Organisations (CEMVO)
Boardman House
64 Broadway
Stratford
London E15 1NG
T el: 020 8432 0200
Fax: 020 8432 0001
Email: enquiries@cemvo.org.uk
www.cemvo.org.uk

Department for Business, Innovation and
Skills (formerly the DTI and BERR)
1 Victoria Street
London SW1H 0ET
Tel: 020 7215 5000
email: enquiries@bis.gsi.gov.uk
www.bis.gov.uk

Department for Children, Schools and
Families
Castle View House
East Lane
Runcorn
Cheshire WA7 2GJ
Tel: 0870 000 2288
Fax: 01928 794248
www.dcsf.gov.uk

Department for Social Development in
Northern Ireland
www.dsdni.gov.uk

Directory of Social Change (DoSC)
www.dsc.org.uk

London Office
24 Stephenson Way
London NW1 2DP
Tel: 020 7391 4800
Fax: 020 7391 4808
Email: training@dsc.org.uk

Liverpool Office
Directory of Social Change
Federation House
Hope Street
Liverpool L1 9BW
Tel: 0151 708 0117
Fax: 0151 708 0139
Email: research@dsc.org.uk

Ethnic Minority Fund (EMF)
Forbes House
9 Artillery Lane
London E1 7LP
Tel: 020 7426 8950
Fax: 020 7426 8429
Email: enquiries@ethnicminorityfund.org.uk
www.ethnicminorityfund.org.uk

Federation of Small Businesses (FSB)
Sir Frank Whittle Way
Blackpool Business Park
Blackpool FY4 2FE
Tel: 01253 336000
Fax: 01253 348046
www.fsb.org.uk

Financial Reporting Council (FRC)
5th Floor, Aldwych House
71–91 Aldwych
London WC2B 4HN
Tel: 020 7492 2300
www.frc.org.uk

Financial Services Authority (FSA)
25 The North Colonnade
Canary Wharf
London E14 5HS
Tel: 020 7066 1000
www.fsa.gov.uk

Fundraising Standards Board (FRSB)
1st Floor
89 Albert Embankment
London SE1 7TP
Tel: 0845 402 5442
Fax: 0845 402 5443
www.frsb.org.uk

Gambling Commission
Victoria Square House
Victoria Square
Birmingham B2 4BP
Tel: 0121 230 6666
Fax: 0121 230 6720
Email: info@gamblingcommission.gov.uk
www.gamblingcommission.gov.uk

Health and Safety Executive (HSE)
Caerphilly Business Park
Caerphilly
CF83 3GG
Tel: 0845 345 0055
www.hse.gov.uk

HSE Incident Centre (RIDDOR reporting)
Contact Centre Address as above
Tel: 0845 300 9923
www.riddor.gov.uk

HM Revenue & Customs
www.hmrc.gov.uk
HMRC Birmingham Stamp Office
9th Floor, City Centre House
30 Union Street
Birmingham B2 4AR
Tel: 0845 603 0135
Postal applications only

Information Commissioner's Office
Wycliffe House
Water Lane
Wilmslow
Cheshire SK9 5AF
Tel: 01625 545 745
email: mail@ico.gsi.gov.uk
www.ico.gov.uk

Institute of Fundraising
Park Place
12 Lawn Lane
London SW8 1UD
Tel: 020 7840 1000
Fax: 020 7840 1001
www.institute-of-fundraising.org.uk

ICSA Information & Training Ltd
16 Park Crescent
London W1B 1AH
Tel: 020 7612 7020
Fax: 0207 612 7034
Email: publishing@icsa.co.uk
www.icsainformationandtraining.co.uk

Institute of Internal Auditors (IIA)
13 Abbeville Mews
88 Clapham Park Road
London SW4 7BX
Tel: 020 7498 0101
Fax: 020 7978 2492
www.iia.org.uk

The Institute of Chartered Secretaries and Administrators (ICSA)
16 Park Crescent
London W1B 1AH
Tel: 020 7580 4741
e-mail: info@icsa.co.uk
www.icsa.org.uk

Investors in People
7–10 Chandos Street
London W1G 9DQ
Tel: 020 7467 1900
Email: information@iipuk.co.uk
www.investorsinpeople.co.uk

APPENDIX A

Land Registry
32 Lincoln's Inn Fields
London WC2A 3PH
Tel: 0844 892 1111
Email: customersupport@landregistry.gsi.gov.uk
www.landregistry.gov.uk

National Council for Voluntary Organisations (NCVO)
Regent's Wharf
8 All Saints Street
London N1 9RL
Tel: 020 7713 6161
Fax: 020 7713 6300
Email: ncvo@ncvo-vol.org.uk
www.ncvo-vol.org.uk

National Housing Federation (NHF)
Lion Court
25 Procter Street
London WC1V 6NY
Tel: 020 7067 1010
Fax: 020 7067 1011
Email: info@housing.org.uk
www.housing.org.uk

Northern Ireland Council for Voluntary Action (NICVA)
61 Duncairn Gardens
Belfast BT15 2GB
Tel: 028 9087 7777
Fax: 028 9087 7779
www.nicva.org

Office of the Scottish Charity Regulator (OSCR)
2nd Floor
Quadrant House
9 Riverside Drive
Dundee DD1 4NY
Tel: 01382 220446
Email: info@oscr.org.uk
www.oscr.org.uk

Office of Public Sector Information
www.opsi.gov.uk

Office of the Third Sector
2nd Floor, Admiralty Arch
South Side
The Mall
London SW1A 2WH
Tel: 020 7276 6400
Email: OTS.info@cabinet-office.x.gsi.gov.uk
www.cabinetoffice.gov.uk/third_sector

The Pensions Regulator (TPR)
Napier House
Trafalgar Place
Brighton BN1 4DW
Tel: 01273 811800

Privy Council
2 Carlton Gardens
London SW1Y 5AA
Tel: 020 7747 5310
Fax: 020 7747 5311
Email: pcosecretariat@pco.x.gsi.gov.uk
www.privy-council.org.uk

Scottish Council for Voluntary Organisations (SCVO)
Mansfield Traquair Centre
15 Mansfield Place
Edinburgh EH3 6BB
Tel: 0131 556 3882
Email: enquiries@scvo.org.uk
www.scvo.org.uk

Tenant Services Authority (TSA)
2nd Floor, Lateral
8 City Walk
Leeds LS11 9AT
Tel: 0845 230 7000
Email: enquiries@tsa.gsx.gov.uk
www.tenantservicesauthority.org

Wales Council for Voluntary Action (WCVA)
Tel: 0800 2888 329
Email: help@wcva.org.uk
www.wcva.org.uk

Appendix B

Outline document retention checklist

CA = Companies Act 2006

Record description	Regulatory retention period and source	Comments/Recommended retention
Statutory registers – charitable companies		
Register of directors; directors' residential addresses and secretaries	Life of charity ss. 162; 165; 275 CA) (For charitable companies.)	
Register of charges	Life of charity (CA, s. 876 CA. (For charitable companies.)	
Register of members	Life of charity ss. 113–121 CA. (For charitable companies.)	Entries in relation to former members may be removed after ten years (s. 121 CA). However, a copy of any entry included in the register immediately before 6 April 2008 that is removed under s. 121 must be retained until 6 April 2018 or, if earlier, 20 years after the person ceased to be a member
Constitution		Copies of the current version must be kept for business reasons. Previous versions are usually also kept for life of company.

APPENDIX B

Other Companies Act records

Certificate of incorporation		Life of charity.
Certificate of change of company name		Life of charity.
Printed copies of resolutions filed at Companies House	While resolution or agreement is in force (s. 29 CA). (For charitable companies.)	Life of charity.
Register of trustees' declarations of interest		If such a register is kept, it probably needs to be treated in at least the same way as the minutes of meetings of trustees. Accordingly, an absolute minimum of ten years, although probably longer
Register of documents sealed		If such a register is kept, it probably needs to be treated in at least the same way as the minutes of meetings of trustees. Accordingly, an absolute minimum of ten years, but probably longer

Statutory returns

Acknowledgements of receipt issued by Companies House in respect of filed documents	Until entry on Companies House file has been confirmed.
Annual return	Three years.
(Forms regarding Directors and Secretaries appointments)	Until entry on Companies House file has been confirmed.
Copies of other statutory returns filed at Charity Commission & Companies House	Until entry on Charity Commission and Companies House file has been confirmed.

Meetings of trustees

Agenda papers		Minimum of seven years, or same as minutes if necessary in order to understand the minutes.
Board minutes (signed copy)	Ten years from date of meeting (s. 248 CA). (For charitable companies.)	Life of charity.
Board committee minutes (signed copy)	Ten years from date of meeting (s. 248 CA). (For charitable companies.)	Life of charity.
Written resolutions of the board	Ten years from date of meeting (s. 248 CA). (For charitable companies.)	Life of charity.
Attendance record		If required by constitution, life of charity.

General meetings

Notices of general meetings (signed copy)		Ten years minimum, but life of the charity recommended. If notice is necessary to understand the minutes, it should be given at least the same retention period.
Certificate of posting of notices		Two years minimum suggested.
Minutes of general meetings	Ten years from date of meeting (s. 355 CA). (For charitable companies.)	Life of charity.
Record of statutory written resolutions of company	Ten years from date of resolution (s. 355 CA). (For charitable companies.)	Life of charity.
Written record of decision of sole member	Ten years from date of decision (s. 355 CA). (For charitable companies.)	Life of charity.
Proxy forms – no poll demanded		One month after meeting.
Proxy forms and polling cards – poll demanded		One year after meeting.

Agreements and related correspondence

Major agreements of historical significance

Permanently.

Contracts with customers, suppliers or agents
Licensing agreements
Rental/hire purchase agreements
Indemnities and guarantees
Other agreements/ contracts

Six years after expiry or termination of the contract Six years is generally the time limit within which proceedings founded on a contract may be brought If the contract is executed as a deed, the limitation period is twelve years Actions for latent damage may be brought up to fifteen years after the damage occurs.

Property

Deeds of title

Permanently or until property disposed of.

Leases

Fifteen years after expiry.

Accounts

Company accounts and accounting records

Accounting records must be retained for private companies or a minimum of three years from the date they are made (s 388(4) CA).

If the charity is not a company the Charities Act 1993, Part VI requires that accounting records are retained for six years.

Best practice suggests also retaining company accounting records for six years from the year end Some accounting records will be required for tax purposes.

Annual report and accounts (signed)

Six years (Value Added Tax Act 1994 Sch. 11).

Tax

VAT records	Six years	Note in general that where there is an enquiry into a tax return, records should be retained until the enquiry is complete.
PAYE	For PAYE records not required to be sent to the Inland Revenue, not less than three years after the end of the tax year to which they relate (Income Tax) (Pay As You Earn REgs 2003 reg. 97).	Note however that payroll records should be kept for five to six years.

Banking records

Cheques, bills of exchange and other negotiable instruments		Three years.
Bank statements	Three years (s 388 CA).	
Instructions to banks		Six years after ceasing to be effective.

Index

accountability C1-5
  objective C1-5.8
  stakeholders, to C1-5.6, C1-5.7
accounting E3
  accruals E3-3.9
  current assets E3-13.10
  exempt charities E3-3.4
  grant funding E3-10
  gross income E3-3.7
  heritage assets E3-13.8
  incoming resources E3-7
  intangible fixed assets E3-13.6
  investments E3-13.9
  liabilities E3-13.11
  notes to E3-13.12
  receipts and payments E3-3.8
  recognition of income E3-8
  recognised gains and losses E3-12.2
  requirement to keep accounting records
      E3-13.15
  requirements E3-3
  resources expended E3-9
  small companies, thresholds for E3-15
  SORP requirements E3-4
  structure E3-5
  support costs E3-11
  tangible fixed assets E3-13.7
  timing for submission E3-13.13.4.1
  transfers E3-12
accounting records B1-11
  adequate B1-11.5
accounting reference date E3-13.4
adoption D1-3.8
annual general meetings C3-3.4
annual report E3-2
  contents E3-2
annual returns
  Charity Commission, to B2-2.1
  companies B2-4.11
  individual and provident societies B2-3
assignment
  contract, of B3-9

audit E3
  independent examination, and E3-18
  requirements by size and type of charity
      E3-16
  Scottish requirements E3-17
auditors
  appointment E3-20
  procedures on change E3-22
  removal E3-21
  resignation E3-21

balance sheet E3-13
board
  role of C2-2
board composition C2-25
board meetings C3-7
  alternatives to C3-7.9
  attendance at C3-7.7
  chairman of trustees C3-7.8
  frequency C3-7.4
  information C3-7.6
  notice of C3-7.3
  planning C3-7.5
  written resolutions C3-7.9
borrowing E1-3.14
  unsecured E1-3.14.7, E1-3.14.8
branches A2-12.1–A2-12.4
breach of trust C2-8
bullying D1-5.14

Cadbury Report C1-2.2
chairman
  main duties C2-35
  main responsibilities C2-34
  powers C2-43
  role of C2-33
charitable assets E1
charitable companies
  secretary B2-6.10
charitable incorporated organisations A2-
      7.1–A2-7.14
  constitution A2-7.6–A2-7.8

conversion to A2-7.10–A2-7.12
establishment of A2-7.9
  forms A2-7.5–A2-7.7
  key features A2-7.4
charitable law obligations
  England and Wales B2-5.2
charitable purposes A1-2
charitable trusts A2-3.1–A2-3.3
charity
  advantages A1-1.4
  assessing public benefit A1-9
  fee-charging A1-7
  key features A1-1.4
  meaning A1-1
  people in poverty not excluded A1-8
  public benefit presumption A1-3
  public benefit requirement A1-4
    general guidance A1-5
    not meeting A1-10
  reasonable restrictions A1-6
  reporting obligation A1-12
Charity Commission
  annual returns to B2-2.1
  challenging decisions of A1-4.1–A1-4.6
  decision review process A1-4.5
  electronic filing with B2-2.3
  enabling powers A1-3.6
  information to A3-6.15
  investigations A1-3.1–A1-3.3
  key features A2-2.4
policemen, as A1-3.2
power to determine members C2-31
power to disclose information A1-3.4
powers A1-3.1–A1-3.3
public benefit, and A1-11
registration with A3-6
regulation A1-3.1–A1-3.3
  excluded charities A3-6.16
  exempt charities A3-6.16
representing interests of charities A1-3.5
responsibilities A1-2.1–A1-2.4
role A1-2.1–A1-2.4
section 8 inquiries A1-3.3
spending permanent endowments E1-3.10
summary information return B2-2.2
visits A1-3.7
Charity Tribunal A1-4.6
chief executive officer (CEO)
  relationship with C2-52
  role of C2-50
committees C3-8
  appointing to C2-63
  audit C2-55
  delegation to C2-53

finance and general purposes C2-57
governance C2-61
nominations C2-59
performance C2-60
policy C2-60
remuneration C2-58
reporting lines for C2-63
terms of reference C2-62
typical C2-54
Common Deposit Funds E1-3.12.15
Common Investment Funds E1-3.12.15
Community Interest Companies A2-10.1–A2-10.7
  key features A2-10.6–A2-10.12
  types A2-10.4
Companies House
  annual return B2-4.11
  electronic filing B2-4.9
  notification to B2-4
    allotments of shares B2-4.6
    change of accounting reference date B2-4.2
    change of articles B2-4.7
    change of directors and secretary B2-4.5
    change of registered office B2-4.3
    charges B2-4.8
    mortgages B2-4.8
    SAIL B2-4.4
companies limited by guarantee A2-5.1–A2-5.17
  advantages A2-5.9
  articles of association A2-5.6
  key features A2-5.1
  limited liability A2-5.4
  membership A2-5.10
  memorandum of association A2-5.6
  powers of members A2-5.11
  requirements A2-5.8
  resolution A2-5.13–A2-5.16
  two-tier structure A2-5.3
  ultra vires rule A2-5.5
company limited by shares A2-8.2
compliance and filing requirements B2-1–B2-6
  Charity Commission requirements B2-2
  summary B2-2.1
conflicts of interest
  trustees C2-24
constitutions A2-11.1–A2-11.19
  amending A2-11.17
  asset lock A2-11.12
  benefits to trustees A2-11.9
  charitable companies A2-11.5
  conflicts of interest A2-11.11

contents of A2-11.3
dissolution clause A2-11.14
guarantee clause A2-11.13
limited liability clause A2-11.13
location A2-11.6
name A2-11.4
nature of A2-11.2
non-distribution clause A2-11.12
notification A2-11.18
objects A2-11.7
paid trustees A2-11.10
powers A2-11.8
purpose of A2-11.2
registered providers A2-11.19
rules for members A2-11.15
trustees, rules for A2-11.16
types A2-11.1
constructive dismissal D1-4.11
contract
   acceptance B3-2.3
   assignment B3-9
   authority to enter in B3-3.2
   basics of contract law B3-2
   clarity, need for B3-3
   conditions B3-3.5
   consideration B3-2.4
   electronic signatures B3-6
      certifying B3-6.3
      methods B3-6.2
   implied terms B3-7.4
      custom, by B3-7.4.4
      fact, by B3-7.4.2
      law, by B3-7.4.3
   intention to create legal relations B3-2.5
   meaning B3-1
   name in which entered into B3-3.4
   non-performance under B3-10
   offer B3-2.2
   oral B3-1.2
   privity of contract B3-8
   seal, and *see* deeds
   signing B3-4.1
   standard terms and conditions B3-7
      key features B3-7
   terms B3-3.5
   ultra vires B3-3.2
   unenforceable B3-2.2
contract of employment D1-2.4
   changing D1-2.5
corporate killing D1-5.1.5

data protection D3-2
   accuracy D3-3.5
   fair and lawful processing D3-3.2
   fair processing of information D3-5.2
   handling exercise of subject rights D3-6.4
   key business impacts D3-5
   key HR impacts D3-6
   length of time data kept D3-5
   monitoring at work D3-6.5
   notification D3-5.1
   offences D3-4
   outsourcing D3-5.4
   principles D3-3
   processing sensitive data D3-6.3
   purposes D3-3.3
   relevant and appropriate data D3-3.4
   rights of data subjects D3-6
   security of data D3-3.8
   security of personal data D3-5.3
   transfer outside European Economic Area D3-3.9
deeds B3-5
   procedure for execution B3-5.3
   reasons for B3-5.1
delegation
   general principles C2-44
direct mail D3-8.2
direct marketing D3-8
   compliant D3-8.1
directors of charitable companies
   trustees as C2-4
document retention B1-1.2
   policy B1-12.2, B1-12.3, B1-12.4
donations D2-5
door-to-door collections D2-1.13
driving requirements D1-5.13
due diligence
   mergers, and A2-14.7

e-commerce law D3-7
electronic communications C3-4
   company, to C3-4.10
   deemed consent C3-4.9
electronic filing
   Charity Commission, with B2-2.3
   Companies House, with B2-4.9
electronic records B1-10
electronic signatures
   contracts B3-6
electronic voting C3-5
e-mail marketing D3-8.4
emergency leave D1-3.9
employment D1
   changes in status D1-1.12
   consideration D1-1.4
   contract D1-1.2
   disciplinary procedure D1-4.2

appeals D1-4.9
hearing D1-4.3
record D1-4.4
right to be accompanied D1-4.5
sanctions D1-4.7
disciplinary rationale D1-4.1
discipline D1-4
dismissal D1-4
facts of status D1-1.10
family-friendly rights D1-3.5
grievance procedure D1-4.10
intention to create legal relationship D1-1.7
mutuality of obligation D1-1.6
offer and acceptance D1-1.3
personal service D1-1.8
summary dismissal D1-4.8
endowment funds E1-2.39
establishing charitable trust A3-2
establishing company limited by guarantee A3-4
formation A3-4.1
establishing unincorporated association A3-3
expendable endowment funds E1-2.3.12
expenses
volunteers, of D1-1.5
external auditors
role of E3-19
extraordinary general meetings C3-3.5

financial management E1-3.11
fire precautions D1-5.11
first aid D1-5.10
flexible working D1-3.11
founder
role of C2-44
fundraising D2-1
action plan D2-1.10
agreements with professional fundraisers and commercial participants D2-2.11
audit trail D2-1.20
broadcast media D2-1.16
businesses, with D2-2.9
Code of Conduct D2-2
codes of practice D2-2
commercial participator statements D2-2.10
declaration of charitable status D2-1.18
effort-reward ratio D2-1.7
events D2-1.14
good practice D2-1.11
joined-up thinking D2-1.6
professional fundraisers D2-6

professional fundraising statement D2-2.8
recent changes D2-1.2
reporting costs D2-1.8
responsibility for D2-1.9
restricted funds D2-1.19
rules D2-1.11
selecting consultants D2-2.7
sources D2-1.4
strategy D2-1.3
telephone D2-1.16
timescale D2-1.5
unauthorised D2-5
funds E1-2

general meetings C3-3
annual C3-3.4
chairing C3-3.11
convening C3-3.6
extraordinary C3-3.5
notice of C3-3.8
proxies C3-3.12
quorum C3-3.13
requisition of C3-3.7
resolutions C3-3.14
short notice requirement C3-3.9
voting at C3-3.10
Gift Aid D2-5.4
declaration D2-5.8
Good Governance Standard for Public Service C1-2.5
governance of charities
accountability C1-5
agency theory C1-3.2
background C1-1
behavioural C1-3.6
books C2-64.2
Cadbury Report C1-2.2
Good Governance: A Code for the Voluntary and Community Sector C1-2.6
Good Governance Standard for Public Service C1-2.5
history of C1-2
influences on C1-1.4
Internet resources C2-64.3
leadership, as C1-3.5
legislation C1-4
Myners Report C1-2.2.8
Nolan Report C1-2.4
On Trust C1-2.3
policy governance C1-3.4
proportionate C1-3.7
regulation C1-4
relationship with management C2-51

INDEX

resources C2-64
sources of useful information C2-64
stewardship theory C1-3.3
theories C1-3.3
group accounts E3-14
group structures A2-12.1–A2-12.4

health and safety D1-1.14, D1-5
  HSE D1-5.9
  on-site data D1-5.8
  policy D1-5.7
holidays D1-3.3
honorary officers C2-32
  constitutional position C2-42
honorary secretary
  main duties C2-41
  main responsibilities C2-40
  role C2-39
honorary treasurer C2-36
  main duties C2-38
  main responsibility C2-37
  role of C2-36

incorporation A3-7
  advantages A3-7.3
  investigations A3-7.4
incorporation of charity trustees A2-9.1–A2-9.7
independent examination
  audit, and E3-18
industrial and provident societies A2-6.1–A2-6.12
  advantages A2-6.10
annual returns B2-3
  forms A2-6.1
  key features A2-6.2–A2-6.9
  mergers A2-14.14
  reform proposals A2-6.12–A2-6.16
insurance E2-2.6
  trustee indemnity insurance E2-2.6.10
  types E2-2.6.9
internal audit E2-2.5
  benefits E2-2.5.10
  governance E2-2.5.7
  model job description E2-2.5.18
  possible structures E2-2.5.14
  process E2-2.5.17
  risk management E2-2.5.4
  role E2-2.5
internal controls E2
  benefits E2-2.4
  board, role of E2-2.2
  Charity Commission checklist E2-2.4.20
  components of system E2-2.4.5

control activities E2-2.4.13
control environment E2-2.4.6
definition E2-2.4.3
fundamental principles E2-2.4.4
information systems E2-2.4.9
monitoring E2-2.4.14
specific risk areas E2-2.4.20
Internet resources C2-64.3
investment managers E1-3.12.17
investments E1-3.12
  ethical E1-3.12.10
  policy E1-3.12.9
  taxation, and E1-3.12.19
  trustees' duties E1-3.12.6
  types E1-3.12.13

land and property
  acquisition E1-3.13
  disposing of E1-3.13.12
  managing E1-3.13.11
  sale of land checklist E1-3.13.26
legacies D2-1.17
legal forms and structures A2-1.1–A2-14.17
  key factors A2-1.10
  risk and unlimited liability A2-2.1–A2-2.12
lotteries D2-1.15

maternity D1-3.6
  keeping in touch D1-3.6.6
  job on return D1-3.6.7
meetings C3
  board C3-7
  effective, guidance for C3-9
  electronic communications C3-4
  electronic voting C3-5
  general *see* general meetings
  meaning C3-2
  members' statement C3-6
  minutes C3-3.15
  teleconferencing C3-2.3–C3-2.8
members
  admission C2-30
  powers of Charity Commission to determine C2-31
  removal C2-30
  rights C2-29
  role of C2-27
  trustees as C2-28
members' statement C3-6
membership charities C2-27
mergers A2-14.1–A2-14.17
  documents A2-14.12
  due diligence A2-14.11

industrial and provident societies
A2-14.17
practical steps A2-14.13
process A2-14.9
register A2-14.14
restrictions on assets A2-14.10
small unincorporated charities A2-14.16
types A2-14.4–A2-14.8
vesting declarations A2-14.15
microfilm records B1-10
minutes B1-8
contents B1-8.8
evidence, as B1-9
meetings, of C3-3.15
natures of B1-8.2
mortgages E1-3.14.3
Myners Report C1-2.2.8

name of charity A3-5
name of company A2-11.4
names
use of B2-5.4
national minimum wage D1-1.13, D1-3.2
networks A2-12.1–A2-12.4
independent charities A2-12.4
Nolan Report C1-2.4
Northern Ireland
charity regulation A1-5.2

observer
role of C2-44
On Trust C1-2.3

payroll giving D2-5.2
parental leave D1-3.10
paternity D1-3.7
patron
role of C2-44
pensions D1-3.4
permanent endowment funds E1-2.3.10
portfolio trustees
role of C2-44
pregnancy
risk assessment D1-5.6
president
role of C2-44
privity of contract B3-8
programme related investments E1-3.12.16
projects A2-12.3
Protected Online Filing (PROOF) Scheme
B2-4.5
proxies
general meetings, at C3-3.12

records B1-1
electronic B1-10
microfilm B1-10
recruitment D1-2
job offers D1-2.2
objective selection D1-2
right to work in UK D1-2.3
redundancy D1-4.12
consultation D1-4.16
determining correct staffing levels D1-4.14
genuine D1-4.13
notice D1-4.18
procedure D1-4.15
selection for D1-4.17
state redundancy pay D1-4.19
register of charges B1-5.5
register of directors B1-5.3
register of members B1-5.2
register of sealing B1-7
register of secretaries B1-5.4
register of trustees' interests B1-7
registered name
display of B2-5.8
registers B1-1
charitable companies B1-3
charities that are not companies B1-2
contents B1-5
format B1-4
inspection B1-6
location B1-4
Regulation of Investigatory Powers Act 2000
D3-6.6
resolutions
general meetings, at C.3.3.14
restricted funds E1-2.3.4
restricted income funds E1-2.3.6
restructuring A2-14.1–A2-14.217
risk assessments D1-5.5
pregnancy D1-5.6
safety D1-5.5.1
risk management E2
appetite E2-2.3.5
assessing risk E2-2.3.13
board, role of E2-2.2
compliance with laws and regulations
E2-2.3.13
elements E2-2.3
environmental/external factors E2-2.3.13
evaluation of action E2-2.3.23
financial E2-2.3.13
governance and management E2-2.3.13
identifying risks E2-2.3.11
monitoring and assessment E2-2.3.28
operational E2-3.3.13

risk map E2-2.3.22
scoring system E2-2.3.22
self-assessment checklist E2-2.3.31
strategy E2-2.1.3
Royal Charter body A2-8.3

Scotland
  charitable law obligations B2-5.3
  charity regulation A1-5.1
secretary B2-6
  cessation of office B2-6.11
  charitable companies B2-6.10
  deputy B2-6.9
  joint B2-6.9
  officer of charity, as B2-6.8.3
  requirement for B2-6.3
  responsibilities B2-6.8
  role B2-6
  status of B2-6.7
setting up a charity A3-1–A3.7
Statement of Financial Activities E3-6
stationery
  charitable law obligations
    England and Wales B2-5.2
    Scotland B2-5.3
  company law requirements B2-5.5
  display of registered name B2-5.8
  legal requirements B2-5
  meaning B2-5.7
  other names, use of B2-5.4
  VAT registration B2-5.6
statutory corporations A2-8.4
street collections D2-1.12
stress
  workplaces, in D1-5.12
subsidiaries A2-13.11
summary information return B2-2.2
  name A3-5
  rules on charity information on materials A3-6.14

taxation D2-6
  claiming refunds D2-6.1
telephone marketing D3-8.3
texting D3-8.4
trading D2-3
  financial risk D2-3.5
  types that may be undertaken D2-3.6
trading companies D2-4
  when to set up D2-4.7
trading subsidiaries A2-13.1–A2-13.10
transfer of undertakings D1-2.6
trustees
  appointments C2-15

conclusion C2-22.4
group discussions C2-22.2
implementation C2-22.4
independent consultant C2-21
individual interviews C2-22.3
internal C2-21
method C2-20
procedure C2-15.2
purpose C2-19
questionnaire C2-22.1
timing C2-19
  appraisals C2-18
  beneficiaries, as C2-14
  benefits C2-23
  board composition C2-25
  board performance review C2-18
  collective responsibility C2-45
  conflicts of interest C2-24
  contractual liability C2-7
  delegation C2-45
    constitutional position C2-46
    legal position C2-46
    matters reserved to board C2-48
    schemes C2-49
    staff, to C2-50
    standing orders C2-49
    sub-delegation C2-47
  directors of charitable companies, as C2-4
  disqualification C2-26
  diversity issues C2-13
  duties C2-3
  governing documents D2-3.4
  identifying board's requirements C2-11
  induction C2-17 legal liability C2-9
  liabilities C2-6
  members, as C2-28
  payments C2-23
    conditions for C2-23.5
    key factors C2-23.11
  potential new, checks for C2-16
  powers C2-5
  recruitment C2-10, C2-12
  relationship with CEO C2-52
  removal C2-26
  resignation C2-26
  responsibilities C2-3
  retirement C2-26
  role of C2-2
  selection C2-10
  training C2-17

ultra vires B3-3.2
unincorporated associations A2-4.1–A2-4.4
unrestricted funds E1-2.3.1

VAT D2-6.2–D2-6.8
  branches, and D2-6.6
  business or non-business D2-6.3
  fundraising events D2-6.5
  records B1-11.9
  zero-related supplies D2-6.4
vesting declarations A2-14.15
volunteer D1-1.1
  agreement D1-1.9
  changes in status D1-1.12
  expenses D1-1.5
  facts of status D1-1.10
  mutuality of obligation D1-1.6
  personal service D1-1.8
  supporting status D1-1.11
voting
  electronic C3-5
  general meetings, at C3-3.10

website compliance D3-7.1
  information requirements D3-7.2
working hours D1-3.1